Arduino Internals

Dale Wheat

Apress®

Arduino Internals

ISBN 978-1-4302-3882-9

ISBN 978-1-4302-3883-6 (eBook)

President and Publisher: Paul Manning
Lead Editor: Ralph Moore
Technical Reviewer: Sam Kelly, Jordi Muñoz
Editorial Board: Steve Anglin, Mark Beckner, Ewan Buckingham, Gary Cornell, Morgan Ertel,
    Jonathan Gennick, Jonathan Hassell, Robert Hutchinson, Michelle Lowman, James Markham,
    Matthew Moodie, Jeff Olson, Jeffrey Pepper, Douglas Pundick, Ben Renow-Clarke,
    Dominic Shakeshaft, Gwenan Spearing, Matt Wade, Tom Welsh
Coordinating Editor: Corbin Collins
Copy Editors: Tiffany Taylor, Heather Lang
Production Support: Patrick Cunningham
Indexer: SPi GlobalArtist: SPi Global
Artist: SPi GlobalArtist: SPi Global
Cover Designer: Anna Ishchenko

Distributed to the book trade worldwide by Springer Science+Business Media, LLC., 233 Spring Street, 6th Floor, New York, NY 10013. Phone 1-800-SPRINGER, fax (201) 348-4505, e-mail orders-ny@springer-sbm.com, or visit www.springeronline.com.

For information on translations, please e-mail rights@apress.com, or visit www.apress.com.

Apress and friends of ED books may be purchased in bulk for academic, corporate, or promotional use. eBook versions and licenses are also available for most titles. For more information, reference our Special Bulk Sales–eBook Licensing web page at http://www.apress.com/bulk-sales.

Any source code or other supplementary materials referenced by the author in this text is available to readers at www.apress.com. For detailed information about how to locate your book's source code, go to http://www.apress.com/source-code/.

Contents at a Glance

About the Author xv

About the Technical Reviewers xvi

Acknowledgments xvii

Preface xviii

■Chapter 1: Hardware 1

■Chapter 2: Software 25

■Chapter 3: Atmel AVR 39

■Chapter 4: Supporting Hardware 71

■Chapter 5: Arduino Software 89

■Chapter 6: Optimizations 99

■Chapter 7: Hardware Plus Software 133

■Chapter 8: Example Projects 165

■Chapter 9: Project Management 213

■Chapter 10: Hardware Design 231

■Chapter 11: Software Design 255

■Chapter 12: Networking 281

■Chapter 13: More Example Projects 305

Index 359

Contents

About the Authors.. xv

About the Technical Reviewers xvi

Acknowledgments xvii

Preface xviii

■Chapter 1: Hardware 1

What Is an Arduino?..1

The Arduino Uno 2

    Processor.. 3

    Serial Port... 5

    Power Supply.. 5

    Expansion Connectors 6

    Shields 9

The Arduino Mega 2560..14

Previous Hardware 16

    Arduino Serial 16

    Arduino USB.. 17

    Arduino Extreme 18

    Arduino Nuova Generazione (New Generation)... 18

    Arduino Diecimila 18

    Arduino Duemilanove 18

    Arduino Mega 19

Who Makes Arduinos? 19

    Officially Licensed Products 19

    Everybody Else 20

Build Your Own 21

    Arduino Printed Circuit Boards 21

    Breadboard Arduinos 22

Summary 23

Chapter 2: Software 25

Hosts and Targets 25

Step by Step 26

    Step 1: Write Some Code 26

    Step 2: Compile the Code 31

    Step 3: Program the Device 33

    Step 4: Test and Debug 33

    Step 5. Repeat 34

Semiautomatic 34

    Blinking in C 34

Going Further 37

Summary 37

Chapter 3: Atmel AVR 39

Origins 39

AVR Device Families 39

When in Doubt: Product Datasheets 40

Device Packaging 40

    Through-Hole DIPs.. 40

    Surface-Mount Devices (SMDs).. 41

    Extra Pins.. 42

Pin Descriptions..43

    Power Pins...43

AVR Core..50

    Clock Sources...54

    Address Spaces...55

    Instruction Set..58

Internal Peripherals 65

    General Purpose Input/Output (I/O)..65

    External Interrupts...66

    Timer/Counters..66

    USART...67

    Two-Wire Serial Interface (TWI), a.k.a. I^{2}C.......................................68

    Analog Inputs...68

Summary 68

Chapter 4: Supporting Hardware 71

Schematic Diagrams..71

    Component Types...72

    Reference Designators 72

    Component Values..73

    Component Value Tolerances 74

    Other Component Parameters 74

    The Connections..75

Getting Power to the Board..75

    The Barrel Connector...76

    Input Power Conditioning 76

    Voltage Regulator 78

    Power Circuit Evolution 79

Serial Interface 81

    RS-232 Interface 81

The Processor 83

    Power Consumption 83

    I/O Drive Capability 84

    The -RESET Signal 84

    The Time Base 84

    Decoupling Capacitors 85

    Blinky Lights 85

Room for Expansion...85

The Mechanical Form Factor 86

Universal Serial Bus (USB): Signals Plus Power 87

Summary 88

Chapter 5: Arduino Software 89

Open Source Software..90

Multiplatform Support...90

The Arduino Heritage 91

Installing the Software...91

The Process, or "How to Arduino" 91

A Tour of the User Interface..93

    The File Menu 94

    The Edit Menu and the Edit Context Menu 94

    The Sketch Menu..95

    The Tools Menu 95

    The Help Menu...97

Summary 97

■Chapter 6: Optimizations 99

How Will You Know It Worked? 99

Shrink Blink 100

How Blink Works 100

Measuring Space-Saving Optimizations 100

Code Analysis 101

Life Without pinMode() 101

Abbr. & Shrtcts 102

Binary Notation 103

Further Analysis 103

Easy Toggling 104

Further Reduction 105

Wasting Time More Efficiently 105

Using Lower-Level Code 106

Saving Space with Simple Serial Communication 107

What "Hello, world!" Does 107

Writing to Configuration Registers 108

Transmitting Data 109

A String of Characters 111

Printing Numbers 112

Saving SRAM 112

Measuring SRAM Requirements 113

The Bare Minimum 114

Memory Sections 116

Where Variables Live 117

Using the Appropriate Data Type 117

Strings of Characters, Revisited 118

Low Power or High Speed? 120

Electronic Measurements 121

    The Arduino as Test Equipment 121

    As Fast As Possible 124

    Slowing It Down 127

    Further Power Reductions 128

Summary 130

■Chapter 7: Hardware Plus Software 133

Available Peripherals 133

    Serial Port(s) 133

    General-Purpose Digital Inputs and Outputs 139

    Timers and Counters 143

    Pulse-Width-Modulation (PWM) Outputs 147

    Analog Inputs 152

    External Interrupts 156

    Interrupt Reference 159

Summary 163

■Chapter 8: Example Projects 165

Beyond the Blinking LED: Starting Simply 165

    Slow Enough 168

    Mostly Optimized Six-Channel Dimmer 170

    It's Dim, Alright 173

Other Uses for a Blinking LED 182

    Infrared Remote Control 182

    TV-B-Gone 183

A Lot of Blinking LEDs 185

    A Direct-Drive Example 185

    Direct-Drive with LED Drivers 187

    Multiplexing Techniques 188

A Digital Clock..205

    Accuracy..210

    User Interface...211

    Additional Features..212

Summary 212

Chapter 9: Project Management 213

Documentation 213

    Source-Code Comments...214

    Whitespace..215

    Code What You Mean, Mean What You Code 216

    Automated Documentation..217

    Writing For Your Audience...217

    Hardware Documentation..218

    Going Further..220

Teamwork and Collaborative Development 221

    Blogs...221

    Forums 222

    Wikis...222

    Revision Control Systems...223

    A Note About Revision- or Version-Numbering 223

    Project-Hosting Web Sites...224

Licensing Your Work..226

    Patents and Trademarks 227

    Copyright...228

    Open Source...229

    The Public Domain..230

Summary 230

■Chapter 10: Hardware Design 231

Learning About Hardware 231

Things You Must Have 232

Things You Want 233

Infrared Proximity Sensor 234

A Modest Prototype 236

Some Modest Improvements 238

Printed Circuit Boards 241

PCB Layout Techniques 243

A First Attempt 244

A More Compact Version 245

Making the Connection 246

Your Own Custom Arduino 247

Compatibility with Existing Arduinos and Shields 247

Power Supply Options 249

Processor Selection 249

Anything Else? 250

Design Software 251

CadSoft EAGLE 251

EAGLE Tips 252

Summary 253

■Chapter 11: Software Design 255

Advanced Topics Within Arduino 255

Writing Arduino Libraries 255

Alternate Cores 262

And Without Arduino 273

    The Bare Metal, Revisited 273

    Other Development Environments 275

Summary 279

Chapter 12: Networking 281

Point-to-Point Networking 281

    Talking Over the Serial Port 281

    Arduino to Arduino 283

MIDI: Musical Instrument Digital Interface 296

The Internet 301

Summary 304

Chapter 13: More Example Projects 305

An Autonomous Robot 305

Power Supply 306

Motion Control 306

    Electric Motors and Actuators 307

Sensors 312

    Light Sensors 312

    Touch Sensors 313

    Noncontact Sensors 314

    Audio Sensors 315

    Indicators, Controls, and Other Forms of Communication 315

Control Systems 316

    Open-Loop Systems 317

    Closed-Loop Systems 317

Example Robot Projects..**319**

A Practice Robot... 319

The Next Robot 341

Your Ultimate Robot.. 357

Summary **358**

Index..**359**

About the Author

Dale Wheat is a full-time freelance writer, specializing in electronics and embedded systems. He has written several articles for technical and hobbyist magazines such as *Circuit Cellar*, O'Reilly's *MAKE* magazine, and *Elektor*. He teaches classes on electronics, microcontrollers, and soldering skills. He designs and sells DIY electronics kits from his website, `dalewheat.com`. Before becoming a full-time writer, Dale consulted as a computer programmer and systems analyst for several companies, including IBM, MCI, and GTE (now Verizon). Dale is a two-term past president of the Dallas Personal Robotics Group, the world's oldest personal robotics club. He is a member of the National Honor Society, Phi Theta Kappa, and intends to continue his education as long as they keep the doors open. He lives with his wife, Anne, near Dallas, Texas.

About the Technical Reviewers

Sam Kelly is an electronic design engineer at 3D Robotics, the open-source hardware side of the DIY Drones amateur UAV community. He is a native San Diegan, but got his Electronics Engineering degree in Tijuana, Mexico in 2009, specializing in digital systems. He has been at 3D Robotics since 2010, doing PCB design for internal and community OSHW (open source hardware) projects, as well as product photography. He enjoys eating his own dog food with the rest of 3D Robotics, spending any free time flying prototype and production quadcopters and drones.

Jordi Muñoz is from Ensenada, Baja California, Mexico. He grew up in Tijuana and was influenced by California in all ways, specially in technology. He spent most of his childhood building complex Lego projects and opening any electronic device in his possession. He moved to Riverside, CA in 2007 (legally) and while waiting for his residency started an Arduino aircraft autopilot project. He and Chris Anderson from the small community of DIY Drones founded 3D Robotics, an Arduino-based autopilot company. The company started in a garage, using DIY stuff and Arduino to create many products. In 2010 he and Chris won the Sparkfun UAV competition. Jordi has been featured in many newspapers and magazines in Mexico and the USA. 3D Robotics grew exponentially from a house garage to a 10,000 square-foot facility in just one year. Now the company is located in San Diego, CA—close to his hometown.

Acknowledgments

You see a single name on the cover of this book. That's because I did it all myself! Bwahahahaha!

Ahem. Actually, that's not entirely true. It seems I had some help. Okay, a lot of help, from a lot of people. I didn't actually invent the Arduino, myself, per se. That was actually the Arduino Team, and they *keep* inventing and re-inventing the Arduino. Thanks go to the Arduino Team for giving us something wonderful upon which we can build to our heart's content.

Several companies and individuals contributed ideas, hardware, software, and photos to help make this book possible. I'd like to thank Marc de Vinck for giving me my very first Arduino (a Duemilanove with an ATmega328—woot!) as well as the ever-so-useful Maker Shield, which he designed. Marc also inspired me to bring my very first DIY electronic kit to market. Jimmie P. Rodgers gave me the LoL (lots of LEDs) Shield that appears in Chapter 8. Andy of Spikenzie Labs gave me the fabulous Solder : Time watch you see in Chapter 8 as well.

I'd also like to make special mention of those kind folk that contributed many of the photographs, including the Arduino Team, Critter & Guitari, Seeedstudio, Gravitech, SparkFun Electronics, Fundamental Logic, Jimmie P. Rodgers, Wayne and Layne, Spikenzie Labs, and SparkFun Electronics.

The crew at Apress runs a first-class operation. I'd like to thank my editorial team for their professionalism, courtesy, enthusiasm, and most of all patience in getting this book from concept to reality: Corbin Collins, Frank Pohlmann, Michelle Lowman, Ralph Moore, Jim Markham, Sam Kelly, Jordi Muñoz, and the eagle-eyed Tiffany Taylor.

I'd like to thank James Floyd Kelly for his words of wisdom and encouragement, when they were needed the most.

On the home front, I especially want to thank my parents and my children for their enthusiasm on behalf of this project. My wife, Anne, deserves extra special thanks for leaving me alone when I needed that and keeping me company when I needed that.

Preface

Let's investigate the inner-workings of your Arduino. It appears to be a simple machine, but it is not. Much effort has been invested to make it easy to learn and use. Unfortunately, these good intentions can mask some of the Arduino's underlying capabilities. You suspected that there was more, much more, under the simplistic veneer.

You were right.

This book is about how Arduino actually works. The Arduino is a successful composite of design decisions that has evolved over time. By giving you a more in-depth understanding of the complex technologies involved, you will see the Arduino "internals" as elements to be changed and re-arranged to suit your design goals.

Intended Audience

This book is written for Arduino users of all stripes, from energetic newcomers to seasoned professionals. You already know what an *Arduino* is, and you have some ideas about what it can accomplish for you. You most likely already own one or have access to one. These are not requirements, just guesses. Your interest in Arduino and its inner mysteries is enough.

We don't have to spend any time going over the *very* basics here; introductory Arduino tutorials are everywhere. This book both covers a lot of ground in depth and hopes to follow you on your journey; it's not meant ot be discarded and useless after you blink your first LED.

What This Book Isn't

This book does not attempt to teach you basic electronics in any structured manner. However, because you're an inquisitive and clever sort of person, you will probably pick up a lot of valuable electronic basics by looking at the example projects and exercises. Much effort and technical review has been invested to ensure the examples presented are based on sound design principles.

This is also not an introduction to programming. It is assumed that you know how to manipulate code with an editor and follow simple instructions to accomplish specific tasks. Again, your curious nature will let you absorb "by osmosis" some of the programming examples and styles illustrated in the book, which strive to be clear and well-written.

In no way do any of these chapters contain *all* the information available on a particular subject. Practical and useful information is presented; references to more detailed information is given. Arduino, like any other complex system, is a moving target. As Heraclitus observed more than 2,500 years ago, you cannot step into the same river twice. It was true then and it remains true today, especially with the swiftly evolving Arduino.

You should know that this book is not merely a collection of technical information without a context. The shiny polish of the Arduino, as the world see it, hides layer after layer of complex solutions to complex design challenges. Revealing these layers in a meaningful and understandable order is what this book is all about.

Finally, this book is not just a collection of random, unrelated Arduino projects. The projects and exercises in this book are included to illustrate and reinforce important design principles, to incrementally build from simple to more complex designs, and finally to help you better imagine what is possible, both with Arduino and beyond.

Chapter Overview

Have a look at the table of contents and get an idea of just how far down the rabbit hole we're going to go. This book strives to be a balanced source of technical reference material, so each chapter should be able to stand on its own.

It wouldn't kill you to read the chapters in the order presented. However, feel free to jump around and sample what you like. There's more here than meets the eye. As a rule, the chapters go from the general to the specific. If you skip around a lot and get stranded, try backing up a chapter or two to make sure you have the proper grounding and then proceed forward again.

- Chapter 1: Hardware
  We look at the available Arduino models and take a peek inside.

- Chapter 2: Software
  We run into software at every level of Arduino development. Here is the overview.

- Chapter 3: Atmel AVR
  The "brain" of the Arduino is a microcosm in itself. Knowing what it can and cannot do can be the difference between success and failure in your project.

- Chapter 4: Supporting Hardware
  The rest of the components play important roles, as well. Knowing what they can do and their limits helps you build a better mousetrap.

- Chapter 5: Arduino Software
  The free Arduino-provided software will get you started quickly and easily. It looks simple but it isn't.

- Chapter 6: Optimizations
  Many optimizations are possible in your sketches, and this chapter shows you how to both implement them and verify them with precise measurement techniques.

- Chapter 7: Hardware and Software Combined
  The cooperation of hardware and software, when they cooperate at all, can produce amazing results. A detailed tour of the built-in peripherals in the AVR helps you do more with less code. The general purpose I/O ports, the USART (serial port), counters. timers, PWM outputs, and analog inputs are examined in detail, with examples. The use of interrupts helps to maximize the cooperation between hardware and software.

- Chapter 8: Example Projects
  A blinking LED? Seriously? What it takes to actually blink an LED with *authority*. What it takes to make a more complex project: a digital clock.

- Chapter 9: Project Management
  Dealing with development issues, such as documentation, collaboration, and licensing.

- Chapter 10: Hardware Design
  Starting from the ground up, literally, we cover the areas of expertise needed to design your own Arduino-compatible or not-so-compatible hardware. This includes power requirements, processor selection, and shield design. Several hardware design automation tools are examined.

- Chapter 11: Software Design
  Beyond sketches: Making sound software decisions depends on knowing your options. Alternative development environments, library development and documentation, and PC-side applications are discussed. You can even design your own software tools.

- Chapter 12: Networking
  Networking your Arduino is as easy as deciding who you want to talk to and what you want to talk about; in theory, that is. In reality, it's always more complicated. Leverage the built-in communication capability of your Arduino to talk to a variety of interesting devices. Add application-specific hardware to extend your network as far as you want. Even a simple web server is possible with the addition of some inexpensive hardware.

- Chapter 13: More Example Projects
  A small autonomous robot is in reality a collection of individual projects that must work together. You'll need everything you've learned so far in this book to make this one work.

Summary

The goal of this book is to be an exploration, compendium, and reference for the neglected inner-workings of the Arduino architecture. Leveraging this knowledge will save you time and improve the quality of your Arduino projects. Hopefully it will also spark your interest in embedded system design and prompt you towards more ambitious projects in the future.

Good luck! Don't forget to have some fun along the way!

CHAPTER 1

Hardware

The hardware of the Arduino has evolved slowly since its introduction in 2005. Because *Arduino* as a concept is very much a combination of hardware and software, it's important to have a good understanding of what's involved in both areas, as well as the areas where they overlap. Let's undertake a broad outline of the hardware part of the Arduino in this chapter, going into some detail in a few areas, as well as its history and how you'll play a part in its future.

What Is an Arduino?

Because of Arduino's history and evolution, there are many variations on what can be called an Arduino. The list grows longer every day. The official offering from the Arduino Team consists of the Arduino Uno and the larger Arduino Mega 2560.

When most people think of Arduino, they imagine the small, rectangular (and probably blue) printed circuit board (PCB). This is properly called the *I/O Board*. See Figure 1-1.

Figure 1-1. The Arduino I/O Board. This is what most people think of when you say "Arduino," even though it's only one piece of a larger system.

The I/O Board is the physically tangible part of the Arduino system. Technically speaking, the term *Arduino* covers the hardware, software, development team, design philosophy, and *esprit de corps* of the user community. Yet you'll often hear people say things like, "Please hand me that Arduino," or "Careful with that Arduino, Eugene."

Arduino was originally developed in Ivrea, Italy. Arduin of Ivrea was the king of Italy about a thousand years ago and is celebrated in local history. The Piazza Gioberti hosts a pub named after this famous king, which some say is only named after the road it's on, the Via Arduino.

The name *Arduino* is a masculine Italian name meaning "strong friend." Being a proper name, *Arduino* is always capitalized. The model name Uno is stylized in all capitals only in the logo on the PCB. For more on the history and heritage of Arduino, as well as mountains of other fascinating information, please see the Arduino web site, `http://arduino.cc`.

The Arduino I/O Board has traditionally been based on the Atmel AVR ATmega8 and later derivatives. The I/O Board also contains a serial port, power supply circuitry, expansion connectors, and miscellaneous support components. The official Arduino FAQ states, "It's just an AVR development board" (`www.arduino.cc/en/Main/FAQ`). This assumes that you know what an AVR is. If you read Chapter 3, you will. (Hint: an AVR is a programmable microcontroller chip.) See the simplified block diagram in Figure 1-2.

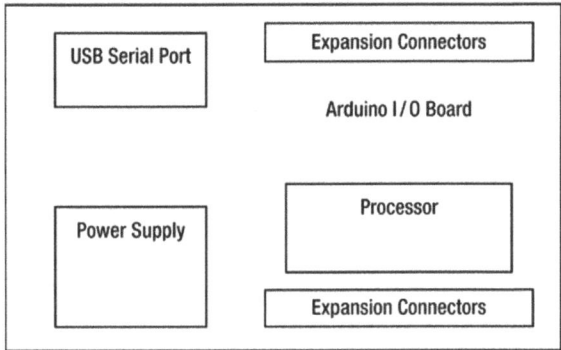

Figure 1-2. The Arduino I/O Board block diagram

The Arduino Uno

The Arduino Uno was announced on September 25, 2011 at the New York Maker Faire. The model name Uno is Italian for the number one and is intended to correspond with the *Uno Punto Zero*, or 1.0 release of the Arduino software. Previous releases, numbered 0001 through 0022 have been considered *alpha*, or preliminary releases.

The Arduino Uno maintains a remarkable resemblance to its forebears. The physical form factor has remained the same. Over the years, the processor has been upgraded twice from the original ATmega8 with 8KB bytes of program memory, first to the ATmega168 with 16KB of program memory and then to the ATmega328 with 32KB bytes of program memory, while remaining pin compatible. The nine-pin RS-232 serial connector and interface circuitry has been replaced with a virtual serial port using various USB interface chips. The power-supply circuitry has seen some refinement with extra over-current protection and intelligent power-source selection.

Due to a temporary worldwide shortage of the beloved 28-pin dual inline package (DIP) version of the ATmega328 processor (whose Atmel part number, to help differentiate it from the other packaging options, is ATMEGA328P-PU, the first *P* being for picoPower technology and the second *P* meaning plastic DIP), a surface-mount version of the Arduino Uno was released, dubbed the Arduino Uno SMD. It's functionally identical in operation to the Uno. The only drawback is that the surface-mount processor can't easily be removed from the PCB, as was the case with the socketed DIP versions. See Figure 1-3.

 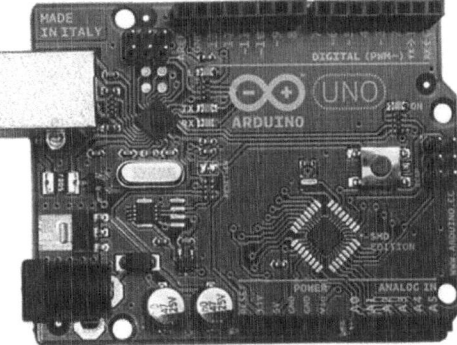

Figure 1-3. The Arduino Uno (left) and the Arduino Uno SMD (right)

If you're starting to get interested in the details of the Atmel AVR, you're in luck! All will be revealed in Chapter 3, including packaging options, how all the pins work and what they do, as well as a good introduction to the inner workings of this very capable device. For now, let's focus on how the Atmel AVR fits into the big picture, Arduino-wise.

Processor

The main brain of the Arduino Uno is the Atmel AVR ATmega328, the black, rectangular plastic block with two rows of pins protruding from its sides. On the SMD version, the processor is one of the two miniscule black squares soldered directly to the PCB.

This device is essentially a computer on a chip, containing a central processing unit (CPU), memory arrays, clocks, and peripherals in a single package. See Figure 1-4.

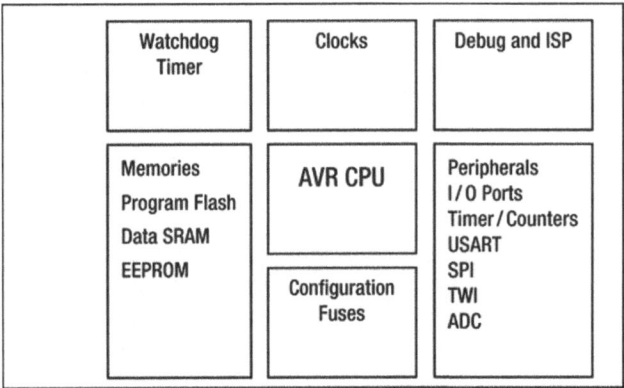

Figure 1-4. Simplified block diagram of the ATmega328

The ATmega328 chip is derived from the original Arduino processor, the ATmega8. It contains more memory and more peripheral capability than its predecessor while using less power. The ATmega328 processor can operate from a wide range of power-supply voltages, from 1.8V to 5.5V. This makes it well-suited for battery-powered applications. At the lowest voltages, the processor has a maximum clock rate of 4MHz (millions of cycles per second). Increase the supply voltage to at least 2.7V, and you can increase the clock rate to 10MHz. To run at the rated maximum clock rate of 20MHz, the chip needs at least 4.5V. The Arduino I/O Board provides 5.0V for the ATmega328 chip, so it can run at any speed, up to the maximum of 20MHz.

The current crop of ATmega328 chips from Atmel feature the company's picoPower technology, which dramatically reduces power consumption in the device. These parts are designated with a *P* suffix: for example, ATmega328P. The previous versions available were able to run either at lower voltages (such as the ATmega328V) but not full speed, or at full speed but not at voltages below 2.7V. The picoPower technology eliminates this limitation, allowing both full speed (at appropriate supply voltages) and low power operation at reduced speeds. The picoPower parts don't even have a speed rating as a component of their part number, as the previous generation did (for example, ATmega328P-PU vs. ATmega328-20PU).

■ **Note** Some specialized I/O Board models are designed to be run at 3.3V. This limits the maximum clock rate to 10MHz.

Although the new ATmega328 chip can run up to 20MHz, the original ATmega8 topped out at 16MHz. The 16MHz clock rate has been maintained in all subsequent Arduino models to preserve compatibility.

See Chapter 3 for more detailed information about the Atmel AVR family of processors.

Serial Port

The function of the serial port remains unchanged from the earliest days of Arduino. The connectors have changed, but everyone pretends that everything is the same. From a functional perspective, this is certainly true.

The serial port is used to communicate. In the development stage of your Arduino project, the communication is between the Arduino and your PC, where you're writing, compiling, and uploading your sketch to the I/O Board. In the application (or *deployment*) phase of your project, when your Arduino is performing its intended purpose, the serial port may continue to communicate with your PC, if that is part of the plan, or it may communicate with another serial device. The use of the serial port is optional at the application stage, so it may be communicating with nothing at all. If this is the case, the receive (RX) and transmit (TX) pins can be used as general-purpose input/output (I/O) lines.

There are several types of serial communication protocols. The Arduino's serial port (internally referred to as the USART peripheral, or Universal Asynchronous/Synchronous Transmitter/Receiver) is used in an *asynchronous* mode, meaning it doesn't provide or require an independent clock signal. This mode of operation is identical to the serial ports of most PCs, also known as *RS-232 ports*. The built-in serial port hardware on the ATmega328 chip is capable of other modes of operation, including *synchronous* mode, where a separate, dedicated signal carries the clock information. The asynchronous method uses one signal to transmit data and another to receive data. Depending on your application requirements, you may need to transmit, receive, do both, or do neither.

■ **Caution**   Don't connect RS-232 signals directly to your Arduino. The typically higher-voltage RS-232 signals can damage the circuitry on the board, including the processor. Always use an RS-232–to-TTL adapter when interfacing an Arduino to an RS-232 port.

Power Supply

The power supply circuit doesn't actually *supply* any power to the Arduino. It only routes, regulates, and filters power supplied from an external source. The present circuit has evolved over the years to make it a convenient and almost foolproof process. The circuit selects the highest available voltage and uses that source to supply the remainder of the circuit. There is even a resettable fuse installed on the board to help prevent damage in the event of a short, thus lessening the likelihood of an unauthorized thermal event. This is a great example of how the Arduino Team has listened to the user community and added incremental improvements to the product over the years.

There are several ways to get power to your Arduino. The simplest, at least initially, is to use the power supplied with the USB cable, which comes from your PC. The USB standard allows for the supply of up to 100mA (milliamps, or 0.1 amps) of current at 5.0V for an unenumerated USB device (that is, a device plugged into the USB bus but not properly identifying itself to the host, such as a USB power tap) and as much as 500mA (0.5 amps) for a properly enumerated USB device. This is more than enough electrical power to light up several LEDs and a few low-power sensors. It isn't sufficient for larger electrical loads, such as relays, heaters, fans, motors, or solenoids.

When the Arduino isn't connected to a PC via the USB cable, regulated 5V power can be supplied to it through the power expansion connector pins labeled 5V and GND.

■ **Caution** A *regulated* 5V supply is required when supplying power via the 5V and GND pins. An unregulated supply's voltage fluctuates with line voltage and load, with the distinct possibility of exceeding the narrow voltage range and very likely causing permanent damage to one or more components, including the processor. The standard Arduino I/O Board provides a voltage regulator. Use it.

For unregulated supply voltage, a modular barrel connector is provided, with input voltages from 7V to 12V. It's directly connected to a 5V regulator circuit. In theory, the input voltage could be as high as 20V, but the likelihood of the voltage regulator chip overheating increases, which can permanently damage the PCB.

The latest design revisions of the Arduino PCBs have greatly improved the ground planes where the voltage regulators are mounted, increasing their ability to dissipate waste heat. However, even with this improved cooling capability, a conservative estimate of the thermal resistance of the device is over 100°C/W, meaning that the temperature of the device will rise over 100°C from the ambient air temperature if 1W is dissipated via the device. That's hot! Don't push it too far!

The barrel connector has a 2.1mm diameter pin. This center pin of the barrel connector is the positive terminal. The outer sleeve connector is ground. The positive connection is also wired to the Vin pin on the expansion connector. The Vin pin can be used to either supply power *to* the shield(s) or route external power *from* shields back to the main I/O Board.

One very nice design feature of modern Arduino I/O Boards is the ability to have multiple, different power supplies connected at once. The intelligent power-switching circuitry selects the highest available voltage and routes that to the voltage regulator.

If you bypass this circuitry and provide regulated 5V power directly to your Arduino (which you most certainly can do), be careful that it truly *is* regulated 5V that you're pumping in. You just bypassed all the safety devices that were put there for your protection. Again, if you know what you're doing, that's fine.

The Arduino Uno also has a dedicated 3.3V regulator installed. Previous I/O Board designs relied on the small 3.3V regulator built into the FTDI USB interface chip. This smaller regulator, although effectively free of additional cost to the system, is only capable of supplying a maximum of 50mA (0.05 amps) of current at 3.3V to the system. The Arduino Uno sports its own 3.3V regulator (the LP2985 from National Semiconductor) that can supply a maximum of 150mA (0.15 amps) of current, but the Arduino web site still only admits to being able to supply 50mA.

Expansion Connectors

To make it easier to connect your Arduino to additional circuitry, four sets of expansion connectors are provided. The two connectors across the top edge of the PCB contain the digital pins, along with the analog reference input and an additional ground connection. The USART TX and RX pins are among these pins, as well.

Along the bottom edge of the PCB are the power and analog connectors. The power connector provides connections to the main supply voltages (Vin, 5V, 3V3, and ground) along with a connection to the microcontroller's -RESET pin. The analog connector brings out the six analog inputs, which can also be used as digital I/O lines if need be.

A very handy feature of the Arduino PCB artwork is that every pin is clearly labeled. This considerably reduces or eliminates tedious cross-referencing between data sheets and code listings. See Figure 1-5.

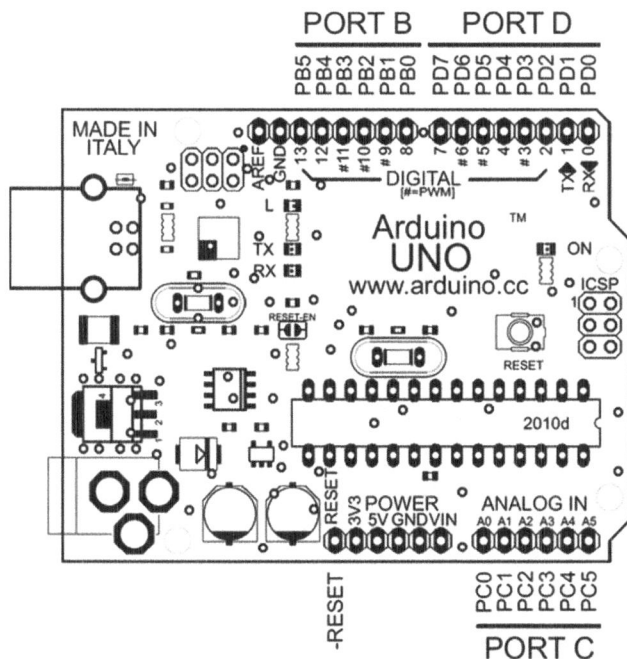

Figure 1-5. The I/O Board's expansion connectors allow additional circuitry to be easily connected.

One of the buried technical details of the Arduino is the naming and grouping of the I/O pins within the expansion connectors. In Arduino-speak, the pins are simply numbered: D0–D13 for the 14 digital pins and A0–A5 for the 6 analog pins. The digital pins run along the top edge of the board, and the analog pins are on the bottom edge.

This naming convention, although widely adopted and referenced extensively in the Arduino documentation and software, is both misleading and inaccurate. Some of the digital pins provide the analog outputs (see the `analogWrite()` function) but are in reality pulse-width-modulation (PWM) or purely digital outputs. The analog inputs can just as easily be used in exactly the same manner as any of the other digital pins, either as digital inputs or as digital outputs, but *never* as analog outputs.

■ **Note**   You can use the analog pins A0–A5 just like any of the other digital pins by referring to them as D14–D19. See Table 1-1.

In AVR-parlance, the ATmega8 family, of which the Arduino Uno's ATmega328 is a derivative, has three general-purpose I/O ports. On the ATmega8, these ports are named Port B, Port C, and Port D. Each port can have a maximum of eight I/O pins associated with it. There's much more information about the details of the AVR I/O ports in Chapter 3.

Some of this confusion over pin names and functions, and the subsequent misleading nomenclature, follows from the multifunctional nature of the device pins. Every one of the general-purpose I/O pins on the ATmega328 has an alternate peripheral function, which can be selected in software. One example already mentioned are the serial port pins, RX and TX. Pin 2 (on the 28-pin DIP) from the AVR side is called PD0 (I/O Port D, bit 0), RXD (received data input pin) to the USART peripheral, *as well as* PCINT16 (pin-change interrupt 16). From the Arduino side, it's called D0 (digital pin 0) or RX.

There is a happy side to all this conflicting naming and renaming. Both the Arduino and the AVR naming conventions work quite well for their intended purposes and provide a nice overlapping symmetry to the circuit design. Just to be thorough, however, Table 1-1 provides a list of all the expansion connector pin information.

Table 1-1. *Arduino I/O Board Expansion Connector Pin Names*

Connector	Arduino	AVR
J1/IOL	D0/RX	PD0/RXD
	D1/TX	PD1/TXD
	D2	PD2/INT0
	D3/PWM	PD3/INT1/OC2B
	D4	PD4
	D5/PWM	PD5/OC0B
	D6/PWM	PD6/OC0A
	D7	PD7
J3/IOH	D8	PB0
	D9/PWM	PB1/OC1A
	D10/PWM	PB2/OC1B
	D11/PWM	PB3/OC2A
	D12	PB4
	D13/LED	PB5

Connector	Arduino	AVR
J2/AD	A0/D14	PC0/ADC0
	A1/D15	PC1/ADC1
	A2/D16	PC2/ADC2
	A3/D17	PC3/ADC3
	A4/D18	PC4/ADC4/SDA
	A5/D19	PC5/ADC5/SCL

■ **Note** The surface-mount version of the ATmega328 chip (but not the DIP version) has two additional analog inputs available, ADC6 and ADC7. Unfortunately, these pins weren't connected to anything on the Arduino Uno SMD PCB. With a steady hand and some good soldering skills, it would be possible to tack some tiny wires onto these pads if you *really, really* needed one or two more analog inputs. Sometimes you do.

Shields

The expansion connectors are where *shields* are installed. Shields allow the I/O Board to act like a miniature motherboard, providing mechanical and electrical connections to additional circuitry. A wide variety of shields are available, providing a mind-boggling array of expansion possibilities for your Arduino.

■ **Tip** The Arduino Shield List is an excellent source of information on available shields and is available online at http://shieldlist.org. The Arduino Shield List provides links to shield makers as well as information about compatibility, resource requirements (such as which pins are used), and licensing information.

Some, but not all, shields have the same board outline as the main I/O Board. When installed, these full-sized shields completely cover, or *shield*, the underlying I/O Board. The Maker Shield, designed by Marc de Vinck, is a versatile prototyping shield that uses *stacking* connectors to make mechanical and electrical contact with the Arduino I/O Board underneath. Instead of just providing mating pins to connect the shield to the Arduino I/O Board, the stacking connectors replicate the expansion connectors, allowing yet another shield to be installed on top of it. The prototyping area in the center of the Maker Shield gives you a place to solder more components to extend the capabilities of your Arduino. See Figure 1-6.

Figure 1-6. The Maker Shield is a full-size Arduino shield that completely covers the Arduino underneath. Stacking connectors allow all the signals from the expansion connector to be replicated above, allowing another shield to be installed on top. The "sea of holes" in the middle is for mounting additional components, extending the fuctionality of your Arduino.

For shields that don't need that much space, or that only require a few closely placed electrical connections, a smaller shield form factor can be used. Only 4 output pins are required to drive a 12-LED array if you use a clever wiring technique called *charlie-plexing*. You'll learn more about charlie-plexing in Chapter 8. Figure 1-7 shows some prototype shields that can be installed across any four contiguous I/O pins on the expansion connectors.

Figure 1-7. *Smaller shields that use only a few I/O lines can be installed in the expansion connectors. The use of multiplexed connections allows up to a dozen LEDs to be individually addressed while only requiring four dedicated control lines from the Arduino.*

It's even possible to build shields that are substantially larger than the I/O Board. One example is the Arduino Piano Shield by Critter & Guitari (www.critterandguitari.com), which gives the user a two-octave piano-like keyboard and other user controls, turning your Arduino into a musical synthesizer. See Figure 1-8.

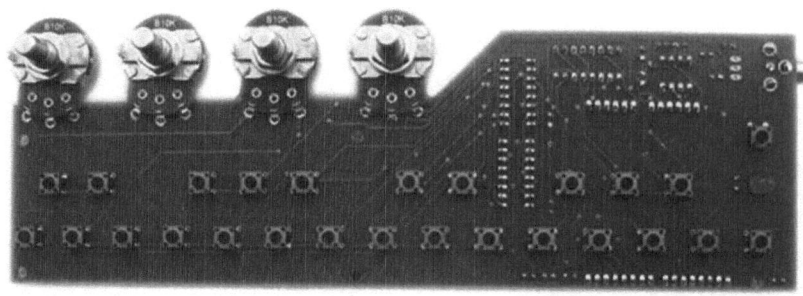

Figure 1-8. The Arduino Piano Shield from Critter & Guitari. This just might be the world's largest Arduino shield. It converts an Arduino into a complete music synthesizer with a two-octave button keyboard and additional user controls. Photo by Critter & Guitari. Used with permission.

The spacing of the expansion connectors has a slight irregularity. The connectors on the top edge are spaced 0.160" apart, pin center to pin center, making them incompatible with the 0.100" grid of solderless breadboards and many other prototyping tools. This aberration has been maintained down through the years in the interest of continuity, despite loud outcries for its rectification. The overriding argument is that although it would be easy enough to correct this issue, doing so would effectively decommission a large number of existing shields whose usefulness stems from reusability. So, the irregularity persists.

Various workarounds have been implemented to correct the expansion connector spacing. Seeedstudio added two additional rows of on-the-grid header pins to its Seeeduino Arduino-compatible product. See Figure 1-9.

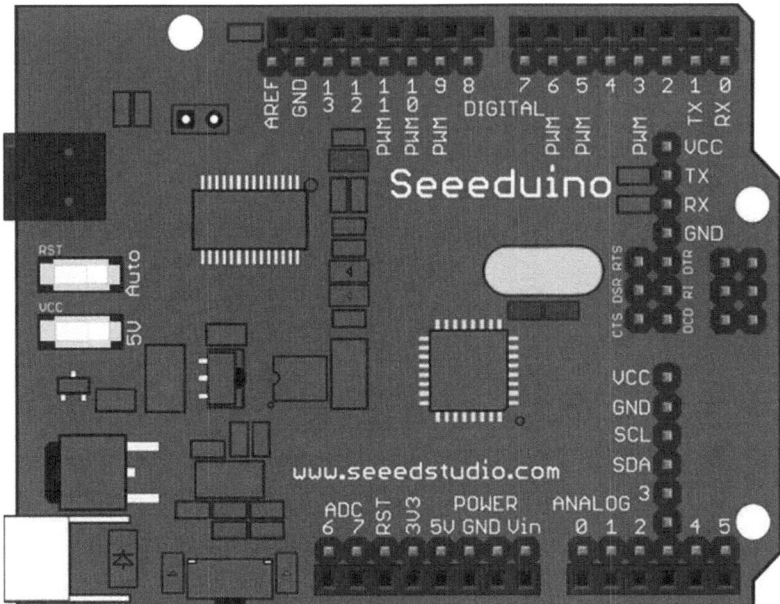

Figure 1-9. The Seeeduino from Seeedstudio adds locations for installing additional expansion connections that are all on a strict 0.100" × 0.100" grid, making it much easier to install in solderless breadboards and other standard prototyping products. Image by Seeedstudio. Used with permission.

Another solution to the pin-spacing problem is to abandon shield compatibility completely. A US company, Gravitech (www.gravitech.us), manufactures the Arduino Nano. The Arduino Nano is designed to be directly installed on a solderless breadboard, with all connections (except the USB mini-B connector) being brought out as header pins with a 0.100" spacing. See Figure 1-10.

Figure 1-10. *Gravitech manufactures the Arduino Nano, which can easily be installed in either a DIP socket or solderless breadboard. The Nano contains all the electronics of the Duemilanove (see section "Arduino Duemilanove" for more) except for the barrel connector and resettable fuse. Photos by Gravitech. Used with permission.*

The Arduino Mega 2560

In almost every respect, the Arduino Mega 2560 is identical to its smaller sibling. It runs at the same speed of 16MHz, requires approximately the same amount of power, executes the same software, and uses the same development tools.

The primary difference between the Uno and the Mega is the processor, the ATmega2560, which has more memory and more peripherals than the ATmega328. The PCB is also larger, but it maintains form-factor compatibility with the standard Arduino, adding three additional expansion connectors along the right side and extending the PCB by approximately an inch in length. The remainder of the circuit is essentially identical to the Arduino Uno. See Figure 1-11.

Figure 1-11. The Arduino Mega 2560

The main difference between the original Mega and the Mega 2560 model is the processor used. The original Mega uses the ATmega1280 with 128KB of program memory. The Mega 2560 model uses the ATmega2560, with 256KB of program memory. The remaining characteristics of the two chips are basically identical.

For a comparison between the Arduino Uno, the original Arduino Mega, and the Arduino Mega 2560, see Table 1-2.

Table 1-2. Comparison of Arduino Uno and Arduino Mega Capabilities

Specification	Arduino Uno	Arduino Mega 1280	Arduino Mega 2560
Processor	ATmega328	ATmega1280	ATmega2560
Program memory	32KB	128KB	256KB
Data memory	2KB	8KB	8KB
EEPROM	1KB	4KB	4KB
Device pins	28/32*	100	100
Digital I/O pins	14	54	54
Analog inputs	6	16	16
PWM outputs	6	14	14
Serial ports	1	4	4

28 pins for the DIP version of the ATmega328, and 32 pins for the SMD version.

Previous Hardware

The Arduino Uno is the result of a relatively short but active evolution. The original production boards date back only to 2005, so not a lot of time has elapsed.

Several prototype versions of the Arduino I/O Board floated around before the familiar form factor emerged. These boards were designed to be easy to build from scratch. The goal was to get boards into the hands of students, artists, and designers as quickly as possible.

Arduino Serial

The first Arduino board with the canonical form factor as you see it today was simply called the Arduino. See Figure 1-12.

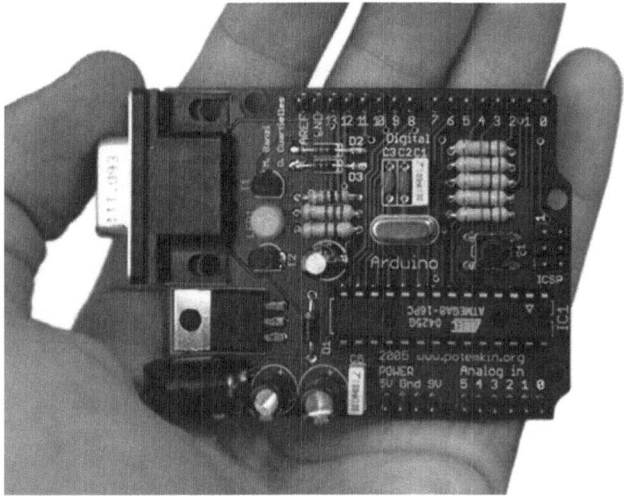

Figure 1-12. The Arduino Serial. Photo by Nicolas Banzetti.

The Serial designation came later to distinguish this design from the later ones that implemented a virtual serial port through USB. Technically, all versions of the Arduino I/O Board use serial communication, so this is something of a misnomer.

The Arduino Board - Serial Interface sported an ATmega8 processor in a 28-pin DIP, running at the (then) maximum clock rate of 16MHz. It had a nine-pin female RS-232 connector (DE9) and discrete level-shifting and inverting hardware to convert the RS-232-level signals into a 0–5V TTL-level that was compatible with the ATmega8's USART pins. Only three of the digital I/O lines had PWM capabilities.

The power supply consisted of a single 5V regulator. Unregulated power could be supplied to the board via a barrel connector or the Vin pin on the expansion connector. Regulated 5V could also be supplied directly via the 5V pin of the expansion connector. No 3.3V power was used on this board. A single LED indicated when power was applied.

A 1KB resistor was installed inline with digital pin 13 (D13). This allowed the user to easily install a single LED in the expansion connector pin, which conveniently was adjacent to a GND pin. Later versions of the board included the D13 LED as a standard feature.

A reset switch was connected between the processor's -RESET line and ground. When pressed, the processor rebooted into the bootloader firmware and waited a short time for a new sketch to be sent from the PC. Failing this, the resident sketch (that is, whatever had been programmed into the part most recently) was then executed. This required the user to physically push the reset button and time the sketch-uploading correctly. Later versions added auto-reset capability via the serial port, eliminating the need to physically reset the Arduino before each upload. Unlike later boards, the processor's -RESET line wasn't brought out to a pin on the expansion connector.

The expansion connectors were typically populated with rows of male pins instead of the more familiar female sockets that are used today. Because these boards were generally distributed as bare boards, the final decision was left to the builder.

One additional six-pin connector was provided for initially programming the blank processors with the bootloader firmware. This connector was erroneously labeled ICSP for In-Circuit Serial Programming. ICSP, however, is the Microchip nomenclature for its PIC line of microcontrollers, popular then and now. The correct AVR terminology is In-System Programming (ISP). This connector can be used to connect the Arduino I/O board directly to a device programmer, such as the Atmel AVRISP or clones, bypassing the on-board bootloader.

Additional (and sometimes expensive!) hardware, such as the AVR Dragon or JTAGICE mkII, along with the right software, allow on-chip debugging of the user's sketch in real time. Hardware debugging, however, isn't supported by any Arduino software.

Arduino USB

The next major mutation of the Arduino I/O Board lost the nine-pin RS-232 connector and replaced it with a USB interface. Both the PC-side software and the microcontroller hardware continued to believe it was a real, live serial port with baud rates and all that jazz. The FTDI USB interface chip basically emulated a legacy serial port. See Figure 1-13.

Figure 1-13. The Arduino USB. This is the second USB version, which corrected a wiring error on the original USB design.

This step was necessary because conventional serial ports were beginning to disappear from the PC landscape. The transition brought along the possibility of being powered directly from the host PC via the USB cable. The user could move a jumper on the PCB to select between USB or external power sources.

Arduino Extreme

The Arduino Extreme began the trend of using female sockets for the expansion connectors. It also used more surface-mounted components than previously, including LEDs to indicate TX and RX activity on the serial port.

Arduino Nuova Generazione (New Generation)

This Arduino model used an improved FTDI USB interface chip that required fewer external components than the previous version, thus simplifying the layout and lowering the cost. Here is where you saw the built-in LED installed on D13 as a standard feature.

It was during the Arduino NG's tenure that the switch from ATmega8 to the newer ATmega168 occurred, doubling the program memory space from 8KB to 16KB.

Arduino Diecimila

Diecimila means 10,000 in Italian, and this model commemorated the milestone of more than 10,000 Arduino boards produced. That's a lot of Arduinos!

Auto-reset was added to the Arduino Diecimila, relieving the user from having to reach over and push the reset button every time a new sketch was uploaded.

Also added was a resettable positive thermal coefficient (PTC) polyfuse in the power-supply section, which temporarily cut off power from the USB port if too much current was drawn. This protected both the Arduino and the host PC. Technically, the host PC's USB hardware is supposed to monitor current consumption and shut down any excessively power-hungry devices, but it turns out that not all manufacturers adhere as strictly to the published USB standard as they might. An extra fuse costs little and saves much.

■ **Caution** Please remember that any pre-Diecimila Arduino carries a potential risk of damage to your PC's motherboard, if *you* manage to short out the 5V power supply.

Arduino Duemilanove

The name *Duemilanove* is Italian for 2009, the year in which this model was introduced. The power source selection jumper was gone, replaced by intelligent highest-voltage-seeking circuitry. During the Duemilanove's reign as flagship Arduino, the ATmega168 processor was upgraded to the ATmega328, again doubling the program memory capacity, this time from 16KB bytes to 32KB. See Figure 1-14.

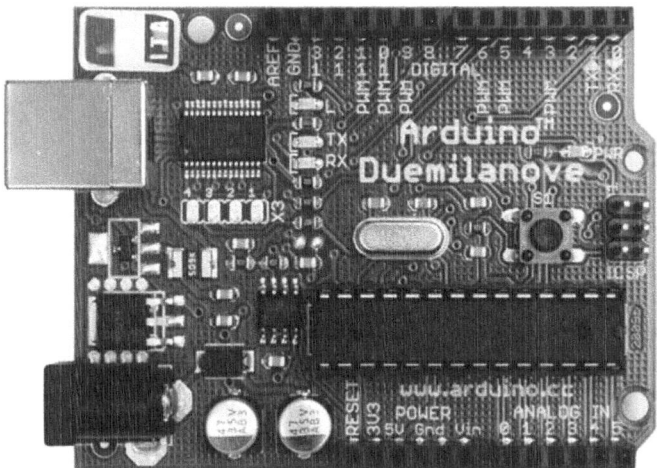

Figure 1-14. The Arduino Duemilanove, which is Italian for 2009, the year it was introduced. Photo by Wikimedia Commons user H0dges and placed in the public domain.

Arduino Mega

The original Arduino Mega is very similar to the standard Arduino I/O Boards, just a little bigger. It uses a physically larger processor chip, the ATmega1280, which is only available in a surface-mount package. The PCB has been extended on the right side to accommodate all the extra I/O lines while maintaining form-factor compatibility with existing Duemilanove-compatible shields.

Who Makes Arduinos?

The Arduino Team makes available all the design files, schematics, board layouts, source code, and other documents so that everyone who wants to can build and use their own Arduino. The only restrictions imposed are on the usage of the name *Arduino*, which should refer to anything designed and supported by the Arduino Team. The rules concerning the terms *Arduino* and *Arduino-compatible* are evolving over time as needs change.

The upshot is that anyone can make an Arduino. You can make an Arduino. Get busy.

Officially Licensed Products

The official Arduino manufacturer is Smart Projects in Italy (`www.smartprj.com`), which builds the Arduino Uno and Mega boards. Additionally, SparkFun Electronics in the United States (`www.sparkfun.com`) builds the Arduino Pro, a minimalist Arduino implementation that lacks a dedicated USB interface and is intended for designs that are to be directly embedded into other devices. Because it has no built-in USB interface, an additional adapter is required to upload sketches to the Arduino Pro. The thinking is that a developer needs only one programming cable rather than redundant USB interfaces on every deployed circuit board. See Figure 1-15.

Figure 1-15. The SparkFun Arduino Pro is a stripped-down, minimalist Arduino circuit. It requires an external USB adapter to upload sketches. Photo by SparkFun. Used with permission.

SparkFun also manufactures the LilyPad Arduino, which is the basis of an entire ecosystem of wearable electronics, or *e-textiles*. The LilyPad Arduino was developed by Leah Buechley and designed by Leah and SparkFun. See Figure 1-16.

Figure 1-16. The LilyPad Arduino was developed by Leah Buechley of the MIT Media Lab. It's designed to be sewn into fabric using conductive thread to produce e-textiles, or wearable computers. Photo by SparkFun. Used with permission.

The LilyPad Arduino can easily be used in noncrafty designs, where a minimalist approach is needed, or if you just like circular things that are purple. It's certainly a more aesthetically pleasing design than that boring old blue rectangle.

Everybody Else

Lots of manufacturers make and sell their own Arduino-compatible boards and shields. This is perfectly in keeping with the Arduino Team's goals of getting the hardware and software out there and into the hands of as many people as possible. Again, as long as the name *Arduino* is reserved for products specifically designed and supported by the Arduino Team, everybody is happy.

A comprehensive index of Arduino and Arduino-compatible hardware designers and vendors is way, *way* beyond the scope of this book. A quick Internet search will uncover more manufacturers and vendors every day.

Build Your Own

You are empowered. Everything about the Arduino is open. You have access to the schematics, the board layouts, the source code, the tutorials, the user forums, and everything else that is Arduino. With all this at your disposal, why not build your own Arduino?

Arduino Printed Circuit Boards

You can buy a blank Arduino-compatible PCB from several sources, collect the necessary components, solder them into place, and voilà! You can say that you built your very own Arduino. The Freeduino project (`www.freeduino.org`) aims to help you do just that.

You can also download the artwork for a (mostly) single-sided PCB design directly from the Arduino web site (`http://arduino.cc/en/Main/ArduinoBoardSerialSingleSided3`). This lets you fabricate your own PCB using a few different methods.

One method is the toner-transfer method. Using specially treated printer paper, you print the PCB artwork using a laser printer or toner-based copier. The toner particles are then transferred to a blank, copper-clad board using either an iron or a modified badge laminator. After cooling, you remove the paper backing by soaking the board in water, leaving the toner pattern adhered to the copper. Then, you slosh the board in an acid bath or wipe it with an acid-soaked sponge to remove the unwanted copper. The remaining copper forms the wiring of the board. You drill holes for the components, ideally using a drill press. The components are then installed and soldered into place.

Another method uses copper-clad panels that are pretreated with photo-sensitive chemicals. The PCB artwork is printed on transparency material and placed over the coated side of the copper panel (for best results, this should be done in a dark or dimly lit area). You then expose the board to sunlight, a strong UV (ultraviolet) lamp, or a really bright desk lamp. Doing so alters the chemical nature of the coating. The parts that were exposed to the light become resistant to the copper etch (acid). The process of removing the unwanted copper is the same as the toner-transfer method.

It's also possible to use a computer numerical control (CNC) machine to route out the unwanted copper on the board as well as to automatically drill the component holes in the right places. Not all hobbyists have access to this type of equipment today. Perhaps in the near future…

If you don't want to actually make the PCBs yourself by hand, it's not too terribly expensive to send the available design files to a professional PCB manufacturer and have it make you a few boards. Richard James Neal, a.k.a. Laen of DorkbotPDX (`http://pcb.laen.org`), offers a low-cost prototyping service to hobbyists for small runs of PCBs. At one time, the cost was $5 per square inch of PCB (for three copies), with no minimum order and free shipping within the United States. See his web site for current terms. This gets you three blank Arduino PCBs (2.1" × 2.7") for $28.35. The nice thing is that you can change up the board layout to suit your needs or artistic temperament, such as adding additional components, more connectors, or even a picture of your smiling face. Laen can accept CadSoft EAGLE files (the format provided on the Arduino web site) or industry-standard Gerber files.

The next step up, which is also cheaper per board, is to send the artwork to a short-run PCB house, such as Gold Phoenix in China (`www.goldphoenixpcb.biz`), where you can get a couple of dozen boards made for just over US$100. This lowers the cost per board significantly, but it's practical only if you need that many blank boards for your projects. You have to export the Arduino-provided CadSoft EAGLE files into industry-standard Gerber files for Gold Phoenix.

■ **Tip**   You'll have to edit the files a bit to get all the helpful pin labels and component legends onto the proper silkscreen layers. The Arduino-provided files seem to have their own idea of where all this information belongs.

Gathering the rest of the components for your home-built Arduino is straightforward, if you live in the United States or United Kingdom. A complete parts list for the Arduino Serial, with Farnell, ELFA, and DigiKey part numbers thoughtfully provided, is available on the Arduino web site (http://arduino.cc/en/Main/PartsSerialV2). Other than the PCB, the only tricky part to get is the ATmega device of your liking, *already preloaded with the Arduino bootloader.* Without the bootloader programmed into the chip, your board really is "just an AVR development board," as per the Arduino FAQ. Herein lies the famous Arduino bootloader chicken-and-egg conundrum.

Factory-fresh ATmega AVRs don't have a bootloader. An AVR-specific device programmer or ISP is required to initially burn the bootloader image into the program memory. From then on, you can easily upload sketches over the serial port from your PC.

Breadboard Arduinos

A printed circuit board isn't required. You can have all the hand-crafted-Arduino fun you want and not even have to learn to solder. A complete Arduino-compatible computer can be built on a very useful prototyping platform called a *solderless breadboard.* See Figure 1-17.

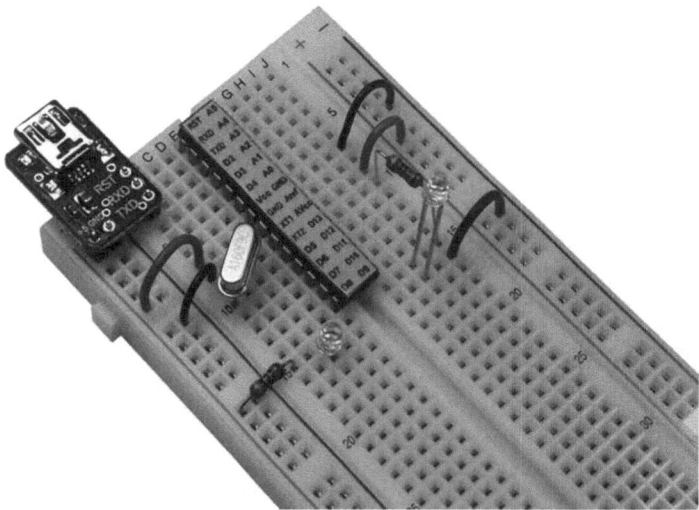

Figure 1-17. An Arduino-compatible physical computing platform can be assembled on a solderless breadboard.

The term *breadboard* is a hold-over from a very-much-bygone age. Believe it or not, before the Internet, people had to make things out of whatever they happened to have on hand. Using a scrap piece of lumber as a substrate, you can tack down component leads using small nails or brads and connect the leads together to make a circuit. Often, the kitchen cutting board was enlisted when a more suitable piece of wood couldn't be found.

Talented technology popularist Collin Cunningham demonstrates building a simple electronic circuit on a real breadboard, using a hammer, nails, and a pair of pliers. You can see the video at `http://blog.makezine.com/archive/2011/04/collins-lab-the-real-breadboard.html`.

Summary

The Arduino I/O Board, although the most recognizable piece of the Arduino puzzle, is only one of many components within the entire system. The basic idea of a small, low-cost, easy-to-use microcontroller has persisted through several generations of electronics and software. Each nuova generazione (new generation) makes incremental improvements to the performance, reliability, and usefulness of the system as a whole.

Although primarily targeted at the Atmel AVR line of microcontrollers, there is nothing written in stone that says an Arduino can't be built on a completely different foundation. Several non-AVR variants have emerged, as well as other designs based on other members of the vast Atmel AVR family.

The basic idea remains simple: a dedicated, reprogrammable microcontroller, with the bare minimum of support components, that can perceive and interact with the world in some limited fashion, both as a building block for more sophisticated systems and a learning tool for aspiring design engineers.

The open source nature of the project has allowed many thousands of developers to create their own Arduino-flavored variations to meet their project needs. Arduino has drastically lowered the barrier to fairly advanced embedded controller design, while maintaining an accessible and easy-to-use user interface. This allows a much broader audience of potential Arduino users more opportunities to create new and fascinating solutions. It's especially empowering to put this sort of accessible technology within the reach of ever younger children, providing them with the tools to build and create, instead of merely consume.

The downside of the program is the oversimplification of the system, which masks the hidden potential of the hardware and software. Amazing things can happen when you tap into the true potential of any complex system. This is correctly called *emergent behavior* when surprising and perhaps unimagined capabilities arise from the interaction of the various components.

This chapter has covered the basics of Arduino hardware and its origins. Now you know a little about the hardware part and a little about the history of the Arduino project. More important, if you weren't previously aware of it, you should be now: you are empowered. Not only does the Arduino project put amazing, enabling technology into the hands of thousands of creative people, it also challenges the traditional concepts of design, manufacturing, and commerce.

The Arduino project belongs to you as much as it belongs to anyone, with the exception of a few little naming issues. What will you do with it? What will be your part in the future of Arduino?

CHAPTER 2

Software

You find software everywhere when you look inside and outside the Arduino. You need software to talk to the Arduino; the Arduino needs software to listen. You use software to write sketches, your sketches get combined with the Arduino libraries, and then *more* software converts (compiles) your programs into the ones and zeros of machine instructions that the AVR microcontroller can understand. In reality, there's even more to it than this.

This chapter serves only as an outline of all the software that is involved in this adventure, to give you an overview of how much software is involved and what functions it serves. Chapter 5 covers the official Arduino software in detail, including the user interface. The clever folks there have spent a lot of time making the software reliable, functional, and, above all, easy to use.

Chapter 11 discusses some of the software design opportunities that exist in the Arduino world. There's always room for improvement. You can tweak the existing software to meet your needs or preferences, or go completely nuts and replace it all with tools of your own imagining.

Hosts and Targets

Working with Arduino today means working with *two* computers at once: the Arduino microcontroller and your PC. In the embedded development world, your PC is the *host* computer, and the Arduino is the *target* computer. This is a different concept than the host and device designations for USB. Although the Arduino, with the appropriate additional USB hardware, can play the part of either a USB device or a USB host, the host computer in the embedded development scenario is the computer on which the software is written and compiled.

The Arduino-supplied software is designed to work on most popular operating systems, including Microsoft Windows, Apple Mac OS, and several varieties of Linux.

Software—lots and lots of software—is needed on both the host and the target computers. Because the internal architectures of the two systems are so different from one another, the process of developing software for one machine on a dissimilar machine is often called *cross-platform development*, or simply *cross development*. You'll also hear similar terms, such as *cross compilers* and *cross toolchains*. These phrases are all talking about tools that help produce executable code for a system other than the one on which the tools are run.

Step by Step

Let's go through the basic steps of programming your Arduino to perform a trivial task: blinking an LED. The actual step-by-step guide for this simple but important exercise is given in Chapter 5. This section only covers the main topics without going into specific, implementation-specific details.

Step 1: Write Some Code

Most beginning Arduino programmers don't write their first *sketch* (Arduino program) by themselves. This is true of most programming languages. There is almost always a traditional, pared-down example exercise that is easy enough to complete in a single sitting yet complex enough to demonstrate that something is actually happening.

A Trivial Example in C

In the C programming language, on which the Arduino programming language is built, the traditional first program is called "Hello, world," because it prints out those words on a console. Once upon a time, that console was a Teletype or CRT-based terminal. These days, it's almost always a console window or terminal window floating on a screen full of other windows or icons. The important thing is that the output is predictable and easily identified as either correct or incorrect.

Printing a couple of words and some punctuation doesn't sound like a big accomplishment (and truly, it's not), but it provides compelling evidence that several key variables are in place, not the least of which is that your *toolchain* (the complete set of all the development tools, both in software and in hardware) is working properly.

■ **Note** Don't underestimate the value of confidence in your tools.

Listing 2-1 shows what the canonical "Hello, world" program looks like in the original C dialect.

Listing 2-1. "Hello, World" in C

```
/* Hello, world */

#include <stdio.h>

int main(void) {
        printf("Hello, world!\n");
        return 0;
}
```

The first line, /* Hello, world */, is a comment, which is ignored by the compiler but very useful to the humans who might need to read this code at some future date. Comments work the same way in the Arduino programming language. Consider adding useful and narrative comments in all your code.

■ **Note**   Self-documenting code is an oxymoron, as well as a poor excuse for laziness. If it was self-documenting, it wouldn't be code, now would it? Don't be lazy. Use comments. Go overboard. Be redundant. It costs little and pays much.

The next line, `#include <stdio.h>`, tells the compiler to add the contents of a *header file*, in this case one with the filename `stdio.h`, into this program file. A header file often contains program definitions and declarations that might prove useful in typical programs and have been collected together to prevent having to reiterate them every time you write new code. Typically, header files (note the `.h` for *header* file extension) exist for each of the major operating system *libraries* (collections of useful functions, snippets, and subroutines) that are made available to the application programmer. The `stdio` system library contains many of the standard input and output functions as provided by the C programming language. In the "Hello, world" example program, a single call to the `printf()` function is used to send a string of characters to the *standard output device*. The Arduino programming language provides many libraries and their associated header files, including `stdio`, which are used in the exact same manner as this example.

Note that most of these terms are specific to the C programming language. You'll often see them used in the Arduino world, because the Arduino programming language is derived from C and still bears a remarkable resemblance, although a few things have been changed along the way.

The remainder of the program listing is the definition of the program's single function, named `main()`. This is where all C programs start execution. Arduino is a bit different, and for a very good reason, but you'll get to that shortly.

The first part of the function definition is where the function is named. The word `void` within the parentheses tells the compiler that the function takes no arguments; it's void of arguments. None are needed. The program is going to print out "Hello, world" no matter what else you try to tell it. The `int` part tells the compiler that the function will return a value, and that this value will be expressed as an *integer number*. This convention reflects the rich heritage of the C programming language, where an application program such as "Hello, world" would be *called* or invoked by an operating system, and a *return value* of some sort would be expected, perhaps to indicate success or failure of the program to the operating system.

In the C programming language, everything is a function. This helps to divide larger programming tasks into smaller, more manageable chunks. The C model of functions taking arguments and returning values is taken directly from algebra. Even the syntax is the same. Arguments and return values are also a part of the Arduino programming language.

Also important is the other punctuation you see in the example program. The opening and closing curly brackets or braces—{ and }–are used to delineate the beginning and ending of the body of the function definition.

The semicolons at the ends of the lines mark the end of complete *program statements*. The two program statements in this example are the call to the library function `printf()` and the `return` statement, which indicates the end of program execution and the *return* to the operating system.

In the Arduino programming language, there is no operating system involved. The `return` statement is supported, but only to return from a *called* function to the *caller* or calling function, along with a supplied return value, if appropriate.

The `printf()` function call and the `return` statement are shown on separate lines, but they need only be separated by a semicolon, as far as the compiler is concerned. Use your best judgment in how you lay out your code. *Whitespace* (the areas between the printable text, assuming your screen background or paper *is* white) is cheap; use it liberally.

■ **Note** Most syntax errors found by the compiler will be due to simple punctuation problems such as omitted semicolons and unmatched parentheses. Look for these first when confronted with a screen full of error messages. Start with the first error message; it probably caused a cascade of other errors.

The argument passed to the `printf()` function is a string of both printable characters and formatting directives, enclosed between double quotes. The `printf()` function interprets the \n sequence to mean "add a new line here." Another useful whitespace code is \t for a tab character, which aligns the next output on a predefined column. A complete guide to the `printf()` function could fill a book all by itself.

This code can be written with paint or charcoal on a cave wall; on paper with pens, pencils, or crayons; or in the air with an airplane equipped for sky writing. But writing it in a form that can be effectively handled by a modern computing device requires the services of some type of *software*, such as a text editor or word processor.

■ **Caution** Word-processing software almost always inserts hidden formatting codes within the text, which will probably confuse or at the least upset your compiler. Always save your computer programs as text-only files, or specify no formatting, if possible. A programmer's editor is preferred, and examples are given later in this chapter

---

Assuming the correctly typed example program has been entered into a computing machine, it then needs to be saved to a *file* (computer document) that can later be found by the compiler. This requires the existence of an operating system (more software) with file-handling capabilities. Luckily, several options are available, depending on your preferences or present situation. For the purposes of this trivial example, a proper operating system is stipulated.

The semi-human-readable document (that is, only partially human-readable, not readable by semi-humans) now exists within the scope of a computer file system. This document is referred to as a *source file*, indicating that it is the origin of the programming process. The file is subsequently processed through various stages to produce object files and eventually an executable binary image. This binary image is composed of the actual ones and zeros that the target computer architecture (the Arduino) can natively execute.

Source files can also be produced by other forms of software, not just by carbon-based programmer types.

Let's skip over the details of the source-file-to-executable-image process for a moment and refocus on achieving the same results for an Arduino.

A Trivial Example in the Arduino Programming Language

It's not hard to port the existing "Hello, world" example program from traditional C to the Arduino programming language. There are, however, a few fundamental differences. These differences correctly reflect the distinctions between the Arduino environment (an embedded system with no operating system) and more traditional application programming scenarios.

The first difference is that there is no explicit reference to any main() function. The main() function exists, because this is, after all, a C-derived language, but it's supplied automatically by the system libraries. It isn't explicitly coded by the programmer.

Instead of a main() function starting everything, Arduino has two important functions: setup() and loop().The setup() function performs whatever one-time initializations need to be made. The loop() function is then called repeatedly, ad infinitum. The calling of the setup() and loop() functions is handled automatically behind the scenes. The minimum Arduino program (that does exactly nothing, other than compile without errors) looks like Listing 2-2.

Listing 2-2. *The Bare Minimum Arduino Sketch*

```
void setup() {
}

void loop() {
}
```

The setup() and loop() function definitions are required, even if they do nothing. If they're missing, you get a nasty "undefined reference to …" error message. Generally, you can find a good use for both of them in every Arduino sketch you write. Many examples are given later in this chapter as well as the rest of the book.

For experienced C programmers, it may help to think of the basic Arduino sketch as already having the code in Listing 2-3 prewritten.

Listing 2-3. *The Assumed C Code in Every Arduino Sketch*

```
void setup(void); // setup() function prototype
void loop(void); // loop() function prototype

int main(void) {

        setup(); // perform whatever one-time initializations are required

        while(1) {
                loop(); // repeat this over and over again
        }

        return 0; // this never happens
}
```

One other minor difference is that the Arduino doesn't know about your intended STDOUT device, which is the implied destination for the output from the printf() function (that is, the system console). You can point it in the right direction using the fdevopen() function and supply a pointer to the function that sends a single character to that device. Then you get to define that function, as well. Within your print-single-character function, you can output the single, printable character via the virtual (or possibly *actual*) serial port using the Arduino's Serial library. This requires that you specify the baud rate in the setup() function beforehand. This all sounds a lot more complicated than it is; see Listing 2-4.

Listing 2-4. *"Hello, World" in the Arduino Programming Language*

```
#include <stdio.h>

int serial_console_putc(char c, FILE *) {
        Serial.write(c); // send a single character out via the serial port
        return 0; // indicate success
}

void setup() {
        Serial.begin(9600); // initialize the serial port
        fdevopen(&serial_console_putc, NULL); // point STDOUT to serial port
        printf("Hello, world!\n");
}

void loop() {
}
```

However, instead of clinging to the past, let's embrace the New Way and simplify this example even further, by talking directly to the serial port without referencing legacy devices. See Listing 2-5.

Listing 2-5. *The Modern "Hello, World" in the Arduino Programming Language*

```
void setup() {
        Serial.begin(9600);
        Serial.println("Hello, world!");
}

void loop() {
}
```

Notice that the Serial.begin() function call in the setup() function remains the same, establishing the communication rate. Instead of jumping through hoops to properly configure everything for the printf() function, you just use the println() method of the Serial object. The println() method automatically appends a newline (specifically, a *carriage return* and a *line feed* character) after the designated text has been output. This effectively performs the same duty as the \n formatting directive within the printf() function's argument.

Move the Serial.println() function call to the loop() function, and you'll have a never-ending supply of "Hello, world!" statements being generated by your Arduino, tirelessly and unflaggingly, until you either reprogram it or remove power.

To detect any of this alleged printing, you have to open a serial terminal window on your host PC. This function is provided within the Arduino IDE.

Another Trivial Example in the Arduino Programming Language

To see your Arduino executing your commands with your bare eyes, you simply change output devices. Most modern Arduino I/O Boards come equipped with a built-in LED on digital pin 13 (D13).

As with the serial port examples, a minimum of device setup is required to properly configure the pin that is driving the LED. On power up, all of the digital I/O pins on the Arduino are configured as *inputs*. You need to change at least one of them (ideally the pin that is connected to the LED) to be an *output.* This configuration only needs to be performed once, so the proper place to do it is within the body of the setup() function.

The pinMode() function configures the device I/O pins. It takes two arguments: the first to specify which pin to configure, and the second to indicate a direction, either INPUT or OUTPUT. See Listing 2-6.

Listing 2-6. Another Trivial Example in the Arduino Programming Language

```
#define LED 13

void setup() {
        pinMode(LED, OUTPUT); // D13 is now an output
}

void loop() {
        digitalWrite(LED, HIGH); // turn on the LED
        delay(1000); // one-second delay
        digitalWrite(LED, LOW); // turn off the LED
        delay(1000); // another one-second delay
}
```

The first line, #define LED 13, is a *macro definition.* This allows you to assign a value to a meaningful name. In this case, you associate the name LED with the number of the pin that (you hope) is attached to an LED. Now, anywhere you type the name LED, the compiler knows to substitute the numeric value 13 in its place. Remember, it helps the humans when source code can be read by humans. Write for your audience.

Within the loop() function, you find two rhyming couplets. In each couplet you see two function calls. The first function is digitalWrite(), which writes a digital (one or zero) value to a device pin. The predefined values HIGH and LOW correspond to the values one and zero, respectively.

Writing a one (HIGH) to digital pin 13 causes the LED to turn on. A zero, or LOW value, causes the LED to turn off.

The delay() function wastes a bit of time. The exact amount of time is specified in *milliseconds* (thousandths of a second) and passed as the argument. This results in a one-second delay between the LED changing state. Without the delay() function calls intermingled between the digitalWrite() function calls, the LED would blink so quickly that it would only appear as a blur, much too fast for the human eye to detect.

Writing (or stealing) the code is the easy part. Compiling it into a form that the chip can understand is a little more complicated.

Step 2: Compile the Code

The nice thing about the Arduino software is that it's generally very easy to use. Not a lot of configuration or tweaking is required to get it to work. You tell it what kind of Arduino you have, you tell it what serial port it's on, and you're done. All the heavy lifting is done behind the scenes.

Let's take a look.

One Button Does It All

The Arduino software does its best to look like it's doing all the work. You push a button, and the software takes your beautiful source code, packs it down into tiny ones and zeros, and then magically beams them into your Arduino.

Trickery! This isn't what happens *at all*. Through some clever misdirection and legerdemain, the Arduino software enlists the help of many, many other software packages, most of which have never even *been* to Italy.

The Arduino software takes your sketch, combines it with some boilerplate code (which looks a lot like Listing 2-3), and then passes it to the `avr-gcc` compiler. The `avr-gcc` compiler is the Atmel AVR port of the popular GNU Compiler Collection (GCC). GCC supports a wide range of computer systems, from the very tiny to the very powerful.

The resulting object code is linked against the standard Arduino libraries (where things like `Serial` are defined) as well as `avr-libc`, the open source C library for the Atmel AVR microcontrollers. The `avr-binutils` collection of tools is used in conjunction with the `avr-gcc` compiler to produce the final executable image, which is formatted as an Intel HEX file: a special file format that encodes a binary image and is recognized by many other software tools.

The resulting HEX file is transmitted to the Arduino using another open source utility called `avrdude` (AVR downloader/uploader).

Within the Arduino's microcontroller, even more software is working to make this one-button process look easy. The Arduino *bootloader* is a tiny bit of resident firmware that remains in place outside of the area where the compiled sketch is stored. The bootloader is activated on power-up or whenever the processor is reset. This allows the Arduino IDE software to remotely reset the I/O Board and then send commands to the bootloader to store a newly compiled sketch.

That's quite a button!

The Tasks of the Compiler

The compiler itself is really a collection of simpler programs that break down the task of source-code translation into smaller, more manageable operations. Here are some enormous oversimplifications of some of the steps that are involved.

The first thing the compiler does is to invoke the *preprocessor*. This software's responsibility is to scan the source code for any required *macro substitutions* as well as splice together any other header files that have been referenced with the `#include` directive.

Next the compiler performs a *lexical analysis* of the aggregated source code, breaking down each program statement into individual *tokens*, or symbols.

The compiler then *parses* the resulting sequence of tokens from the lexical analyzer, or *scanner*, to make sure the program can be successfully converted into machine language instructions. This stage is sometimes referred to as *syntactic analysis*. The order of the tokens within the program is checked against a formal grammar, which states what does and does not constitute a valid program statement.

When all of the original source code has been analyzed and placed into the compiler's internal chart, the process becomes fairly simple, if tedious. Each of the basic programming units recognized by the formal grammar has one or more possible real-world implementations. This varies according to the target device. This is where the `avr-libc` library comes in handy: it's a collection of all the basic computing tasks that may be required in a program, coded specifically for the Atmel AVR line of microcontrollers.

If any additional libraries are needed to finish the process, they're included or *linked* together with the main program. This was once performed by a separate piece of software called a *linker* but has lately been absorbed as yet another task of the compiler.

Next, the resulting conglomeration of bits and bytes is further analyzed to see if any space can be saved or any performance can be improved. This process is called *optimization* and is a mind-bendingly dark art, indeed.

Finally (at least from the standpoint of the compiler suite), the resulting file is written in the appropriate file format for whatever step is next. Normally, this is where the compiler hands off the baton to the device programmer, although in the case of library development, more tasks can be launched.

Step 3: Program the Device

After the source code has been successfully translated all the way to machine code, there remains the job of stuffing all those slippery ones and zeros into that tiny chip. This is where the device programming software and the bootloader do a little dance together.

For most Arduino uploads, the `avrdude` utility is used. This is normally a command-line utility, meaning it doesn't have a fancy, windowed user interface but instead receives its orders directly from the command line. The Arduino IDE knows from your Board and Serial Port settings how to set up this complex set of instructions, along with several other pieces of information contained in the various Arduino configuration files.

The Arduino Bootloader

The final lap of this relay race is handled by the bootloader firmware. This tiny bit of executable code is burned into the AVR's program memory in a special location and can be configured to take over the chip on power-up or after a reset. The Arduino software tells the compiler to skip over this area when compiling a sketch; otherwise the bootloader would be overwritten when a new sketch was uploaded.

The Arduino bootloader presents a bit of a chicken-and-egg problem for hobbyists. You need a dedicated device programmer to program the bootloader into a blank, factory-fresh chip, because chips don't come from the foundry with bootloaders. After the bootloader is programmed, however, it's very easy to upload new sketches to the program memory whenever needed. An Arduino I/O Board can even be used as a device programmer, with some special wiring. But until you have the bootloader installed, you don't yet have an Arduino, per se.

One solution is to buy the chip with the bootloader already programmed. Someday, all microcontrollers will come with bootloaders from the factory. Many non-AVR devices already do.

Step 4: Test and Debug

Now that your sketch is sitting pretty within the confines of the AVR's program memory, it's time to test it and see if it fulfills all your hopes and dreams. This is why it's important to have a simple first project that has a readily identifiable success marker. "Hello, world" served your forefathers well. The blinking LED is another piece of evidence that is hard to argue.

When your Arduino projects become more complex (and they will), it's always a good idea to be thinking about ways to test their performance, even before you start coding. Another good idea is to have a clearly stated goal so you'll know when you're finished.

Step 5. Repeat

This entire process is just one loop through the development cycle. It's almost always reiterated until the behavior of the resulting system meets the expectations of the designer, or until you run out of funding. Code, compile, upload, test, repeat.

Thanks to the sophisticated hardware and software in the Arduino system, this process is now both fast and convenient. You hardly ever have to throw away a shoebox full of punched cards anymore just because of a bad choice in algorithms early in the design phase.

■ **Note** No software project is ever finished.

Semiautomatic

Here is an extra credit mini-project that you may like to try. It gives you some appreciation for how hard your Arduino works to make things look easy and make you, as an Arduino developer, look good.

■ **Caution** Improper use of the commands used in these exercises can render your Arduino inoperable. If you accidentally overwrite the Arduino bootloader (a distinct possibility), you need a dedicated device programmer, such as an Atmel STK500, ARVISP mkII, AVR Dragon, or other, working Arduino to replace it.

You need a plain-text editor or programmer's editor. The editor in the Arduino software thinks you're writing an Arduino sketch and automatically fixes any file-naming mistakes you may make, such as adding a `.c` file extension. In Windows, you can use Notepad. On a Mac, you can use TextEdit. In Linux, gedit or GNU nano will work. You also need access to the command line.

All of the rest of the software that you need for these exercises is provided in the standard Arduino download package. It may be necessary for you to add the location of the AVR-specific tools to your system's path. The location will vary, depending on where you decided to place the Arduino software on your machine: for example, `<Arduino installation folder>/hardware/tools/avr/bin`.

On Windows systems, place a copy of the `avrdude` configuration file (`avrdude.conf`) in that same directory. The configuration file is usually found in `<Arduino installation folder>/hardware/tools/avr/etc`. This allows you to use the `avrdude` utility to program your Arduino without having to specify the location of the configuration file on the command line every time. See the included `avrdude` documentation in `<Arduino installation folder>/hardware/tools/avr/doc/avrdude` for more information.

Blinking in C

Let's blink that LED again, but this time let's do it old school, in C. First, enter the program exactly as you see it in Listing 2-7. The inner workings of the AVR are revealed in Chapter 3. For now, this section glosses over some of the details to illustrate the software process.

Listing 2-7. Blink in C

```
#include <avr/io.h>

int main(void) {

        long i;

        DDRB = 1<<5; // PB5/D13 is an output

        while(1) {
                PORTB = 1<<5; // LED is on
                for(i = 0; i < 100000; i++); // delay
                PORTB = 0<<5; // LED is off
                for(i = 0; i < 100000; i++); // delay
        }
}
```

The #include <avr/io.h> compiler directive reads in a long list of predefined values that pertain to your specific processor. These include the names and addresses of the I/O ports (DDRB, PORTB) that are referenced in the program. The processor is identified in a command-line option passed to the compiler.

The long i; is a long integer declaration, which reserves a spot for a 32-bit value. This value is used as a counter to kill some time.

The 1<<5 notation represents a binary 1 shifted left 5 times. This is only one of many ways to represent this value using C. You can also use binary notation 0b00100000, hexadecimal 0x20, or decimal 32.

Name your new C source file blink.c, and save it in a convenient location. Now open a command-line window and navigate to this location. Enter the following command to compile this simple program:

```
avr-gcc -mmcu=atmega328p blink.c -o blink.o
```

That's a lowercase letter *o*, not a zero. If all goes well, you're rewarded with nothing but another command-line prompt. Otherwise, some possibly enigmatic error messages may pop up. These error messages usually state the offending line number where a problem was found. Start with the first message, if there is more than one, because a single syntax error can cascade into a veritable avalanche of error messages.

Assuming everything goes well, the avr-gcc compiler reads your source file, converts it into machine language instructions specifically for the ATmega328P (the -mmcu=atmega328p command-line option) and writes it out to a file called blink.o, an object file. Object files contains lots of information, such as debugging symbols and other useful tidbits, in addition to the actual machine language instructions you want to send to your Arduino.

You now need to convert this object file into a binary image file that you can program using the avrdude utility. This conversion is accomplished with the avr-objcopy utility, which speaks a variety of object-file dialects. Type this command to perform the conversion:

```
avr-objcopy -O ihex blink.o blink.hex
```

That's a capital letter *O*, not a zero.

Now you have a file suitable for uploading to the Arduino Uno. You use the avrdude utility to send the bits over the wire to the Arduino, like this:

```
avrdude -p atmega328p -c stk500v1 -P \\.\COM11 -U flash:w:blink.hex:i
```

The `avrdude` command syntax is a bit more complex than the previous commands you've used. Let's look at each of the options and see what they do.

- `-p atmega328p`: Tells `avrdude` what kind of chip you want to program. This is similar to the `-mmcu` option for the `avr-gcc` compiler. Different AVR chips use slightly different programming algorithms, and `avrdude` needs to know which one to use.

- `-c stk500v1`: Indicates that the STK500 version 1 protocol is to be used to negotiate the programming of the chip. This is the protocol spoken by the Arduino bootloader.

- `-P \\.\COM11`: Tells `avrdude` which serial port to use. Your serial port will most likely be different. The `\\.\` gibberish is needed under Windows, for some reason, after you've exceeded the single-digit COM ports (1–9).

- `-U flash:w:blink.hex:i`: The complete memory programming instruction, pointing out the memory area of interest (the flash program memory), a *w* for write, the file name (`blink.hex`), and the file format (i = Intel HEX format).

■ **Caution** The avrdude utility is also capable of rewriting the configuration fuses that currently protect the bootloader from being accidentally erased. Don't mess with the configuration fuses until you really, really know what you're doing. You need a dedicated device programmer to recover from such a mistake. The good news is that the bootloader isn't capable of overwriting itself. Decide ahead of time how you want to learn this lesson.

The `avrdude` utility spits out a long series of statements during the programming of the chip, which usually looks like Listing 2-8.

Listing 2-8. Output of the avrdude Utility

```
avrdude: AVR device initialized and ready to accept instructions

Reading | ################################################## | 100% 0.00s

avrdude: Device signature = 0x1e950f
avrdude: reading input file "blink.hex"
avrdude: writing flash (292 bytes):

Writing | ################################################## | 100% 0.07s

avrdude: 292 bytes of flash written
avrdude: verifying flash memory against blink.hex:
avrdude: load data flash data from input file blink.hex:
avrdude: input file blink.hex contains 292 bytes
avrdude: reading on-chip flash data:
```

```
Reading | ################################################## | 100% 0.05s

avrdude: verifying ...
avrdude: 292 bytes of flash verified

avrdude: safemode: Fuses OK

avrdude done. Thank you.
```

If everything has gone according to plan, your Arduino should be flashing its LED at you right now. The flash rate should be a little faster than the `Blink` example sketch. This lets you know that you're officially old school.

Going Further

Even though your fingers are probably exhausted from all this typing, try to bear in mind that your PC is still doing most of the work. You can lighten your load a little by including the three previously mentioned commands (`avr-gcc -mmcu=atmega328p blink.c -o blink.o`, `avr-objcopy -O ihex blink.o blink.hex`, `avrdude -p atmega328p -c stk500v1 -P \\.\COM11 -U flash:w:blink.hex:i`) in a batch file.

An even better alternative is to use the `make` utility, which has been specifically designed to help automate the programming development cycle. A version of the `make` utility is provided in `<Arduino installation folder>/hardware/tools/avr/utils/bin`. You need to also add this to your path, unless you want to type that entire path in every time (which seems like it would defeat the purpose of trying to making things easier).

Chapter 11 contains more information about setting up your projects to use the `make` utility.

Summary

By now, you should have a good idea of just how much software is involved in even the simplest Arduino projects. That LED doesn't blink itself!

Next up, Chapter 3 dives headlong into the heart of the classic Arduino, the Atmel AVR microcontroller.

CHAPTER 3

Atmel AVR

Let's get to know the little computer chip at the heart of your Arduino. You start on the outside and work your way in, with a brief look at the origins and background of the AVR line.

Chapter 1 spent a little time talking about the AVR, mostly as a single component within a larger system. But what a component! There's an entire world inside that little chip. To really be able to take advantage of the potential of your Arduino in your past, present, and future Arduino projects, you need a good understanding of how this part works, what it can do, and how to make it do it. It all starts here. Remember, your Arduino is "just an AVR development board."

The Arduino Team has taken elaborate measures to hide the complexity of this device from the casual user. This is good when you're first approaching the idea of physical computing or embedded development, but it becomes cumbersome and hindering once you've grasped the basic concepts.

This chapter should serve as a good introduction to the AVR, but it's by no means complete. After you've read and understood the material presented here, you should have a better appreciation of just how powerful the hidden, underlying computer within your Arduino can be, as well as where its major limitations lie. You'll also know where to go for even more detailed information, which you may eventually need for more complex projects.

Origins

The AVR architecture was designed by two students on a cold, winter night. Well, it probably took more than one night, but the winter nights in Norway are *really long*.

Alf-Egil Bogen and Vegard Wollan developed a reduced instruction set computer (RISC) architecture design while students at the Norwegian Institute of Technology in Trondheim, Norway. Both men are now employed by Atmel in Trondheim.

To this day, the official explanation from Atmel concerning the meaning of the acronym AVR is that it means nothing in particular. Theories abound, the most popular postulating it stands for Alf and Vegard's RISC.

AVR Device Families

The 8-bit AVR family from Atmel has several branches. The ATmega328 at the heart of modern Arduinos is a member of the ATmega family, but so is the ATmega2560, the computer chip of the Arduino Mega. This could possibly lead to the idea that one version is mega and the other one is somehow less than mega, when in truth they're both technically ATmega.

There is also an AVR tiny family and a classic family. Additionally, Atmel has introduced a USB line (a member of which functions as the USB serial port adapter on the Arduino Uno and Arduino Mega) and an enhanced XMega family, with higher clock speeds and more functionality. More specialized families continue to be developed by Atmel.

Atmel has also designed and produced a 32-bit version of the AVR line, imaginatively called the AVR32. It bears little resemblance to the 8-bit AVR line that is used in the Arduino products and isn't discussed here further.

Each product family addresses a different product sector. The ATmega family is a good blend of affordability and ease of use. The tinyAVR family is directed toward more simplistic or severely cost-constrained applications. The classic family consists of the original AVR offerings from Atmel, including the venerable AT90S1200 and AT90S8515. The majority of the classic family has been discontinued, replaced with higher-performance and lower-power versions.

When in Doubt: Product Datasheets

This chapter is only an overview of the AVR architecture, with special emphasis on the ATmega328 and ATmega2560 devices. The final word on all things AVR lies within the product datasheets, which are freely available from the Atmel web site:

- *ATmega328:* www.atmel.com/dyn/resources/prod_documents/doc8271.pdf

- *ATmega2560:* www.atmel.com/dyn/resources/prod_documents/doc2549.pdf

Be sure to also look for any applicable errata sheets on your particular device. Any machine as complex as the AVR microcontroller is going to have a few adjustments along the way. Each revision of the silicon has incremental improvements, bug fixes, and documented workarounds that are collected and published by the manufacturer.

You're encouraged to browse the datasheets as well as the detailed application notes that are available. They're an invaluable reference. The AVR Team at Atmel is constantly updating the available information and welcome comments and bug reports from users.

Device Packaging

Inside every AVR device is a silicon chip that contains the actual electronics that perform all the duties of the microcontroller. That integrated circuit (IC) or chip is then packaged in a plastic body with almost-microscopic wires running from the edges of the chip to the package pins. Several packaging options are available for AVR devices, accommodating a wide range of end-user applications. Mobile devices naturally put a premium on small size and low weight, whereas hobbyists generally prefer larger-format parts that are easier to handle by hand.

Through-Hole DIPs

The most popular packaging option for the ATmega328 chip is the plastic dual-inline package (PDIP). The last two letters of the complete part number indicate the packaging option and the temperature range. The typical AVR in a modern Arduino I/O Board is properly called the ATmega328P-PU, indicating the PDIP package option and the industrial temperature range of -40°C to 85°C. (See Figure 3-1.) This package variant has been used since the earliest prototypes of the Arduino began circulating.

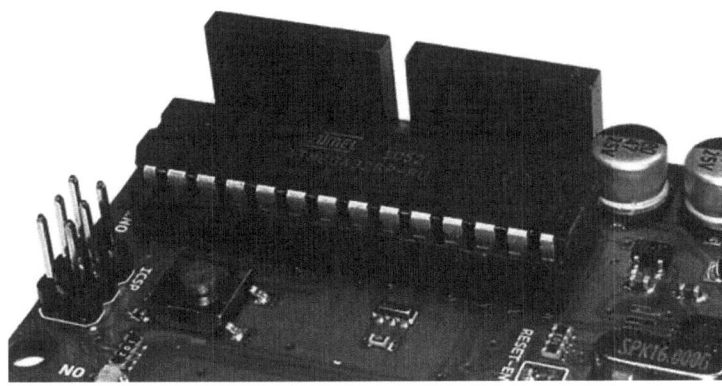

Figure 3-1. *The ATmega328P in a plastic dual-inline package (PDIP). The chip is installed in a socket and can be carefully removed and reinstalled a limited number of times. Note the various markings and indicators on the left end of the package. These orientation marks indicate the location of pin 1. There are two ways to insert the chip into the socket, but only one of them is interesting.*

The pins of the chip (or of its containing socket) are installed through holes drilled through the printed circuit board (PCB) substrate and soldered into place. These are referred to as *through-hole parts*. The holes that the component leads go through are plated with conductive metal, helping to both electrically and mechanically connect the part to the PCB after they're soldered into place.

Surface-Mount Devices (SMDs)

Due to a temporary shortage of devices available in the PDIP format, the Arduino Team released an alternate PCB design for the Arduino Uno that used a surface-mount device (SMD) and called it the Arduino Uno SMD. The SMD version of the PCB layout artfully allows for one of two different SMD package sizes to be populated on the PCB: the 7mm × 7mm Thin Profile Plastic Quad Flat Pack (TQFP) or the 5mm × 5mm Micro Lead Frame Package (MLF). (See Figure 3-2.)

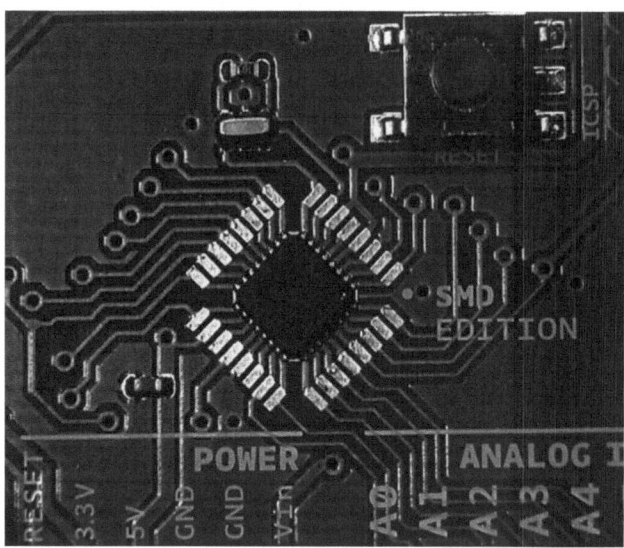

Figure 3-2. *The Arduino Uno SMD was designed to accept either of two different surface-mount device (SMD) packaging variations of the ATmega328 integrated circuit. The smaller of the two PCB footprints, the Micro Lead Frame Package (MLF), is nested within the larger Thin Profile Plastic Quad Flat Pack (TQFP). The silicon chip within the plastic package is smaller still.*

Other packages are available for the ATmega328, including the tiny 4mm × 4mm Thermally Enhanced Plastic Very Thin Quad Flat No Lead Package (VQFN) and the Ultra Thin Fine-Pitch Ball Grid Array Package (UFBGA), also measuring 4mm × 4mm . These wee packages see use in the most space-restricted applications, such as mobile devices.

Extra Pins

Some of the packages for the ATmega328 have 28 pins (the PDIP and VQFN packages), and others have 32 pins (the TQFP, UFBGA, and MLF packages).

The four extra pins on the higher-pincount packages are used as duplicate power and ground connections as well as two additional analog-to-digital converter (ADC) inputs, ADC6 and ADC7. Another way of looking at this is that on the packages with fewer pins, ADC6 and ADC7 aren't *pinned-out*.

Some Arduino (or Arduino-compatible) board designers provide extra connections for these extra ADC inputs, and others don't. The official Arduino Uno SMD, sadly, doesn't (at least in Revision 1 R1 and Revision 2 R2 boards). The Seeedstudio Seeeduino does (see Figure 3-3). This shows the opportunity of open source projects to add additional features without having to start over from scratch with a new design.

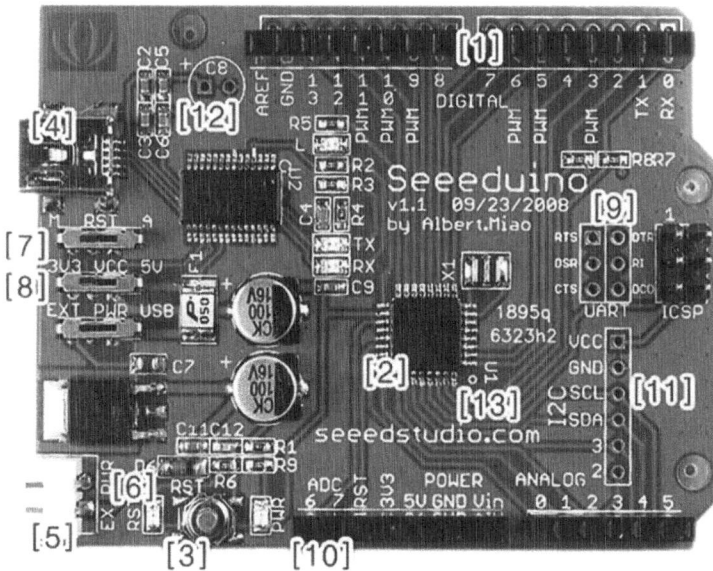

Figure 3-3. *The Seeedstudio Seeeduino uses the SMD version of the ATmega328 chip, and routes the extra ADC6 and ADC7 inputs to connector pins near the power expansion connector [10]. Photo by Seeedstudio. Used with permission.*

Pin Descriptions

The pins of the device, no matter what the package variation, are the microcontroller's electrical and mechanical connection to the outside world. Some pins, such as the power supply connections V_{cc} and ground (GND), have only a single function. Most of the rest of the pins have at least two and sometimes more possible functions. These functions are determined by a combination of device configuration fuse settings and software. See the "Configuration Fuses" section later in this chapter.

Power Pins

The ATmega family runs on direct-current (DC) electrical power, in the range of 1.8V to 5.5V. The higher voltage supplies allow for faster clock rates. See Table 3-1.

Table 3-1. ATmega328 Supply Voltage and Clock Frequency

Maximum Frequency	Minimum Supply Voltage
4MHz	1.8V
10MHz	2.7V
20MHz	4.5V

Curiously, the ATmega2560 on the Arduino Mega has only a single frequency/voltage rating of 0–16MHz at 4.5V–5.5V. No lower-voltage speed ratings are provided in the Atmel datasheet.

Digital and Analog Power Supplies

There are two distinct power circuits within the ATmega chips. One is the digital supply voltage, referred to as VCC or V_{cc}. This is the power supply that provides the CPU core, memories, and digital peripherals with power. The other is the supply for the analog portions of the chip, including the ADC and the analog comparator (AC). The analog power supply pin is called AVCC or AV_{cc}. Both V_{cc} and AV_{cc} should be supplied with the same voltage.

Separate supply pins are used on the ATmega chips so that additional power-supply filtering can be provided for the analog section when low-noise or high-accuracy analog readings are required. This gives the circuit designer the opportunity to reduce the power glitches and high-frequency noise that are generated by the ATmega's digital circuitry.

The 28-pin packages of the ATmega328 have a single V_{cc} pin, a single AV_{cc} pin, and two GND pins. The 32-pin packages have two V_{cc} pins, a single AV_{cc} pin, and three GND pins. The 100-pin ATmega2560 has four V_{cc} pins, five GND pins, and a single AV_{cc} supply pin.

■ **Note** The AV_{cc} power supply *must* be connected, even if no analog circuit functions are used.

The terms VCC (or V_{cc}) and GND don't accurately describe the power-supply pins. These terms are a hold-over from previous semiconductor technologies, such as Transistor-Transistor-Logic (TTL), where the input and output transistor drivers were arranged in a common collector geometry. V_{cc}, therefore, was the voltage of the common collector.

The AVR microcontroller family is based on a low-power Complementary Metal-Oxide Semiconductor (CMOS) transistor technology. *Complementary* means that both N-channel and P-channel transistors are directly implemented in the silicon. MOS transistors don't have collectors, emitters, or bases. They have, instead, a *drain, source,* and *gate* terminal, which only loosely correspond with the terminals of the bipolar junction transistors (BJTs) of older integrated circuits. The correct terminology for the power and ground pins of a CMOS device are V_{DD} and V_{ss}, respectively.

Analog Reference (AREF)

The analog reference (AREF) pin can be used in a variety of ways. It's connected to the reference input of the analog-to-digital converter (ADC) peripheral. The reference input voltage represents the high end of the voltage measurement range. The low end of the voltage measurement range is ground, for single-ended ADC conversions. The ATmega328 only supports single-ended ADC conversions, whereas the ATmega2560 has the ability to make differential voltage measurements across multiple inputs. The ADC takes an analog reading of one of the available analog input pins and compares it to the analog reference input. The resulting numeric value is a ratio of the input value to the analog reference.

Through software, the ADC can select several sources for its analog reference. These sources are an external voltage source applied to the AREF pin, the AV_{cc} analog power supply, or an internal voltage reference. On the ATmega328, the internal voltage reference is approximately 1.1V. On the ATmega2560, the internal voltage reference is selectable between 1.1V or 2.56V.

If you use AV_{cc} or one of the internal voltage references, you can attach an external decoupling capacitor between the AREF pin and ground, thus increasing the stability of the reference voltage.

Another option is to use an external voltage reference source. This option is used in several circumstances: for example, when you require a more accurate reference or need a particular voltage. In this case, it's important not to select via software any of the other reference options, because doing so would directly connect the internal and external voltage sources.

The Arduino Uno connects the AREF pin to the power expansion connector, making it available to users. The Arduino Mega 2560 does the same thing but also connects a 0.1µF (100nF) capacitor (reference designator C3) between AREF and ground.

RESET

The RESET pin provides a mechanism to reset or restart the microcontroller. The bar over the name indicates that it's an active low input, meaning that the RESET function occurs when the input is taken low.

The ATmega2560 has a dedicated RESET input, pin 30. On the ATmega328, the RESET input is multiplexed with the general-purpose I/O pin PC6. The function of the pin is determined by the setting of the reset disable (RSTDISBL) configuration fuse. When this fuse is programmed, the normal reset function of the pin is disabled. You can then use the pin as a general-purpose I/O pin, Port C, bit 6 (PC6). The chip can still be reset from a variety of sources, including the power-on reset (POR) detector, the brown-out reset (BOR) detector, or the Watchdog system reset.

■ **Caution** Disabling the external RESET pin function prevents reprogramming of the device by either the Arduino bootloader using Auto-Reset or an ISP device programmer. Consider this the I/O pin of last resort.

You should note that the RESET pin is designed to withstand higher-than-normal voltage inputs. This is because the RESET pin is also used to signal the chip to enter a programming mode. Bringing the RESET line low and keeping it low causes the chip to enter In-System Programming (ISP) mode, or Low Voltage Serial Programming (LVSP) mode. Raising the RESET pin to approximately 12V (11.5V to 12.5V) causes the chip to enter High Voltage Parallel Programming (HVPP) mode. Because of this special function, the RESET pin lacks the protective clamping circuitry that is present on all other pins, and it's therefore more susceptible to damage from static discharge.

XTAL1 and XTAL2

The XTAL1 and XTAL2 pins are the input to and output from the internal inverting oscillator amplifier, respectively. You can also use XTAL1 as the input to the internal clock circuit, if an external clock source is available.

These pins are normally connected to a quartz crystal to form the time-base of the microcontroller's clock system. The abbreviation XTAL traditionally refers to a crystal of some sort. However, you can also use a ceramic resonator. Ceramic resonators perform much the same function as quartz crystals but are generally less accurate and cost less.

The system clock is the heartbeat of the entire microcontroller. Other clock options are available that don't require the use of the XTAL pins. See the "Clock Sources" section later in this chapter for more details.

The 100-pin ATmega2560 has dedicated XTAL1 and XTAL2 pins. The ATmega328 multiplexes the XTAL1 and XTAL2 pins with the general-purpose I/O port pins PB6 and PB7. A typical Arduino circuit uses either a quartz crystal (Arduino Duemilanove and earlier) or a ceramic resonator (Arduino Uno) to provide a highly accurate time base for the system. The choice between using I/O port pins and clock pins is a by-product of the CKSEL0-3 clock selection configuration fuses. When the quartz crystal or ceramic resonator option is selected, PB6 and PB7 can no longer be used for general-purpose I/O.

General-Purpose Input/Output (I/O) Ports

You've covered all the specific-purpose pins on both the ATmega328 and the ATmega2560 (power and ground connections and AREF, RESET, and XTAL pins). Each and every one of the remaining pins can be used as a general-purpose input/output pin, among (many) other things.

The I/O ports on the AVR are quite versatile. Each port can have up to eight pins associated with it. Each pin within the port can be configured as an input or an output. For more information about the general-purpose I/O ports, see the "Internal Peripherals" section.

Alternate Pin Functions

Every one of the general-purpose I/O pins on the ATmega328 and all but three of the pins of the ATmega2560 (PJ7, PL6, and PL7) performs an alternate function, usually associated with one or more of the other internal peripherals. The alternate pin functions of the ATmega328 are outlined in Table 3-2.

Table 3-2. *Alternate Pin Functions of the ATmega328*

Pin Number		I/O Pin	Function	Description
DIP-28	TQFP-32			
14	12	PB0	D8	Digital pin 8
			CLKO	Divided system clock output
			ICP1	Timer/counter 1 input capture input
			PCINT0	Pin-change interrupt 0
15	13	PB1	D9	Digital pin 9 (PWM capable)
			OC1A	Timer/counter 1 output compare match A output
			PCINT1	Pin-change interrupt 1
16	14	PB2	D10	Digital pin 10 (PWM capable)
			OC1B	Timer/counter 1 output compare match B output
			-SS	SPI bus master/slave select
			PCINT2	Pin-change interrupt 2
17	15	PB3	D11	Digital pin 11 (PWM capable)
			OC2A	Timer/counter 2 output compare match A output
			MOSI	SPI bus master output, slave input (ISP)
			PCINT3	Pin-change interrupt 3
18	16	PB4	D12	Digital pin 12
			MISO	SPI bus master input, slave output (ISP)
			PCINT4	Pin-change interrupt 4

Continued

Pin Number		I/O Pin	Function	Description
DIP-28	TQFP-32			
19	17	PB5	D13	Digital pin 13 (LED)
			SCK	SPI bus master clock input (ISP)
			PCINT5	Pin-change interrupt 5
9	7	PB6	XTAL1	Quartz crystal or ceramic resonator input, external clock input
			TOSC1	Timer/counter 2 oscillator input
			PCINT6	Pin-change interrupt 6
10	8	PB7	XTAL2	Quartz crystal or ceramic resonator output
			TOSC1	Timer/counter 2 oscillator output
			PCINT7	Pin-change interrupt 7
23	23	PC0	A0	ADC0, analog input 0
			PCINT8	Pin-change interrupt 8
24	24	PC1	A1	ADC1, analog input 1
			PCINT9	Pin-change interrupt 9
25	25	PC2	A2	ADC2, analog input 2
			PCINT10	Pin-change interrupt 10
26	26	PC3	A3	ADC3, analog input 3
			PCINT11	Pin-change interrupt 11

Pin Number		I/O Pin	Function	Description
DIP-28	TQFP-32			
27	27	PC4	A4	ADC4, analog input 4
			SDA	I²C/TWI serial bus data input/output line
			PCINT12	Pin-change interrupt 12
28	28	PC5	A5	ADC5, analog input 5
			SCL	I²C/TWI serial bus clock line
			PCINT13	Pin-change interrupt 13
1	29	PC6	-RESET	Reset input, active low
			PCINT14	Pin-change interrupt 14
2	30	PD0	D0	Digital pin 0
			RXD	USART serial input
			PCINT16	Pin-change interrupt 16
3	31	PD1	D1	Digital pin 1
			TXD	USART serial output
			PCINT17	Pin-change interrupt 17
4	32	PD2	D2	Digital pin 2
			INT0	External interrupt 0
			PCINT18	Pin-change interrupt 18
5	1	PD3	D3	Digital pin 3 (PWM capable)
			OC2B	Timer/counter 2 output compare match B output
			INT1	External interrupt 1
			PCINT19	Pin-change interrupt 19

Continued

Pin Number		I/O Pin	Function	Description
DIP-28	TQFP-32			
6	2	PD4	D4	Digital pin 4
			XCK	USART external clock
			T0	Timer/counter 0 external counter input
			PCINT20	Pin-change interrupt 20
11	9	PD5	D5	Digital pin 5 (PWM capable)
			OC0B	Timer/counter 0 output compare match B output
			T1	Timer/counter 1 external counter input
			PCINT21	Pin-change interrupt 21
12	10	PD6	D6	Digital pin 6 (PWM capable)
			OC0A	Timer/counter 0 output compare match A output
			AIN0	Analog comparator input 0 (positive)
			PCINT22	Pin-change interrupt 22
13	11	PD7	D7	Digital pin 7
			AIN1	Analog comparator input 1 (negative)
			PCINT23	Pin-change interrupt 23

AVR Core

Refer back to Figure 1-4 in Chapter 1 for a simplified block diagram of the ATmega328. At its center is the AVR Core, containing the arithmetic logic unit (ALU) that performs mathematical and logic calculations, a set of 32 general-purpose 8-bit registers, a status register (SREG), the program counter (PC), an instruction decoder, and interfaces to the built-in memory arrays and the on-board peripherals. See Figure 3-3.

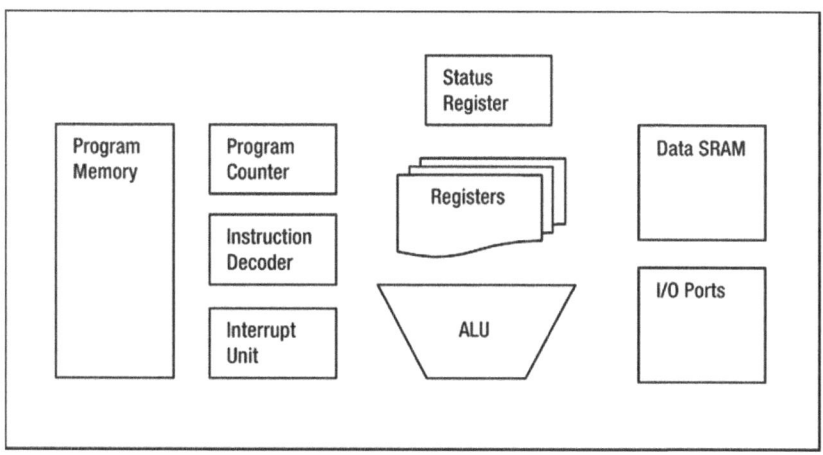

Figure 3-3. The AVR Core contains the essential components of the AVR central processing unit (CPU). It's tightly integrated into the rest of the microcontroller.

■ **Note**   The ATmega2560 also has an external memory (XMEM) interface, allowing up to 64KB of additional SRAM or other memory-mapped peripherals to be added to the system.

After the chip is reset, the PC is set to zero. The first instruction is fetched from a location in the program memory (which can change based on settings in the MCU Control Register), which is called the *reset vector*. It generally contains an instruction to jump (transfer execution) to the proper location in the code to begin any initialization processes needed, and then onward through to the application program. These details are usually handled by the compiler software.

■ **Note**   The term *vector* is used throughout the Atmel AVR documentation. Vectors are generally pointers to specific locations (addresses). The AVR vector table contains a list of executable instructions, but these instructions can be (and usually are) unconditional branch instructions that encode a particular destination address.

The next several locations at the beginning of the program memory are the interrupt vectors. *Interrupts* are events that occur during program execution that cause the chip to stop what it's doing, save its place, execute a specific bit of code, and then return the original program as if nothing ever happened. Table 3-3 lists the reset vector and all the interrupt vectors available on the ATmega328. The ATmega2560 has a similar but longer *vector table*, due to the larger number of built-in peripherals.

Table 3-3. *Vector Table for the ATmega328*

Vector	Address	Interrupt	Description
1	0x0000	RESET	Power-on reset, brown-out reset, watchdog reset, RESET pin
2	0x0002	INT0	External interrupt 0
3	0x0004	INT1	External interrupt 1
4	0x0006	PCINT0	Pin-change interrupt 0
5	0x0008	PCINT1	Pin-change interrupt 1
6	0x000A	PCINT2	Pin-change interrupt 2
7	0x000C	WDT	Watchdog timer
8	0x000E	TIMER2_COMPA	Timer/counter 2 compare match A
9	0x0010	TIMER2_COMPB	Timer/counter 2 compare match B
10	0x0012	TIMER2_OVF	Timer/counter 2 overflow
11	0x0014	TIMER1_CAP	Timer/counter 1 capture
12	0x0016	TIMER1_COMPA	Timer/counter 1 compare match A
13	0x0018	TIMER1_COMPB	Timer/counter 1 compare match B
14	0x001A	TIMER_OVF	Timer/counter 1 overflow
15	0x001C	TIMER0_COMPA	Timer/counter 0 compare match A
16	0x001E	TIMER0_COMPB	Timer/counter 0 compare match B
17	0x0020	TIMER0_OVF	Timer/counter 0 overflow

Vector	Address	Interrupt	Description
18	0x0022	SPI	SPI serial transfer complete
19	0x0024	USART_RX	USART receive complete
20	0x0026	USART_UDRE	USART data register empty
21	0x0028	USART_TX	USART transmit complete
22	0x002A	ADC	Analog-to-digital conversion complete
23	0x002C	EE_READY	EEPROM ready
24	0x002E	ANA_COMP	Analog comparator
25	0x0030	TWI	Two-wire interface (I^2C) event
26	0x0032	SPM_READY	Self-programming event

See Chapter 7 for examples of how to use hardware interrupts in Arduino sketches.

You can enable or disable (mask) individual interrupts in software. There is a master interrupt enable bit in the SREG (bit 7) called the Global Interrupt Enable bit, or simply I. When this bit is set to a 1, interrupts can occur. When the bit is cleared, no interrupts occur. The Global Interrupt Enable bit is cleared by default.

An interesting design decision in the AVR architecture is that when an interrupt occurs and program execution jumps to the designated *interrupt handler* routine, the Global Interrupt Enable bit (I) is cleared. This prevents any further interrupts from being handled. If you need *nested interrupts* (interrupts within interrupts), you must set the I bit explicitly within the interrupt handler routine. Specific machine-language instructions are allocated for setting and clearing the I bit within SREG: SEI for Set Global Interrupt Flag (opcode 0x9478) and CLI for Clear Global Interrupt Flag (opcode 0x94F8). There is also a specific machine-language instruction for returning from an interrupt handler, enigmatically called RETI or Return from Interrupt (opcode 0x9518). This instruction automatically re-enables the Global Interrupt Enable bit when executed.

The SEI and CLI instructions are specific codings of the more general-purpose BSET (Bit Set in SREG) and BCLR (Bit Clear in SREG) instructions. Having the ability to quickly and easily set and clear individual bits within the SREG was considered important enough to warrant their own instructions. You can also test the SREG bits with a variety of *conditional branch* instructions. If the appropriate conditions are met—for example, an arithmetic overflow occurs, or the result of a calculation is negative—then the PC is reloaded with a new value, effectively causing the CPU to jump to a new location in the program memory. The bits in the SREG are listed in Table 3-4.

Table 3-4. Status Register (SREG) Bits

Bit	Name	Description
0	C	Carry
1	Z	Zero
2	N	Negative
3	V	Overflow
4	S	Sign
5	H	Half-carry
6	T	Test bit
7	I	Global interrupt enable

The C, Z, N, V, and H bits are set or cleared depending on the result of certain arithmetic or logical instructions. The S bit is set if either the N or V flag is set, but not both.

The T bit can be manipulated by specific instructions, BLD and BST (Bit Load and Bit Store, respectively). These instructions allow individual bits within the registers to be moved and copied. You can test the value of the T bit using the conditional branch instructions BRTC and BRTS (Branch if T bit Cleared and Branch if T Bit Set, respectively).

Clock Sources

The timing of all internal functions within your Arduino is controlled by the system clock. The standard Arduino circuit uses either an external quartz crystal or a ceramic resonator to provide the fundamental frequency that drives the rest of the system. This is only one of several clock options available with the AVR microcontroller.

The clock systems of the ATmega328 and ATmega2560 are effectively identical. Both have an on-board oscillator whose frequency can be set by an external crystal or resonator. This oscillator has two modes of operation. The low-power mode uses the least amount of power but is unable to drive additional clock signals external to the device. The full-swing mode increases power usage.

Additionally, both devices have the option of being clocked from an external signal. If a suitable signal is already available, this allows the device to be clocked without a dedicated timing component.

There are also two RC oscillator circuits available, with frequencies of 8.0MHz and 128KHz, respectively. The 8MHz oscillator can be calibrated (adjusted) in software, but it isn't as accurate as a quartz crystal or even a ceramic resonator.

A system clock prescaler is available to divide the system clock by integer powers of two from 1:1 to 1:256. Slowing the system clock reduces the amount of power required.

If the main system clock is generated by one of the calibrated resistor/capacitor (RC) oscillators, you can use an external low-frequency clock crystal (typically 32KHz) to drive Timer/counter 2 in a real-time clock application. The timer peripheral can continue to run and keep accurate time even when the main processor shuts down in sleep or power-saving mode.

Address Spaces

The AVR Core has access to several arrays of memory and I/O devices. The AVR architecture itself is based on a Harvard architecture, where the program and data memories are separated, as opposed to a Von Neumann architecture, where the two memories are intermingled, overlapping, and interchangeable.

Program Memory

The actual machine-language instructions for the processor to execute are stored in the *program memory*. On AVR devices, this memory is implemented as a 16-bit wide array of in-system reprogrammable flash memory. Because the program memory is also self-reprogrammable, a certain amount of data can be stored in it, but the programming time and limited number of writes limit its usefulness for transient data storage.

This program memory section is sometimes referred to as ROM, or *read-only memory*. This is yet another anachronism that no longer accurately describes the present function or capabilities. The term ROM was often used to describe the permanent or *non-volatile* bit codings that persisted in a system's memory even during power outages. This term was used to differentiate this type of memory from RAM, or *random-access memory*, yet another misnomer used to identify rewritable or *volatile* memory devices. The flash memory technology used by Atmel in its AVR products as well as other semiconductor devices has all the advantages of non-volatility while being easily reprogrammable without complex or expensive device programming hardware.

Arduino software takes advantage of the AVR's self-programmable nature by implementing a *bootloader*: a small piece of resident firmware that communicates with the host PC and allows compiled sketches to be sent from the PC and stored in the program memory of the AVR. This eliminates the need for any sort of special device-programming hardware.

The PC is used to keep track of the AVR's place within a program. On reset, the PC is cleared to all zeros. Execution begins with the *reset vector*, which is almost always the unconditional branch instruction RJMP (Relative Jump). The destination of the jump is the beginning of the program-initialization code.

The Atmel datasheets suggest that the contents of the program memory should be stable for many years.

Data Memory

The microcontroller usually needs to store variables and changing data during the course of the program's execution. This memory is implemented in the AVR as static, random-access memory (SRAM). Technically, all the memory arrays within the microcontroller are random access, in that any individual memory location can be directly accessed. The memory array is based on *static* bit cells that require no active clock signal to retain their contents, as opposed to *dynamic* RAM cells that require periodic refresh. The SRAM designation is yet another hold-over from previous memory technologies.

The SRAM memory array maintains its data integrity as long as power is applied to the chip. When the power has been removed, however, the status of the memory contents is indeterminate. It's *not* prudent to assume that SRAM contents take on any special value (such as all zeros) after power has been applied. The C programming language, on which the Arduino programming language is based, takes steps to ensure that *uninitialized data* isn't used in a way that assumes an expected value.

The ATmega328 chip has 2KB of SRAM, and the ATmega2560 has 8KB of SRAM. The ATmega2560 can also address *external* SRAM using its XMEM peripheral. This peripheral converts some of the available I/O ports into address and data buses, along with dedicated control lines. Typically, you can add up to 64KB of additional SRAM to the ATmega2560 chip, with more being possible if you implement a *bank-switching* arrangement.

Registers

Every AVR chip from the smallest to the largest has a generous *general-purpose register file*. There are 32 registers in the file, numbered R0 to R31. Most of the arithmetic and logical instructions of the CPU can read and write to the individual registers within the register file directly, often in only one clock cycle. Even the smallest tinyAVR devices with no built-in SRAM have these registers at their disposal. This large register array permits fast and complex algorithms to execute quickly, without having to copy data back and forth from the SRAM memory.

Six of the registers have a special use. They can be combined to form three 16-bit index pointers to the data space. These index registers are called X, Y, and Z. The X index register is composed of registers R26 (low 8 bits) and R27 (high 8 bits). The Y index register is composed of R28 and R29, and the Z index register is composed of R30 and R31.

The AVR Core has many useful and complex addressing modes for accessing both program memory and data memory spaces. These addressing modes are encoded into the individual machine-language instructions that are executed by the AVR Core. For example, a single instruction can load an 8-bit *immediate value* (a form of constant value) from the program memory and write it into any one of the upper 16 registers in a single clock cycle. A variation of this instruction can copy a value from a specific SRAM location into a register, and vice versa. Building in complexity, instructions can use one of the X, Y, or Z index registers as a data pointer, with optional *displacements* or offsets contained within the instruction added to the index register to form the effective address desired. It gets more complicated when you add *post-increment* or *pre-decrement* options, which modify the index register either before or after the operation. This is very handy when you're iterating through arrays of data.

Input/Output Registers

The I/O address space is where all the internal peripherals are accessed. Each peripheral contains one or more registers whose constituent bit settings determine the behavior of the peripheral: for example, the baud-rate setting of the serial port or the direction (input or output) of one of the general-purpose I/O pins.

The SRAM, register file, and peripheral I/O registers are all contained within the data memory space, as opposed to the program memory space. This division of program and data permits more throughput, because separate buses and control lines are used to move data and program instructions back and forth without interfering with each other, and is a performance advantage of the Harvard architecture used by the AVR.

EEPROM

The ATmega328 contains 1KB of *electrically erasable, programmable read-only memory (EEPROM)*. The ATmega2560 has 4KB of EEPROM. Again, you see the residue of generations past lingering in the *read-only* portion of the admittedly conflicted name. It's read-only, but it's also programmable, somehow. Not only that, it's electrically erasable (as opposed to optically erasable, a dim memory of semiconductor devices that had transparent quartz windows over their chips, to allow amnesia-producing, forgetfulness-inducing ultraviolet light to enter and cleanse the memory array of old data).

EEPROM is similar to the program memory, except it's rated to endure many more write and erase cycles. This makes it better suited for storing user-alterable configuration settings or other long-term data that needs to be non-volatile but easily modified.

The EEPROM data can't be directly addressed by the AVR Core. Instead, the address of the desired EEPROM location is written to a special register, a bit in another EEPROM-related I/O register is set to cause a read operation to be performed, and then the EEPROM data can be read from yet another register. Writing to the EEPROM array is accomplished in a similar manner: an address is written to the EEPROM address register, the data to be written is copied to the EEPROM data register, and a slightly more complex bit-twiddling process is invoked. This more complex procedure helps guard against inadvertent EEPROM writes.

The contents of an EEPROM byte are automatically erased prior to writing. The reading process is nearly instantaneous: the data is waiting to be read as soon as the address is set up and the read-strobe bit is engaged. The timing of the writing process is completely controlled by the on-board EEPROM logic. The write process takes approximately 3.3 ms (milliseconds) per byte. A user program can either monitor the status of the program-enable bit (which remains set until the write process is complete) or set up an interrupt to let the processor know asynchronously when the process has completed.

Configuration Fuses

The configuration fuses control several operational aspects of the chip. This gives the devices a great deal of flexibility in how they can be used. The configuration fuses are normally read and written by an external device programmer. The chip can read its fuse setting and lock bits using the LPM instruction (discussed shortly). It can also write to the bootloader lock bits (but none of the other configuration fuses) using the SPM instruction.

■ **Note**   The choice of the term *fuses* to describe the hardware configuration settings on the chip is an unfortunate one. Other manufacturers offer devices with fuses that can be programmed once and then never again. All the AVR configuration settings can be set, erased, and reprogrammed multiple times. Many people associate the word *fuse* with a disposable, one-time device.

Both the ATmega328 and ATmega2560 have three fuse bytes: a high byte, a low byte, and an extended byte. Each byte contains up to eight individual fuse settings.

■ **Caution**   Certain combinations of fuse settings can render your AVR inoperable, or at least inaccessible without specialized device-programming hardware. Always use Smart warnings or Fuse warnings when programming your AVR device directly. This isn't a concern when you're using the Arduino bootloader and the standard Arduino programming software.

Instruction Set

The collection of executable machine-language codes or *instructions* form the AVR *instruction set*. The ATmega328 has 131 unique instructions, and the ATmega2560 has 135. The larger program memory space of the ATmega2560 requires some additional instructions.

■ **Note**   The term *reduced instruction set computer* (RISC) is somewhat confusing, to say the least. It's supposed to indicated that the *complexity* of the instructions themselves is reduced, not that the instruction set, as a whole, has been reduced in size. Simplified executable instructions translate well into simplified silicon implementations, which often translates into smaller, faster, cheaper devices. Although it's possible to develop computers with very few executable instructions (a reduced set), they often prove to be ineffective in practice.

Arduino programmers don't need to know anything about the instruction set of the AVR. The Arduino software completely handles the task of translating the human-readable source code into the appropriate sequences of machine codes needed to accomplish the desired goal.

Knowing more about the inner workings of the AVR Core will, however, give the advanced Arduino programmer a decided advantage when approaching new coding challenges. Knowing the strengths and weaknesses of the internal machinery helps you take advantage of the strengths and avoid, when possible, the weaknesses.

Machine Language Instructions

AVR instructions are either 16 or 32 bits long. Most instructions execute in a single cycle. The main instructions fall into four major categories, plus a small number of system-control instructions.

Arithmetic and Logic

The arithmetic instructions perform very basic binary arithmetic, such as addition, subtraction, and multiplication. All of these instructions are performed by the arithmetic logic unit (ALU) within the AVR Core. The *operands* (numbers used in the calculations) are taken either from the register file or constant (*immediate*) values contained in the instructions themselves, and then processed by the ALU. The results are then stored back in the register file.

The addition and subtraction instructions work on a single byte (8 bits) of data at a time. The AVR implements both carry propagation and zero propagation, which considerably simplifies math on larger data types, such as 16- or 32-bit values.

For example, to add an 8-bit value in one register (the *source* register, or Rr) to another 8-bit value in another register (the *destination* register, or Rd), you use the ADD Rd, Rr instruction:

```
ADD    R0, R1
```

This instruction adds the contents of R1 to R0. Expressed algebraically, this is R0 = R0 + R1. This assumes the proper values for the addition were already present in R0 and R1. You can read more about how to get those values into the registers in the first place in the "Data Transfer" section of this chapter.

To add two 16-bit numbers together, four of the 8-bit registers are needed: two for the first *addend* and two for the second addend. Let's use R1:R0 (low byte in R0, high byte in R1) for the first addend and R3:R2 for the second. The registers need not be adjacent or in any particular order:

```
ADD     R0, R2     ; add low bytes together - this sets the carry flag if necessary
ADC     R1, R3     ; add high bytes together with carry flag
```

As you may have guessed, text after a semicolon (;) on the line is considered a *comment* by the assembler and is ignored.

Note that the second instruction is ADC (Add with Carry). The first ADD instruction properly disregarded any carry flag set from a previous calculation. You can extend this process for larger numbers by appending more ADC instructions. Using all of the 32 available registers at once, a maximum of 128 bit values can be added or subtracted without having to stop, store, and fetch intermediate values elsewhere.

The multiplication instructions take two 8-bit operands and produce a 16-bit result. There are instructions for unsigned (MUL) and signed (MULS) multiplication, as well as for multiplying a signed value by an unsigned value (MULSU). These instructions execute in two cycles.

■ **Note** *Signed* values contain both a numeric sign (positive or negative) and a magnitude. *Unsigned* values contain only a magnitude and are considered to always be positive. If possible, don't mix signed and unsigned values. Strange things will happen.

The additional math instructions INC and DEC allow a register to be incremented or decremented by one. Interestingly, these instructions don't affect the carry flag in the SREG but do affect all other flags. This was intended to help simplify the implementation of an integer loop counter within multiple-precision calculations.

Logical operations work on the individual bits within a register without considering them to represent a numeric value. The logical functions are often referred to as *Boolean algebra*, named after George Boole, the patron saint of ones and zeros. The simplest operations in logic are *and*, *or*, and *not*.

■ **Caution** Don't confuse these *logical* operations at the machine-language level with the logical operators in the C language. The logical operations at the chip level are performed on all bits of the target registers simultaneously. These best correspond with the bit-wise operations of C.

The easiest to explain is *not*, sometimes called *opposite* or *complement*. The complement of 1 is 0, and the complement of 0 is 1. *True* (1) and *False* (0) are often used as operands in logical calculations. This relationship has a nice symmetry to it, which makes it easy to understand and remember. True is the opposite of false, and false is the opposite of true. If this sounds too ridiculously simple, just wait.

The *and* logical operator has two operands instead of one. Let's call them A and B. The result of the computation is called Y, so you can write Y = A and B. The basic rule of *and* is that Y is true if A *and* B are true; otherwise Y is false. This also means that if either A or B is false, then Y must also be false. Table 3-5 illustrates these relationships in a *truth table*, which lists all the possible combinations of inputs and their associated outputs.

Table 3-5. *Truth Table for the Logical* and *Function (True = 1, False = 0)*

A	B	Y
0	0	0
1	0	0
0	1	0
1	1	1

The AND instruction performs the logical *and* function on all eight bits within a register. This is sometimes called bit-wise AND. For example, if R0 contains 0x5F (or 0b01011111 in binary) and R1 contains 0x33 (or 0b00110011 in binary), then the result of AND R0, R1 is 0x13, or 0b00010011 in binary. Note that the corresponding bits in *both* registers must be 1 for the result to be 1. See Table 3-6.

Table 3-6. *Examples of the AND Instruction on R0 and R1*

	7	6	5	4	3	2	1	0
R0	0	1	0	1	1	1	1	1
R1	0	0	1	1	0	0	1	1
Result	0	0	0	1	0	0	1	1

The ANDI (Logical AND with Immediate) instruction does the same thing, except that a constant value is specified in the instruction. This is useful for masking bit positions within a register or selectively clearing some bits while leaving others intact.

The logical function *or* is similar to *and*, except that its basic rule is that if A *or* B is true, then the result is true. Only one of the operands, A or B, need be true for the result to be true. This is reflected in the truth table shown in Table 3-7.

Table 3-7. Tuth Table for the Logical or Function

A	B	Y
0	0	0
1	0	1
0	1	1
1	1	1

The logical *or* function is useful for setting particular bits within a register while leaving the other bits intact. There is also an ORI (Logical OR with Immediate) instruction available.

A variation of the *or* function is called *exclusive-or*, XOR, or EOR. The logic behind the exclusive-or operator is similar to *or*, but with a twist. The rule states, "Y is true if A *or* B is true, *but not both*." See Table 3-8 for the truth table for the exclusive-or function.

Table 3-8. Exclusive-Or Truth Table

A	B	Y
0	0	0
1	0	1
0	1	1
1	1	0

The symmetry of the inputs and outputs makes the exclusive-or function a favorite of cryptographers. You get the same number of ones and zeros out as you put in, which helps to mask any sort of digital bias that could be used to crack the code.

A Word About Missing Instructions

To prevent redundancy within the limited instruction space, complementary instruction pairs have been omitted. An example is the absence of an Add Immediate instruction. An identical result can be obtained by the creative use of the Subtract Immediate instruction, SUBI, and providing the two's complement of the desired constant value. This can easily be implemented in an assembly language *macro* definition, allowing you to use the ADDI macro just as if it were a real instruction. Here is what the macro definition looks like:

```
.macro    addi                  ; there is no addi (add immediate) instruction
      subi    @0,    -(@1)       ; subtract the opposite
.endmacro
```

And here is how it's used in a simple example:

```
ADDI    R0, 7
```

The resulting instruction is actually `SUBI R0, -(7)`, which accomplishes the same thing. Unless you tell it otherwise, the assembler isn't *case-sensitive*—that is, it makes no distinction between upper- and lowercase letters.

Branch

The conditional and unconditional branch instructions allow the program to take various turns in its execution. The *unconditional branch* simply jumps to another program location and begins executing there. *Conditional branches* test a particular condition and then perform the jump only if the condition proves to be true.

The most compact form of the unconditional branch is the `RJMP` (Relative Jump) instruction. It adds a relative offset from the present PC location to determine the destination address. If that relative offset is positive, the branch is forward. If the relative offset is negative, the branch goes backward. The range of the jump is limited to +2,047 and -2,048 *program words*. Recall that all AVR instructions are a multiple of 16 bits (16 or 32) in length. The `RJMP` instruction is a single word long.

The `JMP` (Jump) instruction is two words (32 bits) long. It allows a direct jump to any point within the program memory. Because most program branches are to nearby destinations, it makes sense to use the `RJMP` instruction where possible, to save program space.

Conditional branches test the setting of the flags in the SREG. The flags are generally set after any sort of mathematical computation; you can explicitly set them with the Compare instructions (`CP`, `CPI`, `CPC`, and `CPSE`), which subtract one value from another, set the flags accordingly, but then discard the result.

An example of a conditional branch instruction is Branch if Equal (`BREQ`). This branch takes place if the Z (zero) flag of the SREG is set. The Z flag is set if a comparison of two equal values was recently performed. This code snippet illustrates a conditional branch that will be taken:

```
LDI     R16, 32
CPI     R16, 32     ; Z flag will be set, because R16=32
BREQ destination
...
destination:        ; program execution resumes here
```

The conditional branch instructions use a relative offset from the present PC value to calculate the destination address, similar to the `RJMP` instruction. The relative offset in an unconditional branch instruction, however, is limited to +63 and -64 program words from the present location. This turns out to be sufficient for most situations. If a longer jump is required, you can test the *opposite* branch condition, with the destination being a short hop across an interspersed `RJMP` or `JMP` instruction to the distant point.

There are ten conditional branch variations for comparisons between signed values, ten variations for unsigned values, and eight simple branches that examine a single status bit.

Two special versions of the branch instructions are the `CALL` (Call to Subroutine) and `RCALL` (Relative Call to Subroutine) instructions. These instructions branch to another location but first *push* the current value of the PC onto the *stack*. The destination location is a *subroutine*, meaning that it's a modular piece of useful, reusable code that you can access from various points in the main program without having to rewrite its function every place you need it. A subroutine is expected to exit and return to it caller by *popping* the return value of the PC from the stack. A Return from Subroutine (`RET`) instruction is provided to do exactly that.

The stack is a last-in, first-out data structure that is supported in the hardware of the chip. A special register, the stack pointer, keeps track of what has been pushed onto and popped off of the stack. The stack itself is usually located in the SRAM section. Special instructions, PUSH and POP, allow arbitrary data to be stored in and retrieved from the stack, as well.

Data Transfer

Moving data around inside the chip is where the data-transfer instructions come into play. Data can be moved, loaded, stored, pushed, popped, and sent in or out. Most data transfers are 8 bits, but some allow 16-bit transfers as well.

The MOV (Move) instruction moves an 8-bit value from one register to another. Because the value in the original register remains unchanged, the effect is actually that of a data *copy*, with both source and destination registers being now equal, and the original contents of the destination register lost.

The MOVW (Move Word) instruction performs a similar task, except that two registers are moved at once. The instruction is limited to even-numbered registers.

The simplest of the Load instructions is LDI, or Load Immediate. This instruction loads an 8-bit constant value into a register. The LDI instruction is limited to the upper 16 registers, R16-R31:

```
LDI     R16, 0x99    ; R16 will now contain the value 0x99, or 144 decimal
```

The other Load instruction variations copy data from the data-address space into a specific register. The LDS (Load Direct from SRAM) instruction specifies a 16-bit address within the data-address space, which includes the register file, the I/O space, as well as the internal (and possible external, if provided) SRAM array:

```
LDS     R0, 0x180    ; Copy contents of SRAM at location 0x180 to R0
```

The bulk of the Load instruction variations use the index register X, Y, or Z as the basis for the address to use and then copy the data into a register. Options for post-increment or pre-decrement of the index register are available. Additionally, you can use the Y and Z index registers with a constant displacement in the range of 0 to 63 bytes:

```
LD      R0, X    ; R0 <- (X)
LD      R1, Y+   ; R1 <- (Y), Y is then incremented (post-increment)
LD      R2, -Z   ; Z = Z - 1 (pre-decrement), then R2 <- (Z)
LD      R3, Z+4   ; R3 <- (Z+4) index plus displacement (Y and Z only)
```

LPM (Load from Program Memory) is a special-purpose variation of the Load instruction that copies a byte value from the program memory space, using the Z index register, and stores it in a register. You can also use this instruction on both the ATmega328 and the ATmega2560 to read the fuse and lock bits.

The Store instructions, ST and STS, perform the complementary functions of storing data from the registers to the data memory in much the same way as the Load instructions. The exception is the SPM instruction (Store Program Memory), which takes a little more preparation. The program memory is organized into pages (see Table 3-9), and each page must be entirely erased before it can be reprogrammed. This self-programmability is the basis of the Arduino's bootloader function.

Table 3-9. *Program Memory Page Size*

Device	Page Size	Pages
ATmega328	64 words	256
ATmega2560	128 words	1,024

Data can be pushed onto and popped off of the stack using the PUSH and POP instructions, respectively. After a register is pushed onto the stack, the stack pointer is decremented by one. Conversely, the stack pointer is incremented by one before a POP instruction is executed, copying the value pointed to by the stack pointer to the destination register.

The IN and OUT instructions are used to access the I/O register space, where most of the peripheral device configuration settings are located.

Bit Manipulation

The AVR architecture allows individual bits to be easily set, reset, and tested. This is especially critical in embedded systems, where a single bit may represent a relay output or a sensor input.

The BSET and BCLR instructions that control the bits in the SREG have already been discussed. The SBR (Set Bits in Register) instruction is really a special coding of the Logical OR with Immediate (ORI) instruction, where the operand is bit-wise or'ed with the contents of any one of the upper 16 registers, R16-R31. The CBR (Clear Bits in Register) instruction likewise is a special coding of the Logical AND with Immediate (ANDI) instruction, except that the constant value supplied is automatically complemented.

You can set individual bits in the lower end of the I/O space (I/O registers 0–31) using the SBI (Set Bit in I/O Register) instruction, or clear them with the CBI (Clear Bit in I/O Register) instructions. These instructions don't affect the other bits within the accessed register. This is accomplished by using a read-modify-write cycle and causes these instructions to take two cycles to complete. This is still faster and more code-compact than reading the I/O register into the register file using an IN instruction, making the necessary modification, and then writing the result back using an OUT instruction.

System Control

Some random instructions that just don't seem to fit in anywhere else get stuck in the MCU Control heading.

The SLEEP instruction puts the processor into a low-power state. Several levels of sleep are available, depending on how much power needs to be consumed (or not consumed, as the case may be) as well as the length of time needed to resume normal program execution given a proper stimulus.

The WDR (Watchdog Reset) instruction explicitly resets the Watchdog Reset counter, which causes either a system reset or interrupt (depending on configuration) if ignored for long enough.

The NOP (No Operation) code simply takes up space and wastes time. Fortunately, it takes up exactly one program word of space and exactly one CPU cycle of time. This comes in handy when you require very accurate timing: for example, when one particular branch of a program takes exactly three cycles longer than another, yet they must both finish on the same exact cycle-count to maintain timing. These things happen.

Internal Peripherals

What separates a mere *microprocessor* (such as the Z80, the 6502, the 8088, or even an Intel Pentium) from a *microcontroller* is the inclusion of all those other bits that are required for a complete computer circuit, including memory banks, clock circuits, and interface peripherals.

The AVR family of microcontrollers offers a wide variety of internal peripheral interfaces that make it easy to communicate with other devices. Let's look at some of the major peripherals you can use.

General Purpose Input/Output (I/O)

The ATmega328 has three I/O ports: Port B, Port C, and Port D. The ATmega2560 has 11 I/O ports: Port A, Port B, Port C, Port D, Port E, Port F, Port G, Port H (they skipped Port I), Port J, Port K, and Port L.

When configured as an output, the voltage on the pin can be set to either a logic-high level (V_{cc}) or a logic-low level (GND) by writing a 1 or a 0 to the output port register (called the *data register*) bit, respectively. Additionally, each port pin can be individually addressed using bit-manipulation instructions.

When configured as an input, each pin can be read as either a logic-high or logic-low level. Voltages above $0.7 \times V_{cc}$ are considered a logic-high level and read as a 1. Voltages below $0.3 \times V_{cc}$ are considered a logic-low level and are read as a 0. Voltages between these two levels are indeterminate.

■ **Note** You can read the approximate *analog* voltage values of inputs only by using the ADC peripheral, which is only available on either 6, 8, or 16 pins, depending on the processor. *Digital* inputs (0 or 1) can be read on any general-purpose I/O pin.

Input pins can also enable a built-in pull-up resistor, if needed. This allows the signal to remain in a known state when no external circuit is attached.

Each I/O port is programmatically controlled by setting bits within three I/O registers. The data direction register for each port contains a programmable bit corresponding to each pin. Programming the direction bit of a pin to a 1 makes it an output. Programming a 0 makes that bit an input. After reset, all port pins are inputs by default.

The data register for each port serves two functions. When an I/O port pin is configured as an output, the state of the corresponding pin in the data register determines the voltage level on the pin. When the pin is configured as an input, writing a 1 to the corresponding data register bit enables the built-in pull-up resistor.

The input pins address reflects the current logic level on the associated pin. Don't make the mistake of trying to read from the data (output) register (for example, PORTB), because it only reports the last value, if any, written to that port. Reading from the input pins address (PINA, PINB, and so on) is the correct method of interrogating the outside world.

You can also use the input pins address to toggle the value of an output pin. Writing a 1 to a bit in the input pins address flips the corresponding bit in the data register. This is much faster than reading the bit, performing a logical inversion, and rewriting the bit.

External Interrupts

The AVR Core recognizes and can respond to two different types of external interrupts. The classic external interrupts are the INT0 and INT1 pins of the ATmega328 and INT0-7 of the ATmega2560. Additionally, up to three banks of eight I/O pins can be configured as pin-change interrupts, having the ability to notify the processor should a change occur.

The INT pins are a little more versatile than the pin-change interrupts. Each INT pin has its own, separate interrupt vector, whereas each bank of eight pin-change interrupts shares a vector. Also, the INT pins can be configured to trigger an interrupt on a low-level input, a rising-edge, a falling-edge, or either rising-or-falling-edges. The pin-change interrupts trigger on any change in level; but only a port-level flag is set, indicating which of the three pin-change interrupt ports caused the interrupt, but not which specific pin.

Each external interrupt source can be individually enabled or disabled.

External interrupts are an excellent resource for embedded applications. Proper use of external interrupts can free the main application program from having to constantly poll a device or condition to see if it needs attention. A classic example is a push-button input. If the main application is performing many tasks, it may not be looking at the push-button input line at exactly the moment the user presses the button. This can lead to the appearance of a nonresponsive system. Using a properly configured external interrupt for the push-button allows the main application program to describe the conditions on which it should be interrupted and the appropriate actions to take place in that event. Now the main application program can busy itself with other tasks. Whenever the interrupt occurs, the intended behavior is triggered automatically.

Timer/Counters

The ATmega328 has three timer/counter peripherals available. Each one is a little different. The ATmega2560, as you might expect, has even more.

Let's start with the ATmega328 and its three unique timer/counters. They're referred to as Timer/Counter 0, Timer/Counter 1, and Timer/Counter 2.

Timer/Counter 0

At the heart of Timer/Counter 0 is an 8-bit counter. You can directly read from and write to this counter using the 8-bit TCNT0 register. The behavior and operation of the counter are controlled by the bit settings in two configuration registers, TCCR0A and TCCR0B. Many possible combinations allow a wide variety of uses for this versatile peripheral.

As its name suggests, this peripheral can be used as either a timer or a counter. When clocked (triggered) by an external signal, it performs as a counter. When clocked from the system clock (or a signal derived from the system clock), it can be used as a timer or frequency generator.

The timer/counter can be set up to generate interrupts. This is a handy thing to have when you need to schedule something to happen on a regular basis.

Another popular function is the generation of pulse-width-modulated (PWM) signals. Two different PWM outputs can be controlled, although they share the same period and resolution. These PWM outputs, OC0A and OC0B, are connected to PD6 and PD5, respectively. On the Arduino Uno, these signals are called D6 and D5.

Timer/Counter 1

Timer/Counter 1 shares many characteristics with the other timer/counters. Its principle distinction is that the internal counter is 16 bits long instead of only 8.

Two PWM channels are also available for this timer/counter, just like Timer/Counter 0. These signals can be routed to output pins OC1A and OC1B, also known as PB1 and PB2, or D9 and D10 on the Arduino Uno.

Timer/Counter 1 also has an input capture unit. This hardware allows very accurate timing measurement of incoming signals.

Timer/Counter 2

Another 8-bit counter is found at the heart of Timer/Counter 2. It's almost identical to Timer/Counter 0, with two PWM channels (OC2A and OC2B, routed to pins PB3 and PD3, a.k.a. D11 and D3, respectively), interrupts, the works.

What makes Timer/Counter 2 special is its ability to dance to the beat of its own drummer. It has an asynchronous mode of operation that allows it to be clocked from a source other than the system clock or external signals. Assuming the system is being clocked by the calibrated RC oscillator, the otherwise-unused crystal oscillator driver can be used to drive a low-frequency watch crystal. This configuration is ideal for low-power, real-time clock applications. Unfortunately, there's no easy way to do this using an Arduino without extensive hardware and software hacks.

Timer/Counters of the ATmega2560

The ATmega2560 has all of the timer/counters of the ATmega328, and then some. The two 8-bit counters (0 and 2) are effectively identical in operation. The ATmega2560 adds three more of the 16-bit timers (named 3, 4, and 5), for a total of four. Each timer/counter has 3 PWM channels instead of 2, bringing the total PWM count up to 14. That's a lot of PWM channels!

The pin-number license taken on the Arduino Mega 2560 allows all of the PWM outputs to be grouped together as digital pins D0–D13.

USART

Now here is a grand-sounding name for a peripheral: Universal Synchronous/Asynchronous Receiver/Transmitter. It's synchronous *and* asynchronous! It's a receiver *and* a transmitter! It's *universal!*

It's a serial port. Get over yourself, already.

The ATmega328 has one USART (still called USART0, even though it's the only one). The ATmega2560 has a total of four USARTs, which is very nice. If they aren't needed, the TX and RX pins of the unused serial ports can be used as general-purpose I/O pins.

Just like the PWM pins of the Arduino Mega 2560, the additional USART pins are all grouped together, immediately adjacent to the existing RX and TX pins that are found on the Arduino Uno. An extra pair of serial interface pins are also included on this connector, but they're a horse of a different color.

Two-Wire Serial Interface (TWI), a.k.a. I^{2}C

The extra serial interface pins mentioned previously are the serial data (SDA) and serial clock (SCL) pins of the I^{2}C peripheral. I^{2}C is arcane shorthand for IIC, or Inter-IC, which in turn stands for the Inter-Integrated Circuit bus, a communication specification developed by Philips (now NXP) to cut down on the number of wires running between chips inside of television sets.

The I^{2}C name, logo, specification, and just about everything pertaining to it is copyrighted, trademarked, restricted, and otherwise so nailed to the ground that Atmel calls it TWI for two-wire interface, or sometimes 2-wire interface, just to be different. Don't tell anybody, but it works exactly the same.

Although not marked as such, the ATmega328 also has a TWI peripheral, whose SDA and SCL pins are routed to the analog input pins A4 and A5 on the Arduino Uno.

I^{2}C bus is a popular interface standard for many chip manufacturers. You can find memory chips, ADCs, accelerometers, real-time clocks, temperature sensors, and many more devices that communicate over the I^{2}C bus.

The Arduino supports communication on the I^{2}C bus using the Wire library.

The I^{2}C spec allows up to 127 devices on a bus, although most systems have between 2 and 6 devices. The TWI interface is completely compatible with the I^{2}C spec. If you run into weird problems, perhaps you're not properly terminating the clock and data lines. When all else fails, lower the clock speed and look at the signals with an oscilloscope to see what's going on. Also, make your driver software more forgiving of error conditions. All I^{2}C drivers must be interrupt driven, and that is its own kind of madness.

Analog Inputs

Both the ATmega328 and ATmega2560 have an ADC peripheral. The main difference between the two chips is the number of multiplexed inputs provided to the converter. The ATmega328 provides 6 inputs (8 in the SMD versions), and the ATmega2560 offers a whopping 16 inputs.

On both the Arduino Uno and Arduino Mega 2560, the analog inputs are collected together on one or two connectors. The Arduino Uno has inputs numbered A0–A5, and the Arduino Mega 2560 has numbered inputs A0–A15.

These analog inputs can measure voltages in the range of 0–5V. The actual range is determined by the settings in the peripheral configuration registers and the voltage, if any, applied to the AREF input pin.

The ADC, when properly configured and triggered, can convert the incoming analog voltage into a number in the range of 0–1,023. Zero represents a voltage at or near ground, and a reading of 1,023 indicates a voltage at or near AREF. This corresponds to ten bits of resolution.

The reading of the analog inputs is directly supported in the Arduino programming language using the analogRead() function. This function takes a single parameter (the number of the analog pin to be read) and returns a value between 0 and 1,023.

Summary

You've only scratched the surface of the AVR. There's a world of details inside that little silicon chip.

If all this information has threatened to overwhelm you, take heart. You don't need to memorize every fact and specification concerning these devices. It's enough at this point to be aware of them in a general way. More important, you should have a good idea about where to start looking when you need more detailed information about a particular aspect of the system.

Download a local copy of the datasheet for your favorite AVRs, and take some time to browse through them, even if only to remember where the information can be located so you can look it up quickly when you need it.

Even if you don't plan to write your own assembly-language programs for the Arduino, a good baseline knowledge of the lowest-level building blocks will serve you well, especially when you start wanting to optimize your sketches for either speed or size. Chapter 6 goes into tremendous detail about how you can do that, and it relies on your understanding of what is involved, if not the exact implementation details.

CHAPTER 4

Supporting Hardware

In Chapter 3, you explored the deep-down-inside parts at the heart of the Arduino, the Atmel AVR. With so much internal complexity, it's hard to believe that you would need anything else; but you do.

First, the chip needs power to perform all that magic. Second, if you don't connect the chip to something, no one will ever be able to tell that anything is happening.

Let's take a detailed look at each of the major areas in the basic Arduino circuit. These areas include the following:

- Power supply

- Serial interface

- Processor and associated components

- Expansion connectors

The chapter also looks at the mechanical form factor in some detail and includes a special section on the Universal Serial Bus (USB) interface on modern Arduinos.

Schematic Diagrams

When a circuit has more than one or two components, it begins to be difficult to clearly describe it using words alone. A simplified, stylized diagramming technique has been developed over the years to help facilitate this necessary form of communication. An *electronic schematic diagram* represents individual components as symbols, usually connected with solid lines to indicate the wiring connecting the components. See Figure 4-1.

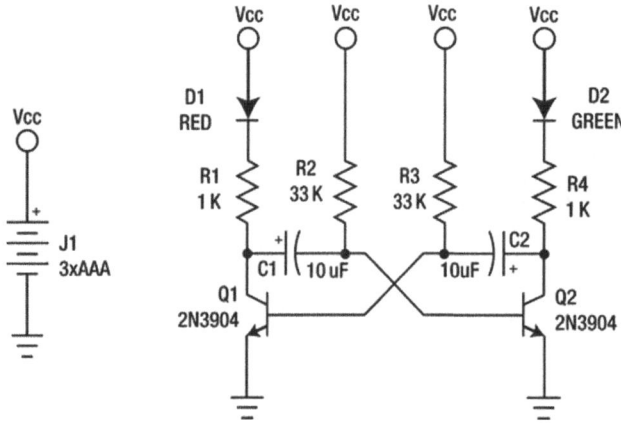

Figure 4-1. *An example schematic diagram*

Other technical occupations also have their own version of schematics. Any sort of stylized representation that focuses only on the essential components and their interrelationships can be classified as a schematic. Electrical or electronic schematics are just one example.

If you're already familiar with modern electronic schematics, please feel free to skip to the next section. If not, here are the very basics you need to identify individual components and start to see the relationships expressed with all those squiggly lines.

Figure 4-1 represents a classic LED blinker circuit, the *astable multivibrator*. It's called *astable* because it doesn't stay in any one state for very long; it blinks back and forth with only one LED on at a time.

One side or the other is on, conducting current through the LED, the current-limiting resistor, and the transistor. Meanwhile, the capacitor is charging; when it reaches a certain threshold, it causes the other side of the circuit to turn on, lighting its LED and extinguishing the other side. The cycle repeats as long as power is applied to the circuit.

Component Types

Five types of electrical components are used in the blinker circuit: LEDs, resistors, capacitors, transistors, and batteries. Technically speaking, there is only one battery in this circuit, and it happens to be composed of three individual cells, but most people refer to the individual cells as batteries.

Each of the components has a distinctive appearance in the drawing. The thin lines connecting the components are wires or electrical connections on a printed circuit board (PCB). Each component should also be clearly labeled with enough information to properly identify it.

The schematic should contain enough information to build, examine, or repair the circuit. Additional notes are often found on schematics to help explain non-obvious aspects of the circuit or provide any necessary advice or warnings that may apply.

Reference Designators

The most obvious components, due to the purpose and design of the circuit, are the two LEDs, labeled D1 and D2. The names D1 and D2 are called *reference designators*. Reference designators are usually a combination of a short abbreviation (D for diode; LEDs are *light emitting diodes*) and a unique number. Because there are only two LEDs in this circuit, they're simply named D1 and D2. They could just as well have been named Red LED and Green LED. As long as each individual component is uniquely identifiable, you can name them whatever you want.

Even if multiple, identical components are used in a circuit, it helps to carefully number them when compiling a *bill of materials* (BOM). This is an important document in the manufacturing process, and it's also very helpful when you're publishing assembly instructions to share with others.

In more complex schematics with many sections, each section may have its own range of numbers for its components: for example, the power-supply section may have seven LEDs numbered D101–D107, and the CPU section may have two LEDs numbered D201 and D202. Nothing says the numbers must be sequential.

Some circuit designers prefer to number the components according to the logical layout as expressed in the schematic. Other designers prefer to arrange the numbering of the components to more accurately represent their physical location in the final, assembled circuit.

The choice of abbreviations for component types varies considerably from one schematic (or continent) to the next. This book uses the abbreviations shown in Table 4-1.

Table 4-1. Schematic Diagram Component Abbreviation Prefixes

Component Type	Abbreviation	Unit of Measure	Symbol
Resistor	R	ohms	Ω
Capacitor	C	farads	F
Diode	D		
LED	D, LED		
Transistor	Q		
Integrated circuit	U		
Crystal	X		
Connector	J		

Integrated circuits are also sometimes labeled X or IC. The U convention, interestingly enough, comes from the Bad English phrase *un-repairable subassembly*. Connectors are sometimes also abbreviated X, as in the Arduino documentation.

Component Values

Each nontrivial component should also have a clearly stated value. The needs of the circuit determine the level of detail given. Noncritical components can get by with just a simple numeric value, usually representing the component's characteristic function. For example, *resistors* are placed in a circuit to *resist* the flow of electrical current, and the amount of that *resistance* is measured in *ohms*, whose symbol is the capital Greek letter omega, Ω.

Component values can be abbreviated by using multiplier prefixes. Resistors, for example, are available in values from less than one ohm to many millions of ohms. Instead of writing 1,000 Ω , you could write 1K Ω , prefixing the unit of measure (Ω) with the uppercase letter *K* (from the Greek prefix *kilo*, meaning one thousand). Other common multipliers are given in Table 4-2.

Table 4-2. Common Component Value Prefixes

Symbol	Value	Exponent	Prefix
p	0.000000000001	10^{-12}	pico
n	0.000000001	10^{-9}	nano
μ	0.000001	10^{-6}	micro
m	0.001	10^{-3}	milli
K	1,000	10^{3}	kilo
M	1,000,000	10^{6}	mega
G	1,000,000,000	10^{9}	giga

Both larger and smaller multipliers have been defined, but they're rarely used in specifying electronic component values.

Component Value Tolerances

Very often, component values only have to be close enough to a particular value to be effective. For example, when you're selecting a value for a current-limiting resistor to be used in conjunction with an LED, it won't make any visible difference to the naked eye if a 1,000 Ω or a 1,007 Ω resistor is used. Common resistors, such as those found on the Arduino PCB, often have value *tolerances* of ±1% for resistors, meaning that the actual value of the resistor could vary as much as +1% or -1% from the labeled value and still be close enough. Capacitor values can be much looser with the tolerances, sometimes rated at +80%, -20%.

Due to the relatively low precision of most component values, only a small number of *significant digits* are required in their specification. This is generally limited to two or at most three digits, in most cases. An example is a resistor rated at 2,200 ohms. It can be written as 2.2K Ω or even as just 2.2K.

You also see a further compacting of component values by replacing the decimal point with the multiplier and omitting the unit of measure (when it's understood): for example, 2,200 ohms can be written as 2K2.

Other Component Parameters

When appropriate, a component on a schematic may also be labeled with other important ratings, such as maximum working voltage (in volts, or V) or power-handling capability (in watts, or W). These indicators tend to be the exception and not the rule in electronic schematics, and they may only be found in a detailed bill of materials.

In more complex electronic components, such as semiconductors, there is no *primary* component value other than a manufacturer's part number. When this is the case, the schematic lists the part number as its value.

The Connections

Solid lines are generally used to represent electrical connections between components. Each component has one or more electrical terminals or pins that allow it to be electrically connected to the other components. These components leads are often drawn as short lines emanating from the body of the component symbol. Even unused component leads are generally shown in schematics, even if just to show that they aren't supposed to be connected to anything in particular. These pins are sometimes labeled N/C (no connection) or not labeled at all. One convention is to place a small × at the end of unconnected pins, but this isn't universal.

There are two special conventions concerning electrical connection notation that may not be obvious to the casual observer. The first is the use of *implicit* or *explicit* connections among signals (often referred to as *nets*) that have more than two endpoints. One style is to show explicitly connected nets with an obvious dot at their intersection, whereas unconnected signals can cross without indicating that they're electrically connected at all. The opposite convention is to show a small arch in the horizontally drawn line to indicate that it hops over the other signal without making contact. The first convention is more prevalent these days and is the one used in this book.

The other important notational convention is the use of buses where multiple electrical components are connected to the same signal. There are several ways of indicating these connections without explicitly drawing a line for every one of them.

A very common example is the use of the ground symbol. *Ground* is an electrical concept from which all other voltages are referenced within a circuit. It's sometimes, although infrequently, actually attached to the ground (that is, the Earth; ground is sometimes replaced with the term *earth*). The ground symbol appears three times in the schematic in Figure 4-1: a short, vertical line with three horizontal lines of diminishing length. Can you find them?

At the top of the schematic in Figure 4-1 you can also see five round symbols labeled V_{cc}, which literally means the voltage of the common collector. All five of these points in the circuit are considered to be electrically connected to each other, even though they aren't explicitly shown as connected with solid lines.

Getting Power to the Board

The very first Arduino I/O Boards had a very simple power-supply circuit. Despite its simplicity, it was quite versatile, allowing you to provide either regulated or unregulated power, as well as routing power to the expansion connectors to power any *shields* that might be attached. The power-supply section of the original Arduino schematic is shown in Figure 4-2.

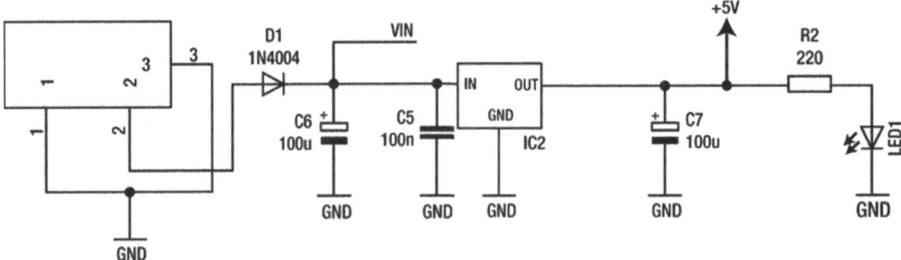

Figure 4-2. *Power-supply section of the Original Arduino serial schematic*

The Barrel Connector

The unlabeled block on the left side of the drawing is the barrel connector for unregulated *direct current* (DC) power input. The part outline vaguely resembles the side view of the barrel connector itself, although the electrical connections aren't physically arranged in the same order as the part. The symbols used in both the Arduino Serial schematic and the present Arduino Uno schematic are the same, but they don't correctly reflect the manufacturer's pin-numbering scheme, the physical connector itself, or industry standard conventions.

Two of the electrical connections to the barrel connector (labeled pins 1 and 3 in this schematic) are connected to ground. Note that the power connector has no preference as to polarity; it's the circuit designer's responsibility to establish this important arrangement and adequately document it.

The barrel connector has a center pin in the middle of a circular opening. The diameter of the pin is nominally 2.1mm, and the inside diameter of the opening is 5.5mm. At the bottom of the housing is a spring-loaded terminal that presses against the outside of the power plug when inserted. These two terminals make electrical and physical contact with the power plug. The third terminal coming from the barrel connector housing is attached to a mechanical switch. This switch is *closed* (shorted to the spring-loaded side terminal) when no plug is inserted and *open* when a plug is present. This could be used to switch from internal to external power when a plug is inserted or removed, but it isn't used for this purpose on the Arduino.

This is a very common connector for low-voltage DC power supplies. It's produced by several different manufacturers. Depending on the exact manufacturer and part number, the connector is rated at 16V–24V and from 2.5A–4.0A of current. You must take this into account when budgeting power to external circuitry.

CUI, Inc. manufactures a connector like this, and you can see the company's detailed datasheet with all the part dimensions and electrical specifications at http://products.cui.com/CUI_PJ-002A_Datasheet.pdf?fileID=4458.

The barrel connector remains the same on every standard form-factor Arduino produced so far.

Input Power Conditioning

The second pin on the barrel connector is the positive voltage connection and is connected directly to the *anode* or positive lead of D1, a diode here employed as a *rectifier*. A rectifier allows current to pass in one direction but blocks the flow of current in the opposite direction. D1's job is to prevent current from flowing at all, should the input voltage be of the wrong polarity (that is, plugged in backward). This is a nice product safety feature that costs little and potentially saves much.

Note the arrow-like appearance of the diode schematic symbol. This helps orient the reader as to the *allowed* or *intended* direction of current flow. The bar of the cathode terminal is often printed on the physical part, helping to orient it during assembly. Unfortunately, it only indicates the flow of conventional current, which turns out to be exactly the reverse of the reality of electron flow. Electrons (the charge carriers in metallic solids, such as copper wire), having a negative charge, actually flow from negative to positive potentials.

The input rectifier, D1, is specified in the original schematic as a 1N4004, which is a generic manufacturer's part number for a 1.0A (maximum) rectifier diode. The 1N4004 is only one in a whole family of similar diodes, numbered from 1N4001 to 1N4007. The main difference between the various part numbers is the maximum DC blocking voltage (V_R), ranging from 50V for the 1N4001 to 1,000V for the 1N4007. The 1N4004 is rated at 400V.

A rating of 400V is a bit of overkill for this application, but many of these design decisions are based on parts' availability and cost, rather than the best fit from a specification standpoint. It's common to see very wide variations in both pricing and availability, both critical factors to manufacturing. Considering that the input voltage was previously limited by the power connector, any of the diodes from this series would serve adequately.

The modern Arduino Uno has a surface-mount version of the 1N4007 (dubbed the M7) in this position.

The limiting factor to consider, as far as the reverse-polarity-protection diode D1 is concerned, is the 1.0A maximum current rating. The Arduino circuitry draws merely a small fraction of one *ampere* (usually shortened to amp or A) of current. Additional circuitry must not push this over the 1.0A limit, or D1 will overheat and eventually fail, usually with burny and sometimes smoky and even flamy results. The smell isn't nice, either.

If power is being supplied from another source, such as the USB adapter or another connector, the limitations of the barrel connector and the reverse-polarity-protection diode D1 can be overlooked. Note that D1's rectification characteristic prevents power from being *supplied* to external circuitry via the barrel connector.

D1's *cathode*, or negative terminal, is connected to several other points within the circuit. Note the use of the explicit connecting dot to show that the several lines are, indeed, electrically connected.

From the connecting dot upward, then over to the right, is a connection to the voltage bus VIN, or input voltage bus. On the original Arduino Serial, this went to only one other location: a pin on the power-expansion connector, also labeled VIN. This additional connection allows the unregulated input voltage to be supplied to expansion shields. Alternatively, it can also be the *source* of unregulated power to the Arduino board, bypassing the barrel connector and reverse-polarity-protection diode D1.

On more modern Arduino boards, the VIN signal is also used to help decide what power source is selected to power the board. This involves a little more circuitry and is described in more detail in the "Power Circuit Evolution" section, later in this chapter.

After the diode, the power signal is attached to two different kinds of capacitors, C6 and C5. Notice that although the two capacitor symbols are similar (two separated plates, which succinctly describes how a capacitor is built), there is a subtle but important distinction. C6 is *polarized*, and the positive connection is labeled in the schematic with a small plus sign (+). Oddly enough, the *negative* lead of a physical capacitor is the one that is usually marked. C5, on the other hand, is nonpolarized and can be installed in the circuit in either possible configuration. Installing C6 backward in the circuit can lead to component failure, including possible expansion and rupture of the containing sleeve or can.

The two capacitors C6 and C5 form a filter, serving as small reservoirs of electrical charge and filtering out much of the electrical noise from the power-supply input.

C6 is rated at 100u, which is understood to mean 100μF (for micro-farads; the lowercase Greek letter mu or μ being sometimes difficult to reproduce in all computer-aided design, or CAD, software packages).

C5 is rated at 100n, which is understood to mean 100nF (for nano-farads), even though it's more likely to see this expressed as 0.1µF in the United States.

Not documented in this schematic are the maximum working voltages of the two capacitors. This is a critical component specification for capacitors. Applying voltages in excess of a capacitor's rated working voltage will result in the deterioration and eventual failure (perhaps catastrophic) of the capacitor's *dielectric*, which is the material used to separate the two conducting plates that form the capacitor. Lower working voltages allow smaller capacitors to be built, so a prudent design engineer specifies a working voltage that is high enough to perform safely in a circuit but low enough not to take up excessive space or increase costs. Common working voltages for electrolytic capacitors range from 4V to 50V. The capacitors serving this function on the Arduino Uno, PC1, and PC2 are rated 47µF at 25V.

Voltage Regulator

Now it's time to *regulate* the incoming voltage for use with the rest of the Arduino circuitry. IC2 is a three-pin, fixed positive voltage regulator of some sort. No part number is given in the original schematic. Remember, the very first Arduino boards were intended to be spread by word of mouth as much as by postal carriers. It was up to the individual building the circuit board to make the final parts selection based on their needs, availability, and best judgment.

The LM7805 fixed positive voltage regulator was often used in this position. It's quite common in hobby electronics and widely available. Although the part has been discontinued by National Semiconductors, it's still produced by many other vendors. National Semiconductor also provides a detailed data sheet for the device: `www.national.com/ds/LM/LM7512C.pdf`.

This part was available in several fixed voltage outputs, including 5V, 12V, and 15V. The 5V version, the LM7805, required a minimum of 7V at the input to guarantee stable 5V output. The current rating was stated as in excess of 1A, assuming that adequate provisions were made to keep the device cool (that is, heatsinking).

The original Arduino documentation recommended an input voltage in the range of 7V–12V. This type of voltage regulator is called a *linear regulator*, because the supply voltage is carried straight through the device. Excess voltage is wasted as heat. This becomes a problem as either the input voltage or the output current consumption rises.

For the TO-220 package (the LM7805 was also available in a larger, TO-3 package), the *thermal resistance* (junction to ambient) was listed as 50°C/W. With a minimum 7V input and only 0.5A of current being drawn, this amounted to 1W (7V - 5V = 2V, 2V × 0.5A = 1W) of power dissipation, raising the temperature of the device 50°C greater than its surroundings. That's hot! Increase either the input voltage or the current draw by very much at all, and the device will enter a self-imposed *thermal shutdown* until the temperature drops back to a reasonable level.

The output of the voltage regulator is supposed to be 5V with a tolerance of 5%, or anything from 4.75V to 5.25V. The 5V output is connected to another filter capacitor, C7. C7 is identical to C6, a polarized electrolytic capacitor rated at 100µF, and does a similar job, filtering out transients and glitches from the voltage supply. On the original Arduino Serial, the +5V supply bus was routed to the power-expansion connector (to a pin labeled +5V), making regulated power available to additional circuitry. The +5V bus also directly powered the ATmega8 microcontroller chip and the RS-232 to TTL level shifter circuit, described later.

Also shown in the schematic is a connection from the regulated 5V supply line to LED1, which served as a power-on indicator. A 220Ω current-limiting resistor, R2, was interposed to control the amount of current flowing through the LED. This LED is on the entire time the Arduino has power.

If a *regulated* source of +5V power is available, the Arduino can be powered directly via the +5V pin of the power-expansion connector.

Power Circuit Evolution

The modern Arduino Uno and Arduino Mega 2560 have basically the same power input and conditioning circuitry as their forebears. The Arduino Uno moves the 100nF capacitor from the input of the voltage regulator to the output. The Arduino Mega 2560 doesn't.

There have been a couple of interesting developments along the way. Looking at the Uno or Mega 2560 schematics, there appear to be *two* 5V voltage regulators in the circuit. This is a technique for providing multiple *component footprints* on the PCB, and only one of the two voltage regulators is eventually populated on the PCB. To prevent confusion, you can name the duplicate parts with the same reference designator but with an alternate suffix: for example, if both a through-hole and a surface-mount version of a resistor are drawn on the schematic, you can label one R1A and the other R1B. If one particular package variation isn't available at manufacturing time, then the equivalent device in a different package can be substituted without requiring the PCB to be modified, or *reworked*. This same technique was used for the surface-mount version of the ATmega328 processors on the Arduino Uno SMD, as illustrated in Chapter 1.

When the USB interface was introduced, replacing the older RS-232 interface, more changes to the power-supply circuit occurred. The USB specification allows the interface to provide a limited amount of regulated power to devices, along with the communication facilities. A regulated 5V supply is taken directly from the USB connector and can be used to power the circuit. The first USB models required you to correctly install jumpers to complete the wiring of the power-supply section. Later models used an analog comparator and low-impedance metal-oxide-semiconductor field-effect transistor (MOSFET) switch to intelligently switch to the highest available voltage. Additionally, a 500mA resettable fuse was included in the USB power tap to prevent Bad Things from happening to the host PC should something untoward occur on the Arduino or any attached circuitry. This resettable fuse normally has a very low resistance and passes up to 500mA (0.5A) of current. If the current draw exceeds this value, the fuse begins to heat up, increasing its internal resistance and thereby lowering the amount of current allowed to pass through the circuit. When the current draw decreases, the fuse cools off and its internal resistance drops. This process, it should be noted, can't be repeated indefinitely, because the thermal stress to the fuse will eventually cause it to fail.

The first several Arduino USB versions employed an FTDI USB interface chip, which included an on-board 5V to 3.3V regulator. This allowed 3.3V at up to 50mA of current to be made available to additional circuitry, should the need arise. Voltages lower than 5V are becoming more common as the demand for lower power consumption increases in electronic devices.

The Arduino Uno and Arduino Mega 2560 have dropped the FTDI USB interface chip in favor of an additional AVR microcontroller, dedicated to USB communication tasks. They have also added a stand-alone 3.3V regulator chip on-board to replace that functionality lost with the change in USB chips. The National Semiconductor LP2985 low-dropout regulator can supply up to 150mA of current at 3.3V, tripling the amount of current previously available.

Looking at Figure 4-3, you can see that not much has changed in the front end of the Arduino power supply over the years. Figure 4-3 is taken from the schematic of the Arduino Mega 2560. The Arduino Uno moves C2 from the input of IC2 to the output; otherwise it's identical to Figure 4-3.

Not shown in Figure 4-3 is the power-on LED indicator, which now has a 1K resistor (RN3C) to limit the current. Instead of a discrete (individual) resistor, the modern Arduinos use a *resistor network*, a small package that contains several identical resistors. This makes them easier to assemble via automation, placing a single component instead of a bunch of individual ones.

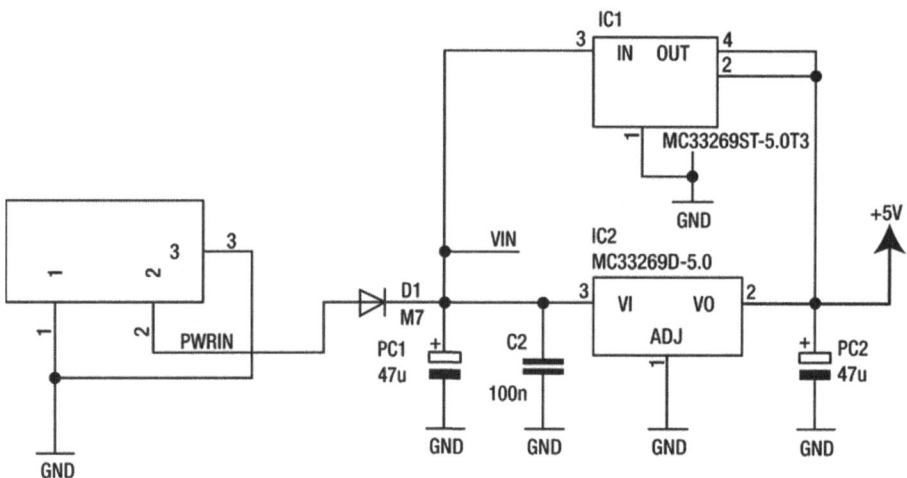

Figure 4-3. *Power-supply section of the Arduino Mega 2560*

The additional power-supply circuitry, including the intelligent voltage-selection circuit and 3.3V regulator, is shown in Figure 4-4. Not shown is the resettable fuse, which is inline with the USBVCC voltage bus, coming from the USB connector.

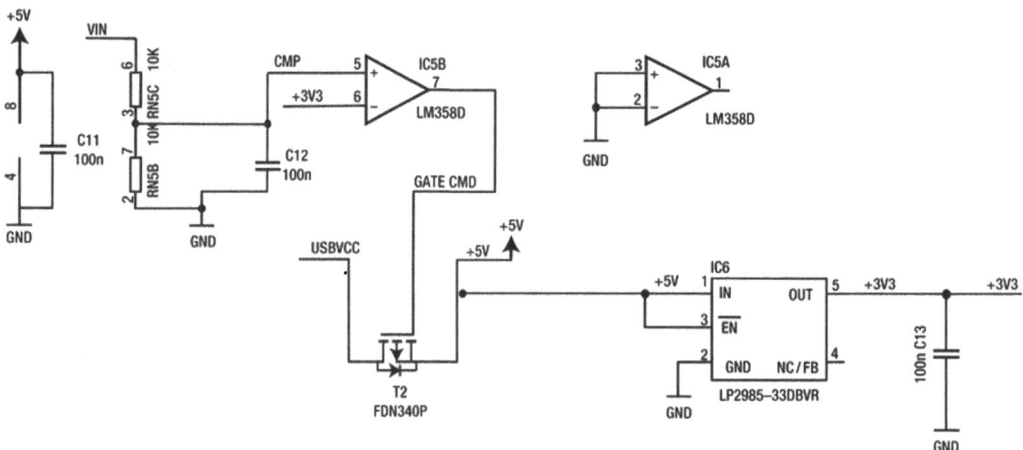

Figure 4-4. *Additional power-supply circuitry found on modern Arduinos*

Serial Interface

The serial interface of the Arduino survives functionally intact from the very earliest prototypes until today. A good case can be made for the argument that the serial bootloader arrangement *defines* the Arduino development methodology, separating it from bare-metal embedded development.

There are, in fact, several distinct serial interfaces available on the modern Arduino, thanks to the wide variety of peripherals offered by the Atmel AVR processor. The most famous serial port in the Arduino world is the Universal Synchronous/Asynchronous Receiver/Transmitter (USART) peripheral, which sends or receives data over a single wire *asynchronously* (one wire for each data direction, plus a ground reference connection) at a predetermined rate. Other useful serial peripherals include the two-wire interface (a.k.a. TWI or I^{2}C) and the serial peripheral interface (SPI), both of which use a separate clock and data line to communicate with other devices. Ethernet is another serial peripheral that can easily be added to the basic Arduino circuit using a special shield.

Unfortunately, there is no standard PC serial port that can work directly *and* reliably with the Atmel AVR chips used with most Arduinos. A buffer or level-shifter circuit is needed, at minimum, to allow the 0–5V signals of the AVR to talk properly to the most common PC serial port standard, RS-232. The modern alternative, the USB standard, is generally thought to be too complex, when fully realized, to be accommodated by a simple microcontroller like the AVR. Effective solutions to both interfacing challenges have emerged, and you look at them in a little detail here.

RS-232 Interface

The oldest Arduino prototypes, and some modern reproductions, provided a level-shifter circuit to convert the RS-232 voltage levels to the appropriate 0–5V levels used by the Arduino. This circuit was built of discrete components and is shown in Figure 4-5.

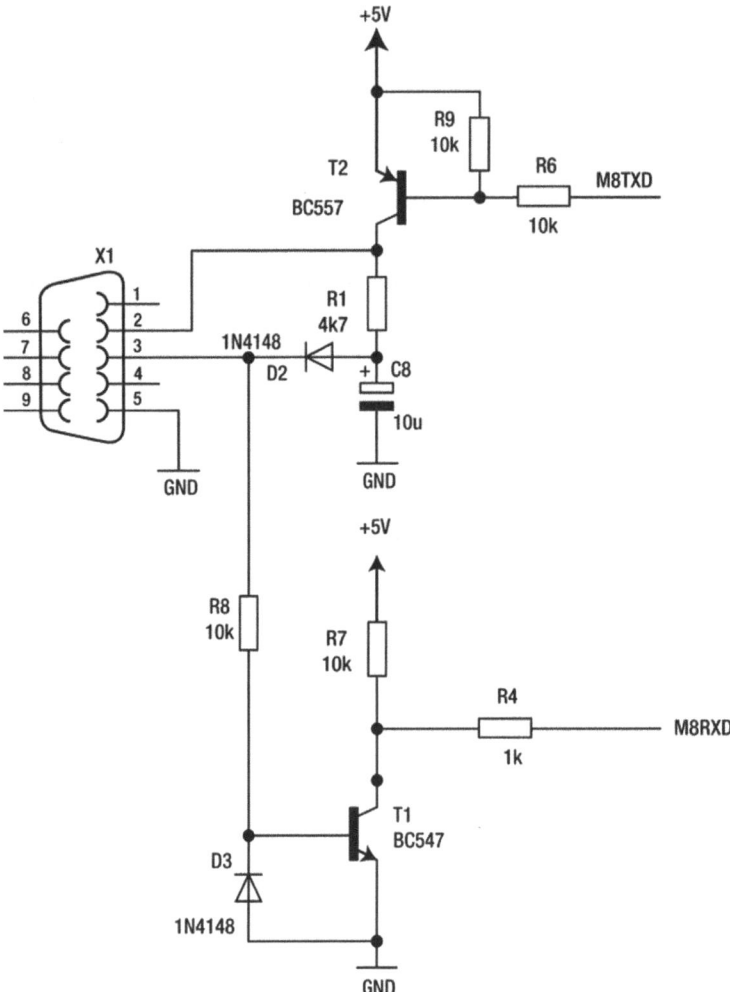

Figure 4-5. The RS-232 to TTL level-shifter circuit from the original Arduino serial

This circuit bears a striking resemblance to the RS-232 interface used in both the original AVR ISP device programmer as well as the example programmer described in Atmel's AVR application note AVR910, "In-System Programming."

A more robust interface circuit can be built using a dedicated RS-232 adapter chip and some capacitors. The Maxim IC MAX232 chip contains a built-in charge-pump circuit to generate the required RS-232 voltage levels and all the level-translation circuitry needed, while providing much higher isolation levels and protection. This circuit was never used by the Arduino Team but was picked up by several versions of the Freeduino project, including the MaxSerial from Fundamental Logic. See Figure 4-6.

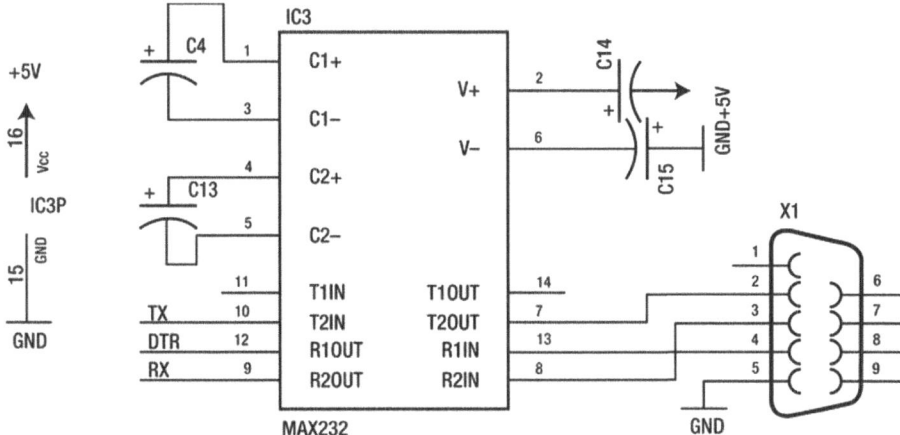

Figure 4-6. *The Fundamental Logic Freeduino MaxSerial serial port. From the Fundamental Logic Freeduino MaxSerial. Designed by CircuitJoy and Spiffed. Based on the Arduino Diecimilia reference design:* www.arduino.cc/en/Main/ArduinoBoardDiecimila. *Released under a Creative Commons Share-alike attribution license: see* www.creativecommons.org/licenses/by-sa/2.5/.

This circuit also introduces the use of the RS-232 handshaking signal *Data Terminal Ready* (DTR) to be used to remotely reset the microcontroller (the *auto-reset* feature), which in turns invokes the bootloader firmware. Previous hardware required you to manually reset the Arduino board before starting the sketch-upload process.

Although the Arduino documentation indicates that the RX and TX lines (D0 and D1, respectively) can be used as normal I/O lines if serial communication isn't needed in your application, this isn't entirely true. The TX line (D1) can be used as either an input or an output but will continue to wiggle the TX circuitry of the serial port, which may or may not cause problems on the other end.

The RX signal (D0), however, remains connected to the receiver circuitry and must be physically disconnected before it can be used as either an input or an output. There is no convenient way to do this on most Arduino boards. The options are to either remove components or cut traces, either one of which will render the Arduino unprogrammable via the bootloader.

Later Arduino boards replace the RS-232 with a USB port, which is described in more detail in the section "Universal Serial Bus (USB): Signals Plus Power," later in this chapter.

The Processor

In Chapter 3, a great deal of information was presented concerning the internal workings of the Atmel AVR chip. Here you look at the AVR as just another (if complex) electronic component.

Power Consumption

Both the ATmega328 and the ATmega2560 share an absolute maximum supply voltage of 6.0V. Operation at or even near the absolute maximum value "may affect device reliability," according to the Atmel datasheet. The normal voltage range for both parts is 1.8V to 5.5V. Note that lower voltages reduce the maximum possible clock speed.

The power requirements of the AVR depend mostly on the operating frequency of the CPU. The higher the frequency, the higher the current consumption. At 16MHz, the ATmega328 draws just under 10mA (0.010A) of current at 5.0V, or 1/20W in *active* mode. Current consumption in *idle* mode is less than 2.5mA (0.0025A). This drops to less than 1μA (0.000001A) in *power-down* mode.

The larger chip on the Arduino Mega 2560, the Atmel AVR ATmega2560, draws only twice the active current of the smaller ATmega328 at 5V and 16 MHz: 20mA (0.020A). The idle current consumption is under 6mA (0.006A), whereas the *power-down* mode draws less than 1μA (0.000001A) at or near room temperature. This can increase to as much as 3μA at elevated temperatures (85°C).

The clock speed, as well as other power-consumption options, such as the Watchdog Timer and Brownout Detector, are configured using the device's configuration fuses. These fuses can't be changed under software control and require a dedicated device programmer to alter.

The power-saving modes (idle and power-down) are entered when the chip is put to sleep and halts execution. The difference between the two modes is that in idle mode, the peripherals continue to operate normally and can bring the processor out of the sleep state by generating interrupts. The power-down mode achieves its low-current usage by also shutting down the peripherals.

I/O Drive Capability

Each I/O pin on either chip can *source* or *sink* up to 40mA (0.040A) of current. This is sufficient to interface with most external electronics, as well as light up a few LEDs. It isn't nearly enough to drive even small electric motors, fans, or solenoids. 5V relays with coil resistance of greater than 125Ω can be directly driven, but a flyback diode should be placed across the coil to prevent a collapsing magnetic field (once the relay coil has been de-energized) from creating a hazardous voltage with respect to the chip.

■ **Note** Bear in mind that the total current of all I/O lines is 200mA (0.2A), so it isn't possible to drive 40mA from all I/O lines at the same time.

The -RESET Signal

The reset signal to the AVR is attached to several components in a typical Arduino. The DTR signal from the serial port is capacitively coupled to the reset line via a 100nF (0.1μF) capacitor. This capacitor allows the change in signal level to trigger a reset on the chip, but it prevents the serial port from holding the chip in a reset state indefinitely. A 10KΩ pullup resistor is also connected between the reset line and +5V, to prevent random electrical noise from falsely tripping the reset circuit. A momentary-contact push button can also short the reset line to ground, thereby causing a device reset.

The reset signal is also connected to pins on both the in-circuit serial programming (ICSP) connector and the power-expansion connector.

The Time Base

Either a quartz crystal or a ceramic resonator is attached to the AVR to provide a stable and accurate time base. You can use additional discrete components depending on the choice of component. Quartz crystals generally have very small value-loading capacitors attached between each of their leads and ground. These capacitors help provide enough load to start the oscillator circuit at power-up. The values are typically only a few pico-farads (22pF is a common value), and the capacitance resulting from the routing of the signals on the PCB is often sufficient to ensure stable operation.

Ceramic resonators often employ a high-impedance resistor (typically 1MΩ or larger) across their leads to help stabilize their operation and reduce unwanted harmonics.

Decoupling Capacitors

The Arduino Uno has a single 100nF (0.1μF) decoupling capacitor, C6, physically located near the processor to help filter out any noise on the power bus generated by the processor itself. It also helps provide a tiny reservoir of power for the chip, whose power consumption comes in sharp spikes during different phases of the clock cycle.

The Arduino Mega 2560 has three similar decoupling capacitors, C4, C5, and C6, located in close proximity to the ATmega2560 chip, performing the same duty.

Both the Arduino Uno and the Arduino Mega 2560 have a 100nF (0.1μF) capacitor between the analog reference (AREF) pin and ground to stabilize the analog reference voltage used by the analog-to-digital converter (ADC) peripheral.

Blinky Lights

Both the Arduino Uno and Arduino Mega 2560 have a dedicated LED attached to D13 (PB5 on the Arduino Uno and PB7 on the Arduino Mega 2560) via a 1KΩ resistor to ground. This is sometimes known as the *programmable LED*, because its function is based entirely on software. In contrast, the green power-on LED indicator is always on whenever power is applied. The TX and RX LEDs are connected to the USB interface chip and indicate activity on the serial port.

Room for Expansion

By itself, the Arduino I/O Board doesn't do much at all. It's possible to have a semi-intelligent conversation with it over the serial port, if you're willing to stretch the definitions of the words *conversation*, *intelligent*, and *possible*. For more useful and practical applications that can actually be accomplished today, let's take a look at the provisions that have been made to extend the reach of the humble Arduino.

Even the earliest Arduino prototypes had some sort of expansion headers installed. The basic idea of the Arduino was to incorporate a generic microcontroller and its associated circuitry onto a standard form-factor device, to prevent unnecessary reinventing of the wheel each and every time a project required some new automation hardware. The Atmel AVR was chosen as the microcontroller, mostly due to its low cost and ease of use, both from a hardware and a software standpoint.

Beginning with the Arduino Extreme, the female headers along the edge of the Arduino I/O Board have created their own standard for building shields—that is, boards intended to be installed on top of (and in some cases, underneath) the Arduino I/O Board. It wasn't until the appearance of the Arduino Diecimila that the final composition of the expansion headers emerged, by wisely including the -RESET line along with the power and ground pins of the Power expansion connector.

The Arduino Uno has four sets of female headers along two edges of its perimeter. (See Figure 1-3 in Chapter 1.) These headers are logically, electrically, and functionally divided into four distinct groups: Port B (digital pins D8–D13, AREF, and ground), Port C (analog inputs A0–A5), Port D (digital pins D0 and D1, a.k.a. RX and TX, and D2–D7), and Power (Vin, two ground connections, 5V, 3, 3V, and -RESET).

Each female header on the Arduino Uno contains either six (Port C and Power) or eight (Port B and Port D) individual pins. The spacing between the female pin sockets is 0.100". The spacing between the top and bottom rows is 1.900". The horizontal spacing between the connectors remains irregular and is discussed further in the next section, "The Mechanical Form Factor."

The Arduino Mega 2560 starts with the same set of expansion connectors as the Arduino Uno, thus maintaining shield compatibility with its smaller sibling. (See Figure 1-11 in Chapter 1.) Because the Arduino Mega 2560 has so many more general-purpose I/O lines available, additional connectors were added along the right edge of the board. Along the top edge, the communication expansion connector was added, being the logical extension of the RX and TX pins of the original Arduino Uno Port D connector. The communication expansion header has transmit and receive pins for three more USARTs (TX1–3, RX1–3) along with two more pins from an entirely different serial peripheral, the TWI or I^{2}C bus connection. These pins are labeled SDA for *serial data* and SCL for *serial clock*.

Additionally, the Arduino Mega 2560 extends the Port C or *analog input* section by adding another 8 pins for analog inputs A8–A15, bringing the total number of analog-to-digital inputs from 6 on the Arduino Uno to 16. Note that the analog expansion connector (A0–A5) on the Arduino Uno contains only six pins, whereas the Arduino Mega 2560 expands this to a full eight pins on both analog input connectors.

Bear in mind that any of the analog inputs can also be used as either a digital input or digital output, just like on the Arduino Uno.

And if that wasn't enough, the Arduino Mega 2560 also has an additional 36-pin female socket on the far right end of the board. This 2 × 18 header contains 32 more general-purpose I/O lines along with two connections to both +5V and ground. That's a lot of I/O lines!

The functional grouping of the additional pins on the Arduino Mega 2560 came at the cost of the logical assignment of ports to headers. The Arduino-specific numbering scheme used for addressing the individual I/O lines helps keep the signals straight. You can address each I/O pin using a single number, without regard to which I/O Port the pin belongs.

The function of the expansion connectors is to provide both electrical and mechanical connections from the Arduino I/O Board to a shield containing application-specific circuitry. A wide range of shields are available both commercially and as open source projects that anyone can build.

The Mechanical Form Factor

The very first Arduino prototypes filled up a small PCB with just enough components to make a working microcontroller circuit. There wasn't a lot of extra space left over. Any circuit expansion was done on an expansion shield, which was stacked on top of the base Arduino I/O Board.

The mechanical form factor has been preserved through many versions of the Arduino I/O Board, mostly to maintain shield compatibility between releases, and not because it's the best of all possible arrangements.

Looking at a modern Arduino I/O Board, such as the Arduino Uno or Arduino Mega 2560, you see a lot of spare room. This is mostly due to the continued miniaturization of the components that are used to implement the basic Arduino circuit.

Although it makes sense, from one standpoint, to take advantage of newer technologies and processes, the perpetuation of the classic Arduino form factor also helps those who want to undertake the journey of building an Arduino from the ground up with their bare hands, as it were. It's still entirely possible to design, build, and assemble an Arduino-compatible I/O Board using *through-hole* components, without having to resort to fancy robotic assembly techniques and mass production.

A drawing of the mechanical form factor of the Arduino Uno is shown in Figure 4-7.

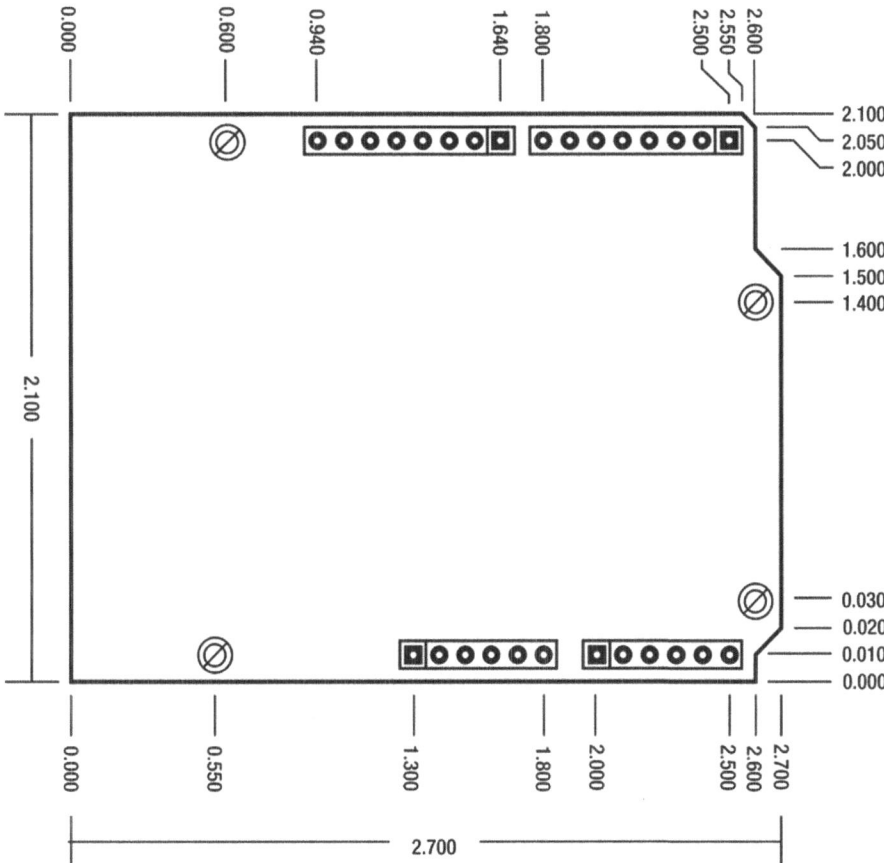

Figure 4-7. *The mechanical form factor of the Arduino Uno*

All the mounting holes shown in the drawing have a diameter of 0.125", or just over 3mm. Note that the fourth mounting hole, at lower left, was added when the Arduino Uno and Arduino Mega 2560 were introduced and isn't present on earlier boards.

Except for the Port B expansion connecter (at upper left), all of the electrical connections on the Arduino Uno are on a convenient 0.100" grid. For some undisclosed reason, this connector was spaced 0.160" from the connector to its right. This spacing irregularity has been preserved to maintain compatibility with shields produced for earlier Arduinos.

Universal Serial Bus (USB): Signals Plus Power

Whereas the first Arduino I/O Boards used an RS-232 connector and associated circuitry to talk to the rest of the world, modern Arduinos use the popular USB. This versatile interface is an industry standard and is maintained by the USB Implementers Forum, Inc. The USB specification and all other information relating to the USB standard can be found at www.usb.org.

The changeover from RS-232 to USB was perhaps inevitable. Most modern PCs and laptops have omitted the once-popular RS-232 port in favor of the smaller USB port. USB-to-RS-232 adapters are available to link older Arduino hardware to more recent PCs.

One major advantage of using USB instead of RS-232 is the availability of a regulated 5V supply along with the communication functions. The USB specification allows an *enumerated device* (one that properly identifies itself to the USB host, such as an Arduino I/O Board) to draw as much as 500mA (0.5A) from this 5V supply. Unenumerated devices can draw a maximum of 100mA (0.100A) of current.

The first Arduinos to use a USB interface instead of the traditional RS-232 port were simply called *Arduino USB*. They were sold as kits, and you had to hand-solder the surface-mount USB interface chip to the PCB. Instructions for the assembly process were published on the Arduino web site.

The first USB interface chip used was the FT232BL from FTDI, Inc. It provided a complete USB-to-serial solution and required only a handful of external components.

Starting with the Arduino NG and continuing until the Arduino Duemilanove, the USB interface chip was another FTDI product, the FT232RL. This chip incorporated many more functions internally than its predecessor and required only a couple of external capacitors for normal operation. The FT232RL contains its own high-precision clock circuit, a 5.0V to 3.3V voltage regulator, and a factory-programmed unique serial number.

Beginning with the Arduino Uno and Arduino Mega 2560, the USB interface has been provided by another Atmel AVR chip, the ATmega8U2. It has a built-in full-speed USB peripheral, which the ATmega328 and the ATmega2560 lack.

Summary

Knowing a little more about the hardware on your Arduino I/O Board enables you to better understand what it's capable of doing by itself and where it needs some help. Now that you have a grasp of the hardware involved and how to read a basic electronic schematic, go ahead and get your own copy of the hardware documentation that matches your Arduino from the Arduino web site, www.arduino.cc. This is the starting point for any additional circuitry you may want to add to your invention. This is true whether you add a commercially available shield or design and build your own interface.

Now you move on from the Arduino hardware to the Arduino software. There's a good chance that you may be spending some time using this software, so let's take a good look at it and see what it's doing for you.

CHAPTER 5

Arduino Software

The officially supported and free Arduino software is certainly a moving target. The alpha versions, ranging from the very first 0001 through 0022, evolved as the needs of the Arduino Team and the growing user base changed and matured.

The goal of a 1.0 version (*Arduino Uno Punto Zero* in Italian) was first announced on the Arduino blog on January 1, 2010 (`http://arduino.cc/blog/2010/01/01/uno-punto-zero`). It was intended to coincide with the continued growth and development of the Arduino hardware and become a reference version, ready to shed its preliminary status. The new generation of hardware, the Arduino Uno and Arduino Mega 2560, were announced at Maker Faire New York City in September 2010.

At the time this edition of the book was going to press, the Arduino 1.0 software was still undergoing frantic work and testing. The Arduino-1.0beta4 prerelease package was posted by David Mellis on September 10, 2011, and was the version used in the examples shown in this chapter.

Arduino 0022, the last of the alpha releases, was used in the bits-and-bytes analyses presented in the next chapter. It has been a stable and dependable release, used by many thousands of Arduino developers all over the world.

It has been suggested that the official release of the Arduino 1.0 software will be made at the 2011 Maker Faire in New York City, and by the time you read this, you'll probably know if this was true or not.

The new version contains many important internal enhancements, as well as a new visual theme. The Arduino logo, a composite of a stylized symbol for infinity with embedded yin-yang-esque negative and positive symbols along with the Arduino name, represents the balanced combination of electronics, imagination, and infinite possibilities. The new theme also features the recombinative use of multicolored 90° arcs in a seemingly random arrangement, invoking a sense of motion, wind, or water, coming together in a slightly off-center stylized heart. See Figure 5-1.

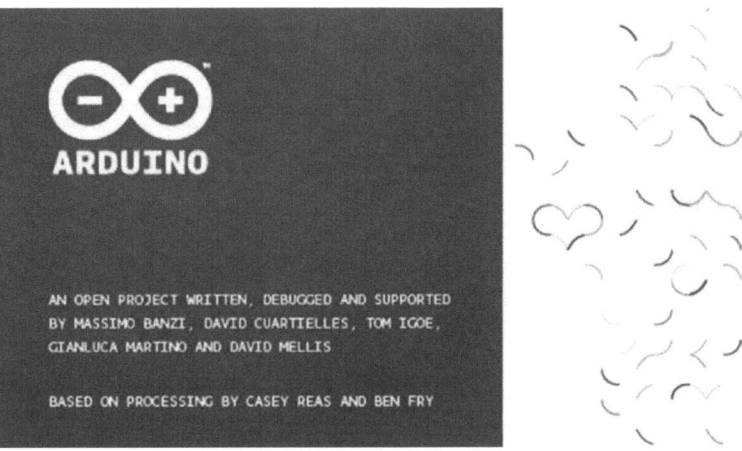

Figure 5-1. The new Arduino splash screen

Please bear in mind that the goal of this book is to provide you with a deeper understanding of the inner workings of both the Arduino hardware and the Arduino software in general. The book won't be rendered useless when the inevitable improvements and enhancements are made to either one or the other.

Open Source Software

The Arduino software is really a collection of many different open source and free software packages. The Arduino software is licensed under the GPL version 2, although the component packages are licensed under a veritable rainbow of different ideas.

The wonderful thing about open source and free software, besides the price, is your access to the actual source code and underlying technologies. You're not just getting a black box that performs a single function. You're *empowered* to take the software to any new heights you wish.

Found a bug? You can report it in the forum, *or* you can fix it yourself, if you have the wherewithal to do so. Missing a feature? You can add it. Hate the way program X does Y? You can adjust it to your own satisfaction.

By now you get the point. Consider following the example of the thousands of people who have contributed code, ideas, testing, and feedback to make the Arduino project the success that it has become, and share *your* brilliance with the whole world.

Multiplatform Support

Perhaps one of the main reasons for the Arduino project's huge success and public acceptance is that virtually the same software is available for use on computer systems running Microsoft Windows, Apple Mac OS, or Linux. That covers a lot of territory! Alternative integrated development environments (IDEs) are being contemplated for use on tablets and smart phones.

The one-size-fits-all magic is due in large part to the Java platform, which was designed from the ground up to be as platform independent as possible. Java, as a programming environment as well as a computer language, has enjoyed tremendous success in the computer software marketplace.

The Arduino software provides a complete Java environment, and a separate Java download isn't required.

The Arduino Heritage

Where did the Arduino software begin? It was originally adapted from the Wiring project (http://wiring.org.co), which was itself an AVR-based embedded development environment with a specialized user interface written in Java.

The canonical wiring board was considered a bit of overkill for the most basic of beginner projects, as well as being beyond the fabrication skills of neophyte electronics hobbyists. The Arduino Team developed a smaller subset of the Wiring functionality and adapted both the hardware and the software to meet those needs.

The Wiring project was derived from Processing (http://www.processing.org), another open source collection of tools for writing interactive and graphically oriented programs on a PC. This is where the idea of a software sketchbook for creative types originated.

A very large body of work exists that explores the frontier between traditional, PC-based computing and the embedded world, using Processing and Arduino in concert. This extends the standard idea of what properly constitutes a computer by moving into the physical computing platform arena. This allows for tangible, interactive devices that can embody rudimentary intelligence and emergent behavior while being both affordable and easy to reproduce.

Installing the Software

The Arduino software comes complete with everything you need to write your own sketches, compile them using a state-of-the-art compiler, and upload them to a variety of Arduino-compatible I/O Boards. It also comes with an entire collection of excellent example sketches to help you get started with the fundamentals. There is also a comprehensive set of libraries included that extend the capabilities of the built-in functions.

The one thing the Arduino software does *not* include is an installation program. No worries; none is needed. Simply unpack the supplied archive file (.zip for Windows, .dmg for Mac OS X, and .tgz for Linux) into a convenient place of *your* choosing on your computer, and there it is.

Uninstalling the Arduino software is just as easy. Can you guess how it's done? You get one hint: erase the folder where you unpacked the downloaded archive file. Need another hint?

The Process, or "How to Arduino"

The optimum way to experience the Arduino is to *possess* or have access to an Arduino I/O Board, the Arduino software, a moderately modern PC, and a USB cable. Oddly enough, the system is pliant enough that the PC is the only required component. The USB cable is only one of many standard interfaces that will suffice. Alternate programming software and development environments are available. The strict definition of what constitutes Arduino-compatible hardware grows more vague every day.

The starting conditions for using the Arduino are straightforward. Turn on your PC. Obtain and install the Arduino software. Use the USB cable to connect the PC to the Arduino I/O Board, and load the appropriate USB drivers (which depend on which Arduino board you have).

The simplest way to get started is to launch the Arduino software and choose the appropriate Board and Serial Port selections from the Tools menu. The Arduino software maintains these settings for you.

An array of example sketches is provided under the Files ➤ Examples menu item. Start with Blink, by choosing Files ➤ Examples ➤ 1.Basics ➤ Blink. The Arduino software loads the sketch into the editor window for you. It should bear a striking resemblance to Figure 5-2.

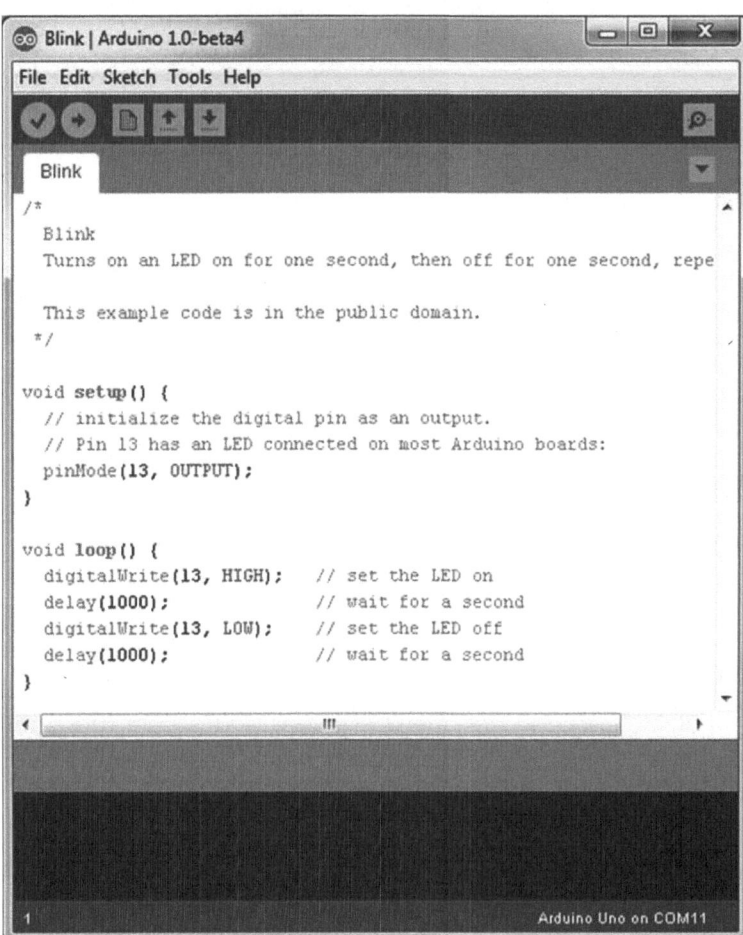

Figure 5-2. *The Arduino software user interface, showing the example sketch Blink*

Click the Upload toolbar icon. Doing so automatically compiles, links, and otherwise translates and prepares the source code you see in the editor pane, transforming it into the ones and zeros understood by the microcontroller on the Arduino board.

If all goes well, and it really should if you're using one of the example sketches, the Arduino software also automatically initiates an *upload* of the necessary information to the Arduino's microcontroller brain. Once stored in the Arduino's program memory, the newly minted sketch is *nonvolatile*, meaning it remains there, unaltered, until it's subsequently overwritten by the upload of another sketch. It doesn't require any power or batteries to maintain this memory.

When the upload process has completed successfully, the sketch begins to execute. Unlike traditional computer programs that run, perform some task, and then terminate, the sketch in the Arduino is generally expected to run indefinitely. In the case of the example sketch Blink, it most certainly does. It blinks an LED over and over again, tirelessly, faithfully, ad infinitum.

That is the first phase of the Arduino dance. You can continue to try the example sketches, if you're curious. This should give you a taste of the variety of tasks the Arduino can perform.

You have two interesting options at this point. The first is to adapt an existing sketch to your needs, making small, iterative changes until it more closely resembles what suits your immediate purpose. The other option is to start completely from scratch, designing a sketch that bears no likeness to any of the existing example sketches.

This choice is up to you.

A Tour of the User Interface

The basic framework of the main user interface remains the same from previous versions, as shown earlier in Figure 5-2. A single editor window dominates the screen, with traditional menu items at the very top and a toolbar of icons directly underneath. A status area is presented at the bottom of the screen.

The main updates from previous versions are partly aesthetic and partly functional. The color scheme has been tweaked a bit, and the icons have evolved from their original pixilated line drawings into more visually identifiable symbols.

The toolbar no longer responds to the Shift modifier of previous versions, which offered the verbose output option for the compile and upload processes and the "…in a new window" option for the New and Open icons. The verbose options, which are exceedingly helpful in debugging, can instead be enabled in the updated Preferences dialog box, accessible from File ➤ Preferences.

The Verify (compile) button is now represented by a check mark instead of the Play transport-control theme. The ever-whimsical Stop button has been eliminated. Did it ever actually do anything?

The Upload button is immediately to the right of the Verify icon, now logically grouped by functionality.

The New, Open, and Save Sketch buttons remain essentially the same. The New Sketch icon looks *somewhat* like a blank page, but the *up* and *down* arrows of the Open and Save icons remain baffling in their interpretation. Their contextual associations are non-intuitive. It's best to rely on the faithful mouse-over labels that appear in the toolbar, just to be sure.

The Serial Monitor icon has been moved to the far right of the toolbar. It shows what appears to be a magnifying-glass symbol poised over a horizontal trail of dots (or perhaps ants).

The editor pane uses the same tab structure for organizing multiple open sketches. The tab control icon operates in exactly the same manner but has received the same bolder refinement in appearance as the other icons; in addition it now points down instead of to the right. The same keyword highlighting is used as in previous versions to help identify elements of the program, which can be of enormous assistance when you're looking for programmatic typos and those pesky syntax errors.

The current line number of the editor's cursor is shown in the lower-left corner of the screen.

Most notable at first glance—to users of the previous software, at least—are the current settings of the Board and Serial Port settings on the Tools menu. This has been a much-requested feature from Arduino users.

Although the most common tasks are handled in the editing pane and via the toolbar icons, the remainder of the user interface is accessed through the menu system. There should be no surprises here for anyone who has used an electric computing device within the last decade or so. The Arduino software, for the most part, complies with industry-standard user interface guidelines, even if it tends to overdo the cascading menus a bit.

The official Arduino guide to the development environment is available from the Arduino web site, `www.arduino.cc/en/Guide/Environment`, as well as locally in the `reference/environment.html` document in the software distribution.

The File Menu

This menu is where you work with your sketches when you think of them in terms of being *files* stored in your computer's idea of an operating system. You can find the usual suspects here: New, Open, Save, Save As, Close, and Print. These options do exactly what you expect them to do. The Page Setup menu item lets you make the most basic choices of page composition for your printed output, including margin sizes and orientation (portrait or landscape), as well as some selections depending on your presently selected system printer, such as paper size. The Upload, New, Open, and Save menu items are echoed in the toolbar icons just below the menu.

In the File menu you also find shortcuts to your Arduino sketchbook as well as a slew of excellent and enlightening example sketches.

You also find the Upload and … drum roll, please… Upload Using Programmer menu items. The Upload option invokes the traditional Arduino bootloader process for most supported Arduino I/O Boards. The new option to upload using a programmer bypasses the bootloader method and writes your sketch directly to your AVR chip using the new programmer option selected in the Tools menu, described shortly.

Probably here because they don't quite fit anywhere else, the Preferences and Quit menu items complete the tour of the File menu. The Preferences menu item brings up the Preferences dialog box, where you can change some of the program's general settings. Your Arduino sketchbook can be located anywhere you like in your computer's file system. The size of the font, but not the font selection itself, can be changed for the editor pane.

The Preferences dialog box has been updated to allow you to specify the verbose output option explicitly, instead of depending on the undocumented Shift modifier of the toolbar icons or editing the cryptic and cleverly hidden `preferences.txt` file.

The remainder of the Preferences you can alter remain the same from previous releases, including the file-extension association, which has been changed from `.pde`, following the Processing tradition, to `.ino` as Arduino impresses more of its own culture and identity on the inherited software framework.

■ **Note** Arduino sketches now have the `.ino` file extension instead of the previously used `.pde` extension.

The Edit Menu and the Edit Context Menu

Again you have the typical populace of an Edit menu, including Undo, Redo, Cut, Copy, Paste, and Find. These work much the same as in any other text-editing application.

There are some nice additions, including Copy for Forum and Copy as HTML, which insert the proper formatting commands to preserve both the formatting and text highlighting provided by the editor.

There are also the same programmer's editor functions found in previous releases, including Increase and Decrease Indent options. In addition, Comment/Uncomment lets you hide large sections of selected code from the compiler as program comments by prepending the double-forward-slash single-line comment symbol to each selected line. Handy!

The Edit menu lacks the keyboard accelerators more commonly found on Microsoft Windows applications. The editor itself implements the ubiquitous Ctrl+X (cut), Ctrl+C (copy), and Ctrl+V (paste) keyboard shortcuts, however.

Right-clicking the mouse in the editor pane opens the edit context menu, which presents the standard editing options of the Edit menu. Missing are the Undo and Redo commands, but included is the handy Find in Reference option that searches through the provided reference hypertext documentation for the selected keyword and launches it in your default browser.

The Sketch Menu

You can find a short list of sketch-related functions in the Sketch menu. The Verify/Compile item is duplicated in the Verify toolbar icon. The Stop item has disappeared, along with its corresponding toolbar icon.

The Show Sketch Folder invokes an OS-dependent file-system explorer application that displays the contents of the otherwise-obfuscated working directory where the intermediate files created by the underlying software elves reside. This is a much simpler solution to quickly and conveniently locating these files when you need them, when compared to rooting out the location from the compiler's verbose output.

The Add File option lets you copy another file into your sketch and open the file in a new tab within the editor pane. The Import Library menu item inserts properly formatted `#include` directives into your code for use with any of the available Arduino libraries. See Chapter 10 for more information about writing your own Arduino libraries, as well as an overview of how libraries are organized and implemented.

The Tools Menu

Here you find some Arduino-specific tools and access to their associated settings.

Auto Format attempts to clean up the format of your code, enforcing consistent indentation and lining up the curly brackets when it can. It is, let's say, problematic at best.

The Archive Sketch item offers to collect all the files in your sketch folder into an archive file appropriate for your operating system. This is handy when you want to share your sketches with others.

No one knows what the Fix Encoding & Reload function does. Perhaps you can be the one to figure it out first!

The Arduino's Serial Monitor is meant to be a useful serial communication tool for talking to your Arduino over the same serial link used to upload sketches. It uses whatever serial port selection you've made in the Serial Port selection item, described shortly in this section. See Figure 5-3.

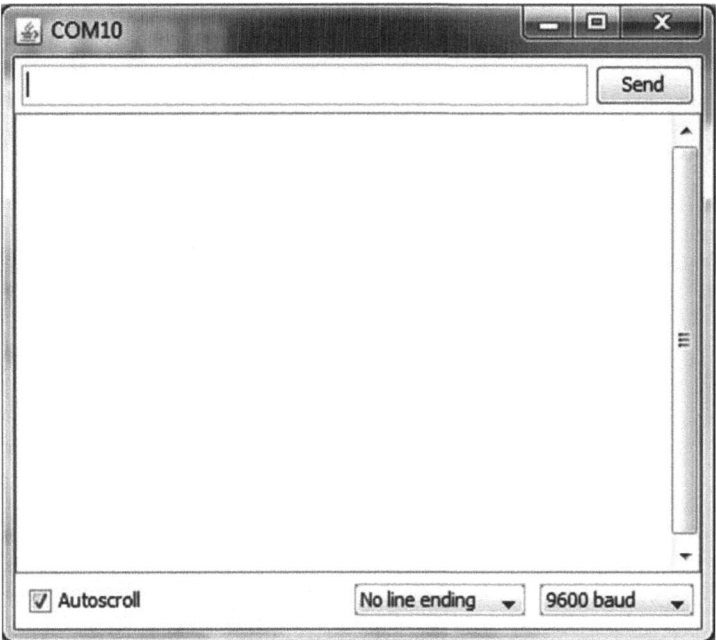

Figure 5-3. *The Arduino's Serial Monitor window permits you to communicate with your Arduino over the serial port.*

It's not a linearly interactive serial terminal, such as minicom or Tera Term Pro. To send characters *to* your Arduino, you type in the text box at the top of the Serial Monitor window and then click the Send button to send, or *transmit*, the text. Any information *received* from the Arduino is listed in the larger, non-interactive text area that makes up the most of the center area.

If your Arduino seems to be emitting nothing but nonsense symbols or nothing at all, be sure to confirm that they are talking at the same rate, using the drop-down list box control in the lower-right corner of the window.

The Serial Monitor can also be invoked by the toolbar icon on the far right.

Don't be surprised if your Serial Monitor windows suddenly goes away when you upload a new sketch to your Arduino. There is only one serial port, and it must be shared between the uploading process and Serial Monitor, and only one of them can use it at a time.

The Board selection menu allows you to tell the Arduino software what kind of Arduino you have, so that it can make the right decisions about how to compile and upload your sketch for you. You can add your own, custom variations if you like. The entire process is outlined in detail in Chapter 11.

The Serial Port menu item lets you indicate which of your system's available serial ports you would like to use. This information is updated every time you plug a USB-equipped Arduino board into your PC, or unplug one. The process of notifying all the interested parties can take a moment or two, so please be patient.

Previous releases of the Arduino software had a Burn Bootloader menu item on the Tools menu, which had its own cascading submenu of selectable device programmers. This has been slightly rearranged in the Arduino 1.0 release, with a separate Programmers selection menu and Burn Bootloader menu item.

The Burn Bootloader menu item uses the programmer selected to properly configure a blank AVR chip to be able to use the Arduino bootloader process of uploading sketches over the serial port. This requires an additional device programmer to be used to perform the actual process, which doesn't actually involve any sort of combustion. You can use your Arduino as a device programmer; this topic is explored in much more detail in Chapter 11.

The Help Menu

A wealth of helpful material is available to help answer your questions when working and playing with Arduinos. The Help menu contains direct links to the most often-used resources. Much of the reference material is provided in the software distribution and is located on your computer for fast and instant access. The Arduino web site (`http://arduino.cc`) is also available, featuring many more helpful resources.

Summary

Getting started with Arduino development is easy. An enormous amount of work has been done to make this possible. The Arduino design process can be as simple or as complex as you need it to be, and the freely provided software is an excellent place to begin.

It's far from perfect, but it's a great start. You're encouraged to make suggestions, provide constructive criticism, help with testing or documenting, and in other ways contribute to the project in any way you like. The Arduino Team doesn't live in an ivory tower, capriciously deciding what gets done and what doesn't. They're energetically engaging the Arduino community, asking for suggestions, and implementing a steady flow of improvements to both the hardware and software over time. Your feedback and creativity are truly needed and appreciated.

The next chapter looks at areas where you can improve some of the performance aspects of the system. There are many possible optimizations you can make when you have a better understanding of the inner workings of the hardware and the software.

CHAPTER 6

Optimizations

As shipped, the Arduino software isn't especially optimized. It's easy to use and simple to install, but there is certainly room for improvement. Let's get started.

Three areas scream out for optimization in any embedded development project: program and data space, program execution speed, and system power requirements. Ideally, you want the smallest program running as fast as possible using the least amount of power. These efforts translate into simpler, cheaper, and more reliable products. In reality, there is almost always some sort of compromise among these three areas, depending on the needs of the project.

This chapter presents a lot of important technical information, grouped into topics. You're not expected to read and digest all this information in a single sitting. Pick out the topics that interest you now and give them a good skimming. File the other headings under "Future Reference" and come back to them when you need some optimizations of those kinds.

How Will You Know It Worked?

You measure the rate of a blinking LED using just your bare eyeballs. For more detailed measurements, you need some different tools. Performing these measurements in your own lab is encouraged but not mandatory.

Some of the optimizations will be very easy to measure. Space-saving optimizations result in a smaller file size. Because the Arduino software reports the resulting binary sketch size after every compilation, it's easy to see if the file got bigger, got smaller, or stayed the same size after you applied a particular optimization. Space-saving optimizations are important because they let you pack more software into your chip, before you have to move up to a bigger (and probably more expensive) device. The available program memory in your Arduino is one of its most precious and limited resources.

Let's try a couple of simple optimizations to see if you can reduce the size of one of the example sketches.

■ **Note** Don't overwrite the sample sketches provided with the Arduino software. If you make changes to the example sketches (available via the menu selection File ➤ Examples) and want to save them, choose File ➤ Save As and give them a new name. Having known working example sketches available is very handy when things start to get Really Weird.

Shrink Blink

Let's see what you can do with your old friend, Blink, found in File ➤ Examples ➤ 1.Basics ➤ Blink. Compiled for the Arduino Uno using Arduino 0022, the resulting binary sketch size is 1,018 bytes (of a 32,256-byte maximum). The same sketch, when compiled for the Arduino Mega 2560, results in a binary sketch size of 1,588 bytes (of a 258,048 byte maximum). The extra size can be attributed to the initialization of the larger number of available peripherals aboard the ATmega2560 chip along with the additional low-level functions needed to talk to them.

How Blink Works

When you look at it a certain way, the Blink example sketch only does three things:

1. Configure digital pin 13 as an output.

2. Change the state of the output pin.

3. Pause for a *human-perceptible* amount of time, and then repeat from step 2.

Because Blink is an example sketch in the 1.Basics category, it makes no attempt at optimization. Its goal is be easy for both the Arduino compiler and the beginning Arduino programmer to understand. It says what it does and does what it says, which is always a good thing. In furtherance of this plainness and simplicity, Blink spells out the discrete commands to turn on the LED, wait, turn off the LED, wait, repeat.

Turning the LED on and off can certainly be accomplished with the code as presented in the Blink sketch, but it can also be looked at, in a more abstract sense, as *toggling* the LED output. If it's on, turn it off, and vice versa. You use this concept shortly to cut the size of the loop() function in half.

Measuring Space-Saving Optimizations

Edit the Blink example sketch using the Arduino code editor. In the setup() function, add two forward slashes (//) to the left of the pinMode() function call. In the Arduino IDE, this modification turns the color of the pinMode() statement from orange (executable code) to gray (program comments).

Everything following the *single-line-comment* marker (//) until the end of the line is considered a program comment and ignored by the compiler. You could have deleted the entire line, but you might want it back shortly for more experiments, so just comment it out for now. This is a useful technique for making small changes to code to compare behaviors, before and after.

Compile the code to see what happens. On the Arduino Uno, the binary sketch size drops from 1,018 bytes to 934 bytes, just by commenting out the pinMode() function call in the setup() function: a space savings of 84 bytes. For the Arduino Mega 2560, the resulting binary sketch size is now 1,504 bytes, showing an identical reduction of 84 bytes. This is explained by the omission of the pinMode() function call, containing 8 bytes, as well as the code for the function itself, containing 76 bytes. Because there was no other reference to the pinMode() function in the program, the compiler wisely omitted the instructions that perform the actual task from the final binary sketch. This form of space-saving optimization has already been done for you, but there is more that you can and should do to get the most out of the limited program memory space.

Code Analysis

The call to the `pinMode()` function required a total of eight bytes of program memory. The `CALL` instruction itself takes four bytes, or two instruction words. Remember that all AVR machine-language instructions are a multiple of 16 bits in length, and each byte contains 8 bits, so it always takes at least 2 bytes of program memory for each machine-language instruction. The subroutine `CALL` instruction is two program words long. The shorter Relative Call (`RCALL`) instruction could have been used here, because the relative distance from the calling program to the subroutine happens to be within the 2KB program word limit of the `RCALL` instruction. In a larger program, however, the `CALL` instruction may be required. There is no simple way to tell this compiler to use the shortest instruction possible in every case.

The other four bytes in the `pinMode()` function call are taken up by the two eight-bit parameters that are passed to the function: the pin number (`13`) and the direction (`OUTPUT`). Each parameter is loaded into a predefined register before the actual function call is performed. Each of these *constant value* parameters is loaded into a register using the Load Immediate (`LDI`) instruction, which is one program word (two bytes) long. The compiler knows if you're using constants (as opposed to variables) so it can easily decide to take this shortcut; this is another optimization provided by the compiler that is already working for you.

You may be thinking at this point that you have completely disabled the humble Blink sketch by failing to configure the one output that it needs to perform its simple function. This isn't entirely true. Try compiling and uploading the sketch to your Arduino, minus the `pinMode()` function call, and observe what happens.

In a brightly lit room or sunlit area, you most likely won't see anything happening. However, this isn't precisely the case. Try observing your Arduino in a darkened room, or wait for the sun to go down. You see that the LED attached to D13 is indeed blinking, albeit *very* dimly. This is because writing a `HIGH` or a `LOW` value to a digital pin that is configured as an *input* causes the built-in pull-up resistor to be activated or deactivated. Even though you didn't explicitly configure D13 as an input, this is the *default state* of all general-purpose I/O pins after reset. The LED is being powered by the very small amount of current flowing from V_{cc} through the pull-up resistor, which is typically only a small fraction of a milliamp.

Although a dimmer LED saves power, it's not saving you any program space, per se. Let's replace the functionality of the `pinMode()` function so that D13 can be configured to be the output it always dreamed of being.

Life Without pinMode()

Setting the direction of an I/O pin is a very straightforward procedure on the Atmel AVR. Recall from Chapter 3 that each of the general-purpose I/O pins belongs to a group called a *port*, and each of the bits within a given I/O port can be either an input or an output. The direction of each of the individual pins is controlled by the bits within the *data direction register* (DDRx) associated with the I/O port.

Arduino hides all this complexity from you and numbers the digital pins starting at zero. The analog pins are likewise numbered. Arduino programmers don't need to worry about ports and addresses and bit positions. You just look at the Arduino I/O Board, find the pin you want to use, and use the number printed on the printed circuit board (PCB). It's quite handy.

Because you know that D13 is PB5 (Port B, bit 5) on the Arduino Uno and PB7 (Port B, bit 7) on the Arduino Mega 2560, you can directly set the single bit in Port B's data direction register (DDRB, bit 5 or 7, depending) and get the same result as the `pinMode()` function call, without all the program overhead.

If you have an Arduino Uno or other ATmega328-based Arduino, add the statement `bitSet(DDRB, 5);` to the `setup()` function of the example Blink sketch. If you're using an Arduino Mega 2560, add bitSet(DDRB, 7); to the setup() function. For the Arduino Uno, your setup() function should now look like Listing 6-1.

Listing 6-1. Directly Setting the Direction Bit of an I/O Port Without Using the pinMode() Function

```
void setup() {
  // initialize the digital pin as an output.
  // Pin 13 has an LED connected on most Arduino boards:
  //pinMode(13, OUTPUT);
  bitSet(DDRB, 5); // D13 (PB5) is now an output
}
```

Compile and upload to your Arduino. You should have a properly blinking LED again, but the binary sketch size should be only 936 bytes. The bitSet(DDRB, 5); statement is reduced to a single instruction (two bytes) by the compiler—and it works.

■ **Tip**   Because you've replaced a *somewhat* human-readable program statement, pinMode(13, OUTPUT), with complete bafflegab and abracadabra, it's more important than ever to use clear, explanatory comments in your code.

Abbr. & Shrtcts

There are several things you need to know and understand about the little code modification just discussed. First, the original designers of the C programming language were pretty ~~lazy~~ *efficient* when it came to typing. If you've ever spent much time working with a Teletype ASR-33, you may begin to understand why. It wasn't exactly a pleasant experience. The designers came up with many shortcuts to help reduce the amount of typing required to perform most functions.

The second thing you should know about the replacement configuration statement is that it isn't truly a function call, even though it looks like one. The bitSet() function is really just a macro definition, defined in the wiring.h header file that is included into your sketch, along with the other Arduino-supplied code, before being compiled into the final binary sketch, ready to upload. This function takes two parameters, value and bit. These parameters are then substituted into a prewritten mathematical formula, ((value |= (1UL << (bit)))). When the substitution is complete, the resulting statement effectively reads as DDRB |= 1<<5, which means "Set bit 5 in DDRB."

The wiring.c and wiring.h files also provide several other bit-manipulation macros that often can be reduced to a single instruction, including bitClear(), bitRead(), and bitWrite(). See the Arduino Reference page (choose Help ➤ Reference in the Arduino software) for more information about these functions.

The DDRB |= 1<<5; statement is a good example of the possible compactness of the C language. Technically, this is an *assignment* statement. The |= operator is called an *augmented* (or *compound*) *assignment operator*. It's *augmented* because it's a composite of the assignment operator = and the bitwise, inclusive-or function, represented by the vertical bar character |. The statement could have been written DDRB = DDRB | (1<<5);. Spelled out, this translates as "Read the value that is currently in the DDRB register, bitwise-or this value with the constant value 1<<5, and then store the result back in the DDRB register."

The term DDRB is used twice in this statement: once as a source (as one of the *operands*) and once as a destination. On the left side of the equals sign (=) is the destination, or *lvalue*. On the right side is the source, or *rvalue*. In either case, the DDRB term represents an address in I/O space. It's defined in the avr/io.h header file, which is included automatically by the Arduino software. Actually, the avr/io.h header file is just a generic header file that looks at which part has been defined as being used: for example, __AVR_ATmega2560__ is a symbol that is defined in the code when the Arduino Mega 2560 board is selected by choosing Tools ➤ Board.

With all this predefinition of terms having already been put in place, you can refer to DDRB like any other variable in the program. It can be read, written, or modified just as any other numeric value can be.

Binary Notation

The 1<<5 notation needs some explaining. This is an example of the *left-handed bitwise shift* operator at work. The 1 on the left side is a constant, representing a single, digital 1 in the least significant binary digit. The 5 tells the operator how many times to shift the bits leftward. The corresponding *right-handed bitwise shift operator* is, you guessed it, written >>. The 5 is used because you're interested in bit 5 of the DDRB register, which corresponds with the fifth pin of the Port B general-purpose I/O port, PB5.

Shifting a bit to the left in a binary number is the same as multiplying it by two. If you shift a decimal base 10) number to the left (and add a zero to the now-empty space on the right), it's the same as multiplying that number by 10. Binary numbers are exactly the same as decimal numbers, except they're base 2 instead of base 10. Inside the computer chip, all numbers (and all data, really) are represented by binary numbers.

So instead of 1<<5, you could use decimal 32 (DDRB = 32;), hexadecimal 0x20, octal 040, or binary 0b00100000. Unfortunately, none of these other (perfectly accurate) representations readily communicate to the reader that you're interested in bit 5 here, and only bit 5. The binary representation 0b00100000 comes close but is more error-prone and takes much longer to type. The compiler understands them all, and they end up as the right bits in the right places after all the dust settles.

Couldn't you write 1<<5 directly into the DDRB register and be done? In this trivial example, yes. You don't care about the values of the other bits in DDRB, and writing a single bit (bit 5) clears all the other bits as an unintentional byproduct. Because this is a trivial example, it doesn't matter. Setting or not setting any of the other bits in that particular register doesn't affect the desired outcome.

Using the bitSet() macro instead of either the direct assignment statement or the augmented assignment statement makes the source code clearer in its intent, without incurring any sort of size penalty or code bloat. The compiler reduces it to the smallest code possible. When it's within the range of the *bit-manipulation* instructions SBI and CBI, it uses those. Otherwise, it cobbles together something brief.

If the 1<<5 notation just isn't your thing, you can use the Arduino-provided bit() macro, which does the same thing. For example, 1<<5 can be written bit(5).

Further Analysis

As just mentioned, you could simply write the desired value directly into the DDRB register, treating it just like any other variable. You'd do so with a statement such as DDRB = (1<<5);. This works because, in this example, you don't especially care if you clobber all the other bits in the DDRB register. You only care if the fifth bit gets set.

One interesting note about writing a value directly to the register (instead of the read/modify/write procedure used with the augmented assignment operator) is that the binary sketch size is now 938 bytes, or 2 bytes *bigger* than the preferred method, using the bitSet() macro. This is because the compiler uses two machine-language instructions to perform this direct write: one to load a constant value into a register, and another to write that value to the I/O port. There is no Load Immediate (LDI) instruction that directly addresses the I/O space. The binary sketch size on the Arduino Mega 2560, likewise, is 1,506 bytes, one machine-language instruction longer than the more compact version.

How, exactly, does the compiler perform this bit of magic? The answer lies in the *highly optimized* AVR-specific libraries that are provided with the Arduino software. They're part of the AVR port of the GNU Compiler Collection (avr-gcc) and collected together into the avr-libc library. The compiler determines that only a single bit is being manipulated and uses the exact machine-language instruction that was created specifically for this job: Set Bit in IO Register (SBI). The SBI instruction performs the complete read/modify/write process in two clock cycles but only uses a single word of program memory to do it.

That's not all you can optimize in terms of space in this example. Let's further use your understanding of the internals of the Atmel AVR to optimize the blinking of the LED.

Easy Toggling

As discussed previously regarding the example sketch Blink, the LED is explicitly turned on and then explicitly turned off again, using two different forms of the digitalWrite() function. The first function call turns on the LED by writing a HIGH level to pin D13, and the second function call turns off the LED by writing a LOW level to the same pin.

Also mentioned previously is that this on-again, off-again cycle can be more abstractly viewed as a *toggling* of the output pin. Luckily, the AVR knows how to toggle the output of its pins using a special write sequence, using an otherwise unused address.

The Input Pins Address (PINx) is normally only ever *read* by the processor, to determine the actual logic levels present on the general-purpose I/O pins.

■ **Tip** Don't make the mistake of trying to *read* the PORTx register. This is the output port data register only and only indicates what value, if any, was last written to the output port. To read inputs from the outside world, you *must* read from the PINx register.

When the AVR design engineers decided to add *pin-toggling* capabilities to the newer AVR chips, they didn't have any extra I/O addresses to use, so they cleverly reused an address that had only been used previously for inputs. Writing a 1 to a bit in the PINx register *inverts* or toggles the output level of the corresponding output pin for that port. Note that this *doesn't work* on older AVR devices, such as the ATmega8, ATmega16, and ATmega32. When in doubt, check the datasheets.

To toggle the LED, you just need to write a single 1 to the correct bit position in the PINB register. You don't need to preserve any of the other bits in this register, because they technically don't exist.

Replacing both of the digitalWrite() function calls with bitSet(PINB, 5); results in a binary sketch size of only 658 bytes for the Arduino Uno and 870 bytes for the Arduino Mega 2560. Please remember to use 7 instead of 5 when using the Arduino Mega 2560, because D13 is mapped to PB7 and not PB5.

This results in a slimming of 278 more bytes. The digitalWrite() function is handy, but it comes with a price.

Further Reduction

A closer look at the resulting code reveals a duplication of efforts. Whereas the original version of Blink's `loop()` function contained four program statements to perform the discrete steps involved, the new version needs only two: the first to change the LED state, and the second to wait a short period of time. Because the `loop()` function automatically repeats itself, it turns on the LED after one pass and then turns off the LED on the next pass.

Eliminating the now-redundant lines of code produces a binary sketch size of 644 bytes, a further saving of 14 bytes of program memory.

Wasting Time More Efficiently

What's left to optimize in this sketch? The only function calls you haven't modified so far are the `delay()` function calls that produce the human-perceptible delay you need in order to be able to detect the blinking of the LEDs with the naked eye.

Just to establish a lower boundary, comment-out the remaining `delay()` function call within the `loop()` function. When compiled, this produces a binary sketch size of 454 bytes. This is the lower boundary for the binary sketch size because no code for the delays has been included at all, and it will take *something* to replace that functionality. Let's look at a couple of alternatives.

First, let's try a simple `for()` loop to kill some time. A `for()` loop is a special kind of *control* (that is, looping) structure. A `for()` loop contains a place for some initialization code, a place for a test to see if the loop should continue, and a place for some code to perform every loop. These code snippets are included as the parameters of the `for()` statement and are separated by semicolons.

Add the program statement `for(int i = 0; i < 32000; i++);` somewhere inside the `loop()` function. It really doesn't matter where you place this statement in such a simple example program.

Suspiciously, after compilation, the binary sketch size is *still* 454 bytes. Uploading the sketch to your Arduino produces perhaps puzzling results. The LED comes on and appears to stay on, but it looks a little dimmer than before. In reality, it's blinking away madly, more than half a million times per second. This is much too fast for the human eye to detect and looks like a blur. What happened?

Optimization happened, that's what. The compiler spied your empty `for()` loop, which contained no executable statements. The compiler then decided that the `for()` loop wasn't needed in the final program. Therefore, the compiler completely omitted the `for()` loop, thinking it had done a Good Thing. Remember, the compiler takes *optimization* very seriously and doesn't understand you wanting to waste time like that.

Add the keyword `volatile` just before the integer type declaration `int` to prevent this optimization. This produces a 498-byte binary sketch (a good sign, because it's bigger) and, better yet, a rapidly yet visibly flashing LED. The `volatile` keyword instructs the compiler to make no assumptions about this particular variable, including assumptions that might have lead to optimizations.

The parameter passed to the Arduino's built-in `delay()` function is the desired delay time expressed in milliseconds. The parameter selected in your `for()` loop is just a big number and doesn't directly correspond to milliseconds. By giving up this accuracy, you save 146 bytes of program memory. This is figured by offsetting the 190 bytes you saved by omitting the `delay()` function by the 44 bytes taken up by the empty `for()` loop.

Using Lower-Level Code

Another approach to adding a perceptible delay is to use the already-ticking Timer0 and its associated interrupt handler, TIMER0_OVF_vect, which increments an unsigned, long integer value called timer0_millis.

■ **Caution** If you ~~mess with~~ improve the built-in Arduino code that uses the timers, you risk losing the proper function of the built-in timing functions, such as delay(), millis(), and so on.

To refer to this new variable in your sketch, you need to add an external variable declaration. The variable timer0_millis is *defined* in the wiring.c source code, but the compiler forgets all about it when it has completed the compilation of that source file and moved on to the next file to be compiled. You remind the compiler about this variable by adding the external variable *declaration* extern volatile unsigned long timer0_millis; somewhere in your sketch but *outside* either of your two functions, setup() and loop(). This declaration needs to be placed somewhere in your sketch *before* the first reference is made to the variable. In other words, it has to be defined before it can be used. Also note that this declaration must match the definition in the other file exactly. You can't say it's an int in one place and a byte in another, or the compiler will become confused.

Now replace the empty for() loop with the following two program statements inside the loop() function:

```
while(timer0_millis < 1000); // wait 1 second
timer0_millis = 0; // reset millisecond timer
```

The first statement is an empty while() loop that waits for timer0_millis to equal or exceed the value 1,000. Because timer0_millis should increment at the rate of one count per millisecond, this loop, excluding any code overhead, should take approximately one second to complete. It won't be *exactly* one second, but it will be very close. When the while() condition is satisfied, execution continues with the next program statement, which resets the millisecond timer count.

Do take note of the fact that this counter-resetting method completely nullifies the intended operation of the millis() function, which is to report the cumulative number of milliseconds since the Arduino sketch began to execute. Because this is a trivial example, and all you want is a one-second delay, you can take this liberty.

Compile and upload this sketch to your Arduino. This alternative delay results in a binary sketch size of 496 bytes on the Arduino Uno and 708 bytes on the Arduino Mega 2560, even smaller than your empty for() loop delay method. Had the lower-level Arduino code not already initialized Timer0 and provided an interrupt routine, you would be required to do so yourself, and the code would be correspondingly larger. As it is, you have creatively used the existing software to do your bidding, at the expense of the original intent of the millis() function.

In summary, you've replaced three function calls and cut the binary sketch size by more than half. In truth, there's still more to cut, because a lot of unused functionality is waiting to be exploited in a plain-vanilla Arduino sketch.

Saving Space with Simple Serial Communication

The Arduino's Serial library is very convenient and does a lot of different, useful things. In Chapter 2, you successfully ported the classic C program "Hello, world!" to the Arduino and replaced printf() with Serial.println(). Sometimes, however, you only need to send a few simple messages or report a reading or two. In these situations, you may want to save some program space by replacing Serial with the bare minimum of code necessary to send or receive data.

■ **Note** *Baud rate* or *bits per second* (bps)? Technically, these terms don't mean the same thing, although they're often used interchangeably. Both the Arduino and Atmel documentation use *baud* when they more properly mean *bps*.

Let's bypass the Arduino's Serial library and write directly to the USART peripheral. In doing so, you lose a *lot* of functionality but should regain some program space. Create a new sketch for these experiments. To begin, add to the setup() function the two lines shown in Listing 6-2. The loop() function must be included as well, but you don't need anything in there just yet.

Listing 6-2. "Hello, World!" Using the Arduino Serial Library

```
void setup() {
  Serial.begin(9600);
  Serial.println("Hello, world!");
}

void loop() {
  // nothing to do here
}
```

Compiled with Arduino 0022 for the Arduino Uno, this two-liner translates into a 1,906-byte binary sketch. The Arduino Mega 2560, as you might expect by now, results in a larger binary sketch that weighs in at 2,744 bytes. Let's see what you can do about reducing those numbers.

What "Hello, world!" Does

Breaking down the "Hello, world!" sketch is even easier than the Blink sketch. You're down to just two major operations in this example:

1. Initialize the serial port to the correct communication format and data rate.

2. Send a string of characters out the serial port, one at a time.

On the Arduino Uno, only one hardware USART peripheral is available, called USART0, and it's already connected to the USB interface that pretends to be a serial port on the PC. This makes the "Which port do I use?" decision simpler. On the Arduino Mega 2560, there are four USART peripherals built-in, and USART0 is connected to the USB interface.

There are several registers associated with each USART peripheral. These registers are the way you communicate with the serial port in the sketch. The Arduino `Serial` library knows all about them and even adds additional capabilities by using the available interrupts that can be generated by the USART hardware, permitting serial transmission and reception to be performed in the background using a set of circular buffers. That's great if you have the extra room to accommodate all that code. If you're adding serial communication features to an already-full chip, you may not.

Writing to Configuration Registers

The AVR USARTs are very flexible peripherals and have many configuration options available. You need to write to four of these registers (UCSR0A, UCSR0B, UCSR0C, and UBRR0) to get everything running smoothly for your sketch. Each of these registers contains discrete bits that configure particular aspects of the USART.

Instead of a long list of `bitSet()` and `bitClear()` macro calls (which would work but would end up being unwieldy and error-prone), let's write all the bits to each of those registers, one whole register at a time. You can use a trick similar to the bit-shifting fun you had back in the "Shrink Blink" section to set each bit, *by name*, to either a one or a zero, as appropriate. Yes, even the bits have names. The names of the bits and the registers are already defined in one of the header files that is automatically included by the Arduino software, so you don't have to look them up in the datasheet.

First, to get a lower bound for your experiment, comment-out the `Serial.begin()` and `Serial.println()` function calls. Doing so effectively guts the sketch as far as functionality, but it still compiles with no errors. On the Arduino Uno, it should result in a binary sketch size of only 450 bytes. The Arduino Mega 2560, likewise, needs 662 bytes to wake up in the morning but not get anything done.

Add the following three lines to your `setup()` function:

```
UCSR0A = 0<<TXC0 | 0<<U2X0 | 0<<MPCM0;
UCSR0B = 0<<RXCIE0 | 0<<TXCIE0 | 0<<UDRIE0 | 0<<RXEN0 | 1<<TXEN0 | 0<<UCSZ02 | 0<<TXB80;
UCSR0C = 0<<UMSEL01 | 0<<UMSEL00 | 0<<UPM01 | 0<<UPM00 | 0<<USBS0 | 1<<UCSZ01 | 1<<UCSZ00 | 0<<UCPOL0;
```

If you're feeling especially lazy, you can type in these shorter lines instead:

```
UCSR0A = 0;
UCSR0B = 1<<TXEN0;
UCSR0C = 1<<UCSZ01 | 1<<UCSZ00;
```

These shortened versions take advantage of the fact that the omitted bits needed to be set to zero, and that's exactly what the compiler puts in those bit positions unless otherwise instructed. If you go ahead and type in *all those words,* you're rewarded later when you want to go back and tweak some of the other USART settings; otherwise you have to go back to the datasheet and look up all the bit positions.

You *must*, however, write a 0 to the UCSR0A register if only to intentionally clear the U2X0 bit, which, when set, doubles the transmission and reception speed. The U2X0 bit is set by the Optiboot bootloader after the chip is reset and remains set after the sketch begins to execute. If you omit that, you're going to get garbage characters in the Serial Monitor window, because the baud rate isn't what you think it is. Note that you haven't set the actual baud rate yet—that will happen shortly. Even if another bootloader is being used, it isn't a good idea to make assumptions about the starting state concerning hardware configuration.

The other bits in UCSR0A mostly reflect the current status of the device. You learn more about the details when you actually get around to sending some data.

The second line enables the USART transmitter, by setting the TXEN0 bit within the UCSR0B register to 1. Because you're only transmitting and not receiving, it isn't necessary to enable the receiver (by setting bit RXEN0 to a 1). Enabling the transmitter actually routes the USART output pin directly to the I/O pin on the chip package and disconnects the general-purpose I/O line. Note that you don't need to explicitly set the pin to be an *output*, because this is taken care of automatically in the hardware.

The other bits in the UCSR0B register enable or disable the possible interrupts that can be generated by the USART hardware, including Receive Complete, Transmit Complete, and Data Register Empty. You don't use any interrupts in this simple example, so all of these other bits can remain set as zeros.

There is one other configuration bit in UCSR0B (UCSZ02) that, along with two other bits in the UCSR0C register (UCSZ01 and UCSZ00) determine the number of bits that are transmitted with each byte. As luck would have it, the UCSZ02 bit should be set to zero to configure the serial port for eight data bits, which is what you want. The Arduino software assumes a serial port configuration of 8N1, meaning eight data bits, no parity bits, and a single stop bit.

UCSR0B also contains a couple of bits (RXB80 and TXB80) for sending and receiving a possible ninth data bit, which is sometimes required by certain serial protocols. The AVR USART hardware is quite versatile, indeed.

You set the remaining data-size bits, UCSZ01 and UCSZ00, in the third configuration statement. They both need to be set to 1 to indicate that eight data bits should be transmitted and received. The serial data format can be anything from five to eight data bits long.

The only remaining configuration task is to set the baud rate. This is accomplished by providing a number to be used as a *prescaler*, or divisor for the system clock. The resulting clock signal should be 16 times (16x) the actual baud rate. This is because the USART *oversamples* the incoming data stream to help eliminate errors due to intermittent line glitches. The formula for determining the baud-rate divisor comes straight from the AVR datasheet.

Instead of wedging yet another magic number into the code, you spell out what you're doing using macro definitions. Add the following two lines just above the setup() function:

```
#define BAUD_RATE 9600
#define BAUD_RATE_DIVISOR (F_CPU / 16 / BAUD_RATE - 1)
```

F_CPU is a predefined symbol that represents the frequency of the CPU. In the case of most Arduinos, this is 16,000,000, which represents the CPU frequency in cycles per second, or Hertz. In any case, it should be correctly defined, and you can rely on its correctness so that you don't have to alter your source code every time you want to try it on a different Arduino. This is one of the many parameters that gets set when you select your specific Arduino model by choosing Tools ➤ Board.

Now if you want to change the baud rate from 9600 to something else, you know where to go.

To configure the USART to operate at this communication rate, add the following program statement to your setup() function:

```
UBRR0 = BAUD_RATE_DIVISOR;
```

Your USART is now completely configured. It took only four program statements. Note that the binary sketch size for the Arduino Uno is only 478 bytes, compared with 1,372 bytes had you used the ever-more-convenient Serial.begin(9600) function call. The Arduino Mega 2560 is a little heavier, at 690 bytes, instead of the previous 2,206 bytes using the Serial library.

Transmitting Data

To transmit a single byte of data, you write an eight-bit value to the UDR0 register. That's all there is to it. The USART hardware does the rest for you.

You need to wait until that character gets transmitted before sending another one, however. To determine when this has happened, you interrogate the USART0 Data Register Empty (UDRE0) bit in the UCSR0A register. When this bit is set, it means that the USART's internal transmit buffer is empty and ready for another byte.

Listing 6-3 contains a simple function to send a single character via the serial port. You can add this function anywhere you want within your sketch, but if you add it *before* it's ever referenced by your other code, you can omit the otherwise-required *function prototype* that clues in the compiler as to the function's parameters and return type, if any.

Listing 6-3. *A Function to Transmit a Single Character via the USART Peripheral*

```
void usart_putc(char c) {
  loop_until_bit_is_set(UCSR0A, UDRE0); // wait for transmit buffer to be empty
  UDR0 = c; // transmit character out the serial port
}
```

From the function declaration, you can see that the function takes a single char (eight-bit value) as an input parameter and doesn't return a value (void).

The loop_until_bit_is_set() function is (as you probably guessed) not a function at all, but rather yet another macro definition. This one is provided by the avr-libc library. You could have also used the Arduino-supplied bitRead() macro inside an otherwise-empty while() loop, which produces the same executable code:

```
while(bitRead(UCSR0A, UDRE0));
```

Use whichever one makes the most sense to you. There is also a convenient loop_until_bit_is_clear() macro definition available for when you want to wait for a zero instead of a one.

The actual transmitting of the byte in question is performed by the last program statement in the function, the assignment of the variable c to the USART0 data register, UDR0.

Note that the order of these two operations could be reversed (write, then wait for the operation to complete), and the function would still work. However, this is less efficient, time-wise, because the USART *may already be ready to transmit*. You know that it *won't* be ready to transmit after you're written a value to the data register (because it will be busy sending it out, one bit at a time, along with the start, stop, and option parity bits), but you know at least some time is going to elapse before the calling routine calls again. It's better to try to find something useful to do instead of waiting around (also known as *blocking*) when there's more work to be done. Returning as soon as possible from low-level device drivers is always a good idea.

Now add the following program statement to the very end of your setup() function:

```
usart_putc('!'); // send a test character
```

Note the use of the *single-quote* character to delineate the single-character parameter of the function. Upload this sketch to your Arduino, and then open the Serial Monitor window. You should be greeted by a single exclamation point. This exclamation point is brought to you by a sketch that is only 492 bytes in size on the Arduino Uno and 704 bytes for the Arduino Mega 2560. It's only one character, but it's a good start.

A String of Characters

Now you have a function that will transmit a single character. What you need is a function that will transmit as many characters as you want or need. This may be 1, or it may be 100, or more. Luckily, that's easy in C. See Listing 6-4.

Listing 6-4. A Function to Transmit a String of Characters

```
void usart_puts(char *s) {
  while(*s) {
    usart_putc(*s);
    s++;
  }
}
```

Add this function definition just after the usart_putc() function definition. Looking at this function declaration, you see that no return value is expected (void), but the parameter is a little different-looking. If you're already familiar with C strings and pointers, feel free to skip over this section.

The canonical Unix puts() function traditionally appends a newline character to the end of the string being printed. You omit that functionality in this simple example, but feel free to add it if you like.

The (char *s) notation indicates a *pointer* to (or address of) a character data type, and not an actual char (8 bit) variable at all. A pointer is a variable that contains a memory address that points to something. Pointers are their own kind of data type and are especially useful when you want to work with a piece of data, and the piece right after that one, and the piece right after that one, and so on. Arrays of data are a good example. A *string* of characters is a variable-length array of characters whose end is indicated with a special null value, usually zero. Traditionally, the unprintable ASCII codes, such as bell, carriage return, and line feed have short, uppercase abbreviations such as BEL, CR, and LF. The very first code, NUL, has a value of zero. This can be expressed in C as \0. This is the character that is used to indicate the end of character strings in C, which are sometimes referred to as *nul-terminated strings*. It isn't the same as the predefined value NULL, which is a pointer that isn't pointing to anything, usually ((void *)0). Believe it or not, sometimes that's just what you want. One example is to use the void return value to indicate that a function has failed and won't be returning a valid pointer.

Within the function is a while() loop. The *test condition* of the while() loop is designated as (*s), which is read as "the value contained in the variable that is pointed to by the pointer s" or, more briefly, "what s points to." While s points to a value that is true, or more specifically *not zero*—that is, a transmittable character and *not* the terminating NUL symbol—the loop continues, sending the value pointed to by s to the usart_putc() function. After this, the pointer s is incremented using the C increment shorthand s++. Because the compiler knows (you told it) that the *data type* of the thing that s points to is a char, it knows what size steps to take when incrementing, decrementing, or otherwise doing pointer math on s. Even though character strings aren't a fundamental data type that is supported by the C programming language, like char, int, long, float, and so on, the standard C library contains many functions that work with strings.

After s is incremented, the loop repeats. If the end of the string is encountered, the function terminates.

Replace the usart_putc('!') test statement at the end of the setup() function with the following and see what happens:

```
usart_puts("Hello, world!");
```

If all goes well, you should have a 520-byte sketch (for the Arduino Uno; 732 bytes for the Arduino Mega 2560) that prints "Hello, world!" on the Serial Monitor. All you can print are either single characters or fixed strings, but sometimes that's all you need. Take all that saved program space and do something excellent with it!

Printing Numbers

Sometimes single characters or fixed strings are sufficient, but what if you need to take readings and report back numbers? That can be easily done with a very few lines of code. See Listing 6-5 for a function to print integers.

Listing 6-5. A Function to Print Integers

```
void usart_puti(long i) {

  char s[25]; // character buffer to build string in

  itoa(i, s, 10); // convert integer to ASCII string, base 10
  usart_puts(s); // now print the string on the serial port
}
```

This function uses the power of the itoa() function from the standard C library. It takes a number and converts it to an ASCII string in the radix (base) indicated by the third parameter, which in this case is ten. You could easily make a different version for hexadecimal numbers by changing the radix to 16.

These three printing functions, along with the appropriate initialization steps, should cover a large portion of your serial transmitting needs, while not saddling your sketch with excess girth.

There is also a dtostr() function in the avr-libc standard library that converts a floating-point number to an ASCII string. You must specify the *width* and *precision* desired in the conversion. The width is the total size of the resulting string, and the precision is the number of places to the right of the decimal place. This clever function comes at a cost, adding almost 2KB to the binary sketch size. Also, it's interesting to note that the function takes a *double* (double-precision floating-point number) as a parameter, even though the math libraries for the AVR treat both the single-precision float type and the double as 32-bit values. One doesn't have twice the precision of the other; they're identical.

For extra credit, move the USART initialization statements to their own function, perhaps called usart_init(). You could even pass the desired baud rate as a parameter to this function, thereby emulating the Arduino's Serial.begin() function. Remember to add a call to usart_init() in your setup() function.

Saving SRAM

Even more precious than the scarce program memory in the Arduino is the amount of available SRAM. Recall from Chapter 3 that the ATmega328 has a mere 2,048 *bytes* of SRAM. That's not *mega*bytes or *giga*bytes. The ATmega2560 has 8,192 bytes of SRAM—more, but only when compared with the little one.

SRAM is mostly thought of as being used for temporary data storage, such as variables and the like. SRAM is also used for the system *stack*, the place where return addresses are stored during subroutine calls and interrupts. The stack is also used in interrupt handlers to preserve the contents of the registers needed by the handler itself, so that no registers are harmed in the handling of this interrupt.

Like any precious commodity, SRAM is valuable not only because it's scarce, but also because it's hard to find. In truth, it's not hard to find but hard to measure. Comparing program space savings is trivial because the Arduino tools publish the resulting sketch size with every compilation. The standard Arduino toolset also includes a utility program, `avr-size`, to tell you how much SRAM is being used, at least initially, in a sketch. This helps you measure the *fixed* (or preallocated) amount of SRAM that your sketch requires when it first starts. How much SRAM it will ultimately need depends on many other factors. Let's cover the easy ones first.

Measuring SRAM Requirements

Before you can get all scientific and perform some SRAM measurement experiments, you need to set up your laboratory. As mentioned previously, the tools you need have already been provided. All you have to do is the following:

1. Get to a command-line prompt.

2. Find the tool you need.

3. Find the ~~victim~~ experimental subject.

4. Perform the experiment.

5. Repeat.

If you're comfortable working at the command line, this process is straightforward. You probably already know what's going on here and know several alternate ways of accomplishing the same thing. Please feel free to use whatever method works for you.

On the other hand, if you aren't so comfortable with the command line and all that cryptic typing stuff, this may not be the experiment you want to perform today. Feel free to skip over this section for now and return when you need to squeeze every last drop of SRAM out of your Arduino.

Step 1 varies depending on your operating system of choice. For example, when using Windows 7, you can navigate to the desired folder using Windows Explorer, hold down the Shift key while right-clicking the folder of interest, and select Open Command Window Here from the context menu. You determine the desired folder in step 3.

Other operating systems, although perfectly cromulent in their own right, have different methods available for getting to a command-line prompt within the correct subdirectory.

Step 2 can be easy or it can be hard. Once you have the command-line window open, simply type `avr-size` and press Enter or the equivalent on your PC. If you get the message `avr-size: 'a.out': No such file`, then you're in luck! The `avr-size` utility can be found from your command-line prompt. If not, you need to add the proper path to your `PATH` environment variable. This varies from one system to the next. Repeat until you get the specified message in response to the `avr-size` command with no parameters given.

Step 3 is a little more complicated. You need to find one of the intermediate files produced by the Arduino software during the compilation process. These files are artfully hidden away from your sight by the Arduino software. You can find them, but it takes some sleuthing on your part.

Holding down the Shift key while clicking the Arduino Verify toolbar icon produces verbose output in the console window. That's the easy way. Note that this only works when clicking the toolbar icon; it doesn't work when you choose Sketch ➤ Verify/Compile. You can get verbose output during the sketch-upload process by using the same trick (hold down the Shift key while clicking the Upload toolbar icon).

Alternately, you can change the Arduino's `preferences.txt` file and get verbose output each and every time you compile. To find the Arduino's `preferences.txt` file location, select File ➤ Preferences in the Arduino software. See Figure 6-1: the file location is given near the bottom of the dialog box.

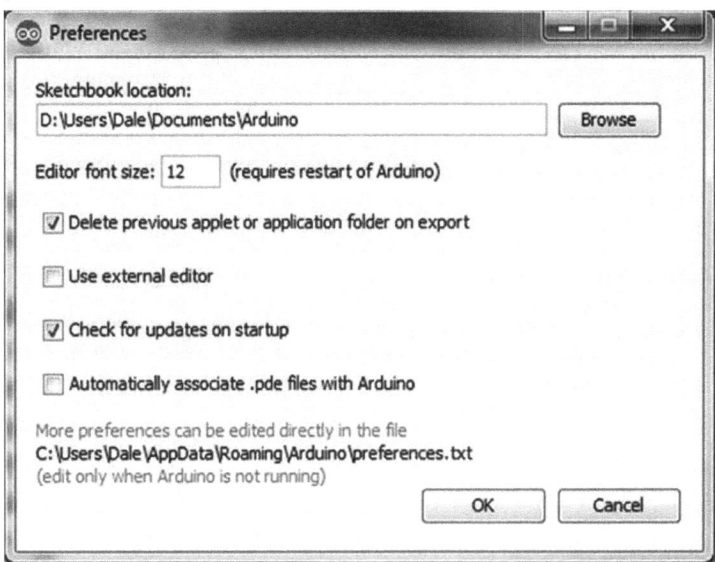

Figure 6-1. The location of the Arduino preferences.txt file is revealed in the File ➤ Preferences dialog box.

In this example, the preferences.txt file is located in the C:\Users\Dale\AppData\Roaming\Arduino folder. Yours will likely be elsewhere.

When you've discovered the secret hiding place of the Arduino's preferences.txt file, edit the file with your favorite programmer's editor and add the line build.verbose=true. Make sure you exit the Arduino software while editing the preferences.txt file. Note that you don't have to make this change in the preferences.txt file if you just hold down the Shift key when compiling.

The Bare Minimum

Reopen the Arduino software, and open the example sketch, BareMinimum, by choosing File ➤ Examples ➤ 1.Basics ➤ BareMinimum. As its name implies, this is the bare-minimum sketch that will compile properly using Arduino. It has skeleton setup() and loop() functions, and that's all.

Compile this sketch with verbose output, and pay special attention to the console area at the bottom of the Arduino window. It should resemble Figure 6-2.

Figure 6-2. *The verbose output option causes the Arduino software to reveal the location of the temporary folder used to compile the sketch.*

In this example, the Arduino software created a temporary folder located at `C:\Users\Dale\AppData\Local\Temp\build6459014193141626380.tmp`. You may want to use the scrollbar on the right side of the console window to scroll up and see what else happened during the compilation process, if you're curious.

This is the temporary folder where all the intermediate files are stored that are created when Arduino compiles your sketch. If you shut down the Arduino software and start it up again, it creates a new, *different* folder to contain these temporary files.

The file you're most interested in at this point is the `BareMinimum.cpp.elf` file. Now that you know where all the good stuff is, navigate to this folder and prepare for step 4.

From your command-line prompt, issue the following command:

```
avr-size -C --mcu=atmega328p BareMinimum.cpp.elf
```

Note the capital C in the command-line option: this instructs the avr-size utility to report its findings in AVR format. Also, the --mcu option has *two* leading dashes and informs the utility as to the storage capacity of the chip's memory banks, allowing it to calculate what percentage has been used. atmega328p has to be spelled out in all-lowercase letters. The avr-size utility won't recognize --mcu=ATmega328P, for example.

The report should resemble the following:

```
AVR Memory Usage
----------------
Device: atmega328p

Program:     450 bytes (1.4% Full)
(.text + .data + .bootloader)

Data:          9 bytes (0.4% Full)
(.data + .bss + .noinit)
```

The avr-size utility reports that the BareMinimum sketch occupies 450 bytes of program memory (confirmed by the binary sketch size report), which constitutes 1.4% of the program memory's capacity. It also shows that 0.4% of the precious, precious SRAM (nine bytes) has already been allocated. The preallocated memory is used by the variables listed in Table 6-1, which were declared in the wiring.c file.

Table 6-1. Preallocated Variables in the BareMinimum Arduino Sketch

Variable Name	Data Type	Size in Bytes
timer0_fract	unsigned char (8 bits)	1
timer0_overflow_count	unsigned long (32 bits)	4
timer0_millis	unsigned long (32 bits)	4
Total		9

Memory Sections

The terms .text, .data, and so on, refer to various memory *sections* within the resultant memory image. Each memory section exists for a different reason. The .text section is where the executable program resides. The .data section is where *initialized* variables are located, whereas the .bss section is for *uninitialized* variables. These are the three primary sections within the compiled program. The avr-gcc compiler is quite familiar with them. They have been around, literally, for decades.

The .noinit section is a special exception. Data values placed in this section aren't automatically initialized when the sketch begins executing. This is useful when you want a piece of data to survive a device reset, for example. You can place a variable into this section using the GNU Compiler Collection (GCC) specific __attribute__ keyword:

```
unsigned char reset_count __attribute__ ((section(".noinit")));
```

Note that the double parentheses are required when using the `__attribute__` keyword. You can also use this technique to allocate and prepopulate variables in the EEPROM section, using the section name `.eeprom`. This normally creates an additional file with the extension `.eep` that can be used to program the device. The Arduino's Optiboot bootloader, however, doesn't currently support writing to the EEPROM. For now, this must be done with dedicated device programming hardware. The `avr-size` utility only reports the `.eeprom` section size if it exists.

It's still handy for you, as a programmer, to know about the `.eeprom` memory section, because even if the *contents* of the EEPROM on the chip don't get programmed, it allows the compiler to know about the *addresses* of the variables within the EEPROM, for use with the `eeprom_*` functions that are available in the `avr-libc` library.

Where Variables Live

The compiler allocates memory locations for variables based on several factors, usually depending on how it thinks they're going to be used. One of the factors that helps the compiler make these decisions is the variables' *scope*, or visibility within the program.

A variable with global scope is visible from anywhere within the program. These are variables that are defined outside of any particular function. A local variable, however, can only be seen from the function or block where it's defined.

The compiler only allocates space within a memory section for either global variables or local variables that have the static modifier, meaning that they remain allocated even outside their scope. Normal local variables, also known as *automatic* variables, are dynamically allocated on the stack and released or deallocated when the function terminates. They don't need to have a permanent address assigned to them by the compiler.

The initialized variables in the `.data` section are the global or static local variables that have a value assigned to them when they're declared. Uninitialized variables in the `.bss` section are cleared to a zero value when the sketch first starts. You should not, however, depend on the value of an uninitialized variable in your programs.

Now it's time to perform those experiments. Try running the `avr-size` utility on sketches with all kinds of different variables, declared in all kinds of different scopes. Mix up the initialized and uninitialized variables, and see which memory section they land in.

Using the Appropriate Data Type

The best way to save SRAM is to use the appropriate data type for your variables. Use the smallest data type that will sufficiently express your data. Table 6.2 lists the standard data types that are available within the Arduino programming language.

Table 6-2. *Available Data Types and Their Ranges*

Data Type	Number of Bits	Number of Bytes	Minimum Value	Maximum Value
unsigned char byte	8	1	0	255
signed char	8	1	-128	127
unsigned int word	16	2	0	65,535
int	16	2	-32,768	32,767
unsigned long	32	4	0	4,294,967,296
long	32	4	-2,147,483,648	2,147,483,647
unsigned long long	64	8	0	18,446,744,073,709,551,616
long long	64	8	-9,223,372,036,854,775,808	9,223,372,036,854,775,807
float	32	4	-3.4028235E+38	3.4028235E+38
double	32	4	-3.4028235E+38	3.4028235E+38

So if you're counting from one to ten, you don't need to declare an int; just use a byte. Likewise, if you're not using fractions, you most certainly want to be using one of the *integer* data types and not floating-point.

Strings of Characters, Revisited

Although the C language makes working with character strings very simple, it doesn't (yet) translate well to a Harvard architecture such as the AVR. The GCC compiler doesn't really understand the idea of separate data spaces for program memory and data memory. It wants to think that *all* memory is located in one big linear array and that there is One Way to access it.

This is especially true when handling strings of characters. Let's look at an example.

Add these two global variable declarations just above the setup() function in the BareMinimum sketch:

```
char c;
char msg[] = "This is a message";
```

Now add this assignment statement within the body of the setup() function:

```
c = msg[0];
```

The assignment statement is necessary for this experiment because any *unreferenced* variables will be optimized out of the program. Compile the program, and take a look at the sizes of the resulting memory sections:

```
AVR Memory Usage
----------------
Device: atmega328p

Program:    476 bytes (1.5% Full)
(.text + .data + .bootloader)

Data:        28 bytes (1.4% Full)
(.data + .bss + .noinit)
```

The character string `msg` was placed in the `.data` section. This is appropriate because you may want to modify the string at some later point. But what if all you want to do is print a banner to the serial port, identifying the program? Most nontrivial programs that have even the most Spartan of user interfaces have several read-only character strings that need to be emitted at some point.

The present solution is to use the `pgmspace` functions that are available from the `avr-libc` library. Listing 6-6 contains an example sketch that illustrates the practice of storing fixed-content strings in program memory, from the Arduino web site (`www.arduino.cc/en/Reference/PROGMEM`), used with permission.

Listing 6-6. Example Sketch Illustrating Use of Program Memory for Storing Read-Only Content

```
/*
 PROGMEM string demo
 How to store a table of strings in program memory (flash),
 and retrieve them.

 Information summarized from:
 http://www.nongnu.org/avr-libc/user-manual/pgmspace.html

 Setting up a table (array) of strings in program memory is slightly complicated, but
 here is a good template to follow.

 Setting up the strings is a two-step process. First define the strings.

*/

#include <avr/pgmspace.h>
prog_char string_0[] PROGMEM = "String 0";   // "String 0" are strings to store.
prog_char string_1[] PROGMEM = "String 1";
prog_char string_2[] PROGMEM = "String 2";
prog_char string_3[] PROGMEM = "String 3";
prog_char string_4[] PROGMEM = "String 4";
prog_char string_5[] PROGMEM = "String 5";
```

```
// Then set up a table to refer to your strings.

PROGMEM const char *string_table[] =        // change "string_table" name to suit
{
  string_0,
  string_1,
  string_2,
  string_3,
  string_4,
  string_5 };

char buffer[30];     // make sure this is large enough for the largest string it must hold

void setup()
{
  Serial.begin(9600);
}


void loop()
{
  /* Using the string table in program memory requires the use of special functions
     to retrieve the data.
     The strcpy_P function copies a string from program space to a string in RAM ("buffer").
     Make sure your receiving string in RAM  is large enough to hold whatever
     you are retrieving from program space. */


  for (int i = 0; i < 6; i++)
  {
    strcpy_P(buffer, (char*)pgm_read_word(&(string_table[i]))); // Necessary casts etc.
    Serial.println( buffer );
    delay( 500 );
  }
}
```

Low Power or High Speed?

You've taken a good first look at space-saving optimizations. These are easy to measure by comparing the before and after sizes of the binary sketch. Measuring execution speed and power consumption is a bit more involved.

Power and speed have a close relationship. More speed generally requires more power. Finding the optimum balance between the two is the goal of overall *performance* optimization.

Let's explore the limits of both power and speed. First, you find out how fast you can make the Arduino run. Then you slow things down a bit. After that, it's time to find out how much this performance costs in terms of power. Before that, however, you need to equip yourself with the proper tools for the job.

Electronic Measurements

To measure things electrical and electronic, you need a variety of *test and measurement equipment*. For example, you can use a *volt meter* to measure voltage. To measure current, an *ammeter* is used. These tools are good for measuring static or slowly changing levels. For more complex measurements, you use more complex tools.

The Arduino as Test Equipment

What test equipment is available on *your* bench? Please don't feel like you must immediately go out and buy thousands of dollars of test gear (unless that's an option and this was the ~~excuse~~ justification you've been waiting for—if so, go nuts!). You may be surprised by what you can do with what's right in front of you.

For some baseline readings on Arduino performance, you can use the Arduino to measure itself. These measurements can be used for *relative* performance increases but not *absolute* readings, because the Arduino must necessarily spend a small amount of time tending to the measurements themselves.

Open the Arduino software, and type in the short sketch from Listing 6-7. If you're super-lazy, rename the stop_time variable to j and omit the comments. It's really a very short sketch.

Listing 6-7. The Arduino Measuring the Performance of the Arduino

```
// arduino_performance

void setup() {
  Serial.begin(9600); // initialize serial port to 9600 bps
  Serial.println("Arduino performance test begins now.");
}

extern volatile unsigned long timer0_millis;

void loop() {

  unsigned long i = 0; // test value
  unsigned long stop_time; // in milliseconds

  // calculate stop time (current time + 1 second)
  stop_time = millis() + 1000;

  while(timer0_millis < stop_time) i++; // count!

  // report performance results:
  // number of loop iterations in one second
  Serial.print(i);
  Serial.println(" loops in one second.");

  while(1); // and stop here
}
```

Compile the sketch, and upload it to your Arduino. After the upload is complete, open the Serial Monitor window. Make sure the communication rate is set to 9600. Opening the Serial Monitor window toggles the Data Terminal Ready (DTR) line on the serial port, which should reset your Arduino and start the test over again. If your Arduino lacks the Auto Reset function, you have to coordinate the pressing of the on-board Reset button after opening the Serial Monitor. In either case, you should be greeted by the program self-announcement, "Arduino performance test begins now." (or whatever text, if any, you decided to include there), followed one second later by the test-result message.

Compiled with Arduino 0022 and running on an Arduino Uno, this performance test reports 836,003 loops in one second. The Arduino Mega 2560 reports 835,901 loops in the same time period. That's a lot of loops!

What do these numbers tell you? These preliminary test results tell you how quickly the Arduino can do *absolutely nothing useful*, while measuring the time it takes to do absolutely nothing useful. This is similar to the BogoMIPS metric used to measure the relative speed of CPUs running the Linux kernel (see http://tldp.org/HOWTO/BogoMips).

As Ralph Tenny once said, "If you can't measure the frequency, measure the period," reminding you of the reciprocal nature of period and frequency. Technically, you're not measuring the time it takes for each iteration of the empty loop. You're measuring the number of times the loop executes in a given time period (the frequency) and using the reciprocal of the frequency to estimate the loop execution time.

Note that you're using the direct timer0_millis trick again to keep track of the Arduino's concept of the current time. Because you're not rewriting the timer0_millis value anywhere in this sketch, you don't abandon the usefulness of the millis() function, as you did previously in the Blink optimization, even though it isn't being used elsewhere. This little optimization almost doubles the number of do-nothing loops that can be performed by the Arduino in a given second by eliminating the overhead associated with the millis() function call and reading the millisecond count directly.

Because a stock Arduino Uno uses a 16MHz oscillator (either a quartz crystal or a ceramic resonator, depending on the batch build date), it can execute up to 16,000,000 instructions per second. Because of the highly optimized machine code that is created for the while() loop that is doing all the counting, the loop executes very quickly. It takes 5 cycles to increment the 32-bit loop counter, i; 8 cycles to compare the timer0_millis millisecond counter with the captured stop_time variable; and 2 cycles to jump back to the beginning of the loop, for a total of 15 cycles.

If the Atmel AVR was doing nothing else, it should have been able to run this loop over a million times in any given second. However, this sketch depends heavily on the fact that Timer0 is running and generating interrupts on a regular basis; otherwise the loop would never end because there would be no incrementing of the millisecond timer. The *average* cycle time is 16,000,000 cycles per second ÷ 836,003 loops per second, or just over 19 cycles per loop.

You can now use this cycle count as your baseline reading. Any additional time spent in the while() loop can be calculated by offsetting the total time by this baseline reading.

Let's see how long it takes to turn the LED on and off again using the digitalWrite() function. You can safely omit the configuration of the LED output pin, because the resulting blink rate will be too high to see with your eyes, anyway. Modify the while() loop to look more like Listing 6-8.

Listing 6-8. Measuring the Performance of the digitalWrite() Function

```
while(timer0_millis < stop_time) {
  digitalWrite(13, HIGH); // LED on
  digitalWrite(13, LOW); // LED off
  i++; // count!
}
```

Compiled with Arduino 0022, the Arduino Uno can execute 112,653 of these loops in one second, whereas the Arduino Mega 2560 can execute only 67,013 of the same loops. The wide variation is explained by the larger number of I/O pins that the Arduino Mega 2560 must account for in the digitalWrite() function.

For the Arduino Uno, these numbers indicate that it takes 16,000,000 cycles per second ÷ 112,653 loops per second, or just over 142 cycles per loop. You subtract out the baseline reading of 19 cycles, leaving 123 cycles per loop. This gives you an average of 66 cycles for each of the two digitalWrite() functions. This translates into 4,125 nanoseconds.

The Arduino Mega 2560, however, takes a leisurely 110 cycles, on average, for each call to the digitalWrite() function, which can also be stated as 6,875 nanoseconds.

Remember that substitution of the single-instruction bit-manipulation for the digitalWrite() function reduced the time to set or clear a single bit to two cycles or just 125 nanoseconds. Let's test that idea by replacing the digitalWrite() function calls with bitSet() and bitClear() macros, as shown in Listing 6-9.

Listing 6-9. Replacing the digitalWrite() Function Calls with Macros

```
while(timer0_millis < stop_time) {
  bitSet(PORTB, 5); // LED on
  bitClear(PORTB, 5); // LED off
  i++; // count!
}
```

For the Arduino Uno, the simple substitution increases the loop count to 690,609 loops in a single second. This corresponds with a cycle count per loop of approximately 23, or just 4 cycles over the baseline reading. Because both the SBI and CBI instructions take exactly two cycles to execute, this is exactly what you expected. It would also appear to confirm the validity of your test.

The Arduino Mega 2560 also shows a similar boost in performance after the substitution, turning in a goodly 682,028 count, remaining right around the average of 23 cycles per loop, which is only 4 cycles above the baseline reading. Remember to set and clear bit 7 of PORTB on the Arduino Mega 2560, although in this example it doesn't really make any difference because the blinking of the LED is too fast to see.

Applying a final optimization to this loop, let's substitute the on-again-off-again commands with a single bit-toggle operation. See Listing 6-10.

Listing 6-10. Using the Bit-Toggling Capabilities of the AVR to Increase Performance

```
while(timer0_millis < stop_time) {
  bitSet(PINB, 5); // toggle LED
  i++; // count!
}
```

This loop runs 756,381 times in a second, which corresponds to 21 clock cycles per loop. Once the baseline overhead is removed, you can see that only two cycles were needed to toggle the LED *really quickly*, and that lines up exactly with your understanding of the SBI instruction, which needs only two cycles to do its job.

As Fast As Possible

It's not especially useful to blink an LED at this ridiculously high rate, but it would be nice in lots of other applications to send and receive data as fast as possible. Let's determine the highest toggle rate you can get on the I/O pin using software alone. To do this, you must abandon the Arduino Serial Monitor as your test instrument and try something else.

Take a look at Listing 6-11. It's a simple program that looks like it ought to be really ripping along.

Listing 6-11. Toggling an I/O Pin as Fast as Possible

```
void setup() {
  bitSet(DDRB, 5); // PB5/D13 is connected to an LED
}

void loop() {
  bitSet(PINB, 5); // toggle LED
}
```

Because the Arduino is quite busy at the moment, it can no longer help you measure itself. This is where you bring in the Big Iron, a piece of test equipment specifically designed to measure high frequencies and display waveforms: the oscilloscope.

An oscilloscope generally displays a graph-like image that represents a voltage level in the Y-dimension over time, which is represented by the X-dimension. Figure 6-3 is an example screen capture from a relatively low-cost oscilloscope manufactured by Rigol, displaying the output of D13 on an Arduino Uno.

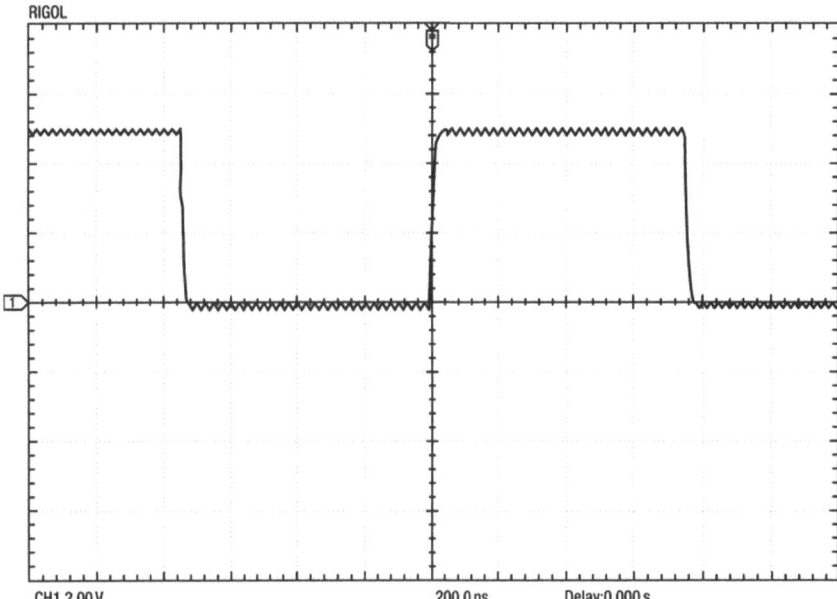

Figure 6-3. Digital signal waveform output from the sketch in Listing 6-11

In addition to displaying a picture of the waveform for you to see, the oscilloscope also provides several other useful measurements, including frequency, as well as the period of both the high-level and low-level portions of the signal. Additional readings can also be selected on most digital storage oscilloscopes (DSOs). See Figure 6-4.

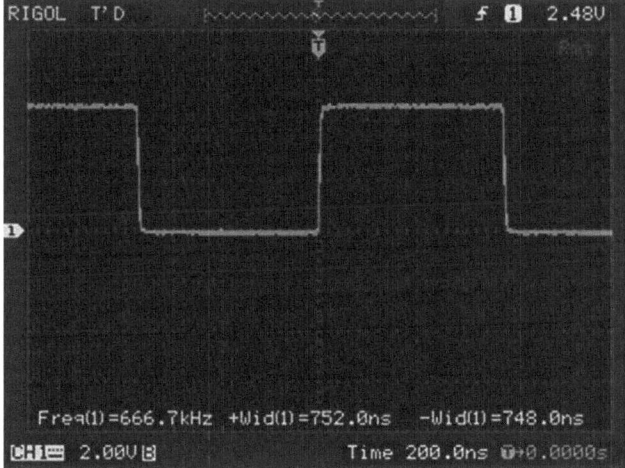

Figure 6-4. *Screen capture from an oscilloscope showing additional measurements*

The scope would appear to be reporting an output frequency of 666.7KHz, with an on time of 750ns and an off time of 748ns. This would lead you to believe that each pass through the `loop()` function was taking 12 cycles. What's going on here?

The answer is something that's easy to forget when programming the Arduino: the `loop()` function is being called repeatedly and ad infinitum by the hidden `main()` function. The apparent slowness of this signal is due to the calling overhead of the `loop()` function itself.

Here is a breakdown of what's happening in this sketch:

1. `main()` calls `loop()`: four cycles on the Arduino Uno, five on the Arduino Mega 2560.

2. `loop()` executes the `SBI` instruction: two cycles.

3. `loop()` returns to `main()`: four cycles on the Arduino Uno, five on the Arduino Mega 2560.

4. `main()` jumps back to the beginning of itself: two cycles.

As you can see, the problem is even worse on the Arduino Mega 2560. Due to its larger address space, it takes one cycle longer to push and pop the larger addresses (22-bit vs. 16-bit) to and from the stack when performing subroutine calls. The same is true for interrupt handling.

To eliminate this slowdown, all you have to do is wrap the `bitSet()` macro in a loop of your own devising. See Listing 6-12.

Listing 6-12. A Faster Loop for Toggling an I/O Pin

```
void loop() {
  while(1) {
    bitSet(PINB, 5); // toggle LED
  }
}
```

This sketch produces a much faster output signal; see Figure 6-5. The entirety of this sketch, after the I/O port has been properly configured as an output, consists of two machine-language instructions: SBI and RJMP. The first instruction toggles the I/O line, and the second instructions jumps back to the first instruction.

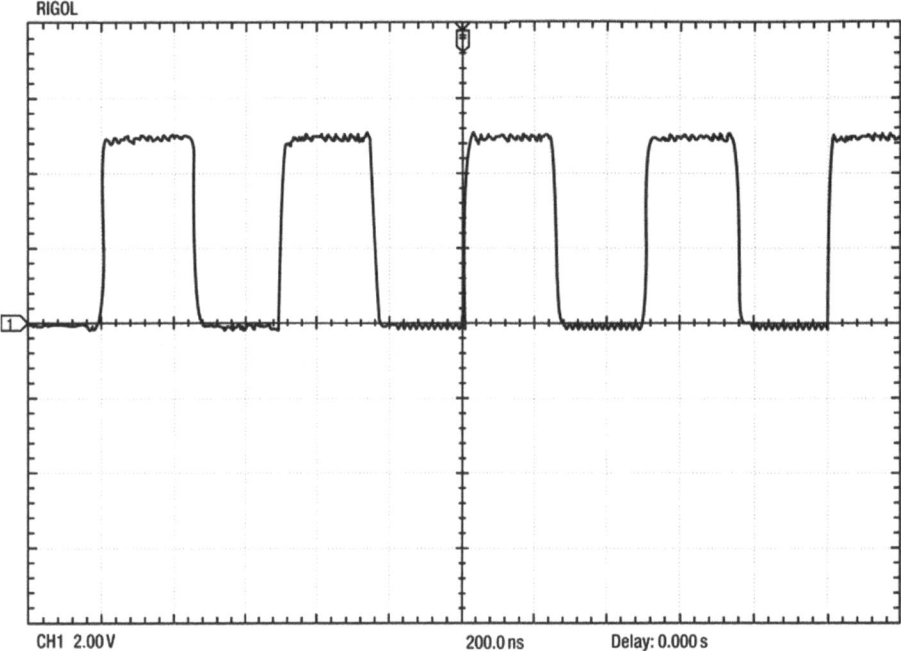

Figure 6-5. A much faster output waveform

Unfortunately, this signal isn't stable. Watching the oscilloscope display for even a short period of time reveals an occasional glitch occurring. Also, the frequency and period readings tend to jump around a little. What is causing this?

You left the millisecond timer running, and it's generating an interrupt about 1,000 times every second. During the time that it takes for the interrupt service handler to execute, the I/O line *does not toggle*. You can fix this by adding the following statement to the setup() function:

```
noInterrupts(); // no!
```

This function call, like so many others, is yet another macro. It turns out to be a single machine-language instruction, CLI, which clears the I (for Interrupt) bit in the CPU's status register, SREG. This, in turn, globally disables all interrupts from being acknowledged. Because you don't want or need interrupts in this example, this is a good solution to the problem.

Slowing It Down

So now you know that you can get the humble Arduino to output a 2MHz signal using software alone. That's pretty fast! It can't do much else at the same time, assuming you want a nice, stable signal. Let's find out how slow it can go.

Lowering the operating speed of the Arduino is the best way to lower its power requirements. If possible, you can also lower the operating voltage, which also saves power.

There are two easy ways to change the operating frequency of your Arduino. The first is to replace the quartz crystal or ceramic resonator, choosing a new component with a lower frequency. The other option is to change the operating frequency in software, using the clock prescale register (CLKPR). Let's try the software method first. You can always mangle improve your Arduino's hardware later, if you feel the need to do so.

The CLKPR register controls the division of the CPU clock according to the values in Table 6-3, assuming your Arduino is currently clocked by a 16MHz oscillator.

Table 6-3. Clock Prescale Register Divider Values

CLKPR Value	Division Factor	Resulting Frequency	clock_prescale_set() parameter
0	1	16,000,000	clock_div_1
1	2	8,000,000	clock_div_2
2	4	4,000,000	clock_div_4
3	8	2,000,000	clock_div_8
4	16	1,000,000	clock_div_16
5	32	500,000	clock_div_32
6	64	250,000	clock_div_64
7	128	125,000	clock_div_128
8	256	62,500	clock_div_256

Changing the CPU's clock affects other peripherals as well, including the analog-to-digital Converter (ADC) and general-purpose I/O ports. The serial port, however, isn't affected, so you can still use common communication rates, even when your CPU is slowed down.

There is a special write sequence to update the CLKPR register. Bit 7, called CLKPCE, must be set to 1 while all the other bits are set to 0 to start the sequence. Then the actual prescaler value must be written to the CLKPR register within four clock cycles. To ensure that this takes place in time, it's wise to disable interrupts for the duration of the write sequence.

Listing 6-13 demonstrates two things. The first is that serial communication still runs at the proper rates. The second is that the LED is blinking very slowly, when it ought to be a high-speed blur.

Listing 6-13. Slowing the CPU Clock

```
void setup() {
  Serial.begin(9600);
  Serial.println("Normal serial communication at 9600 bps");

  pinMode(13, OUTPUT); // D13 is connected to an LED

  noInterrupts(); // disable interrupts temporarily
  CLKPR = 1<<CLKPCE; // enable clock prescaler write sequence
  CLKPR = 8; // select clock divisor of 256
  interrupts(); // re-enable interrupts
}

void loop() {
  digitalWrite(13, HIGH); // LED is on
  delay(10); // 0.01 second delay
  digitalWrite(13, LOW); // LED is off
  delay(10); // 0.01 second delay
}
```

The Arduino's CPU is now running at 62.5KHz instead of the original 16MHz. The LED is on for 2.56 seconds and then off for the same time period. The serial port still works as you would expect.

The clock_prescale_set() function, declared in the avr/power.h header file, does the same thing.

Further Power Reductions

Two more methods are available to you for reducing the power requirements of your Arduino. The first is to put the processor to sleep when it would otherwise just be waiting around for something to happen. You can save additional power by shutting down unused peripherals.

The AVR architecture allows for several depths of sleep to occur. You can think of them as ranging from lightly napping to heavy slumber. To access these sleep modes, you can use some functions from the avr-libc library. Add the following line to the beginning of your sketch:

```
#include <avr/sleep.h>
```

This is a header file that is *not* normally included automatically by the Arduino compilation process, so you need to explicitly add it when you want to use the sleep functions provided by the avr-libc library.

The lightest form of sleep for the AVR is known as *idle mode*. In this mode, the CPU stops executing instructions, which saves a lot of power. All the remaining peripherals, however, continue to run at full speed, thereby consuming some power.

Interrupts are covered in more detail in Chapter 7. For now, you already have a free interrupt configured and running for you: the Timer0 interrupt used to trigger the millisecond counter. The sketch shown in Listing 6-14 demonstrates a method for putting the CPU to sleep while waiting for the timer to increment. This effectively puts the chip to sleep for about 99% of the time: a big savings in power.

Listing 6-14. Putting the CPU to Sleep

```
#include <avr/sleep.h>

extern volatile unsigned long timer0_millis;

void setup() {
  pinMode(13, OUTPUT); // an LED is attached to D13
}

void loop() {
  while(timer0_millis < 1000) {
    set_sleep_mode(SLEEP_MODE_IDLE); // select "lightly napping"
    sleep_mode(); // go to sleep
  }
  timer0_millis = 0; // reset millisecond counter
  bitSet(PINB, 5); // toggle LED
}
```

BONUS: DIGITAL SIGNAL PROBE

A crude *digital signal probe* for use with your Arduino can be built using only a short piece of 22-gauge wire. You can use smaller-diameter wire, but it tends to fall out of the expansion header sockets. Larger diameter wire or repurposed paper clips aren't recommended because they tend to deform the internal spring structure of the header pins, rendering them potentially unreliable in the future.

To build a probe, follow these steps:

1. Take a 6" piece of 22-gauge solid, insulated wire and strip about a quarter (1/4) of an inch of insulation from both ends. If you want to get fancy, you can solder header pins to a similar length of stranded wire of any small gauge, but only a simple wire of some sort is needed for this experiment.

2. Compile and upload the example Blink sketch to your Arduino:

   • File > Examples > 1.Basics > Blink

   • Sketch > Verify / Compile

   • File > Upload to I/O Board

3. Verify that the LED is indeed blinking properly.

4. Using the code editor, change all references to pin 13 to some other pin number, such as 2. The code should now look like this:

129

```
void setup() {
  // initialize the digital pin as an output.
  // Pin 13 has an LED connected on most Arduino boards:
  pinMode(2, OUTPUT);
}

void loop() {
  digitalWrite(2, HIGH);    // set the LED on
  delay(1000);              // wait for a second
  digitalWrite(2, LOW);     // set the LED off
  delay(1000);              // wait for a second
}
```

5. Save this sketch with a different name; don't overwrite your example sketches!

6. Compile and upload the sketch to your Arduino. Verify that the LED is no longer blinking.

7. Install one end of the wire in the expansion header pin socket marked 13.

8. Install the other end of the wire in the expansion header pin socket marked 2.

9. Verify that the LED is now blinking.

Why does this work? Remember that you changed all the references to pin 13 to pin 2 (or some other convenient pin of your choosing). Because D13 was *not* configured as an output in the setup() function, it remains in its default state as an *input*. As an input, it doesn't mind at all if another output is connected to it. The LED and its associated current-limiting resistor remain electrically attached to pin 13, but pin 13 no longer drives it. Any signal you now connect to D13 will show you whether it's high (LED on) or low (LED off).

Try probing the other pins in the expansion headers. Because the modified Blink example sketch didn't specifically configure any other pins as outputs, they normally show up as low (the LED remains unlit). Pay special attention to the relative brightness of the LED as you probe the 5V line and the 3.3V line. Which one is brighter? Why?

More extra credit questions: Why does probing the RESET line cause the Arduino to reset? Why is the RX line always high, even when nothing is being received on the serial port?

You can always use the programmable LED as a digital signal probe as long as pin D13 is left as an input.

Avoid probing the Vin pin if your Arduino is powered by an external power supply of greater than 6V. The LED won't mind, but D13 *certainly* will.

Summary

The Arduino software takes advantage of the many optimizations provided by the avr-gcc compiler and the finely-crafted avr-libc library. The Arduino-supplied libraries, on the other hand, could use a little help.

Speed, size, or power: pick all three. There's plenty of opportunity to squeeze more performance from your Arduino. You just need to know where to start looking. This chapter gives you that start.

You can apply many other optimizations to your Arduino sketches. This chapter is just a brief example of some of them. In the next chapter, you look at ways to obtain more performance from your Arduino by learning about some of the powerful peripherals that are waiting to do some work for you. Synchronizing your hardware and your software allows you to achieve very impressive performance improvements. Using the hardware-signaling system of interrupts lets your software be automatically notified when something interesting happens.

CHAPTER 7

Hardware Plus Software

Software commands hardware. Can hardware command software? Yes! It can and it should, from time to time. When the two cooperate, it's more like a dance and less like a military exercise. Let's look at some ways to make your software more aware of the available hardware, and what benefits you can derive from this more-cooperative relationship.

The first step is to learn more about the peripheral hardware that is already built in to your Arduino and how to use it in your applications. Next you move on to using *interrupts* more effectively, which can make your Arduino look like it can do more than one thing at a time.

Available Peripherals

You've already used several of the Arduino's built-in peripherals in the example sketches. The serial port lets you communicate with the host PC as well as other serial devices. The digital ins and outs let you turn things like LEDs on and off, as well as tell if buttons have been clicked. The pulse-width-modulation (PWM) outputs are an excellent way to simulate an analog output using a digital interface, which is perfect for dimming lights and controlling motor speeds. Driving the PWM outputs are the lower-level timer/counter peripherals, which can be used, as their name implies, for both timing and counting purposes.

The Atmel AVR also has a couple of true analog peripherals, including the analog-to-digital converter (ADC) and an analog comparator (AC). These inputs take a varying voltage, generally ranging between ground (0V) and V_{cc} (5V), and convert it into ones and zeros.

Let's take a look at some of these available devices-within-the-device and see what happens when you flip them over to fully automatic.

Serial Port(s)

The Arduino's serial port gets a lot of use. It's the preferred mechanism for uploading new sketches from the development software to the chip itself. You can use it to debug programs and report readings. It works straight out of the box, using the supplied Serial library, and it uses only two device pins to do so.

The Arduino Uno has a single *hardware* serial port, USART, whereas the Arduino Mega 2560 has four of them. Both flavors of I/O Boards connect their first USART to a serial-USB interface. It's also possible, in a limited fashion, to use any pair of the other digital I/O pins as a serial port using the SoftSerial library. The advantages of using a real hardware USART certainly outweigh any software simulation, assuming you have enough USARTs to go around.

A Small Replacement for the Serial Library

In Chapter 6, you replaced the Arduino-supplied Serial library with a few simple functions. You saved a lot of program memory, but at what cost? No facility was provided to *receive* serial input. The transmission of data was quite wasteful of CPU bandwidth, as the processor waited, patiently, for every single character to shuffle slowly out the serial port, doing no useful work in the interim. No attempt was made to provide *handshaking* with the serial port on the other end of the line, and no contingency plan was in place to handle any errors that might occur.

With all of these shortcomings, the exercise was still worthwhile, because it did implement a very simple method for sending a limited amount of data via the serial port while saving quite a bit of precious program memory. Keep this technique in reserve for when you need to send a small amount of data but don't need all the bells and whistles provided by the Serial library.

Is the Serial library always a better alternative in nontrivial applications? Sometimes, but not always. There are still timing and reliability issues with this software, which should one day be sorted out. In the meantime, you can use the existing USART hardware, taking advantage of its talents and capabilities, which free up the CPU to do other tasks.

What the USART Does

The main job of each of the USARTs on board the AVR is to *serialize* and *deserialize* a stream of data bits. This allows a multibit piece of data, such as an eight-bit byte, to be transmitted or received using a single wire. Otherwise, eight data lines plus some sort of timing signal, or *strobe* line, would be needed to send or receive a single byte of information. That sort of arrangement is usually called a *parallel interface*.

The USART also handles, in hardware, the generation of the proper timing signals and the appropriate framing, error-checking, and synchronization bits that allow it to comply with asynchronous serial communication standards. Beyond these duties, the USART hardware in the AVR also provides a small amount of buffering, which permits a byte of data to be prepared for either transmission or reception while another one is actually being transmitted or received.

The very basic task of shifting bits in and out at the proper rate, with the right framing, *can* be accomplished with software, as illustrated by the abilities of the SoftSerial library. On the smaller AVR devices that lack any hardware USART, this is the only option, short of adding a dedicated USART peripheral to the circuit. Letting the hardware USART do its job frees the CPU to get on with other business.

Talking to the USART

Instead of dealing with the individual bit timings and all the other low-level details for serial communication, you did manage to use the built-in USART hardware to do all that work for you. Once the proper device configuration was performed (a total of four program statements), all you had to do in order to transmit a byte of information over the serial port was to write to a register, a la UDR0 = c;, and you were done. The USART considers it polite to wait for that byte to finish transmitting before transmitting another byte, and it even provides a status bit in one of its control registers to tell you when that moment occurs.

What you did in your first-generation USART code was sit there and watch the USART0 Data Register Empty (UDRE0) bit in the UCSR0A register until it changed. This is ~~a waste of time~~ an opportunity for excellence. In addition to the UDRE0 status bit, the USART also provides an interrupt to let the CPU know when the UDRE0 bit is set, (called the Data Register Empty interrupt), indicating that there is now room in the USART's output buffer mechanism for a new, transmittable byte.

Bear in mind that another, similar interrupt is available from the USART: the Transmit Complete interrupt. From the sound of its name, it would seem like this is the one you would want to use. There has been some confusion over this choice in the past. The Transmit Complete interrupt occurs when the serial transmission is *totally* finished: that is, after the last part of the last bit is sent out the serial port. The Data Register Empty interrupt occurs *before* the Transmit Complete interrupt, due to the internal buffer in the USART hardware. You should use the Data Register Empty interrupt to tell you when to reload the data register, if needed, because you can send out another byte before the previous byte has completely shifted out the serial port.

You *can* use the Transmit Complete interrupt in applications where some action needs to take place to commemorate the end of the serial transmission: for example, when special transmitter hardware needs to be powered down. Because you're just wanting to save some time at the moment, you use the interrupt that happens first and saves you the most time: the Data Register Empty interrupt.

The USART hardware can also generate an interrupt in response to the complete *reception* of a byte from the serial port. This interrupt is called the Receive Complete interrupt. See Listing 7-1 for an example sketch that toggles the LED every time a new character arrives via the serial port.

Listing 7-1. USART Receive Complete Interrupt Example Sketch

```
void usart_init(unsigned long rate) {
  UCSR0A = 0<<TXC0 | 0<<U2X0 | 0<<MPCM0;
  UCSR0B = 1<<RXCIE0 | 0<<TXCIE0 | 0<<UDRIE0 | 1<<RXEN0 | 0<<TXEN0 | 0<<UCSZ02 | 0<<TXB80;
  UCSR0C = 0<<UMSEL01 | 0<<UMSEL00 | 0<<UPM01 | 0<<UPM00 | 0<<USBS0 | 1<<UCSZ01 | 1<<UCSZ00 |
0<<UCPOL0;
  UBRR0 = (F_CPU / 16 / rate - 1);
}

void setup() {
  bitSet(DDRB, 5); // D13 (PB5) is connected to an LED
  usart_init(9600); // configure USART
}

void loop() {
  // nothing happens here
}

ISR(USART_RX_vect) {
  bitSet(PINB, 5); // toggle LED
  unsigned char c = UDR0; // read incoming byte to clear interrupt flag
}
```

There are a few important items to discuss in this sketch. First, the USART initialization code has been collected into its very own subroutine, called usart_init(). The desired communication rate (sometimes called the *baud rate*) is passed as its only parameter, a la the Arduino's Serial.begin() library function.

You can save a few more bytes if you know ahead of time what baud rate you want to use, instead of passing it as a parameter to usart_init(). You can use the BAUD_RATE_DIVISOR macro definition from the previous sketch in Chapter 5 ("Writing to Configuration Registers" section), instead. This is because the compiler sees the constant value indicated and does the math itself, reducing the equation to a single number. Otherwise, the Arduino has to calculate the baud rate on the fly, which involves two division operations and results in the final sketch containing the __udivmodsi4 library function, which is artfully compact but still takes up some space.

Notice the second line of the usart_init() function:

```
UCSR0B = 1<<RXCIE0 | 0<<TXCIE0 | 0<<UDRIE0 | 1<<RXEN0 | 0<<TXEN0 | 0<<UCSZ02 | 0<<TXB80;
```

The RXCIE0 bit (USART0 Receive Complete Interrupt Enable) and the RXEN0 bit (USART0 Receiver Enable) are the only bits that are set to 1 in this assignment statement. This could just as easily have been accomplished with two much shorter lines of code:

```
bitSet(UCSR0B, RXCIE0); // enable receive interrupt
bitSet(UCSR0B, RXEN0); // enable receiver
```

This would have resulted in a slightly larger sketch, however. Because the USART control registers aren't in the addressable range of the SBI and CBI machine-language instructions, the compiler can't use them to directly manipulate the bits in the UCSR0B register. It's forced to perform a read/modify/write operation on the UCSR0B register *twice*. This results in a binary sketch size of 618 bytes, compared with the original, more compact sketch that contained 608 bytes.

The TXEN0 bit isn't set to 1 because you're not using the USART transmitter at all in this sketch. The other bits remain the same from the previous example sketches found in Chapter 5. The setup() function is fairly predictable, configuring the D13 pin (PB5 on the Arduino Uno) as an output so you can see the LED later, and then calling the usart_init() function to get the USART rolling.

Of special interest is the loop() function, which is suspiciously empty. All the fun stuff happens in the interrupt service routine (ISR), which is defined just after the loop() function. ISR() looks like a function but is really a macro defined in the avr/interrupt.h header file. The parameter passed to the ISR macro is the predefined signal name of the interrupt handler, which in this case is USART_RX_vect. Signals are a holdover from long, long ago; the term *signal* described what you now know as interrupts.

■ **Note**　You don't get to name your interrupt handlers. You must use the signal names supplied by the avr-libc library. See Table 7-1 and Table 7-2 in the section "Pin-Change Interrupts." And yes, they all end in _vect, which is short for *vector*.

The interrupt handler works *mostly* just like any other function, except that it never takes parameters and it never returns a value. You cover a few other ISR-specific details shortly.

In the ISR(USART_RX_vect) handler, you see the shortcut LED toggle method:

```
bitSet(PINB, 5); // toggle the LED
```

So every time this interrupt handler executes, you should be able to see the LED change state.

Also in the interrupt handler is a dummy read of the USART0 data register, UDR0. This read is *required* to reset the "receive complete" interrupt flag. Normally an application shows some sort of interest in the incoming data stream, but this example sketch just wants to demonstrate how an interrupt handler is written, and the received value is discarded.

Compile and upload this sketch to your Arduino Uno. Verify that the LED toggles for every character that is sent from the Serial Monitor window. Remember that you must click the Send button or press the Enter key to actually send anything. Sending two characters at a time toggles the LED and then quickly toggles it back again, so you should only see a very short blink.

You can do something more intelligent in the interrupt service routine if you like. Try the code in Listing 7-2, replacing the previous interrupt handler.

Listing 7-2. Alternate USART Receive Complete interrupt handler

```
ISR(USART_RX_vect) {
  unsigned char c = UDR0; // read incoming byte to clear interrupt flag
  if(c =='1') {
    bitSet(PORTB, 5); // turn on LED
  } else if(c == '0') {
    bitClear(PORTB, 5); // turn off LED
  }
}
```

That's all there is to writing an interrupt handler. The hard part is to pick the right interrupt to use, enable it, and then find the correct signal name for it from the available documentation. See Table 7-7 and Table 7-8 in the section "Interrupt Reference." Note that the current avr-libc documentation as supplied by the Arduino software is chock-full of errors and omissions, especially in the signal-names section. This is mostly because the documentation was automatically generated from the source code comments, which suffer from repeated "improvements," usually of the copy-and-paste variety.

This sketch is specific to the Arduino Uno, not only because the LED bit is hardwired to PB5 (recall that the LED is attached to PB7 on the Arduino Mega 2560) but also because the ATmega2560 has *four* USARTs (USART0–3), and the handler names are different:

```
ISR(USART0_RX_vect)
ISR(USART1_RX_vect)
ISR(USART2_RX_vect)
ISR(USART3_RX_vect)
```

■ **Caution** The compiler doesn't check for proper handler names. At this point, it can only look to see whether the handler name ends in _vect. Using USART_RX_vect (for the ATmega328) instead of USART0_RX_vect (for the ATmega2560) will produce no compile-time errors, only runtime errors.

ISR() Options

The avr-libc library provides several options to pass along to the interrupt service vectors, depending on how you want them to behave.

The first parameter to the ISR function is the signal name that is to be handled. It bears repeating that you do *not* get to name your own signals. You must use one of the predefined signal names from the avr-libc library.

As discussed in Chapter 3, interrupts must be *enabled* in two places to ever fire. The first is specific to the hardware that is generating the interrupt, such as the USART peripheral. The second is the *global interrupt enable bit* (I) contained in the processor's status register (SREG). If the I bit isn't set, then no interrupts are recognized, acknowledged, or acted upon by the processor. The Arduino software provides two simple macros for enabling and disabling the global interrupt enable bit:

```
interrupts();
noInterrupts();
```

These two macro definitions resolve into the single machine-language instructions Set I Bit in SREG (SEI) and Clear I Bit in SREG (CLI), respectively.

When enabled, and the right conditions prevail, an interrupt can be generated. This launches a series of actions on the part of the processor. First, the global interrupt enable bit I is cleared. This prevents any further interrupts from being handled until either

- The interrupt handler routine returns or

- The interrupt handler routines explicitly reenables the I bit

The address of the current program instruction is saved on the stack. The processor then *vectors* (jumps) to the specific location in the interrupt vector table that is reserved for that interrupt. The interrupt vector table usually contains jump (JMP) instructions that point the processor to the appropriate interrupt handler routine.

The interrupt vector executes, and when it's complete, issues the special Return from Interrupt (RETI) instruction. This instruction recalls the program counter's previous value by popping it from the stack and reenables the global interrupt enable bit. Program execution resumes from the point where it was interrupted.

Although the processor automatically saves the program counter's contents, this isn't true of either the processor's SREG or the contents of any of the general-purpose registers, R1–R31. All but the most trivial of interrupt service routines need to save the processor's state before performing any calculations; otherwise the interrupted program running in the foreground is in for a nasty surprise.

The compiler knows how to properly save the processor's state, and the code to do so is automatically included both before and after the code written by the application programmer in the interrupt service handler.

Nested Interrupts

To allow the use of nested interrupts—that is, an interrupt handler that allows other events to interrupt it—you can add the ISR_NOBLOCK modifier to the ISR handler:

ISR(USART_RX_vect, **ISR_NOBLOCK**) ...

Using this modifier reenables global interrupts earlier in the execution of the handler than specifically executing the interrupts(); macro call would.

Empty Interrupts

Some interrupt flags are cleared when the interrupt service routine executes, unlike the USART Receive Complete interrupt, which required the data register to be read. In these and similar cases, no other action may be required to be performed by the interrupt handler, and the interrupted program can resume as quickly as possible. This is often the case when the processor is put to sleep and one of the peripherals needs to wake it up. To do this and generate the minimum amount of code, you can use the EMPTY_INTERRUPT() macro instead of the ISR() macro:

EMPTY_INTERRUPT(TIMER0_OVF_vect);

This macro then creates a handler that does nothing except return to the interrupted program using the RETI instruction. No function body is required when using this alternative form.

Bare-Naked Interrupts

When you need the most control over the code going into your interrupt handler routines, you can use the ISR_NAKED modifier, which generates a function body lacking both the standard prolog and epilog for saving and restoring the processor state. You even have to explicitly include the RETI instruction within such a function, because the compiler isn't going to put *anything* in there for you.

If your handler only needs to update a flag or perform some other miniscule task that doesn't affect either the SREG or the general-purpose registers, you can use this option:

```
ISR(TIMER0_OVF_vect, ISR_NAKED) {
  bitSet(PINB, 5);
  reti(); // return from interrupt
}
```

The reti() function is another macro that inserts the correct machine-language code for the Return from Interrupt instruction. It's defined in the avr/interrupt.h header file. You *must* include this macro as the last statement in your interrupt handler if you use the ISR_NAKED modifier.

Undefined Interrupt Behavior

If an interrupt occurs for which no handler has been written, the default action taken by the compiler is to tell the processor to jump back to the beginning of its program, effectively restarting the chip. It does this by filling the interrupt vector table with bad interrupt vectors, unless the application program writer specifies a proper handler for a particular interrupt.

You can change this default behavior by defining your own default function, using the BADISR_vect signal name:

```
ISR(BADISR_vect) ...
```

Undefined interrupts generally indicate software bugs. Restarting the sketch is a bit drastic, however. You can more elegantly handle it using the BADISR_vect option.

General-Purpose Digital Inputs and Outputs

You've been playing with the digital input and output (I/O) pins in almost every example sketch. You've learned how to configure them as either inputs or outputs, either using the pinMode() function or specifically setting the direction bits in the data direction registers (DDRx). You've mostly been working with individual I/O lines using either the Arduino-supplied digitalWrite() function or the bitSet() and bitClear() macros. It's also possible to read the values present on the pins by either using the digitalRead() function or directly interrogating the PINx registers.

Another fun trick is to enable and disable the built-in pullup resistors on each of the input pins, using the otherwise-unused data register, which is normally used when the pins are set up to be outputs. Along the same line, the output state of any pin can be toggled by writing to the Input Pins address; this is very useful when you don't want to disturb any of the neighboring I/O pins.

You can also read and write up to eight bits at a time by talking to the I/O ports' data register and Input Pins address. This can be much faster and more compact than updating or checking each pin individually.

Pin-Change Interrupts

Besides all this general functionality, all of the I/O pins on the Arduino Uno, and up to 24 of the pins on the Arduino Mega 2560, can be configured as pin change interrupts. This permits any of these pins to be set up to notify the CPU if anything changes on their inputs, without forcing the CPU to constantly check in to see what's happening.

Pin-change interrupts are grouped into three banks of up to eight individual lines apiece. Each bank has an interrupt associated with it. These banks generally correspond with the general-purpose I/O ports. See Table 7-1 and Table 7-2.

Table 7-1. Pin-Change Interrupts for ATmega328

General-Purpose I/O Port	Pin Name	Pin-Change Interrupt Bank	Pin-Change Interrupt Name
Port B	PB0	Bank 0	PCINT0
	PB1		PCINT1
	PB2		PCINT2
	PB3		PCINT3
	PB4		PCINT4
	PB5		PCINT5
	PB6		PCINT6
	PB7		PCINT7
Port C	PC0	Bank 1	PCINT8
	PC1		PCINT9
	PC2		PCINT10
	PC3		PCINT11
	PC4		PCINT12
	PC5		PCINT13
	PC6		PCINT14

General-Purpose I/O Port	Pin Name	Pin-Change Interrupt Bank	Pin-Change Interrupt Name
Port D	PD0	Bank 2	PCINT16
	PD1		PCINT17
	PD2		PCINT18
	PD3		PCINT19
	PD4		PCINT20
	PD5		PCINT21
	PD6		PCINT22
	PD7		PCINT23

Note: PC7 (PCINT15) doesn't exist on the ATmega328.

Table 7-2. *Pin-Change Interrupts for the ATmega2560*

General-Purpose I/O Port	Pin Name	Pin-Change Interrupt Bank	Pin-Change Interrupt Name
Port B	PB0	Bank 0	PCINT0
	PB1		PCINT1
	PB2		PCINT2
	PB3		PCINT3
	PB4		PCINT4
	PB5		PCINT5
	PB6		PCINT6
	PB7		PCINT7

Continued

General-Purpose I/O Port	Pin Name	Pin-Change Interrupt Bank	Pin-Change Interrupt Name
Port E	PE0		PCINT8
Port J	PJ0	Bank 1	PCINT9
	PJ1		PCINT10
	PJ2		PCINT11
	PJ3		PCINT12
	PJ4		PCINT13
	PJ5		PCINT14
	PJ6		PCINT15
Port K	PK0	Bank 2	PCINT16
	PK1		PCINT17
	PK2		PCINT18
	PK3		PCINT19
	PK4		PCINT20
	PK5		PCINT21
	PK6		PCINT22
	PK7		PCINT23

To respond to a pin-change interrupt, you must do three things:

1. Enable the appropriate pin-change interrupt bank using the PCICR register.
2. Enable the specific pins to be used using the PCMSK0–2 registers.
3. Write an interrupt handler routine.

Single Pin Interrupt Example

Let's try using a single pin-change interrupt to see how it works. You take advantage of the fact that the pin-change interrupts don't care if the pin that's involved is an input or an output. This way, you can invoke an interrupt through software by changing the state of an output pin, without having to attach any new hardware to the Arduino.

Let's go back to your faithful friend, Blink. Select File ➤ Examples ➤ 1.Basics ➤ Blink from the menu. Add the following lines to the end of the setup() function:

```
Serial.begin(9600);
bitSet(PCICR, PCIE0); // enable pin change interrupt bank 0
bitSet(PCMSK0, PCINT5); // enable pin change interrupt on PCINT5/D13
```

You leave the loop() function alone. It continues to turn on the LED, wait a second, turn off the LED, wait another second, and then repeat. That's what you like about Blink.

Add the following interrupt handler for pin-change interrupt bank 0:

```
ISR(PCINT0_vect) {
  if(digitalRead(13) == HIGH) {
    Serial.println("LED is on");
  } else {
    Serial.println("LED is off");
  }
}
```

Compile and upload this sketch. Open the Serial Monitor window, and observe what happens.

You should get a message about once a second, alternating between "LED is on" and "LED is off." The interrupt handler gets invoked every time there is a *change* in the state of the PCINT5 pin, which you also know as D13 or PB5. You don't get to specify what kind of change. So when the loop() function calls the digitalWrite() function to either turn on or turn off the LED, as long as the new value is different from the present value, a pin-change interrupt is detected, and the interrupt service routine is called.

In the interrupt service routine, the digitalRead() function is called to determine the present state of the pin. If it's HIGH, the LED is on, and a suitable status message is sent. Otherwise, the LED is most likely off, and that status is likewise reported.

This example is quite simplified because only one pin holds your interest. You knew that only one pin had been authorized to generate an interrupt, so it wasn't hard to figure out what happened.

You can use any of the I/O pins on the ATmega328 as pin-change triggers. Each pin-change interrupt bank has its own interrupt handler. It's up to the individual interrupt handler to determine which pin changed, triggering the interrupt request. This can be discovered by reading the status of the port pins, using the Input Pins address (PINx) for the applicable port.

The ATmega2560 also has three banks of pin-change interrupts. The same registers are used to enable the individual pins and banks, although banks 1 and 2 are mapped to different ports.

Timers and Counters

The ATmega328 has three unique timer/counter peripherals, cleverly named Timer/Counter 0, Timer/Counter 1, and Timer/Counter 2. Each timer/counter peripheral is slightly different from the others. Let's look at Timer/Counter 0 first and learn what makes it so special. Once you understand what makes this timer tick, then you can go on to the other two timer/counters and concentrate on how they differ from Timer/Counter 0.

Timer/Counter 0

At the core of Timer/Counter 0 is an eight-bit counter. This means it can count from 0 to 255, at which point it starts over again at 0. It can also count from 0 to 255, then back down from 255 to 0, over and over again. This is the basic thing that it does: its reason for existence.

Several variations on this basic theme can be made with Timer/Counter 0. You can specify a different maximum number instead of 255. It can be either a counter or a timer. In its role as a timer, it can be clocked by the CPU oscillator or through a prescaler with predefined divisors. These divisors can be 1, 8, 64, 256, or 1,024. As a counter, it can be driven from an external input pin.

Timer/Counter 0 has two pulse-width-modulation (PWM) channels associated with it. (PWM is explained in more detail in the section "Pulse-Width-Modulation (PWM) Outputs.")

Timer/Counter 1

The heart of Timer/Counter 1 is a 16-bit counter. This allows it to count from 0 to as much as 65,535. Like Timer/Counter 0, it can either always be counting up or it can count up, then down, then up, then down.

Timer/Counter 1 also has an input capture unit, which lets it put a timestamp on an incoming signal. Two PWM channels are available for use with Timer/Counter 1 on the Arduino Uno, and three PWM channels on the Arduino Mega 2560.

Timer/Counter 2

Timer/Counter 2 is remarkably similar to Timer/Counter 0. It's an eight-bit counter with two associated PWM channels, having both timer and counter facilities as well as the ability to generate several interrupts.

What makes Timer/Counter 2 special is its ability to be driven asynchronously from the CPU clock, via a low-frequency 32KHz watch crystal attached to the TOSC1 and TOSC2 pins. On the ATmega328, these pins serve double duty with the primary XTAL1 and XTAL2 pins, normally connected to the 16MHz quart crystal or ceramic oscillator. This prevents most Arduino Uno–compatible circuits from implementing this feature.

On the ATmega2560, however, the TOSC1 and TOSC2 pins are only shared with the PG4 and PG3 general-purpose I/O lines. The ATmega2560 has dedicated XTAL1 and XTAL2 pins, so no conflict is present. Timer/Counter 2 can be clocked using a low-power (as well as relatively low-frequency) watch crystal. This allows the implementation of a real-time clock that can continue to run when the processor is put to sleep.

ATmega2560

The ATmega2560 has all the same timer/counter peripherals as the ATmega328, and then some.

Timer/Counter 1 on the ATmega2560 is also a 16-bit counter, just like on the ATmega328. It adds an additional PWM channel, for a total of three PWM channels on Timer/Counter 1 alone.

If that weren't enough, the ATmega2560 sports three more 16-bit timer/counter peripherals, which are all clones of Timer/Counter 1. They're aptly named Timer/Counter 3, Timer/Counter 4, and Timer/Counter 5.

Timer Interrupts

You can perform some simple experiments with the timer/counter interrupts to get an idea of how they operate. The Arduino software has already configured all the timer/counter peripherals for use with the analogWrite() function, as well as time-keeping duties for Timer/Counter 0. You use Timer/Counter 1 for this experiment, fully aware that you then lose the use of analog (PWM) outputs 9 and 10 on the Arduino Uno. See Listing 7-3.

Listing 7-3. A Simple Timer Interrupt

```
void setup() {
  bitSet(DDRB, 5); // PB5/D13 has an LED attached
  TCCR1A = 0;
  TCCR1B = 1<<CS12;
  bitSet(TIMSK1, TOIE1); // enable overflow interrupt
}

void loop() {
  // nothing happens here
}

ISR(TIMER1_OVF_vect) {
  bitSet(PINB, 5); // toggle LED
}
```

Compile and upload this sketch. Behold! You have yet another blinking LED. Let's see exactly what's going on here.

The setup() function starts off with the familiar pinMode() function replacement, bitSet(DDRB, 5), just to save a little program space. Then you see some manipulation of the timer control registers, which is where all the magic happens.

The second line of the setup() function clears all the bits in the TCCR1A register. This register controls the assignment of the PWM output pins and also contains two of the four bits used to select the timer mode. Because the Arduino software had already programmed this register to provide for PWM outputs that you aren't using, you clear out all the bits at once by writing a zero to the register.

The next timer configuration statement writes a single 1 to the CS12 bit location of the TCCR1B register, which has the side effect of also writing zeros to all the other bit locations. The other two mode-select bits were in this register, but you wanted to set them to zeros, anyway. The CS12 bit is one of three bits (CS10, CS11, and CS12) that select the prescaler value for the system clock to drive the counter in a timer mode. There are eight possible combinations (see Table 7-3), and you want the one that provides a divide-by-256 prescaler of the system oscillator. Setting only the CS12 bit makes this selection for you.

Table 7-3. Timer Clock Select Bits for Timer/Counter 1

CS12	CS11	CS10	Description
0	0	0	No clock
0	0	1	Divide by 1
0	1	0	Divide by 8
0	1	1	Divide by 64
1	0	0	Divide by 256
1	0	1	Divide by 1,024
1	1	0	Use the falling edge of external input T1
1	1	1	Use the rising edge of external input T1

Timer/Counter 0 has a similar set of predefined clock prescalers that can be selected. The only differences are that the bit names are CS02, CS01, and CS00, and that the last two options select input pin T0 instead of T1. Timer/Counter 2 is different. It doesn't support an external input in the same way that Timer/Counter 0–1 can. See Table 7-5, later in the chapter.

Because the system clock on a standard Arduino is 16MHz, the clock signal provided to the timer circuit is now 16,000,000 ÷ 256 = 62,500Hz, or 62.5KHz. This value was selected with some care, and it nearly approximates the maximum value that the 16-bit counter in Timer/Counter 1 can hold, which is 65,535. In other words, when driven at this clock speed, the counter overflows in just over 1 second. This generates an overflow interrupt, the interrupt service routine executes, and the LED is toggled.

The final timer configuration statement in the setup() function specifically enables the overflow interrupt for this timer, Timer Overflow Interrupt Enable 1 (TOIE1). Because the Arduino software has already enabled the global interrupt bit, things should start happening in just about one second, assuming your interrupt service routine is in place.

The interrupt handler couldn't be simpler:

```
ISR(TIMER1_OVF_vect) {
  bitSet(PINB, 5); // toggle LED
}
```

This example illustrates the normal mode of the timer, which is only one of many possible modes that are available using the timer/counter peripherals. For example, if you wanted an interrupt to occur *exactly* every second, you could use one of the two Clear Timer on Compare Match (CTC) modes. In this mode, you configure a prescaler and select the counter/timer mode in a manner similar to the previous example, but then you program the desired match value used to trigger a reset of the counter, instead of letting it roll over on its own. See Listing 7-4.

Listing 7-4. *Generating a Timer Interrupt Every Second*

```
void setup() {
  bitSet(DDRB, 5); // LED on PB5/D13
  TCCR1A = 0;
  TCCR1B = 1<<WGM13 | 1<<WGM12 | 1<<CS12 | 1<<CS10;
  ICR1 = 15625;
  bitSet(TIMSK1, ICIE1); // enable capture event interrupt
}

void loop() {
  // nothing happens here
}

ISR(TIMER1_CAPT_vect) {
  bitSet(PINB, 5); // toggle LED
}
```

This mode uses the Input Capture Register (ICR1) to hold the compare value. The value is calculated by dividing the system clock by the requested prescaler, which determines the number of clock cycles to count before starting over, which fires the input capture event interrupt. In this case, the largest prescaler, 1,024, is used to divide the system clock, resulting in a clock signal of 15.625KHz driving the timer.

Pulse-Width-Modulation (PWM) Outputs

Each of the timer/counter peripherals has at least two PWM channels associated with it. The Arduino software automatically configures all of the available timers for hardware PWM duty at the beginning of every sketch.

Using the Arduino-supplied analogWrite() function, the hardware PWM channels can be easily programmed with any value between 0 (completely off) and 255 (completely on). Anything in between produces a variable duty-cycle pulse stream at approximately 490Hz.

The Arduino software treats all the PWM channels the same, limiting them to eight-bit resolution and hardwiring them to a relatively slow frequency. It's not hard to reprogram any of the available PWM channels and reconfigure them to your liking. The only trick is choosing among the many operational modes and setting the parameters accordingly.

Listing 7-5 is a short experiment you can try, which illustrates the simplicity of the Arduino's analogWrite() function and the use of PWM.

Listing 7-5. *Fading the LED Using PWM*

```
void setup() {
}

void loop() {

  static byte pwm = 0;
```

```
  analogWrite(11, pwm); // set the PWM duty cycle
  delay(10); // a very short delay
  pwm++; // increase the PWM duty cycle
}
```

Note that you don't have to explicitly set the direction bit for the output pin when using the Arduino's analogWrite() function. It takes care of this for you. If you don't use the analogWrite() function, and you set up the PWM outputs yourself, you need to remember to configure the proper pin as an output, either using the pinMode() function or setting the bits in DDRx appropriately.

Compile and upload this sketch to either an Arduino Uno or an Arduino Mega 2560. Nothing happens. To make something happen, all you have to is connect D11 to D13 using a short length of wire or a small-value resistor (see "Digital Signal Probe" in the Chapter 6).

On the Arduino Mega 2560, you can use D13 instead of D11 and the sketch works without the help of the extra wire. This is because the Arduino Mega 2560 has 14 PWM outputs, which happen to include D13—the one that is already connected to the LED.

Using the Arduino Uno, however, you have only six PWM outputs, and D13 is *not* one of them. That's OK—you can still connect one of the proper PWM outputs (D11 is the closest, so that's what you use) to D13 and light up the LED, as long as D13 itself isn't programmed to be an output.

Without the wire, using analogWrite() on a non-PWM pin produces 1 for values 128 and above and 0 for values less than 128.

PWM Tricks

You can eliminate the jumper wire in the previous exercise and replace it with a bit of software trickery, based on what you previously learned about using pin-change interrupts. See Listing 7-6.

Listing 7-6. Transferring the PWM Output to a Different Pin Using Pin-Change Interrupts

```
void setup() {
  bitSet(DDRB, 5); // LED pin
  bitSet(PCICR, PCIE0); // enable pin change interrupts on bank 0
  bitSet(PCMSK0, PCINT3); // enable PCINT3 (PB3) pin change interrupt
}

byte pwm = 0;

void loop() {
  analogWrite(11, pwm); // set the PWM duty cycle
  delay(10); // a very short delay
  pwm++; // increase the PWM duty cycle
}
```

```
ISR(PCINT0_vect) {
  if(bitRead(PINB, 3)) {
    bitSet(PORTB, 5); // LED on
  } else {
    bitClear(PORTB, 5); // LED off
  }
}
```

Nothing changes in the loop() function. The value of the pwm variable is used to write an analog value to the PWM output pin, using the analogWrite() function. Then the pwm variable is incremented. When it gets to its maximum value (255 for a byte, which is the same thing as an unsigned char), it rolls over to its minimum value, which is 0.

The setup() function now contains the initialization code to enable PCINT3, which corresponds with the digital pin 11 used by the analogWrite() function. Because PCINT3 is contained in the first bank of pin-change interrupts, you write an interrupt handler for the PCINT0_vect signal.

The interrupt handler checks the state of the port pin, using the bitRead() macro. Notice that no explicit comparison is done in this conditional statement. The bitRead() macro returns either 1 or 0, depending on the state of the bit being examined. In the C programming language, conditional statements are evaluated as either true (non-zero) or false (zero). When the output pin is a logical 1, the bitRead() macro returns a value of true, so the LED is turned on. When it returns a false value—that is, zero, indicating the pin is in a logical low state—the LED is turned off. The conditional statement could be more explicitly written as

```
if(bitRead(PINB, 3) == 1) ...
```

This is yet another example of the possible compactness possible in the C language. Those guys were ~~lazy~~ efficient. Compactness and clarity aren't always the same thing, however. It's certainly possible to write such dense code that you, yourself, can't comprehend it. This is even more prevalent in other programming languages, such as Forth, which is considered by many to be a write-only language. Good commenting discipline helps!

Remove the jumper wire from your Arduino Uno, compile and upload the sketch, and observe what happens. If all goes well, the LED should be ramping up in brightness over the period of approximately 2.56 seconds and then starting over again.

More PWM Trickery

The PWM hardware can generate its own interrupts. In the previous example sketch, the PWM signal was present on two pins at once. This is a neat trick and can come in handy when you need to duplicate a relatively slow signal on multiple pins, for example, using the hardware USART to transmit on several different lines at once.

Let's use the PWM interrupt for overflow to increment the PWM duty cycle for you. You continue to use one of the Arduino Uno's PWM-capable pins, D11. You saw from the previous sketch that this pin is also referred to as PB3 (Port B, bit 3). To get even closer to the bare metal, you need to know the timer/counter with which this PWM output is associated. Table 7-4 lists the timer/counters, their PWM outputs, and both the AVR names and Arduino names for the Arduino Uno.

Table 7-4. Timer/Counter PWM Pins on the Arduino Uno

Timer/Counter	PWM Output	AVR Name	Arduino Pin
Timer/Counter 0	OC0A	PD6	6
	OC0B	PD5	5
Timer/Counter 1	OC1A	PB1	9
	OC1B	PB2	10
Timer/Counter 2	OC2A	PB3	11
	OC2B	PD3	3

Working backward through Table 7-4, you see that Arduino PWM pin 11 is connected to Timer/Counter 2's OC2A output. Each of the timer/counters on the ATmega328 has two PWM channels associated with it, referred to as A and B. When configured for PWM usage, the internal counter is continuously compared with the values stored in the two Output Compare Registers, OCRxA and OCRxB. Several options exist for what to do when the values line up properly.

For your second PWM experiment, you configure Timer/Counter 2 for normal counter mode and enable both the Compare Match A interrupt and Overflow interrupt. When the counter overflows, the count starts over at zero. At this point, you want to turn on the LED. When the compare match event takes place, you want to turn off the LED. To do so, you define two interrupt service routines. See Listing 7-7.

Listing 7-7. Reassigning PWM Outputs to Any Output Pins, Using Interrupts

```
void setup() {
  bitSet(DDRB, 5); // LED pin
  TCCR2A = 0; // normal mode
  TCCR2B = 5; // super slow CK/128
  TIMSK2 = 1<<OCIE2A | 1<<TOIE2; // enable match and overflow interrupts
}

byte pwm = 0;

void loop() {
  analogWrite(11, pwm); // set PWM duty cycle
  delay(10); // a short delay
  pwm++; // increase PWM duty cycle
}

ISR(TIMER2_OVF_vect) {
  if(pwm) bitSet(PORTB, 5); // LED on, maybe
}
```

```
ISR(TIMER2_COMPA_vect) {
  if(pwm < 255) bitClear(PORTB, 5); // LED off, maybe
}
```

The setup() function looks pretty familiar, configuring the LED output pin and the timer/counter peripheral. Timer/Counter 2 has a slightly different set of available clock prescalers; see Table 7-5. You also enable two distinct interrupts associated with Timer/Counter 2, the Match Compare A and Overflow interrupts, by setting the appropriate bits (OCIE2A and TOIE2) in the Timer/Counter 2 Interrupt Mask Register, TIMSK2.

Table 7-5. *Timer Clock Select bits for Timer/Counter 2*

CS22	CS21	CS20	Description
0	0	0	No clock
0	0	1	Divide by 1
0	1	0	Divide by 8
0	1	1	Divide by 32
1	0	0	Divide by 64
1	0	1	Divide by 128
1	1	0	Divide by 256
1	1	1	Divide by 1,024

The loop() function slowly adjusts the PWM duty cycle upward by continuously writing to the PWM hardware using the analogWrite() function. You could save 538 bytes of program memory by not using the analogWrite() function and writing directly to the compare register, OCR2A.

There is a bit of finesse going on in the interrupt service routines. You could have simply turned on the LED in the overflow interrupt (where the counter has just restarted from zero) and turned it off again at the compare match interrupt. This mostly works. It fails at the endpoints, 0 and 255. This is because the simplistic approach to PWM (turn on at zero, turn off at compare match) fails to consider that you may not want to turn on the output (for example, when the output is zero) or that you may not ever want to turn off the output (for example, when the output is full-scale).

In the overflow interrupt handler, the zero output scenario is tested by the shortened conditional if(pwm), which returns true as long as the value of pwm isn't zero; otherwise it returns false and the rest of the statement isn't executed. The compare match interrupt, on the other hand, only clears the output if the PWM value is less than full scale (255).

Let's try one more variation of the PWM reassignment experiment. This time, you move all the functionality that is presently in the loop() function—that is, the ramping up of the PWM output value— into the overflow interrupt handler. Why? Because the overflow interrupt handler is being invoked on a regular basis, every time the counter overflows from 255 back to 0. This happens on a fixed, periodic basis.

Either delete or comment-out all the code in the loop() function. Now update the overflow handler as follows:

```
ISR(TIMER2_OVF_vect) {
  if(pwm) bitSet(PORTB, 5); // LED on, maybe
  OCR2A = pwm;
  pwm++;
}
```

Compile and upload the sketch. You should see the same old thing, just a little faster. Why faster? Let's calculate the update frequency.

The system clock remains at 16MHz. The prescaler you selected for Timer/Counter 2 was divided by 128 by writing a 5 to the control register, TCCR2B. This means the counter is being clocked at 16,000,000Hz ÷ 128 = 125KHz. After every 256 clocks, the counter overflows. This occurs at roughly 488Hz. This is when the overflow interrupt occurs. In the interrupt handler, the PWM value (pwm) is incremented by one, which correspondingly adjusts the PWM duty cycle when it's written to the Output Compare Register A for Timer/Counter 2, OCR2A. Because this value, too, overflows when it gets to 255 (or after every 256 interrupts, if you want to look at it like that), this results in an apparent blinking frequency of ~488Hz ÷ 256 = ~1.9Hz, or about twice a second. This can be adjusted in large steps by changing the prescaler value of the timer.

What's interesting about this approach is that the loop() function is now doing absolutely nothing. All the action is happening behind the scenes in the interrupt handlers.

Analog Inputs

Both the Arduino Uno and the Arduino Mega 2560 have a single ADC peripheral on board. Each ADC unit has an input multiplexer with several inputs. The ATmega328 has 8 analog inputs, and the ATmega2560 has 16 analog inputs. Only six of the eight available analog inputs are available on the plastic DIP version of the device. The surface-mount version has all eight inputs available, but only six of them are connected to anything on the Arduino Uno. Several Arduino clones provide extra headers for these two extra ADC inputs.

The inputs to the ADC multiplexer share pins with the general-purpose digital inputs and outputs. This means if you don't want or need to use the analog inputs in your application, you're free to use those pins as regular digital I/O.

If, on the other hand, you're going to use any of the pins in analog mode, you should consider disabling any unused digital inputs by setting the individual bits (ADC0D–ADC5D) in the Digital Input Disable Register 0 (DIDR0). This reduces the amount of power that would have been used by these unused digital inputs.

The ATmega2560 has an additional Digital Input Disable Register to accommodate its larger array of analog inputs, but curiously it's called DIDR2. The missing DIDR1 is found on the earlier ATmega16, which used a completely different bit-mapping in the register, so the name was most likely changed to prevent confusion.

The ADC peripheral measures analog voltages by a method known as *successive approximation*. You may already be familiar with this process, but as the children's game Guess the Number. After each guess at the secret number, the guesser is informed if they're too high or too low until the right number is eventually guessed. The AVR's ADC peripheral methodically guesses at each of the ten bits in the resulting conversion by creating its own internal, adjustable voltage and comparing it to the sampled voltage from the analog input pin. This process is repeated ten times and eventually produces the analog conversion result, which is a number in the range of 0–1,023.

The ADC peripheral runs on its own clock, which in most cases is much slower than the processor clock. The optimum clock frequency ranges between 50KHz and 200KHz. A prescaler is provided to divide the processor clock to an appropriate frequency.

When the conversion process has begun, it takes 13 of these scaled-down ADC clocks to complete the conversion. The exception is the very first conversion performed after the ADC peripheral is enabled, which takes 25 ADC clock cycles to complete.

When the conversion is complete, the result is stored in a register and the peripheral's status flags are updated. The ADC can generate an interrupt once a conversion finishes.

If the ADC function isn't required in your application, consider disabling the peripheral by resetting the ADC Enable (ADEN) bit in the ADCSRA control register. Although this bit is off by default after power-on or a chip reset, the Arduino software turns it on at the beginning of every sketch.

Arduino Uno as Thermometer

The ATmega328 on the Arduino Uno also has an additional, internal ADC channel that is connected to a temperature sensor in the chip. This feature isn't implemented on the ATmega2560 chip.

You need to tweak this sketch to get an accurate reading on your Arduino Uno. Each temperature sensor is relatively linear in response, but the overall accuracy is rated at ±10°C. See Listing 7-8.

Listing 7-8. Arduino Uno as Thermometer

```
void setup() {
  Serial.begin(9600);
  Serial.println("Arduino Uno as Thermometer");
  ADMUX = 1<<REFS1 | 1<<REFS0 | 1<<MUX3; // 1.1V reference, ADC channel "8"
  ADCSRA = 1<<ADEN | 1<<ADSC | 0x07; // enable ADC, start conversion, 125 KHz clock
}

#define OFFSET 343

void loop() {

  Serial.print(ADC - OFFSET);
  Serial.println("C");
  bitSet(ADCSRA, ADSC); // start next conversion
  delay(250); // wait
}
```

Compile and upload the sketch. Open the Serial Monitor, and see what it says. The first few readings may well be way off, but soon it will settle down and start reporting the temperature of the internal sensor.

The setup() function first initializes the serial port and then configures the ADC to measure the special ADC channel assigned to the internal temperature sensor. It specifies that the 1.1V internal voltage reference is to be used instead of the A_{VCC} voltage, which is normally 5.0V. This gives a better match to the output of the temperature sensor, resulting in a more accurate conversion.

The loop() function prints the conversion result, adjusted by the OFFSET value, followed by the unit of measure (C). The code continues on to start a new conversion by setting the Start Conversion bit (ADSC) in the ADCSRA control register. A short delay is performed, and the loop() function repeats.

You need to adjust the OFFSET value to calibrate your Arduino Uno. Bear in mind that the ATmega328 chip will be as much as 3°C warmer than the ambient air.

Arduino as Voltmeter

In Chapter 6 you built a digital signal probe, using just an Arduino and a short jumper wire. This tool is very useful for determining if a digital signal is high or low. It's not especially helpful if the signal is somewhere in between. For measuring voltage levels, you need a *voltmeter*.

You can build a limited-range voltmeter using the same Arduino and jumper wire and a different sketch. It would be nice if you could attach a variable resistor called a *potentiometer* to the circuit or use something like the Maker Shield (see Figure 1-6 in Chapter 1), which already has a potentiometer installed. If not, you can still explore some of the varying voltages on the Arduino itself.

■ **Caution** If you're powering your Arduino via the USB cable, there are no dangerous voltage levels to worry about. If, on the other hand, you're powering your Arduino via the external power connector, take care *not* to connect the Vin connector directly to the pins of the ATmega chip on your Arduino.

Listing 7-9 shows a simple example sketch that repeatedly reads analog pin A0 and then prints out the average value over the serial port.

Listing 7-9. Simple Analog Voltmeter

```
void setup() {
  Serial.begin(9600);
  Serial.println("Arduino Voltmeter");
}

#define SAMPLES 2500

void loop() {

  unsigned long voltage = 0;
  unsigned int i;

  for(i = 0; i < SAMPLES; i++) {
    voltage += analogRead(0); // accumulate samples
  }
  Serial.print((((voltage * 5.0) / 1024) / SAMPLES), 4);
  Serial.println("V");
}
```

Compile and upload this sketch. Then open the Serial Monitor window to see what's going on. You should see the program banner and then a series of voltage measurements.

Connect A0 to the 5V pin on the power expansion header. The readings may vary due to the acceptable tolerances on your Arduino's power supply, so don't be alarmed if you see 4.9785V on the 5V line.

Now try the 3.3V connector and see whether you're getting something in the neighborhood. Finally, try connecting your voltage probe to one of the GND connections and make sure the sketch is reporting something quite close to 0.0000V.

The setup() function initializes the serial port and prints a short announcement as to the application's primary intent. The loop() function takes a large number of samples, specified by the constant defined as SAMPLES, adding all the samples together in a big pile. After all the samples have been gathered together, the actual voltage is calculated based on the number of samples and adjusted by the analog reference voltage (AREF) and the resolution of the ADC. The resulting voltage is reported to four decimal places on the serial port, and the loop() function repeats.

The ADC produces a reading that has a resolution of ten bits. The lowest value, being a signal at or near ground (0V), should be zero. The largest reading, a signal just at or above the AREF voltage, should return a value of 1,023. These numbers are always integers, having no fractional part or digits to the right of the decimal point. Each bit in the result represents AREF/1,024. On the Arduino Uno, AREF is 5.0V, so each bit represents approximately 4.88mV, or 0.00488V. If your Arduino is running on a different voltage—for example, the Arduino Pro or Arduino Mini at 3.3V—you need to adjust the sketch accordingly.

To improve the accuracy of the readings, you can use the technique of *oversampling*. You take more than one reading and calculate the average (technically, the arithmetic mean) of all the readings by dividing the sum of all the readings by the number of readings taken.

The number of samples specified in the example sketch was chosen to produce a summary voltage report about 4 times every second (specifically, it turns out to be closer to 3.496 reports per second). This is fast enough to be useful and slow enough to be fairly accurate.

This reporting frequency wasn't chosen at random, however. The ADC is clocked by a signal derived from the system clock. The optimum ADC frequency is stated in the AVR datasheet as 50KHz to 200KHz. The Arduino software selects a clock prescaler of 128, which produces an ADC clock of 125KHz, well within the optimal range.

Each ADC conversion, after the first calibration conversion has been completed, takes exactly 13 ADC clocks. This results in a maximum sampling rate of just over 9,615 conversions per second, assuming a system clock of 16MHz. This doesn't take into account the time required to read the conversion from the ADC hardware, add it to the running total, or keep track of the loop count.

Theoretically, by using the ADC's conversion-complete interrupt, you could accumulate 2,500 samples and report the resulting voltage as many as 3.846 times per second. That's not a giant increase in reporting frequency—only about 10%. However, it may be a good idea in certain applications to have the ADC conversions happening in the background while a higher-level application executes in the foreground. Let's see what it takes to get that going; see Listing 7-10.

Listing 7-10. *Arduino as Automatic Voltmeter*

```
#define SAMPLES 2500

void setup() {
  Serial.begin(9600);
  Serial.println("Arduino Automatic Voltmeter");
  ADMUX = 1<<REFS0; // select ADC0 (A0), AREF=AVCC (5.0V)
  ADCSRA = 1<<ADEN | 1<<ADSC | 1<<ADATE | 1<<ADIE | 1<<ADPS2 | 1<<ADPS1 | 1<<ADPS0;
  ADCSRB = 0; // free running mode
  bitSet(DIDR0, ADC0D); // disable digital input on ADC0
}

void loop() {
  // nothing happens here
}
```

```
ISR(ADC_vect) {

  static unsigned int i = 0; // sample counter
  static unsigned long voltage = 0; // voltage reading accumulator

  voltage += ADC; // accumulate voltage readings
  i++; // also count samples taken
  ADMUX = 1<<REFS0; // re-select ADC0 (A0), AREF=AVCC (5.0V)

  if(i >= SAMPLES) {
    Serial.print(((((voltage * 5.0) / 1024) / SAMPLES), 4); // report
    Serial.println("V"); // label units of measure
    voltage = 0; // reset voltage readings
    i = 0; // reset sample count
  }
}
```

Compile and upload this sketch, and then open the Serial Monitor window to see the results. It should behave a lot like the previous sketch. Take some voltage readings to make sure things are still in order.

The main difference in this automatic version of the voltmeter sketch starts in the setup() function. The ADC peripheral is configured to generate an interrupt when it completes a conversion, by setting the ADIE bit in the ADCSRA register to 1. In addition, the free-running mode of the ADC is enabled through the combination of the ADC Auto Trigger Enable bit (ADATE), which is also in the ADCSRA register, and the lower bits of the ADCSRB register, which you set to all zeros. This operational mode instructs the ADC to automatically start a new conversion after the previous conversion completes. Other conversion triggers are available as well, including interrupts from the AC, the external interrupt request 0, and select timer/counter interrupts. The free-running mode ensures the fastest conversion turnover, triggering a new conversion immediately after the previous conversion is finished.

Because you're using oversampling to augment the limited resolution of the ADC, it's possible to speed up the ADC clock by choosing a smaller prescale divisor without losing too much accuracy. Selecting the divide-by-64 divisor effectively doubles the sample rate while reducing the effective resolution by one bit.

Shortened conversion cycles means less available time to handle the end-of-conversion interrupt. This leads to another important observation about the example sketch. The optimum interrupt handler gets in quickly, does its job, and exits promptly. Performing a lot of floating-point math, formatting reports, and sending data via the relatively slow serial port aren't the kinds of things you want in a production-ready interrupt handler. Ideally, the interrupt handler aggregates the data and sets a flag, indicating to the foreground process that a report is ready.

External Interrupts

The Arduino software has a little support for using interrupts in your sketches. It uses interrupts internally for timing functions. It makes provisions for enabling and disabling interrupts globally, using the interrupts() and noInterrupts() macro definitions, which resolve to the SEI and CLI machine-language instructions, respectively.

The only other support present in the Arduino software for interrupts is the `attachInterrupt()` and `detachInterrupt()` functions. These functions allow you to connect a function of your own devising to the available *external interrupts* of the AVR core. These interrupts are tied directly to the core, and their inputs share pins with the other general-purpose I/O lines in both the ATmega328 and the ATmega2560. See Table 7-6 (n/c stands for not connected).

Table 7-6. External Interrupts

External Interrupt	Arduino Uno		Arduino Mega 2560	
	Port	Pin	Port	Pin
INT0	PD2	2	PD0	21
INT1	PD3	3	PD1	20
INT2			PD2	19
INT3			PD3	18
INT4			PE4	2
INT5			PE5	3
INT6			PE6	n/c
INT7			PE7	n/c

The ATmega328 has two external interrupts, INT0 and INT1. They share pins with PD2 and PD3, respectively. These I/O pins can be configured as inputs (with or without enabling the built-in pullup resistors) or as outputs.

The ATmega2560 has eight external interrupts, INT0–INT7. They share pins with I/O lines from Ports D and E. Only six of the available external interrupts, INT0–5, are connected to anything on the Arduino Mega 2560 I/O Board.

External interrupts work in a manner similar to the pin-change interrupts discussed earlier. External interrupts, although more scarce, are more flexible in their configurations. Each of the external interrupts can be individually enabled or disabled, just like the pin-change interrupts. However, each external interrupt has its own interrupt vector. You can configure the external interrupts to detect pin changes, like the pin-change interrupts, but also program them to only respond to rising edges, falling edges, or low levels. This allows a bit more discrimination in determining what external signal should generate an interrupt.

Let's take a look at this signal-filtering capability of the external interrupts, using the Arduino-supplied functions; see Listing 7-11. Just add the bold statements to the Blink example sketch.

Listing 7-11. Exploring External Interrupt Trigger Configurations

```
void setup() {
  // initialize the digital pin as an output.
  // Pin 13 has an LED connected on most Arduino boards:
  pinMode(13, OUTPUT);
  Serial.begin(9600);
  attachInterrupt(0, tattle, CHANGE); // jumper D2 to D13
}

void loop() {
  digitalWrite(13, HIGH);   // set the LED on
  delay(1000);              // wait for a second
  digitalWrite(13, LOW);    // set the LED off
  delay(1000);              // wait for a second
}

void tattle(void) {
  Serial.println("I'm telling!");
}
```

In the setup() function, you additionally initialize the serial port and attach the function tattle() to external interrupt 0, INT0, to trigger on any CHANGE in the incoming signal. Notice that the second parameter of the attachInterrupt() function doesn't contain any sort of special punctuation, such as parentheses. In C, this doesn't invoke or call the function, but serves as a reference to its address in the program space. The Arduino-supplied attachInterrupt() function uses this address as a destination to jump to when one of the predefined external interrupt vectors is executed.

The tattle() function is called when the external interrupt fires. If you attach a jumper wire between D13 (the LED output) and D2 (the external interrupt input), you should see some output from the serial port, both in the Serial Monitor window (the preferred method) and also on the TX LED on the Arduino I/O Board. This should coincide with the alternating of the LED.

■ **Note** The tattle() function in the previous exercise is *not* an interrupt handler, per se. It's simply a function, like any other function. The Arduino software has already provided the appropriate interrupt handlers for all the external interrupts—INT0_vect and so on—and these functions in turn call the user-written handler function when enabled by the attachInterrupt() function.

The other possible conditions acceptable to the external interrupts are RISING, FALLING, and LOW. Try them now, in place of the CHANGE parameter of the attachInterrupt() function. RISING should only produce a tattle as the LED begins to illuminate, but not when it's extinguished. FALLING should produce the opposite effect.

When you try LOW, however, something seems to go wrong. The LED quits blinking, and a steady stream of tattling ensues. What happened?

The LOW setting is somewhat special. When the input signal is low, the interrupt fires and *continues* to fire as long as the input stays low. In this case, the external interrupt is detected, and execution proceeds to your little tattle() function. The tattle() function sends out a message via the serial port and then returns. The low condition persists, however, because your foreground program doesn't get a chance to change the state of the LED before the external interrupt again is invoked—and it never will.

Try not to code yourself into this particular corner, if you can help it. Don't interrupt on a low-level signal that won't eventually change of its own volition, or none of your other programs will ever get a chance to run again. The problem is compounded because the external interrupts have the highest priority in the interrupt structure of the AVR, so even another, active interrupt handler won't be able to execute while this condition persists.

It *is* possible, on the other hand, to disable the external interrupt in the interrupt handler routine, thus knocking the computer chip out of its rut. Add a detachInterrupt(0); statement to the end of the tattle() function. This solves the problem of the endlessly reinterrupting interrupt, but it also disables the intended function of the sketch.

Interrupt Reference

Table 7-7 and Table 7-8 provide lists of all the possible interrupt sources for both the Arduino Uno and the Arduino Mega 2560.

Table 7-7. Interrupt Vectors for the ATmega328

Vector	Interrupt	Handler	Description
1	INT0	INT0_vect	External interrupt 0
2	INT1	INT1_vect	External interrupt 1
3	PCINT0	PCINT0_vect	Pin-change interrupt 0
4	PCINT1	PCINT1_vect	Pin-change interrupt 1
5	PCINT2	PCINT2_vect	Pin-change interrupt 2
6	WDT	WDT_vect	Watchdog timer (when used as an interrupt)
7	TIMER2_COMPA	TIMER2_COMPA_vect	Timer/Counter 2 compare match A
8	TIMER2_COMPB	TIMER2_COMPB_vect	Timer/Counter 2 compare match B
9	TIMER2_OVF	TIMER2_OVF_vect	Timer/Counter 2 overflow
10	TIMER1_CAPT	TIMER1_CAPT_vect	Timer/Counter 1 capture
11	TIMER1_COMPA	TIMER1_COMPA_vect	Timer/Counter 1 compare match A
12	TIMER1_COMPB	TIMER1_COMPB_vect	Timer/Counter 1 compare match B
13	TIMER1_OVF	TIMER1_OVF_vect	Timer/Counter 1 overflow

Continued

Vector	Interrupt	Handler	Description
14	TIMER0_COMPA	TIMER0_COMPA_vect	Timer/Counter 0 compare match A
15	TIMER0_COMPB	TIMER0_COMPB_vect	Timer/Counter 0 compare match B
16	TIMER0_OVF	TIMER0_OVF_vect	Timer/Counter 0 overflow
17	SPI	SPI_STC_vect	SPI serial transfer complete
18	USART_RX	USART_RX_vect	USART receive complete
19	USART_UDRE	USART_UDRE_vect	USART data register empty
20	USART_TX	USART_TX_vect	USART transmit complete
21	ADC	ADC_vect	ADC conversion complete
22	EE_READY	EE_READY_vect	EEPROM ready
23	ANALOG_COMP	ANALOG_COMP_vect	Analog comparator triggered
24	TWI	TWI_vect	Two-wire interface (I2C) event
25	SPM_READY	SPM_READY_vect	Self-programming event

***Table 7-8**. Interrupt Vectors for the ATmega2560*

Vector	Interrupt	Handler	Description
1	INT0	INT0_vect	External interrupt 0
2	INT1	INT1_vect	External interrupt 1
3	INT2	INT2_vect	External interrupt 2
4	INT3	INT3_vect	External interrupt 3
5	INT4	INT4_vect	External interrupt 4
6	INT5	INT5_vect	External interrupt 5
7	INT6	INT6_vect	External interrupt 6

Vector	Interrupt	Handler	Description
8	INT7	INT7_vect	External interrupt 7
9	PCINT0	PCINT0_vect	Pin-change interrupt 0
10	PCINT1	PCINT1_vect	Pin-change interrupt 1
11	PCINT2	PCINT2_vect	Pin-change interrupt 2
12	WDT	WDT_vect	Watchdog timer (when used as an interrupt)
13	TIMER2_COMPA	TIMER2_COMPA_vect	Timer/Counter 2 compare match A
14	TIMER2_COMPB	TIMER2_COMPB_vect	Timer/Counter 2 compare match B
15	TIMER2_OVF	TIMER2_OVF_vect	Timer/Counter 2 overflow
16	TIMER1_CAPT	TIMER1_CAPT_vect	Timer/Counter 1 capture event
17	TIMER1_COMPA	TIMER1_COMPA_vect	Timer/Counter 1 compare match A
18	TIMER1_COMPB	TIMER1_COMPB_vect	Timer/Counter 1 compare match B
19	TIMER1_COMPC	TIMER1_COMPC_vect	Timer/Counter 1 compare match C
20	TIMER1_OVF	TIMER1_OVF_vect	Timer/Counter 1 overflow
21	TIMER0_COMPA	TIMER0_COMPA_vect	Timer/Counter 0 compare match A
22	TIMER0_COMPB	TIMER0_COMPB_vect	Timer/Counter 0 compare match B
23	TIMER0_OVF	TIMER0_OVF_vect	Timer/Counter 0 overflow
24	SPI	SPI_STC_vect	SPI serial transfer complete
25	USART0_RX	USART0_RX_vect	USART0 receive complete
26	USART0_UDRE	USART0_UDRE_vect	USART0 data register empty
27	USART0_TX	USART0_TX_vect	USART0 transmit complete
28	ANALOG_COMP	ANALOG_COMP_vect	Analog comparator triggered
29	ADC	ADC_vect	ADC conversion complete

Continued

Vector	Interrupt	Handler	Description
30	EE_READY	EE_READY_vect	EEPROM ready
31	TIMER3_CAPT	TIMER3_CAPT_vect	Timer/Counter 3 capture event
32	TIMER3_COMPA	TIMER3_COMPA_vect	Timer/Counter 3 compare match A
33	TIMER3_COMPB	TIMER3_COMPB_vect	Timer/Counter 3 compare match B
34	TIMER3_COMPC	TIMER3_COMPC_vect	Timer/Counter 3 compare match C
35	TIMER3_OVF	TIMER3_OVF_vect	Timer/Counter 3 overflow
36	USART1_RX	USART1_RX_vect	USART1 receive complete
37	USART1_UDRE	USART1_UDRE_vect	USART1 data register empty
38	USART1_TX	USART1_TX_vect	USART1 transmit complete
39	TWI	TWI_vect	Two-wire interface (I2C) event
40	SPM_READY	SPM_READY_vect	Self-programming event
41	TIMER4_CAPT	TIMER4_CAPT_vect	Timer/Counter 4 capture event
42	TIMER4_COMPA	TIMER4_COMPA_vect	Timer/Counter 4 compare match A
43	TIMER4_COMPB	TIMER4_COMPB_vect	Timer/Counter 4 compare match B
44	TIMER4_COMPC	TIMER4_COMPC_vect	Timer/Counter 4 compare match C
45	TIMER4_OVF	TIMER4_OVF_vect	Timer/Counter 4 overflow
46	TIMER5_CAPT	TIMER5_CAPT_vect	Timer/Counter 5 capture event
47	TIMER5_COMPA	TIMER5_COMPA_vect	Timer/Counter 5 compare match A
48	TIMER5_COMPB	TIMER5_COMPB_vect	Timer/Counter 5 compare match B
49	TIMER5_COMPC	TIMER5_COMPC_vect	Timer/Counter 5 compare match C
50	TIMER5_OVF	TIMER5_OVF_vect	Timer/Counter 5 overflow

Vector	Interrupt	Handler	Description
51	USART2_RX	USART2_RX_vect	USART2 receive complete
52	USART2_UDRE	USART2_UDRE_vect	USART2 data register empty
53	USART2_TX	USART2_TX_vect	USART2 transmit complete
54	USART3_RX	USART3_RX_vect	USART3 receive complete
55	USART3_UDRE	USART3_UDRE_vect	USART3 data register empty
56	USART3_TX	USART3_TX_vect	USART3 transmit complete

Summary

The exercises and experiments in this chapter only scratch the surface of what's possible when hardware and software work together. Sometimes you just have to try it yourself and find out what works, what doesn't work, and, more important, *why*.

You now have an inkling of how to *empower* your peripherals to go out and work on their own without constant supervision. It's a good bet that you've already begun to think about the potential advantages this knowledge will bring in some of your Arduino projects. Some techniques will work better than you expected, whereas others will inexplicably fail. Both are good experiences as long as you learn something from them.

Are you ready to put all this fancy book-learning to good use? You'll find several interesting LED-based projects in the next chapter.

Enjoy the dance.

CHAPTER 8

Example Projects

Making an LED blink is a good first step, but of what other use is it? Specifically, is there any nontrivial application for this interesting technology? Let's look at one particular example: LED lighting.

Here in the first decades of the twenty-first century, LEDs are taking tremendous strides in efficiency, reliability, and cost-effectiveness. They still lag a bit behind some older lighting technologies, but today it's not entirely far-fetched to start experimenting with LEDs for the purposes of illumination, and not only as point-source indicators.

Blinking the house lights on for a second and then off for a second runs out of novelty quickly. By blinking them very quickly and adjusting the duty cycle of the blink rate, you can effectively make a dimmable light. Dimmable lights are perfect for adjusting the ambient light levels to the appropriate function or mood desired. In addition, using the pulse-width-modulation (PWM) technique of adjusting the duty cycle so the perceived light level goes up and down achieves a great savings in power, with almost no waste at all.

In this chapter you look at how to control several dimmable LEDs at once, build high-power LED drivers for high-power LEDs, use infrared LEDs for remote control, and build *really* big arrays of LEDs. You also touch on the beginnings of a popular LED project, the digital clock. Let's get started!

Beyond the Blinking LED: Starting Simply

Listing 8-1 illustrates perhaps the simplest possible Arduino sketch that actually does something useful.

Listing 8-1. Dimming a Single LED with a Single Arduino Statement

```
void setup() {
}

void loop() {
  analogWrite(11, analogRead(0) >> 2);
}
```

For this sketch to work properly, you must attach a variable voltage to the first analog input, A0. This is easily accomplished using a potentiometer, whose endpoints are connected to V_{cc} and ground and whose wiper contact (usually but not always the center pin) provides the variable voltage between the two potentials. A 10K linear potentiometer is perfect. Then connect D11 to D13 using a short jumper wire, so the PWM signal on D11 drives the LED that comes standard on most Arduinos on D13.

On the Arduino Mega 2560, however, D13 *is* a PWM output, so no jumper wire is required. Just modify the `analogWrite()` function to address D13 directly.

Alternately, you can go ahead and wire your Arduino to a small *solderless breadboard* or other prototyping device. This gives you much more flexibility in how you connect your external components, as well as making it easier to make changes as you go along. See Figure 8-1.

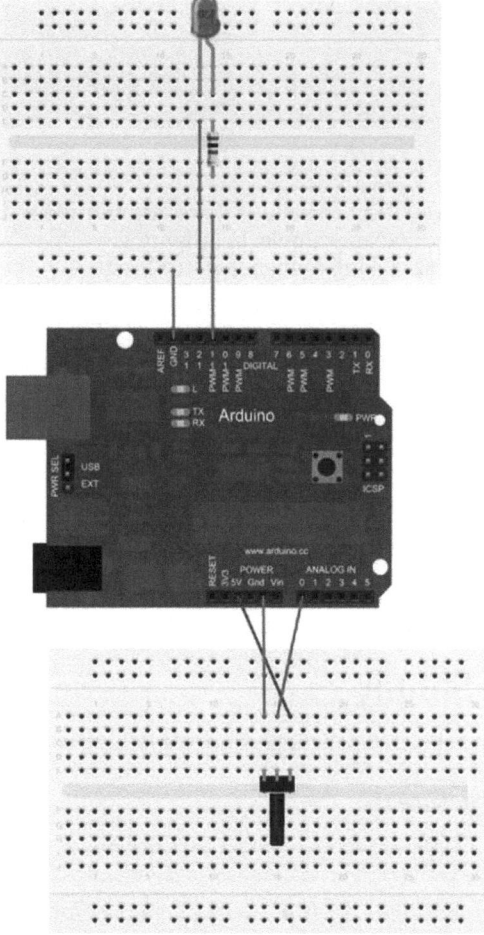

Figure 8-1. *A single 5mm LED and a potentiometer connected to an Arduino using a pair of solderless breadboards*

When connecting additional LEDs to the Arduino, you need to provide a current-limiting resistor in series with the LED. This prevents the LED from drawing too much current, which could damage either the LED or the Arduino itself. The LED installed on modern Arduino boards already has its own current-limiting resistor properly connected to it.

Recall from Chapter 7 that the parametric ranges of the Arduino's analog functions aren't the same. The `analogWrite()` function allows a possible range of 0–255. The `analogRead()` function, on the other hand, can return a value between 0 and 1,023. These ranges correspond to the eight-bit and ten-bit resolutions of the associated hardware, respectively.

To translate the reading from the analog-to-digital converter (ADC) from a ten-bit representation to a more suitable eight-bit format, you use simple bit-shifting math: `>> 2`. Each shift to the right divides the integer value by two. This tells the compiler to take the return value of the `analogRead()` function and shift it to the right (that is, toward the least-significant bit) two times, discarding the lowest two bits and effectively dividing the result by four. You could just tell it to divide by four; but because the result of the function call isn't a constant, the compiler misses this potential optimization and includes the actual integer division subroutine from the `avr-libc` library, thereby increasing the binary sketch size from 1,076 bytes to 1,152 bytes.

Alternatively, you could also use the handy Arduino `map()` function, which scales a value based on supplied ranges. The online documentation for the `map()` function uses this exact ADC-to-PWM scenario as an example:

```
int val = analogRead(0);
val = map(val, 0, 1023, 0, 255);
analogWrite(9, val);
```

These three statements can be more compactly expressed as

```
analogWrite(9, map(analogRead(0), 0, 1023, 0, 255));
```

However, this more-compact rendering is a bit harder to comprehend at first sight, with no measurable performance improvement other than the omission of the declared integer variable, `val`. Example code *should* be as clear as possible in its intent and function.

The problem with using the `map()` function in this instance is that it further expands the binary sketch size to 1,508 bytes. The `map()` function is very handy when the input and output ranges bear no obvious mathematical relationship. Because the values of the Arduino analog functions require only a small nudge to align properly, you can save some program memory. You may need it later. There is an even simpler solution, revealed later in the chapter. Stay tuned.

How, then, to improve on this simple sketch? Is it not already perfect? It performs its intended function. It takes up little space. It's easy for a human to read and perhaps understand, although it could use a few more comments (hint, hint).

There are three major, if non-obvious, areas that could stand some improvement. First, the sketch uses the Arduino analog functions, which can easily be optimized for both speed and size. An additional restriction of the Arduino analog functions is their arbitrary PWM frequency selection, which may or may not be appropriate for your application. Because you haven't exactly defined the application in concrete terms, you have to address that soon.

The second area of improvement relates to the *excess* speed of the sketch's execution. It runs full tilt all the time, executing the `loop()` function over 4,000 times per second. Such a high update rate is quite unnecessary in a lighting application, where the human eye has trouble seeing anything faster than 60Hz. In an optimum situation, the processor would shut itself down for a large percentage of the time, waking only when an adjustment was needed, thus saving a substantial amount of power. The milliwatts saved here are often ignored in projects that control hundreds or thousands of watts of lighting, but that's just bad form, and no excuse for waste.

The third area for improvement is either the most obvious or the least obvious, depending on your perspective. This simple sketch matches one of six available analog inputs to one of six available PWM outputs. The other analog inputs and PWM outputs are completely idle. Let's expand the sketch to address this area of improvement first; see Listing 8-2.

Listing 8-2. A Six-Channel Dimmer Sketch for the Arduino Uno

```
void setup() {
}

void loop() {
  analogWrite(11, analogRead(0) >> 2);
  analogWrite(10, analogRead(1) >> 2);
  analogWrite(9, analogRead(2) >> 2);
  analogWrite(6, analogRead(3) >> 2);
  analogWrite(5, analogRead(4) >> 2);
  analogWrite(3, analogRead(5) >> 2);
}
```

Now the sketch is reading six channels of analog information and updating six PWM outputs correspondingly. It can do this over 600 times per second, which is impressive but totally unnecessary. Let's pace this sketch and make a few other optimizations along the way.

Slow Enough

How fast is too fast? Anything much beyond the perception threshold of the human eye is too fast for a lighting application. Let's go far enough past this threshold to eliminate any visible flicker. Something just over 100Hz should be perfect. Any higher than that, and you start to get into the audible range, which is a problem when you convert this project over to motor speed control (which is easily done, as demonstrated later).

The default PWM frequency when using the Arduino `analogWrite()` function is ~490Hz. That's too high for this lighting application. Let's slow it down by a factor of four by changing the prescaler of the associated timer/counter peripheral.

Recall from Chapter 7 that PWM output D11 is driven by Timer/Counter 2's PWM channel A. (See Table 7-4.) The corresponding output pin is PB3 (Port B, pin 3), which you call OC2A when it's being used as a PWM output. The Arduino software has already set up the PWM functionality for you. You only need to adjust the prescaler to get a more appropriate PWM rate. The prescaler already selected is divide-by-64. This divides the 16MHz system clock into a slower 250 KHz clock that then drives the counter in the Timer/Counter 2 hardware.

If you're doing the math at home (and you really should be), you may be curious how an 8-bit counter produces an overflow ~490 times a second when driven at this clock speed (because 16,000,000 ÷ 64 ÷ 256 = ~976Hz). The answer is that the counter isn't just counting up to the maximum value (255) and then rolling over back to 0. That would be the Fast PWM mode, which is available should you need it. It's one of the other PWM modes, known as Phase Correct PWM mode, or *dual-slope* mode. The counter goes up to the maximum value, then counts down to zero, then counts back up again, ad infinitum. This takes 510 clocks to repeat. You might think it would take 2 × 256 = 512 clocks, but the two endpoints aren't repeated (that is, the upper count sequence is 253, 254, 255, 254, 253… and the lower count sequence is 3, 2, 1, 0, 1, 2, 3). Therefore the formula to calculate the PWM frequency using the phase correct PWM mode is F_CPU ÷ prescaler ÷ 510, which gives you the familiar ~490Hz number when the prescaler is 64.

Change the prescaler to 256, and you get a PWM frequency of ~122Hz. This is good enough for now. Comparing the prescaler selection bits for Timer/Counter 2 from Table 7-5, you see that only a single bit differs between the Arduino-specified prescaler setting of 64 and your desired prescaler of 256. Bit `CS21` in Timer/Counter 2's configuration register `TCCR2B` needs to be a 1 instead of a 0. Let's take the easy road for once and set that bit, assuming everything else is just how you need it to be. Don't fret; you return and address the issue properly in good time. Add this single statement to the setup() function:

```
bitSet(TCCR2B, CS21); // change Timer/counter2 prescaler to CK/256
```

This statement changes the PWM frequency of both D11 and D3, because both of these PWM outputs (OC2A and OC2B) are driven by Timer/Counter 2. You adjust the PWM frequencies of the remaining two timer/counter peripherals before you're done with dimmers.

Just looking at the LED, you shouldn't be able to see any visible difference in appearance. Turning the potentiometer knob up increases the apparent brightness, and dialing it back down again causes the LED to dim. If the knob seems to operate backward from this, try swapping the V_{cc} and ground leads on the potentiometer.

Or at least it *appears* to dim. In reality, the LED is never *partially* on or off. It's either fully on or fully off *part of the time*. This is an important distinction, because it vastly simplifies the additional hardware required to drive larger loads.

So now the PWM frequency is slow enough. What about the update frequency of the sketch? How can you slow it down from 600+ Hz without adding wasteful delay() functions or constructing some complex sleep + wake-up algorithm?

The simplest method is to use an interrupt. You already know that Timer/Counter 2 is overflowing about 122 times every second. You can move the actual code to update the dimmer into an interrupt service handler and enable the overflow interrupt. Instead of copying and pasting all that code into another function, simply rename the loop() function to ISR(TIMER2_OVF_vect) and then create a new, empty loop() function, so that your sketch now looks like Listing 8-3. Don't forget to also add the additional statement in the setup() function to enable the timer-overflow interrupt; otherwise nothing interesting will happen.

Listing 8-3. A Six-Channel Dimmer Using Slower PWM and an Interrupt Handler

```
void setup() {
  bitSet(TCCR2B, CS21); // change Timer/Counter2 prescaler to CK/256
  bitSet(TIMSK2, TOIE2); // enable Timer/counter2 overflow interrupt
}

void loop() {
  // nothing happens here
}

ISR(TIMER2_OVF_vect) {
  analogWrite(11, analogRead(0) >> 2);
  analogWrite(10, analogRead(1) >> 2);
  analogWrite(9, analogRead(2) >> 2);
  analogWrite(6, analogRead(3) >> 2);
  analogWrite(5, analogRead(4) >> 2);
  analogWrite(3, analogRead(5) >> 2);
}
```

Now all the updating is done in the background by the timer-overflow interrupt, leaving the loop() function delightfully empty and ready for other tasks. This approach is still a little faster than you need to actually update a single channel.

The operator of the light dimmer expects a change in the output of the dimmer when the input is adjusted. This change needs to respond in real time; that is, there can be no perceptible delay or lag in the response of the system. The key word here is *perceptible*. As long as something happens within a small fraction of a second, the user is convinced that the system is responding appropriately and briskly to their commands. This generally makes users happy. As you may already begin to appreciate, a small fraction of a second is plenty of time for an Arduino to execute thousands of lines of code.

Let's add a bit of finesse to the interrupt service routine, so that it only updates a single channel each time it's invoked by the overflow interrupt. You add a `static byte` declaration within the function definition to keep track of which channel needs servicing next. The `static` keyword ensures that the value of the variable persists even after the routine exits. You then define a list of the PWM pins in the form of a `const byte` array. You can use the value of the `channel` variable to look up the correct PWM output pin in the list. The `channel` variable is substituted for the constant values used previously in the update statement. The channel number is then incremented for next time through the loop and rolled back to zero when it gets too large. All of these changes are made in the interrupt service handler itself, and no other modifications to the sketch are required. See Listing 8-4.

Listing 8-4. An Even Slower Update Rate for the Six-Channel Dimmer Sketch

```
ISR(TIMER2_OVF_vect) {

    static byte channel = 0;
    const byte pwm_pins[6] = { 11, 10, 9, 6, 5, 3 };

    analogWrite(pwm_pins[channel], analogRead(channel) >> 2);
    channel++;
    if(channel > 5) channel = 0; // roll over
}
```

Each channel is now updated just over 20 times per second. The average person will *perceive* this as an instantaneous response to the adjustment of the potentiometers.

■ **Tip** Listing 8-4 is an example of a simple *state machine*. It's implemented as a function that is periodically invoked, and it retains some record of its present *state*. It quickly performs some *state-specific* action, which may or may not alter the state, and then exits. A state machine can get all kinds of complicated, but this one is very simple. The state in this example is the current channel.

Mostly Optimized Six-Channel Dimmer

As promised, Listing 8-5 shows the mostly optimized sketch for running a six-channel dimmer circuit in the background.

Listing 8-5. The Mostly Optimized Six-Channel Dimmer Sketch

```
void setup() {
  // output ports
  DDRB = 0xFF; // all outputs
  DDRD = 0xFF; // all outputs
  // ADC
  ADMUX = 0<<REFS1 | 1<<REFS0 | 1<<ADLAR;
```

```
  ADCSRA = 1<<ADEN | 1<<ADSC | 1<<ADPS2 | 1<<ADPS1 | 1<<ADPS0;
  DIDR0 = 1<<ADC5D | 1<<ADC4D | 1<<ADC3D | 1<<ADC2D | 1<<ADC1D | 1<<ADC0D;
  // Timer/counter0
  TCCR0A = 1<<COM0A1 | 0<<COM0A0 | 1<<COM0B1 | 0<<COM0B0 | 0<<WGM01 | 1<<WGM00;
  TCCR0B = 0<<WGM02 | 1<<CS02 | 0<<CS01 | 0<<CS00;
  // Timer/counter1
  TCCR1A = 1<<COM1A1 | 0<<COM1A0 | 1<<COM1B1 | 0<<COM1B0 | 0<<WGM11 | 1<<WGM10;
  TCCR1B = 0<<WGM13 | 0<<WGM12 | 1<<CS12 | 0<<CS11 | 0<<CS10;
  // Timer/counter2
  TCCR2A = 1<<COM2A1 | 0<<COM2A0 | 1<<COM2B1 | 0<<COM2B0 | 0<<WGM21 | 1<<WGM20;
  TCCR2B = 0<<WGM22 | 1<<CS22 | 1<<CS21 | 0<<CS20;
  bitSet(TIMSK2, TOIE2); // enable overflow interrupt
}

void loop() {
  // nothing happens here
}

ISR(TIMER2_OVF_vect) {

  static byte channel = 0;
  byte adc;

  adc = ADCH; // read upper 8 bits of ADC conversion result

  switch(channel) {
    case 0: OCR2A = adc; break; // PWM pin D11
    case 1: OCR1B = adc; break; // PWM pin D10
    case 2: OCR1A = adc; break; // PWM pin D9
    case 3: OCR0A = adc; break; // PWM pin D6
    case 4: OCR0B = adc; break; // PWM pin D5
    case 5: OCR2B = adc; break; // PWM pin D3
  }

  channel++;
  if(channel > 5) channel = 0;
  ADMUX = 0<<REFS1 | 1<<REFS0 | 1<<ADLAR | channel;
  ADCSRA = 1<<ADEN | 1<<ADSC | 1<<ADPS2 | 1<<ADPS1 | 1<<ADPS0;
}
```

Despite how lengthy this sketch may seem from a source-code perspective, it compiles down to a skinny 656 bytes, smaller even than your faithful friend Blink. This is mostly due to abandoning the Arduino analog functions and writing directly to the registers when possible.

One additional step that had to be taken was to explicitly set the PWM output pins to outputs, by writing to the data direction registers of both Port B and Port D. The Arduino analogWrite() function took care of this for you in the previous incarnation of this sketch.

The timer/counter peripherals are all properly configured for eight-bit phase-correct PWM duty. Timer/Counter 2's overflow interrupt enable bit, TOIE2, is set to 1 in the TIMSK2 register. This allows the timer to generate a periodic interrupt when it overflows.

The ADC peripheral is configured slightly differently than normal. An option exists to have the 10-bit conversion result left-aligned in the 16-bit result register. You select this option by programming a 1 into the ADLAR bit in the ADC's ADCSRA configuration register. This allows the interrupt service routine to read only the upper eight bits of the conversion result, which is all you want, and disregard the two lowest bits. This obviates the bit-shifting math from the previous sketch.

Because all six of the analog inputs are being used in their analog capacity, the digital input circuits associated with those pins are disabled by setting the bits in the Digital Input Disable Register, DIDRO. This saves a little power, but more important, it prevents Strange Things from happening when the digital inputs try to make heads or tails (that is, ones or zeros) out of the (possibly) constantly varying input voltages. They just wouldn't understand, so you shut them down.

As before, nothing happens in the loop() function. Perhaps you can think of something clever to put there.

The interrupt handler gets a few changes. A switch() statement based on the channel variable replaces the table lookup for the assignment of the conversion result to the proper PWM output register. The channel number is incremented, as before. The ADC's input multiplexer is then pointed at the new input channel, and a new conversion is started.

The ADC's status bits need not be examined because you've given the peripheral more than enough time to complete a conversion.

By reconfiguring the prescaler of the Timer/Counter 0 peripheral, the built-in Arduino timing functions such as delay() and millis() no longer work as expected. You do, however, have a nice, regular heartbeat in the Timer2 overflow interrupt, so you could use that for timing duties, if needed.

Why is this example sketch called *mostly optimized*? Because there are a few more things you could do to it, of course. There always are.

To start, you've been pretending that Timer/Counter 1 is an eight-bit counter with two PWM channels associated with it. In reality, it's a 16-bit counter (with 2 PWM channels associated with it), but it also offers both a 9-bit and a 10-bit counter mode, each with Fast PWM and Phase Correct PWM modes. The ten-bit mode exactly matches the output precision of the ADC peripheral, so it would be a better fit to program it accordingly. Don't waste those two extra bits if you don't have to.

To prevent flickering, especially at the lower end of the dimmer range, you could add some sort of filtering algorithm, such as *slew-rate limiting*, which would prevent the output from jumping rapidly from one value to another. This gives an impression of smoothness to the overall performance of the circuit and, done properly, adds a professional-level fade effect to the lighting transitions.

Finally, if you really can't think of anything clever to put in the loop() function, consider putting the processor to sleep, using the functions provided in the avr-libc library.

Now it's time to hook up all these pots and LEDs and see what happens; see Figure 8-2. It's really not as bad as it may look at first glance. You should be able to see that it's just a repetition of the basic circuit from Figure 8-1, with six input potentiometers and six output LEDs, which are duplicates of each other. Note the use of the power rails along the edges of the solderless breadboards: these allow multiple signals to be connected together. On the top breadboard, all the ground connections for the LEDs are connected together, and a single wire runs back to the GND pin on the Arduino. Similarly, both the 5V and GND connections to all the pots are connected via the two power rails and then routed back to the 5V and GND pins on the Arduino power-expansion connector.

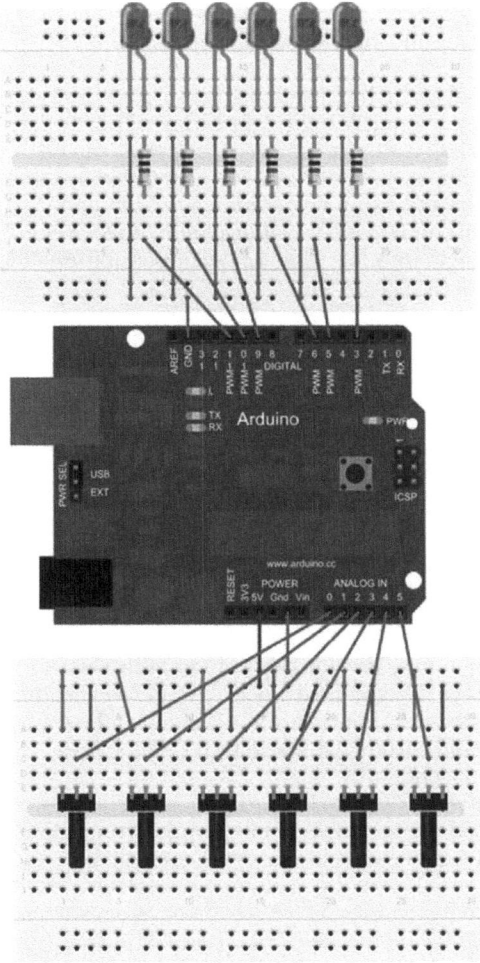

Figure 8-2. *The beginnings of a six-channel dimmer circuit, for experimental purposes*

It's Dim, Alright

You took an LED that was probably none-too-bright to begin with and made it even dimmer. This doesn't qualify as illumination yet. What do you need, to go from a single LED to something that actually lights up a room?

The answer is simple: More Power! This breaks down into two basic areas:

- Getting the power
- Controlling the power

The typical USB-powered Arduino has a little power to play with, as far as lighting up some LEDs goes. Let's figure out exactly how much power there is to go around, before hooking up the jumper cables.

The USB specification, which is available for your perusal at the USB Implementers Forum web site (`www.usb.org`), provides for up to 500mA (0.5A) at somewhere around 5V to be supplied to a USB device that properly enumerates itself on the bus. That's two and a half watts, maximum. This power can be used for whatever purpose the USB device needs. For an Arduino, there is the power consumed by the ATmega processor itself, along with the USB interface and the always-on power indicator LED, and sometimes the TX and RX LEDs, and possibly the built-in LED on D13. All this doesn't add up to even one watt, so there's a little room left in the power budget to light up a few more LEDs, or possibly one *big* LED.

A Little LED Math

How much power does a small LED draw? Electrical power is expressed in units called *watts* and can be calculated by multiplying voltage by current. Voltage is measured in volts (labeled with the capital letter *V*) and current flow is measured in amperes, often abbreviated as *amps* or just the capital letter *A*.

A typical, red indicator LED draws in the range of 20mA (0.02A) at around 2.0V. Other colors generally require more voltage as you go further up the rainbow. In terms of power, this red LED's power requirement is calculated as 0.02A × 2.0V = 0.04W, or 40 milliwatts. That's not very much, which is one of the reasons why you see little indicator LEDs everywhere.

Unfortunately, they add up. Recalling from Chapter 3, you know that each of the I/O pins on the Atmel AVR can sink or source up to 40mA at 5.0V. That's perfect for driving LEDs! However, you can't drive two 20mA LEDs from every pin of the chip (at least not at the same time) because of the 200mA overall device limitation. This limit applies to both the ATmega328 and the ATmega2560 devices. You *could* hook up an LED to every single pin, but you'd have to *promise* not to turn them all on at the same time. At most you could drive ten of these little, red LEDs at full current, which still isn't a good idea because it leaves no room for anything else to be driven by the chip.

Even if you did connect 20 high-efficiency super-bright white LEDs to the Arduino, with suitable current-limiting resistors to keep the current to each LED under 10mA, thus abiding by the overall AVR device current limit, you still wouldn't have that much light output—maybe enough for a night light or even a reading lamp, if it was close enough. More power is available on the Arduino, but you can't run it *directly* through the processor itself. You need an LED driver.

A Small LED Driver Circuit

You can use a single transistor with a couple of resistors to build your own LED driver circuit. The transistor acts as a *current amplifier* in this configuration. It takes a very small amount of current to turn on the circuit, illuminating the LED. This is what you need to lower the current requirement from the processor. See Figure 8-3.

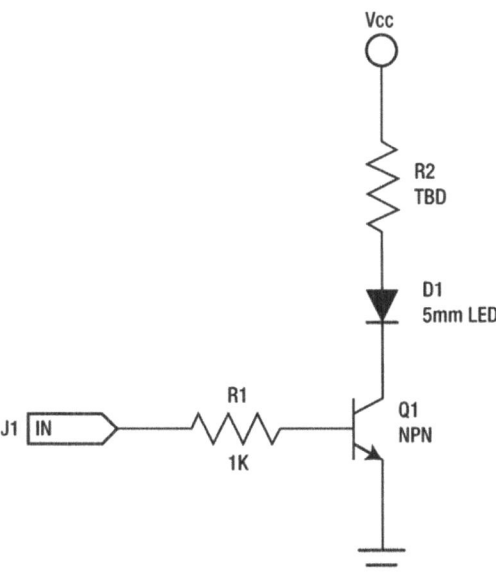

Figure 8-3. *A single LED driver circuit*

J1 is the connection back to one of the Arduino output pins. It could be a PWM output or any of the other digital outputs. R1 controls the amount of current that flows out of the Arduino pin and into the base of the transistor. This is your main concern right now: limiting the amount of current drawn out of the Arduino's pins, because there's only so much to go around.

The amount of current flowing into the base is directly proportional to the amount of current flowing from the transistor's collector to its emitter. Because the output of the Arduino pin will be at 5V when the pin is driven to a high state, the amount of current flowing through the resistor R1 and into the base of transistor Q1 will be at most 5V ÷ 1,000Ω = 5mA (0.005 A), according to Ohm's Law. In reality, the current will be less, because inside the transistor, between the base and the emitter, is a *p-n junction*, the intersection of P-type and N-type semiconductors. This junction is electrically similar to a diode, so there is a voltage drop. In your example circuit, you use a silicon transistor whose typical junction voltage drop is between 0.6V and 0.7V at negligible current levels, going up exponentially (as semiconductor voltage-current curves tend to do) as the current increases. You should see just over 4mA (but no more than 5mA because of the resistor) flowing from the pin of the Arduino through the base resistor R1 and into the base of the transistor.

Drawing only five milliamps or less per pin is perfect for the Arduino Uno. You could, in theory, connect a driver circuit like this one to every single pin at the same time and still be using less than half of the allowed current flowing out of the chip. This assumes a maximum of 20 outputs × 5mA = 100mA, which means you're using the USART pins as outputs as well as all the analog inputs.

You could even attach as many as 40 to 50 of these driver circuits to the Arduino Mega 2560, but this would be pushing it right up to the limit. Increasing the value of R1 from 1KΩ to 1.5KΩ would lower the current requirement of each driver but correspondingly decrease the amount of current that could be switched on and off by the driver circuit.

The amount of current that can flow through the transistor, connecting the circuit that powers the LED, is calculated by multiplying the base current by the transistor's DC current gain factor, abbreviated h_{FE}. A common, small-signal transistor such as the PN2222A has a minimum h_{FE} of 50 when the base current is as little as 1.0mA. This means if you apply 4mA of current to the base of a PN2222A transistor, it can conduct a minimum of 200mA (0.200A) from the collector to the emitter. That's right: this simple circuit can sink as much current as an entire ATmega device. This gives you a little more low-cost electrical muscle for driving your LEDs.

If you apply more current to the base by lowering the value of the base resistor, more current can flow through the transistor. Correspondingly, *less* current into the base *reduces* the maximum current that can flow in the circuit. The maximum collector current (I_C) of the PN2222A transistor is 1.0A.

A Little More LED Math

The actual amount of current that flows through this circuit is determined by two important factors: the forward voltage of the LED and the value of the current-limiting resistor that is in series with the LED. There is also a small amount of voltage dropped across the collector-emitter path of the transistor itself; but it will be very small (dozens of millivolts) when the current is relatively small, as it is in the single LED driver.

The forward voltage of the LED is tricky, because it varies exponentially with the amount of current flowing through the LED. The manufacturer's datasheet for any given LED only publishes a range for the forward voltage, because it varies even further from lot to lot as well as from LED to LED.

The best way to determine the forward voltage of an LED is to connect it to a power supply that allows either the voltage or the current to be varied, while also connecting an ammeter in series with the LED to measure the current flow. Starting at zero, slowly adjust the power up until either the desired brightness is achieved or the maximum current for the LED is reached. The maximum current should be given in the manufacturer's datasheet.

■ **Caution** Remember that *maximum* means *maximum*. It's a bad idea to over-power an LED.

Then, when the current through the LED has been established, measure the voltage across the terminals of the LED. This is the exact voltage drop for this particular LED at this current … at this temperature. Note that the numbers change as the LED heats up. For small indicator LEDs, little heat is generated; but this isn't the case with any of the larger LEDs now available for lighting applications, which can easily get so hot they need a heatsink to draw away the heat, lest the LED burn up.

Using a typical red LED as an example, you can safely assume a maximum current of 25mA and a forward voltage around 2.0V. Fully illuminated, this LED draws only 50mW, or 1/20 of a watt. That's not much power at all; it won't get unduly hot, and you can safely experiment on it without tongs, gloves, or safety masks.

If the LED is dropping 2.0V across its terminals, that means the remaining voltage in the circuit (5.0V - 2.0V = 3.0V) is going to be dropped across the current-limiting resistor, to be dissipated as waste heat. Because you now know what the voltage across the resistor should be, you can select an appropriate value (in ohms) for the resistor to give you the amount of current you want flowing through the circuit; again by using Ohm's Law. To calculate the optimum value of the current-limiting resistor, you divide the voltage across its terminals by the desired current flow in amps to get the resistance value in ohms, or 3.0V ÷ 0.025A = 120Ω.

Because 120Ω happens to be a common resistor value for 5% tolerance resistors, you can stop there. Had the number turned out to be some weird fraction, you would simply round up to the next-most-common value.

That was the process to determine the resistance of the current-limiting resistor. It's also necessary to calculate the power-handling capacity needed in this circuit. You may recall that power is the product of voltage and current, and because you've already calculated these values (3.0V and 0.025 A), you need only multiply them together to find the power that is to be dissipated by the resistor in the circuit: 3.0V × 0.025A = 0.075W, or 75mW.

A very common power rating for small resistors is 1/4W, or 250mW, so you can easily use a quarter-watt resistor in this circuit. There is plenty of excess power-handling capability. You want more capacity than demand in this example. You *don't* want to use a quarter-watt resistor when the power requirement gets above 200mW or so; the resistor will get uncomfortably warm. Move on up to a half-watt resistor to be on the safe side.

Because the current-limiting resistor does away with the excess power in the circuit by converting it into waste heat, the resistor tends to warm up during use. For your little red LED example, it probably won't get very warm at all. This will change when you move on to bigger LEDs.

So all that math tells you that you can use a 120Ω, 1/4W resistor for R2 in your driver circuit, if you're using the red LED you imagined you were going to use. What about other colors? Yellow LEDs tend to share the same forward voltage characteristics as red LEDs, generally somewhere in the 1.8V to 2.4V range. Green and blue LEDs can have forward voltages in the range of 3.0V to 3.6V, as well as white and ultraviolet (UV) LEDs. Your voltage may vary.

Some multimeters offer a diode test mode that measures the forward voltage of diodes or LEDs, but this is usually at miniscule current conditions—typically less than one milliamp. This is useful for giving an absolute minimum value for the LED's forward voltage; in practical applications, it most certainly will be higher.

One additional feature of your simple driver circuit is that it can easily drive more than a single LED, as long as the total current through the transistor is below the maximum collector current (and assuming enough base drive current). Let's add some more LEDs to this circuit. See Figure 8-4.

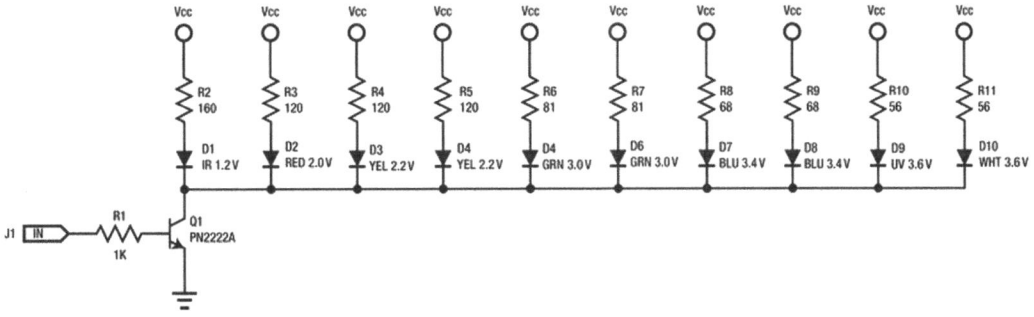

Figure 8-4. Multiple LEDs driven at full brightness by the same output pin

Note that all these LEDs come on and go off together, as one. However, this is sometimes what you want. The values for the individual current-limiting resistors are based on the theoretical forward voltages shown in the schematic.

If each LED in this driver circuit is running at 25mA, this one-driver circuit is now switching 250mA, about half of the total power available if the Arduino is being powered by the USB cable. You could, in theory, attach as many as *two* of these circuits to an Arduino without having to supply power from a different source. Luckily, the Arduino is already provisioned for this eventuality.

This circuit doesn't scale in a perfectly linear manner, however. The additional current flowing through the transistor increases the voltage drop across the transistor, thereby reducing the voltage across the LEDs and their associated current-limiting resistors. This voltage drop should only increase to about 0.250V using the components shown in Figure 8-4, but even this small change diminishes the brightness of each of the LEDs somewhat, with the most visible difference being seen with the higher-voltage LEDs such as the white and UV.

A 1W LED Driver

You have 2.5W of electrical power available on the typical USB-powered Arduino, less a small amount to drive the native circuitry. Let's push one of those watts through one *big* LED. See Figure 8-5.

Figure 8-5. A 1W white LED, attached to an aluminum-core PCB as a heatsink

A 1W LED is becoming more commonplace. The LED in Figure 8-5 was obtained from overseas via eBay for about one US dollar. The only documentation that came with it was a printed on the bag label: "1 pcs 1W White Lumen LED 40lm." There were no electrical specifications, other than the 1W figure. Luckily, most of these (but not all!) LEDs are similarly constructed. It was a good bet that it required about 350mA and had a forward voltage between 3.0V and 3.6V. Empirical testing revealed a forward voltage of 3.250V at 350mA at room temperature, or ~1.14W. Do take note that this 1W rating describes the LED's power requirement and *not* its optical output power.

After the part had been running for about 15 minutes, its temperature stabilized at about 25°C above ambient: not terribly hot, but *not* something you want to touch with your own, personal fingers. The forward voltage also declined to 3.204V at operating temperature. No additional heatsink was attached to the aluminum-core PCB.

■ **Caution**   Don't look directly at LEDs intended for illumination purposes!

Driving this LED directly from a 5V source should require a 5.13Ω resistor ((5.0V - 3.204V) ÷ 0.350A) that can safely dissipate just over 627mW of power. The standard value of 5.1Ω is *really close* but just a fraction of a percent too small. The next standard value in the E24 scale is 5.6Ω. A full 1W power-handling rating for this resistor wouldn't be amiss here.

You can also build one big resistor out of a few smaller resistors. Five 1Ω resistors in series provide enough resistance, and the power rating can be distributed among them, so even 1/4W resistors would work. When in doubt, use a bigger resistor. You can also wire two 10Ω resistors in parallel, halving their resistance but doubling their individual power-handling capacity.

The single LED driver circuit presented in Figure 8-3 will work with this LED, but with *only one* of these LEDs at a time. Dropping the value of the base resistor from 1KΩ to 680 or 560 ohms would help ensure enough current was able to flow from the Arduino pin to the transistor. Again, you only need to make sure that the current flowing either into or out of any Arduino pins is less than 40mA per pin, and that the total of all pins is less than 200mA.

Why can only one of these 1W LEDs be connected at once? Isn't there 2.5W of discretionary power to go around? The LED described in this experiment is using 1.14W all by itself, radiating perhaps as much as 10% of that energy as visible light and the remainder as waste heat. The current-limiting resistor, if you recall, is also spending part of the power budget, radiating 100% of the electrical power flowing through it (1.796V × 0.350A = 0.6286W) as waste heat, almost 2/3 of another one of your precious watts. So that's over 1-3/4W being used already.

Another way to look at it is strictly from the current perspective: You're using 350mA of the available 500mA that can be supplied by your USB cable, not counting what the rest of the Arduino circuit needs.

A 10W LED Driver

Packing even more of a punch, 10W LEDs are now available at reasonable prices. These LEDs *must* be mounted to a heatsink to draw away their excess heat. This step is no longer optional at these power levels. See Figure 8-6.

Figure 8-6. A 10W white LED attached to an aluminum heatsink. The metal tabs on the left and right of the LED are the electrical connections.

As you may or may not be able to see in the photograph, the 10W LED is really an array of 9 individual LEDs, organized in a 3 × 3 array. Each of the individual LEDs buried within the array is similar in characteristics to the single 1W LED examined earlier.

Because there are three parallel strings of three LEDs in series in this array, both the forward voltage and the current requirements are tripled. The LED needs around 10V at 1.0A (10W) to operate at full capacity. This exceeds the power supply of an Arduino that is powered only by a USB cable. Because the Arduino retains its pre-USB power-supply circuitry, all you have to do is find a suitable external power supply, and you'll be on your way to controlling this much larger LED. You're now officially entering the realm of LED lighting, although still at a modest scale. LEDs of this stature generally emit in the range of 500 to 900 lumens of light, which is comparable to a 40W or 60W incandescent bulb. This underlines the higher efficiency of LED lighting when compared to some, but not all, of the preexisting lighting technologies.

Let's build a driver circuit for this LED and connect it to an Arduino. Your faithful friend the PN2222A transistor has to bow out at this point. The 1.0A continuous-power requirement happens to be the PN2222A's absolute maximum collector current (I_c), so you can either look for a larger bipolar junction transistor (BJT) or try a different kind of transistor entirely. Let's look at a proven contender in this field: the IRLZ44, a logic-level power metal oxide semiconductor field-effect transistor (MOSFET), originally from International Rectifier and now produced by Vishay. See Figure 8-7.

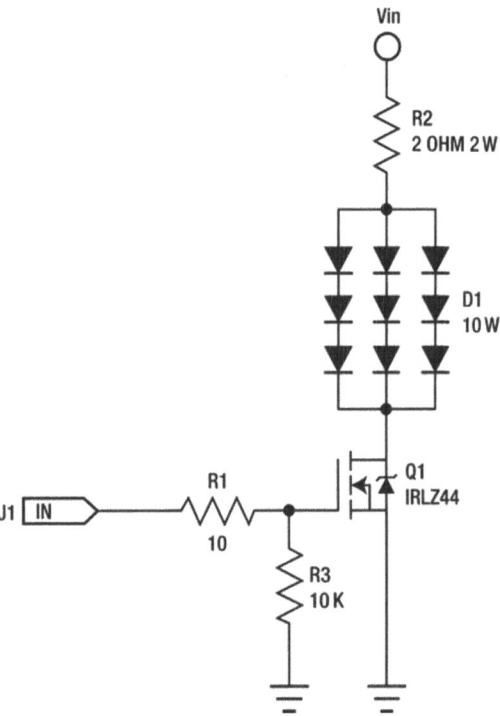

Figure 8-7. A single LED driver for a 10W LED using a MOSFET

The overall layout of this schematic should look quite familiar by now. The BJT has been replaced with a MOSFET, which has its own schematic symbol that more accurately describes its inner workings. The single LED has been replaced with a 3 × 3 array of LEDs, even though they're all packaged within the same device. The values of the two resistors have been modified for this new circuit. A new resistor, R3, has been added.

R1 still limits the amount of current flowing into the *gate* of the MOSFET. This kind of transistor is controlled by voltage instead of current, unlike the previous BJT. You'll note a gap within the MOSFET symbol between the gate and the other two terminals, the *source* (connected to ground) and the *drain* (connected to the LED, and so on). This gap reminds you that there is no direct electrical connection between these terminals. A voltage on the gate induces an electrical field that creates an *enhancement region* in the transistor, causing it to conduct current.

Because the two conductors are separated by an insulator, there is a small amount of capacitance on the gate. This capacitance must be charged before the voltage on the gate will rise high enough to turn on the MOSFET, so for a very short amount of time, a very large current can flow into the gate. You want to limit the peak value of this in-rush current while at the same time *not* introducing much delay. A small-value resistor, measuring just a few ohms, will work nicely. Once the gate has been moved to the higher voltage level, it takes practically no energy to keep it there, unlike the BJT that always conducts the base current out through the emitter.

Due to the capacitive nature of the transistor's gate, it can't be left floating (that is, with no input) at any time. A new component, R3, very loosely ties the gate to ground, keeping the transistor turned off until a real signal arrives from the Arduino. Remember, the Arduino takes a moment to compose itself whenever it has been reset or first powered up, and in that period of time all the I/O pins are still inputs. Stray electromagnetic energy in the atmosphere can easily be converted to enough electrical potential to partially or fully turn on the transistor. This is something that you *do not want* to happen.

If V_{IN} is a regulated 12V supply, R2 should be (12.0V - 10.0V) ÷ 1.0A), or 2Ω with a 2W *minimum* power rating. Three-, four-, or even five-watt resistors would be welcome here. Just as with your friend the PN2222A transistor, let's not ask these parts to run at 100% all the time.

If you're tired of calculating all these resistor values, you can take a break. There are many prebuilt 12V lighting products available now that feature LEDs. Figure 8-8 shows a low-voltage MR-16 lamp being driven by the circuit in Figure 8-7.

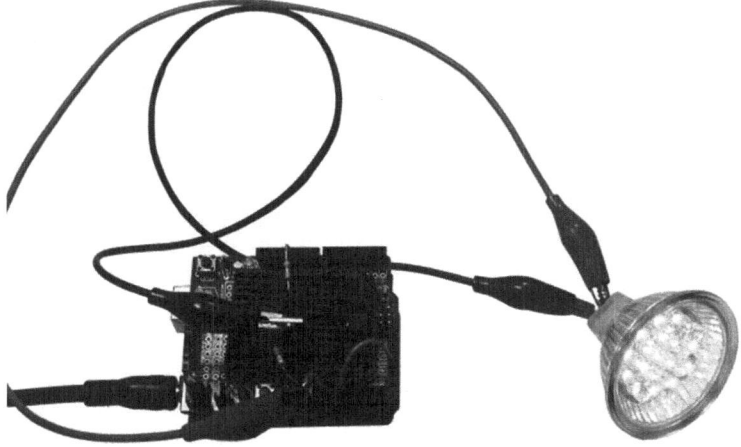

Figure 8-8. A low-voltage LED lamp with built-in drive electronics

One of the decidedly nice things about these self-contained low-voltage lighting devices is that they already contain their own drive electronics. They run on either 12V AC or DC, so it doesn't matter which way you connect the leads. Several of these lamps can be controlled by a single driver circuit such as presented in Figure 8-7.

Other Uses for a Blinking LED

LED lighting is one of the more fascinating applications of blinking LED technology. On a smaller scale, some other uses can prove handy, as well. One of them is using LEDs for communication.

Infrared Remote Control

It's quite possible that you've already used an LED to send a message today. Most consumer electronic devices that support a remote control use one or more variations of infrared (IR) remote-control protocols. These devices blink an infrared LED on and off quickly, using different timing patterns to convey different commands.

The typical IR remote control uses a 940nm IR LED. This wavelength is just past the red end of the spectrum that is visible to humans. You don't see any flashes of light coming from the end of your remote control, but your digital camera or camcorder very probably can. This useful piece of information can also be used to develop see-in-the-dark equipment by building large arrays of infrared LEDs and using suitable cameras to do the actual seeing part. Sadly, no Arduino is required.

However, if you *do* want to use your Arduino to send and receive IR remote-control commands, it's relatively easy, once you've hooked up the right hardware.

The IR transmitter is just an LED, like any LED you've blinked so far. A typical 5mm IR LED usually has a maximum continuous current of 100mA and a typical forward voltage of 1.2V–1.5V. You can attach an IR LED directly to an Arduino pin through a 100Ω resistor, but it won't transmit very far, because it's only getting about 40% of the power it's expecting. In normal service (that is, soldered to a remote-control PCB), these IR LEDs are often badly abused, sometimes simply shorted across the battery terminals for the brief time they need to be on, with little or no current-limiting provided. This increases effective distance at the cost of longevity.

You can get more range by adding the single LED driver from Figure 8-3 and lowering the resistance of the current-limiting resistor to 47Ω. This increases the current flowing through the LED to around 100mA. A half-watt resistor is recommended, even though the low duty cycle of the LED tells you the *average* current of the LED is less than the maximum. It's entirely possible that a software glitch could leave the LED on, and you don't want to have to explain why the lab burned down.

The IR receiver is a bit more complicated. You can build one out of an infrared photodiode and a bunch of other analog circuitry, or you can buy one already made in a tiny module that works perfectly. There are several popular models made by different manufacturers. The PN4602 by Panasonic is a good choice. It has only three connections: power, ground, and decoded signal out. These highly integrated devices are made by the millions for all those consumer electronic gadgets people seem to keep buying, so their cost is quite low.

For best performance in variably lighted environments, the IR signal is usually modulated at some predefined frequency. A very common frequency is 38KHz.

A delightfully useful library for IR communication is available from Ken Shirriff's blog (www.arcfn.com/2009/08/multi-multiprotocol-infrared-remote-library.html). Download the zip file and unpack it in your Arduino's /libraries/ folder. It even comes with several useful demo programs, which you should be able to load from the Arduino's File ➤ Examples ➤ IRremote menu item. Use the IRrecvDump sample sketch to identify, if possible, the codes coming from your IR remote. Jot down the codes emitted from a few buttons; then you can use those codes in your own sketch, simulating the use of the remote control.

The example sketches connect the IR transmitter circuit to D3 and the IR receiver to D11. The output pin is chosen because Ken used the PWM capabilities of the Atmel AVR to help with the modulation of the output signal. The input pin can be any digital input pin.

Listing 8-6 gives a simple sketch that alternately turns on and off an IR remote-controlled RGB LED controller.

Listing 8-6. *A Short Sketch Using the IRremote Library (On and Off Codes Decoded Using the Library's IRrecvDump Example Sketch)*

```
#include <IRremote.h>

IRsend irsend;

void setup() {
}

void loop() {
  irsend.sendNEC(0xFFB04F, 32); // on
  delay(1000);
  irsend.sendNEC(0xFFF807, 32); // off
  delay(1000);
}
```

The library supports Sony, NEC, and RC5/6 codes, which should cover a large number of IR remote-control devices.

Now you have an Arduino that can control several different lights at once. It can also send *and* receive infrared remote-control codes. Can you imagine any interesting combinations of these two capabilities?

TV-B-Gone

Mitch Altman (shown in Figure 8-9) is a very interesting man. He wants you to be happy. He has an idea that if you spent more time doing the things you love and less time watching TV, you'd be a happier person. He may be right.

Figure 8-9. Mitch Altman. Photo by Alexander Klink. Image licensed under Creative Commons Attribution 3.0 Unported.

Mitch travels around the world teaching people to solder, and otherwise empowering people to change the world to be a better place to live. One of his inventions is the TV-B-Gone (`www.tvbgone.com`), which is a universal TV remote control that has one button. Can you guess what that button does? Yes, that's right: it turns off almost every TV known to man that is within range. His invention is quite simple in its mission as well as in its execution. It's an excellent example of a popular open source project.

Looking at the schematic, available from the Adafruit website (`www.ladyada.net/make/tvbgone/download.html`), you can see that it's a tribute to minimalism. It's based on the Atmel AVR ATtiny85, which shares the same processor as your Arduino. The ATtiny85 lives in an eight-pin plastic DIP and needs only a few volts to operate. The TV-B-Gone circuit has only a single pushbutton input and two outputs. One of the outputs is connected to a high-current driver circuit that drives four infrared LEDs. The other output drives a visible green LED to let you know it's doing something when you press the button.

These little blinking LEDs can either bring a tiny bit of peace and quiet to your immediate vicinity, or they can get you barred from attending the Consumer Electronics Show for life. True story.

Think about that the next time you hear a comment about Arduinos only being good for blinking LEDs.

A Lot of Blinking LEDs

An Arduino Uno can light up about 20 LEDs individually. In the absence of a driver circuit, as many LEDs as you want can be driven directly by the Arduino's I/O pins, as long as the total power drawn remains less than 200mA. This can be guaranteed by limiting the current to each LED to 10mA or less, or by limiting the duty cycle of the LEDs in software so that no more than 200mA is drawn at any given time.

A Direct-Drive Example

Here is a simple circuit that connects 20 LEDs in the form of a bar graph, implemented as an Arduino shield. See Figure 8-10 for the schematic and Figure 8-11 for an example PCB layout.

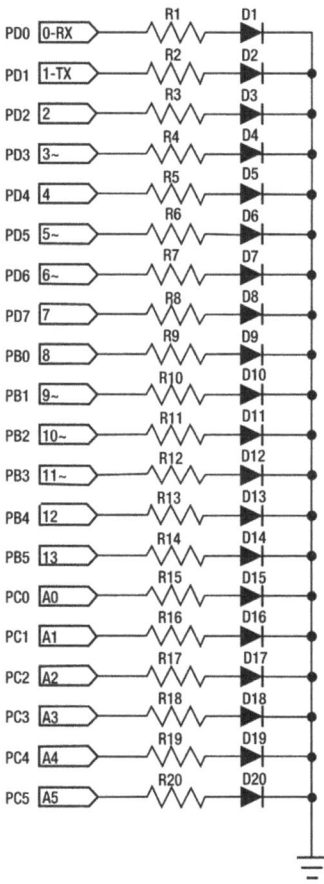

Figure 8-10. The schematic diagram of the 20-LED bar-graph shield

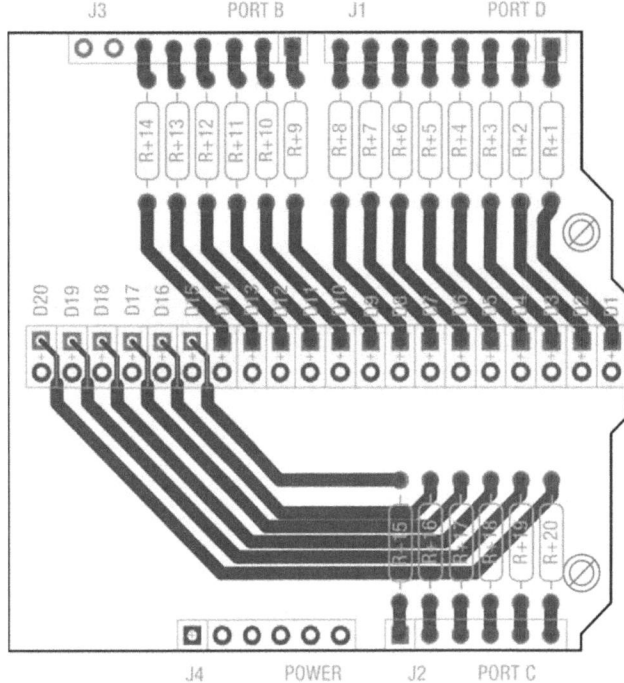

Figure 8-11. *The PCB layout of the 20-LED bar-graph shield, showing only the solder side (bottom) connections. The cathodes of all the LEDs are connected to GND via a ground plane on the top side (not shown).*

This is a direct-drive configuration, meaning that each LED can be addressed directly. Each LED is connected to a single I/O pin, which should be configured as an output.

This particular implementation also uses the USART serial input line as an output. Because the Arduino Uno installs a couple of 1KΩ resistors between the USB interface and the ATmega328, the lower impedance of the I/O pin's output driver wins, swinging the output fully from 5V to ground and turning on and off the LED under program control.

This technique usurps the USART's receiver pin, but only temporarily. The Arduino can still be reprogrammed later using the Arduino software, because the first thing that happens during a sketch upload is to reset the processor; this invokes the on-board bootloader, which properly configures the USART for communication. The Arduino forgets all about the misuse of the USART's serial input line as an output.

There are two ways to go with the resistor value selection. If you want to light up all the LEDs at once, you must restrict the current to each LED to under 10mA. This will keep the total current under the 200mA device maximum, which you have to respect when driving the LEDs directly with the I/O pins.

For typical red LEDs of normal brightness, use a minimum of 330Ω, 1/4W resistors for R1–20. For other colors, you need to calculate the resistance using the formula $V_R \div I_{LED}$, where V_R is the voltage dropped across the resistor (that is, V_{CC} - the LED's V_F, or forward voltage) and I_{LED} is the current desired; in this case, use 0.010A (10mA) for I_{LED}.

If you anticipate only needing a few LEDs on at any given time, you can push more current through each of the LEDs by lowering the value of the current-limiting resistors used on the PCB. You must not exceed the 40mA limit for each I/O pin.

A good method to enforce this self-imposed LED limit is to use a single function in your sketch to control the LEDs. This keeps all the hardware rule-enforcing policies in one location, at the cost of being able to turn on or off LEDs randomly throughout the sketch.

To fit all 20 LEDs in a single line across the Arduino shield, you use a smaller, rectangular LED measuring 2mm × 5mm × 7mm. Alternately, you could use a pair of ten-segment bar graph modules. The spacing of the pins would have to be increased from 0.100" to 0.300" to accommodate the larger bar-graph modules, but this makes it a lot easier to populate the PCB and keep all the LEDs aligned attractively.

Not shown in the PCB layout is the ground plane on the top layer that connects all the ground connections together and wires them to the GND pins on both the POWER and PORT B expansion connectors.

You spend some more time on PCB layout tools and techniques in Chapter 10.

Direct-Drive with LED Drivers

Why do you have to choose between many LEDs and bright LEDs? You don't; you can have both. All it takes is a few LED driver circuits between the ATmega and the LEDs.

Wiring 20 individual driver circuits is possible but may become tedious, especially if more than one assembly is being built. A low-cost alternative is to use a prebuilt transistor driver chip, such as the ULN2003. It contains seven transistor driver circuits. Each driver contains two NPN BJT transistors configured in a Darlington arrangement. The output of the first transistor drives the base of the second transistor, thereby amplifying the current even more. See Figure 8-12.

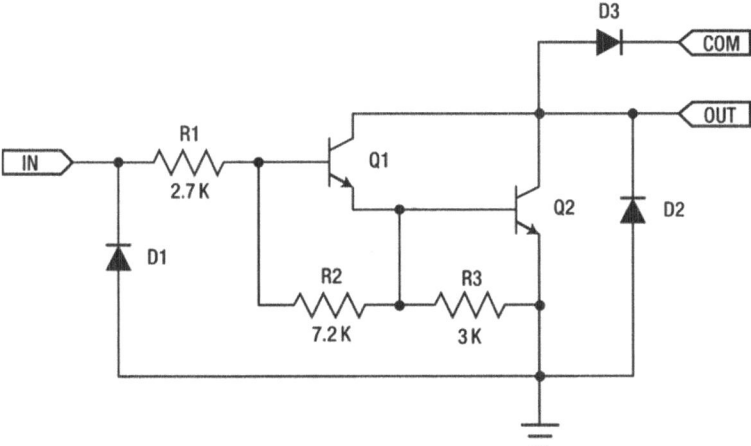

Figure 8-12. Each of the driver circuits in the ULN2003 contains a Darlington pair of transistors and associated resistors.

You can use three of these chips to drive up to 21 LEDs. In keeping with the spirit of using component arrays instead of discrete components, you can also use two LED bar-graph modules (ten

LEDs each) and three *resistor networks*, each containing seven resistors, with one common terminal connected to 5V. This reduces your component count (not counting connectors or the PCB) to only eight. See Figure 8-13.

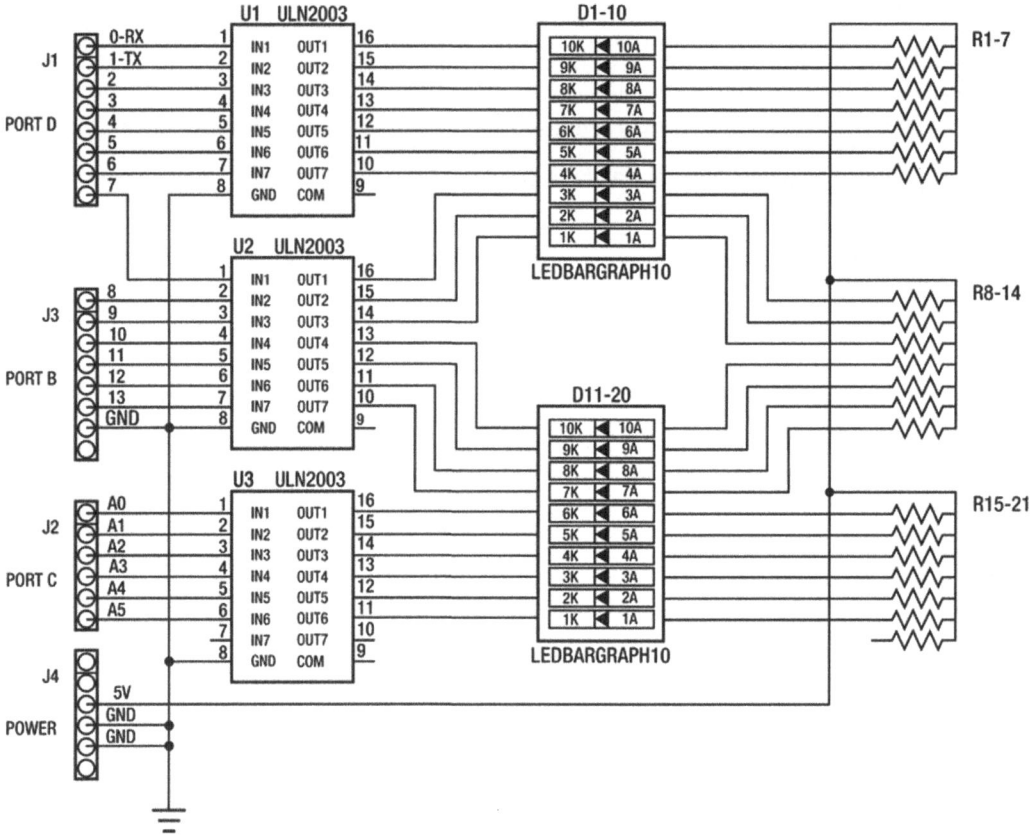

Figure 8-13. *Driving 20 LEDs directly using the ULN2003 driver chip*

Multiplexing Techniques

So far you've limited the LED count to one LED per I/O pin. This is fine when you have lots of I/O pins, such as the Arduino Mega 2560. But sometimes even the 84 available I/O pins of the ATmega2560 chip (70 of which are available on connectors on the Arduino Mega 2560) isn't enough. In those cases, you have two alternatives.

The first alternative is to use additional hardware to expand the number of available I/O lines. This is certainly a viable choice when a large number of individual LEDs need to be controlled. One example is the use of *shift registers*, a type of dedicated hardware logic that allows a serial stream of data bits to be *shifted* through a bank of single-bit memories called *flip flops*.

The Arduino library supports the shiftOut() function, which *serializes* eight bits of data out on a single data pin and an associated clock pin. This works perfectly with one or more shift registers. An excellent tutorial on using both the shiftOut() library function and the 74HC596 shift register chip is available on the Arduino web site: http://arduino.cc/en/Tutorial/ShiftOut.

Another technique for increasing the number of LEDs is *multiplexing*. There are several types of multiplexing that allow larger numbers of LEDs to be controlled by a circuit. Let's look at a few of the more popular multiplexing techniques.

Row-Column Multiplexing

One example is *row-column* multiplexing. A rectangular array of LEDs is wired in a grid, with all of the LED anodes (positive terminals) connected to the grid *rows* and the LED cathodes (negative terminals) connected to the grid *columns*. This example is called an *anode-row grid*, to indicate which type of terminal (anode or cathode) is attached to which dimension (row or column). The rows and columns can be switched around, if necessary. See Figure 8-14.

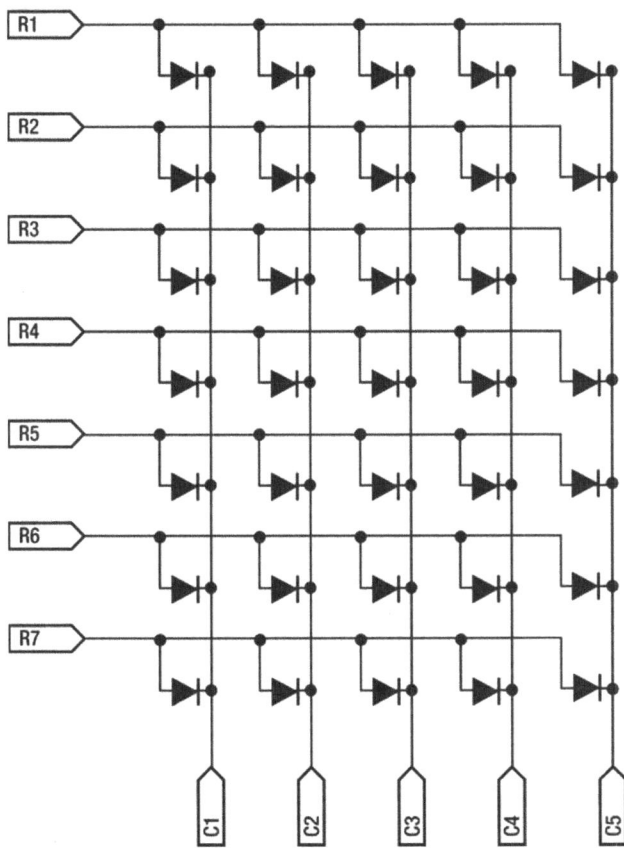

Figure 8-14. An anode-row LED array, illustrating row-column multiplexing

There are 5 columns and 7 rows of LEDs in this example matrix, for a total of 35 LEDs. This is enough LEDs to represent the uppercase letters, numerals, and punctuation of the English language, for the most part. Smaller and larger representations are also possible, but this is a good place to start.

It doesn't take many I/O lines to control this array: 5 for the columns and 7 for the rows, for a total of 12. Twelve is better than 35, especially when you're talking about a precious commodity like programmable I/O lines on an Arduino. That leaves a few I/O lines left over on the Arduino Uno to interface with other circuits.

Previously, you used *direct* control of each LED by connecting one terminal of the LED to its very own I/O line or LED driver. The other terminal of the LED was wired to either 5V or ground, depending on the circuit configuration.

Now you control each of the LEDs in the matrix by manipulating the underlying grid. As before, you light up each LED by connecting a higher potential (voltage) on the anode and a lower potential on the cathode. This results in current flow though the LED, causing it to emit light. Just as before, you also need to make provision for some sort of current-limiting device to be in series with the LED to control the amount of current flowing, as well as be mindful of the current-handling capabilities of each I/O line.

To illustrate the basic idea of row-column multiplexing, let's omit the current constraints from the simplified model matrix and concentrate on the fundamental techniques. You go back and add the appropriate real-world circuitry later.

To light up a single LED in this array, you first identify which row and column uniquely addresses it. Let's use the numbering scheme illustrated in Figure 8-14, with rows numbered 1–7 from top to bottom and columns numbered 1–5 from left to right. The top, left LED then has row-column coordinates 1,1, or row 1, column 1.

Assuming Arduino I/O lines are connected to all the rows and columns, you first place all the pins in a high-impedance state by making them inputs with no pull-up resistors active. This happens to be the default state of all Arduino I/O lines; but let's not assume things are the way you want them, and *specify* how things should be. See Listing 8-7.

Listing 8-7. Blinking a Single LED in a 5 × 7 LED Array

```
const byte row_pins[7] = { 2, 3, 4, 5, 6, 7, 8 };
const byte column_pins[5] = { 9, 10, 11, 12, 13 };

void leds_off() {

  byte i;

  // reset all row pins
  for(i = 0; i < 7; i++) {
    digitalWrite(row_pins[i], LOW); // turn off row pin
    pinMode(row_pins[i], INPUT); // make row pin high-impedance
  }

  // reset all column pins
  for(i = 0; i < 5; i++) {
    digitalWrite(column_pins[i], LOW); // turn off column pin
    pinMode(column_pins[i], INPUT); // make column pin high-impedance
  }
}
```

```
void one_led(byte row, byte column) {
  row--;
  column--;
  leds_off(); // turn off all the LEDs
  pinMode(row_pins[row], OUTPUT); // turn on row pin
  digitalWrite(row_pins[row], HIGH); // rows = anodes = high
  pinMode(column_pins[column], OUTPUT); // turn on column pin
  digitalWrite(column_pins[column], LOW); // columns = cathodes = low
}

void setup() {
}

void loop() {
  one_led(1, 1);
  delay(1000);
  leds_off();
  delay(1000);
}
```

Nothing interesting happens in the setup() function, but it's required, so there it is. The loop() function calls another function, one_led(), with the coordinates of the single LED you want illuminated. In this case, it's row 1, column 1.

The first thing that the one_led() function does is adjust the two parameters row and column to be *zero-based* instead of *one-based*. People-types tend to number things starting at one (one-based), but computers, well, they like to start at zero. You're calling the upper-left corner of the LED matrix row 1, column 1. The two lookup tables used for translating the row and column designators to Arduino pin numbers—row_pins[] and column_pins[], respectively—are zero-based arrays. The Arduino pin number for row 1 is stored in row_pins[0], and the pin number for column 1 is stored in column_pins[0]. So each of these parameters is decremented by one before proceeding on to the rest of the function.

Next, the one_led() function calls yet another function, leds_off(). As its name might suggest, this function turns off all the LEDs in the array by flipping the direction bits of all the I/O lines being used to address the LED matrix into inputs. It also turns off any pull-up resistors that may have been previously activated. This effectively shuts off all current flowing through the LED array, rendering it dark.

Now that the one_led() function has specified its starting conditions, it can turn on a single LED in the matrix by programming a single row pin and a single column pin to be outputs and setting their logic levels appropriately. For anode-row LED matrices such as the example in Figure 8-14, you set the anode HIGH using the digitalWrite() function, and the cathode LOW. For the other flavor of LED matrices (anode-column or row-cathode, however you want to call them), reverse those two levels to allow the current to flow in the more interesting direction. Remember, LEDs are diodes and conduct current in only one direction.

The loop() function blinks this one LED in the corner by alternately calling the one_led() function and the leds_off() function, interleaved with a one-second delay to make the blink more visible.

To let all those other LEDs have a turn, replace the loop() function with the following code:

```
void loop() {

  byte row, column;

  for(row = 1; row <= 7; row++) {
    for(column = 1; column <= 5; column++) {
      one_led(row, column);
```

```
        delay(100);
      }
    }
  }
}
```

This creates a walking-dot pattern, with a single pixel scanning across each row and then down to the next row, repeating when it reaches the bottom of the LED matrix.

As fascinating is this display is at this point, it still doesn't spell out *A* for Arduino (our goal). To do this, you have to resort to trickery.

It may or may not be obvious from the schematic alone, but it isn't possible to control every LED individually in this array. Yes, it's possible to turn on any *one* LED, but only as long as all the other LEDs are off. Using the simplistic row-column addressing, if you turn on the LED in the upper-left corner (1, 1) and also want to turn on the LED in the lower-right corner (7, 5) at the same time, you may be surprised by the mysterious illumination coming from the other two corners. Then again, you may not.

The current applied to the grid flows through every possible combination of rows and columns. The best you can do is to enable a single column at a time and light up only the LEDs in that column by turning on their respective rows. Then the next column can be illuminated, then the next, and so on. If this process is repeated fast enough, it looks like a solid pattern of LEDs.

It's also possible to scan through the rows, enabling the individual columns. You want to keep the update rate as fast as possible while doing the least work. Because this example array has fewer columns than rows, it takes less time to scan through the columns.

Listing 8-8 contains a sketch that displays a capital letter *A* on a 5 × 7 LED matrix, this time using a column-anode, row-cathode module.

Listing 8-8. *Displaying A for Arduino on a 5 × 7 LED Matrix Using Row-Column Multiplexing*

```
const byte row_pins[7] = { 2, 3, 4, 5, 6, 7, 8 };
const byte column_pins[5] = { 9, 10, 11, 12, 13 };

void setup() {

  byte i;

  for(i = 0; i < 7; i++) {
    digitalWrite(row_pins[i], LOW);
    pinMode(row_pins[i], OUTPUT);
  }

  for(i = 0; i < 5; i++) {
    digitalWrite(column_pins[i], LOW);
    pinMode(column_pins[i], OUTPUT);
  }
}

void draw_column(byte bits) {

  digitalWrite(row_pins[0], bits & 0x40 ? LOW : HIGH);
  digitalWrite(row_pins[1], bits & 0x20 ? LOW : HIGH);
  digitalWrite(row_pins[2], bits & 0x10 ? LOW : HIGH);
  digitalWrite(row_pins[3], bits & 0x08 ? LOW : HIGH);
  digitalWrite(row_pins[4], bits & 0x04 ? LOW : HIGH);
```

```
  digitalWrite(row_pins[5], bits & 0x02 ? LOW : HIGH);
  digitalWrite(row_pins[6], bits & 0x01 ? LOW : HIGH);
}

const byte bitmap[5] = {
  0b00011111,
  0b00100100,
  0b01000100,
  0b00100100,
  0b00011111
};

void loop() {

  byte column;

  for(column = 0; column < 5; column++) {

    digitalWrite(column_pins[column], HIGH); // enable this column
    draw_column(bitmap[column]);
    delay(2);
    digitalWrite(column_pins[column], LOW); // disable this column
  }
}
```

The setup() function turns all the necessary I/O pins into outputs and then sets their outputs to a LOW level. The loop() function iterates through the five columns, enabling only one column at a time.

The actual dots are drawn in the draw_column() function, which is passed a slice of the letter's pixels from the bitmap[] array. Each bit in the column is examined, and if it's supposed to be on, it's turned on (by setting the corresponding row pin LOW); otherwise it's turned off.

The C ? operator tests a conditional statement and returns either the first value (LOW in this example) if the condition is true or the second value (HIGH in this example) after the colon (:) if the condition is false. This is more compact than writing a bunch of if(condition)... statements.

You can just see the outline of the character to be drawn if you look at the bitmap[] array's declaration sideways. The ones represent lit pixels, and the zeros represent dark pixels. Can you see it? The 0b... notation allows a binary number to be written as a series of ones and zeros, which makes it easier to see bitmapped patterns.

The short delay() in the loop is required. If omitted, column *ghosting* will occur, where LED pixels seem to bleed over from one column to another. This is caused by not giving the I/O lines enough time to change states. The additional delay gives the I/O lines time to properly synchronize and eliminates ghosting. Try it without the delay() function to see what it looks like, if you're curious.

This sketch works, after a fashion, with only seven current-limiting resistors between the Arduino I/O pins and the row pins of the matrix. The column pins can be connected directly to the Arduino pins. The display isn't very bright, however. See Figure 8-15.

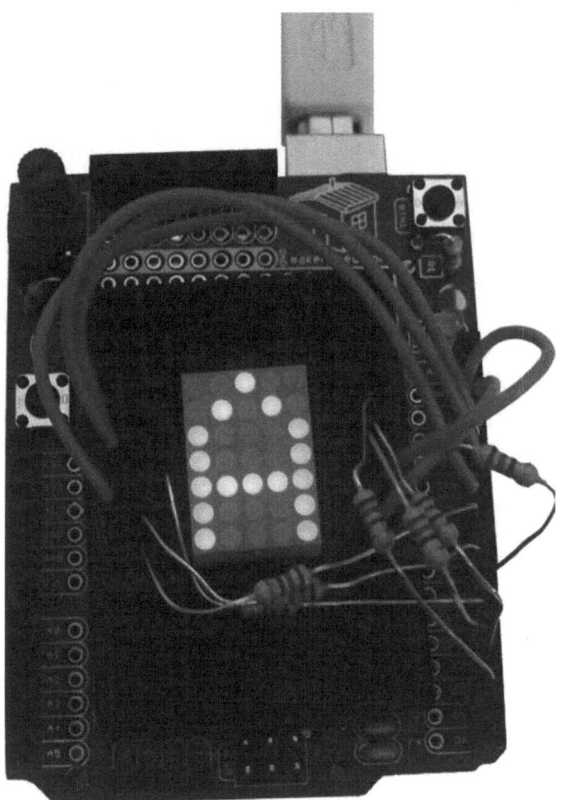

Figure 8-15. A 5 × 7 LED matrix driven by the Arduino pins, without column drivers. A is for Arduino.

This is caused by two important factors. The first is that all the current to drive an entire column of LEDs is being switched on and off by a single I/O pin. Remember that an Arduino's I/O lines are only supposed to handle up to 40mA of current. You can augment this current-handling bottleneck by adding a column-driver circuit. Remember to change the logic of your sketch if you add an *inverting* driver to the circuit.

The second factor is that the duty cycle of each column is only one in five. If the LED is supposed to be on, it's really on only 20% of the time, meaning it's *dark* 80% of the time. Once you've got your matrix-scanning sketch working properly, feel free to increase the current through each LED. It's only the *average* current over time that counts.

Extending this project requires more LEDs, more I/O pins (or additional hardware), and certainly more sophisticated software, unless your communication needs are satisfied with a single capital *A* or single LEDs. Tiny Pong, anyone?

Also available are preconfigured arrays of LEDs, complete with semi-intelligent controllers. Figure 8-16 (top) shows a 32 × 16 LED module from Sure Electronics in China. It's powered by 5V and has four Holtek HT1632 driver chips installed. Each pixel has both a red and a green LED installed. This allows for four possible color combinations: red, green, yellow, and black. More information about how to connect it to your Arduino can be found in the Arduino Playground: www.arduino.cc/playground/Main/HT1632C.

But wait, there's more! Why stop at two-dimensional LEDs when you can go 3D? See Figure 8-16 (bottom).

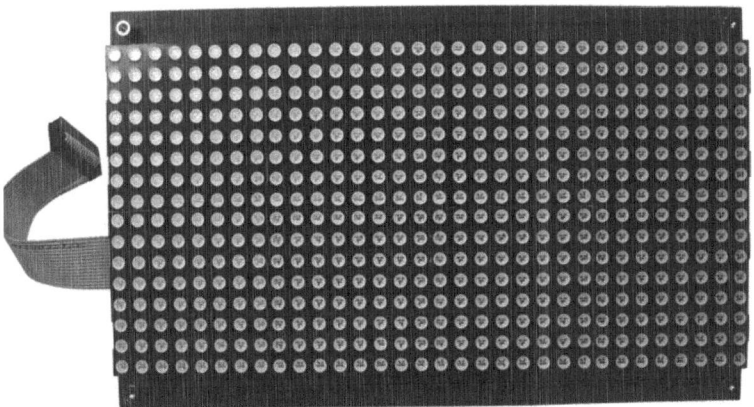

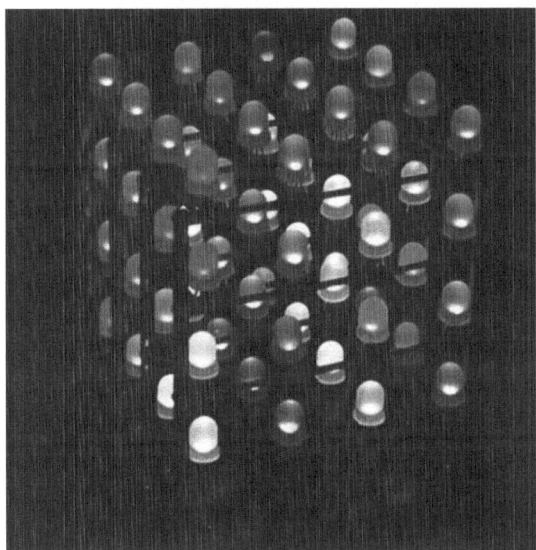

Figure 8-16. *A 32 × 16 bicolor (red + green) LED array with embedded drivers from Sure Electronics (top) and the 3D 4 × 4 × 4 RGB LED Cube kit from Seeed Studio (bottom).*

This beautiful sculpture in Figure 8-16 uses 64 LEDs, each one containing a red, green, and blue LED die.

Segment-Digit Multiplexing

You don't need 35 LEDs to display a message if your message is composed entirely of numerals. You can represent the Latin numerals 0–9 using just seven carefully arranged LEDs. See Figure 8-17.

Figure 8-17. *A seven-segment LED array can represent the numerals from 0–9, and a few letters, too. An eighth LED forms a right-hand decimal point.*

The LED segments of the numeric display are labeled *a* through *g*, starting at the top and going clockwise, and ending with the middle segment. Arrays such as this one are usually configured with either all the LED anodes or all the cathodes wired in common, and referred to as either *common anode* or *common cathode*. A common-cathode seven-segment LED module is shown schematically in Figure 8-18.

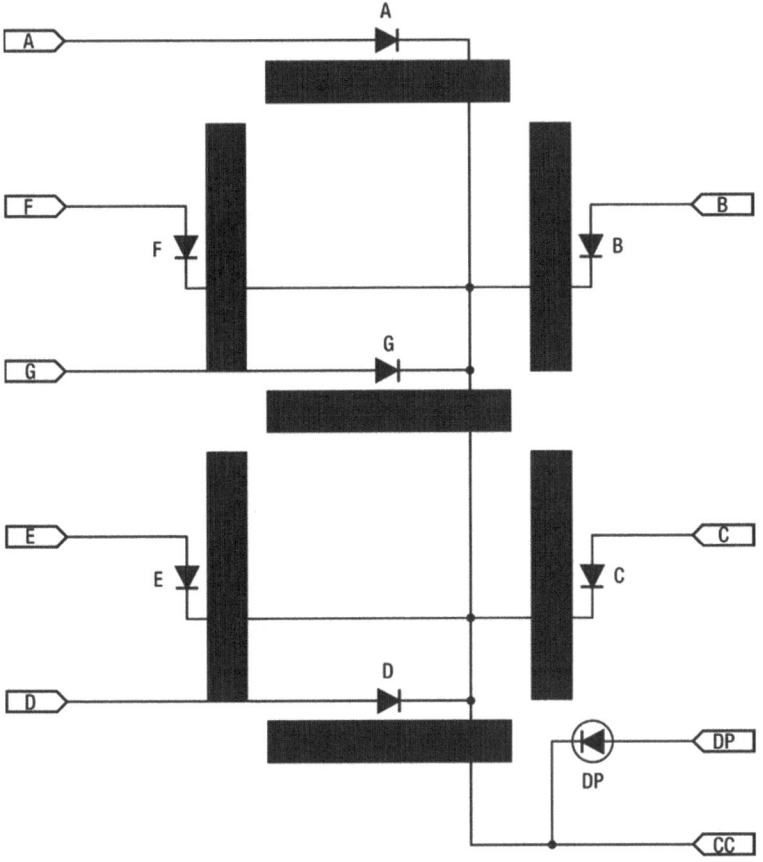

Figure 8-18. *The schematic diagram of a common-cathode, seven-segment LED module, with right-hand decimal point*

A single numeric digit can count from zero to nine. It can also display a limited number of letters and punctuation. See Listing 8-9.

Listing 8-9. *Demonstration Sketch for a Single Seven-Segment LED Display and a Pushbutton*

```
#define PUSH_BUTTON_INPUT 5

#define SEGMENT_A 6
#define SEGMENT_B 7
#define SEGMENT_C 8
#define SEGMENT_D 9
#define SEGMENT_E 10
#define SEGMENT_F 11
```

```
#define SEGMENT_G 12
#define SEGMENT_DP 13

void setup(void) {

  // push button input

  pinMode(PUSH_BUTTON_INPUT, INPUT); // this is an input
  digitalWrite(PUSH_BUTTON_INPUT, HIGH); // enable built-in pull-up resistor

  // turn off all LED outputs

  digitalWrite(SEGMENT_A, LOW);
  digitalWrite(SEGMENT_B, LOW);
  digitalWrite(SEGMENT_C, LOW);
  digitalWrite(SEGMENT_D, LOW);
  digitalWrite(SEGMENT_E, LOW);
  digitalWrite(SEGMENT_F, LOW);
  digitalWrite(SEGMENT_G, LOW);
  digitalWrite(SEGMENT_DP, LOW);

  // LED segments are all outputs

  pinMode(SEGMENT_A, OUTPUT);
  pinMode(SEGMENT_B, OUTPUT);
  pinMode(SEGMENT_C, OUTPUT);
  pinMode(SEGMENT_D, OUTPUT);
  pinMode(SEGMENT_E, OUTPUT);
  pinMode(SEGMENT_F, OUTPUT);
  pinMode(SEGMENT_G, OUTPUT);
  pinMode(SEGMENT_DP, OUTPUT);
}

// buttonPress() function returns TRUE if button is pressed, FALSE otherwise

#define TRUE 1
#define FALSE 0

int buttonPress(void) {

  if(digitalRead(PUSH_BUTTON_INPUT) == LOW) {
    return TRUE;
  } else {
    return FALSE;
  }
}

// LEDnumber() displays a single digit on the 7-segment LED display, 0-9

const byte LEDsegment[] = {
  // GFEDCBA
  0b00111111, // 0
```

```
    0b00000110, // 1
    0b01011011, // 2
    0b01001111, // 3
    0b01100110, // 4
    0b01101101, // 5
    0b01111101, // 6
    0b00000111, // 7
    0b01111111, // 8
    0b01101111, // 9
};

void LEDnumber(int number) {

  unsigned char i;

  if(number < 0) {
    for(i = SEGMENT_A; i <= SEGMENT_G; i++) digitalWrite(i, LOW); // turn off all segments
  } else {

    digitalWrite(SEGMENT_A, LEDsegment[number] & 0x01); // segment A
    digitalWrite(SEGMENT_B, LEDsegment[number] & 0x02); // segment B
    digitalWrite(SEGMENT_C, LEDsegment[number] & 0x04); // segment C
    digitalWrite(SEGMENT_D, LEDsegment[number] & 0x08); // segment D
    digitalWrite(SEGMENT_E, LEDsegment[number] & 0x10); // segment E
    digitalWrite(SEGMENT_F, LEDsegment[number] & 0x20); // segment F
    digitalWrite(SEGMENT_G, LEDsegment[number] & 0x40); // segment G
  }
}

#define DELAY_TIME 100 // 100 milliseconds = 0.1 seconds

void loop(void) {

  unsigned char x = 0;

  if(buttonPress()) {
    digitalWrite(SEGMENT_DP, HIGH); // turn on decimal point if button is pressed
  } else {
    digitalWrite(SEGMENT_DP, LOW); // else turn it off
  }

  LEDnumber(0); // display a 0
  delay(DELAY_TIME); // a short delay
  LEDnumber(1); // display a 1
  delay(DELAY_TIME); // a short delay
  LEDnumber(2); // display a 2
  delay(DELAY_TIME); // a short delay
  LEDnumber(3); // display a 3
  delay(DELAY_TIME); // a short delay
  LEDnumber(4); // display a 4
  delay(DELAY_TIME); // a short delay
  LEDnumber(5); // display a 5
```

```
    delay(DELAY_TIME); // a short delay
    LEDnumber(6); // display a 6
    delay(DELAY_TIME); // a short delay
    LEDnumber(7); // display a 7
    delay(DELAY_TIME); // a short delay
    LEDnumber(8); // display a 8
    delay(DELAY_TIME); // a short delay
    LEDnumber(9); // display a 9
    delay(DELAY_TIME); // a short delay

    LEDnumber(-1); // clear the LED display

    // now loop here forever & ever

    while(1) {

        while(buttonPress() == FALSE); // wait here for button to be pressed
        while(buttonPress() == TRUE); // wait here for button to be released

        LEDnumber(x);
        x++;
        if(x >= 10) x = 0; // start back over at zero
        delay(DELAY_TIME);
    }
}
```

This sketch starts out with some pin assignments in the form of several #define statements. Each segment, including the decimal point, is assigned to an individual I/O pin.

A momentary-contact pushbutton is connected between pin 5 and ground. The built-in pull-up resistor on pin 5 is enabled so that when the button isn't being pressed, the input pin's logical level is HIGH. When the button is pressed, the input pin is shorted to ground, and the input pins reads as a LOW.

A function called buttonPress() encapsulates this button logic, returning a TRUE value when the button is being pressed and a FALSE value when it isn't being pressed. This allows you to test the button's state using (semi-) intuitive statements such as if(buttonPress())....

The segment patterns for the numeric digits 0–9 are encoded in a const byte array called LEDsegment[].

Another function defined in the sketch is LEDnumber(), which takes a single parameter. If the parameter is negative, the LED display is blanked. Otherwise, the parameter is used as an index to the LEDsegment[] array, and the individual bits are tested to determine if the I/O lines should be set to a HIGH or LOW value, either turning on or turning off the respective segment.

The loop() function counts from 0 to 9 on the display and then goes into an infinite while() loop, waiting for the user to press a button. Each time the button is pressed (and released), the number on the LED display is incremented, starting back over at zero once the number exceeds nine.

Two digits can count from 0 to 99. This would be good for a seconds counter, for example. A two-digit, seven-segment display can be wired directly because it requires only 14 (2 × 7) LED drivers, which can be Arduino I/O pins.

You can control more digits with fewer I/O lines by using a variation of the row-column multiplexing technique. The individual segment lines are connected together (that is, all the a segments bussed together, all the b segments together, and so on), and the common lines—either common-anode or common-cathode—can be used to enable the individual modules. See Figure 8-19.

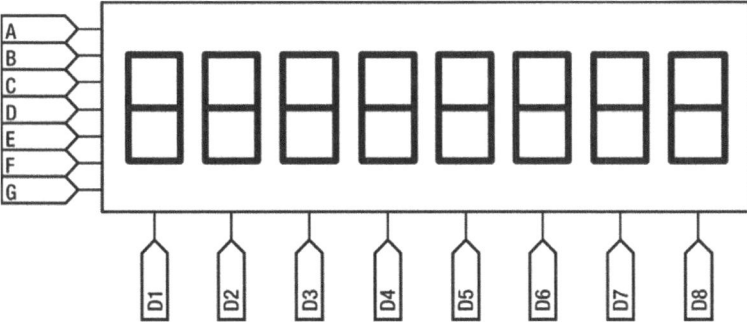

Figure 8-19. *An eight-digit, seven-segment LED display*

Just like the row-column multiplexing you did previously, there are two ways to scan a seven-segment LED display like this one. The first, and perhaps the more obvious approach, is to enable one digit at a time and then light up only those segments that belong to that digit. If repeated fast enough, all the digits appear to be illuminated simultaneously. Trickery! It serves you well.

Alternately, the opposite approach is to enable each of the segment lines individually and then drive all of the digits that currently want to display that segment.

A third approach, and one more suited for battery-powered applications such as digital watches, is to illuminate only one segment at a time. This works better than you might first imagine. It's the technique used on the delightful Solder : Time watch by SpikenzieLabs. See Figure 8-20.

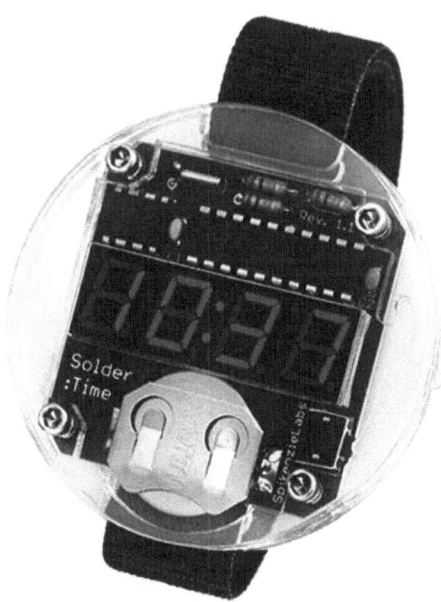

Figure 8-20. *The Solder : Time watch kit from SpikenzieLabs turns on only one segment at a time to conserve battery power, while still presenting a very readable LED display.*

Time-Domain Multiplexing (Persistence of Vision)

Another form of multiplexing substitutes one of the physical dimensions of the display with the time axis. This is properly called *time-domain multiplexing*, but you may know it by the more popular phrase *persistence of vision*.

For a basic persistence of vision (POV) display, only a single row of LEDs is required. The Blinky POV kit by Wayne and Layne is a perfect example. See Figure 8-21.

Figure 8-21. *The Blinky POV kit is a simple persistence of vision LED circuit that is available in kit form from Wayne and Layne (*http://wayneandlayne.com*). Photo by Wayne and Layne. Used with permission.*

The single row of LEDs flashes out a pattern of dots. Wave the unit around, and your eyes stitch together the dots to form a two-dimensional image. See Figure 8-22.

Figure 8-22. Wayne and Layne's Blinky POV kit in action. Photo by Wayne and Layne. Used with permission.

POV applications require maximum brightness from the LEDs, because their output is spread out over a larger area than normal. Make sure you give your POV LEDs all the power they can handle.

Charlieplexing

Need to light up a *lot* of LEDs but can't spare a lot of I/O lines? Charlieplexing may be the answer.

The LoL Shield

Jimmie P. Rodgers is an inventor, speaker, and teacher. Like Mitch Altman (and often *with* Mitch Altman), he travels the world, checking out crazy stuff and teaching people to solder and make things.

One of the things Jimmie makes (and sells) is the LoL Shield. *LoL* stands for Lots of LEDs. It's basically an experiment to see how many 3mm LEDs can fit on a standard Arduino shield. The answer to that question is: 126. See Figure 8-23.

Figure 8-23. *The LoL (Lots of LEDs) Shield by Jimmie P. Rodgers: a charlieplexed LED array in the form of an Arduino sheild*

At first glance, you might assume some sort of multiplexing was going on here, and you'd be right. But count again: that's a 9 × 14 rectangular matrix. It would take 9 + 14 (23) I/O lines to wire that up using row-column multiplexing. There are no hidden shift registers underneath, either. It uses a different type of multiplexing that is almost unique to LEDs: charlieplexing.

Charlieplexing was mentioned in application note 1880 from Maxim IC (`www.maxim-ic.com/app-notes/index.mvp/id/1880`) published February 10, 2003. Charlie Allen was mentioned as an early promoter of this technique to drive LEDs and save I/O pins, hence the name. Maxim IC also manufactures several LED driver chips that implement this technique in hardware. Earlier, in August 2001, Don Lancaster described this technique in his *Tech Musings* column (`www.tinaja.com/glib/muse152.pdf`), but he credits Microchip Technology with the idea. Mr. Lancaster, the inventor of the original color organ and author of dozens of technical books, describes charlieplexing as a problem in *n*-connectedness and compares it to string art.

Microchip published an application note titled "Complementary LED Drive" by Jean-Claude Rebic (`http://ww1.microchip.com/downloads/en/AppNotes/91029a.pdf`) in 1998.

Charlieplexing takes advantage of the both the *tri-state* capabilities of modern microcontroller I/O lines and the single-direction current-flow characteristics (polarization) of LEDs. The topology of charlieplexed LED displays is unique. An attempt at a simple explanation follows.

If you have three I/O lines available, how many LEDs can you uniquely address? Using a direct-drive approach, you can get up to three LEDs going. Using a row-column arrangement, only two (a 2 × 1 array).

Using charlieplexing, you can get six. How? By connecting an LED between every available I/O line and then connecting *another* LED *backward* between the same I/O lines. This gives you $n \times (n - 1)$ possible LEDs, where *n* is the number of I/O lines you can allocate to the LED display. The LoL Shield uses 12 I/O lines. See Figure 8-24.

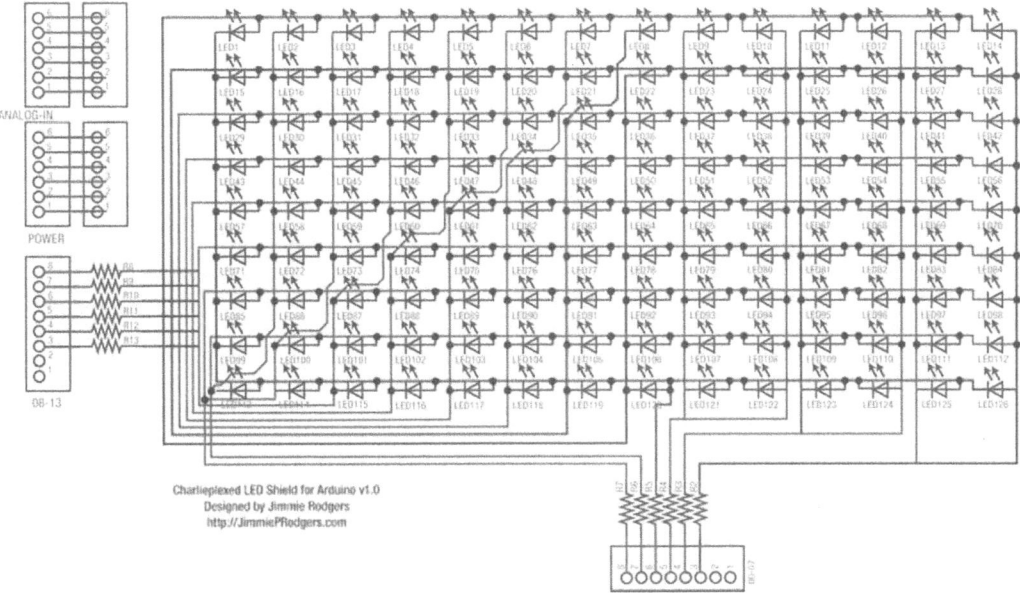

Figure 8-24. *The schematic of the LoL Shield by Jimmie P. Rodgers*

This is version 1.0 of the LoL Shield. The current version corrects a small ghosting problem caused by the preinstalled LED on D13 that comes with most modern Arduinos. You can, alternatively, remove either the LED or its associated current-limiting resistor to avoid the ghosting problem.

So here you have 126 (of a possible 132) LEDs controlled by only 12 I/O lines. Amazing!

A Digital Clock

First, a disclaimer: This is *not* a very good digital clock. It's the beginning of a really nice digital clock project, but only that: a beginning. Let's look at what it does and how it does it. Then you can think about possible (mandatory?) upgrades and some of the ways you might want to implement them.

Building a *good* digital clock is a bit outside the scope of this chapter. But after working on this project, you should have a good idea of what would be involved in taking this project to the next level, should you desire to do so. If not, please feel free to skip to the next chapter.

Figure 8-25 is the schematic of the clock. It's drawn as an Arduino shield, but unless your digital clock needs an USB interface, it may be easier to drop a processor and related support circuitry onto this circuit and have a stand-alone clock.

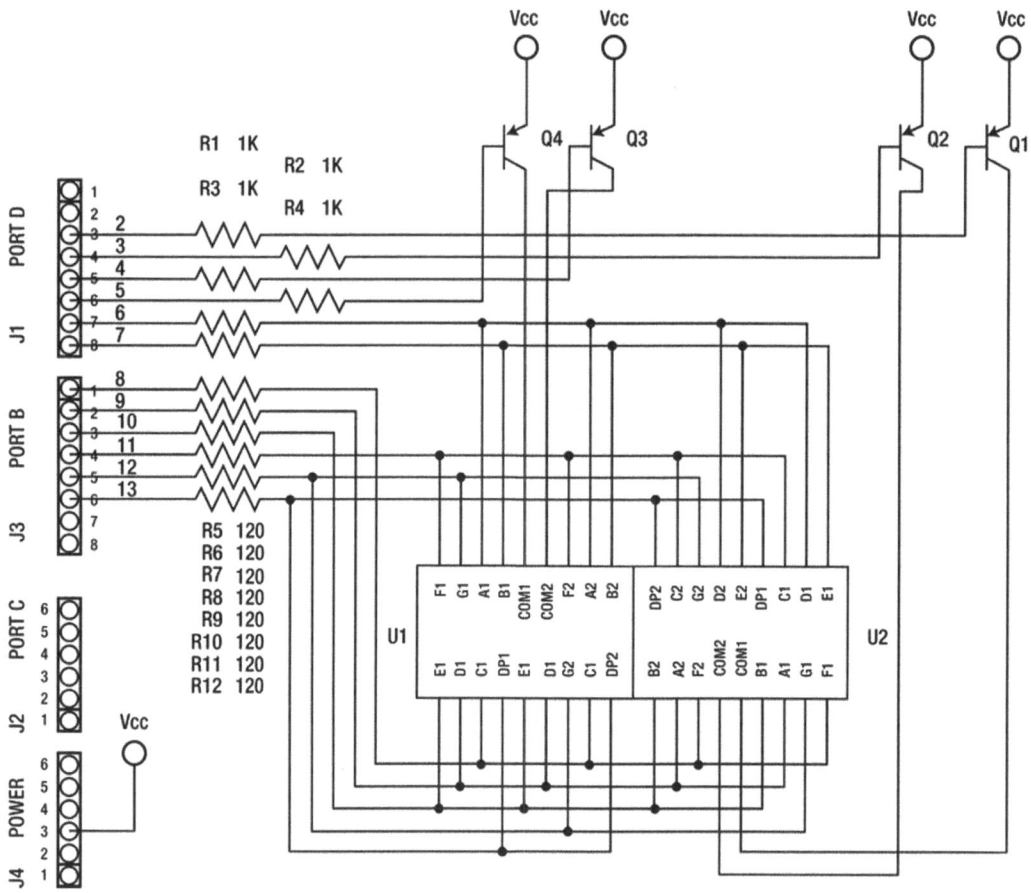

Figure 8-25. *The schematic diagram of a digital clock shield*

Arduino pins 2–5 provide the digit-driver signals. The PNP BJTs, Q1–Q4, switch the common anodes of the MAN6110 dual 7 segment LED display modules to V_{cc} when their bases are driven low. This is the opposite behavior that you saw with the other polarity, NPN, in previous driver circuits.

Arduino pins 6–13 drive the segments directly, with current-limiting resistors in series. Because the segments of the module are the cathodes of the LEDs inside, the voltage presented on the Arduino pin must be low to turn on the segment.

Each of the MAN6110 modules has two complete seven-segment arrays with right-hand decimal points. The pins on the module aren't bussed together. What may not be obvious from the schematic is that the right-hand module is rotated 180° so that its decimal points are on the top side instead of the bottom. The wiring of the segments accommodates this rotation. This was done to create a colon between the two center digits. See Figure 8-26.

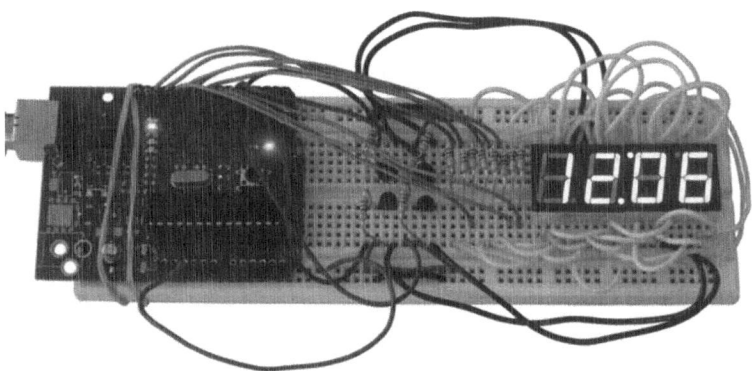

Figure 8-26. The digital clock prototype built on a solderless breadboard

Listing 8-10 shows the sketch for the prototype digital clock.

Listing 8-10. Outline for a Digital Clock Sketch

```
volatile byte seconds_units = 0;
volatile byte seconds_tens = 0;
volatile byte minutes_units = 0;
volatile byte minutes_tens = 0;
volatile byte hours_units = 2;
volatile byte hours_tens = 1;

const byte numerals[10] = {
  ~0b00111111, // 0
  ~0b00000110, // 1
  ~0b01011011, // 2
  ~0b01001111, // 3
  ~0b01100110, // 4
  ~0b01101101, // 5
  ~0b01111101, // 6
  ~0b00000111, // 7
  ~0b01111111, // 8
  ~0b01101111, // 9
};

void setup() {

  // digit drivers - active low
  pinMode(2, OUTPUT); // digit 1 - right
  pinMode(3, OUTPUT); // digit 2
  pinMode(4, OUTPUT); // digit 3
  pinMode(5, OUTPUT); // digit 4 - left

  // segments - active low
  pinMode(6, OUTPUT); // segment a
```

```
    pinMode(7, OUTPUT); // segment b
    pinMode(8, OUTPUT); // segment c
    pinMode(9, OUTPUT); // segment d
    pinMode(10, OUTPUT); // segment e
    pinMode(11, OUTPUT); // segment f
    pinMode(12, OUTPUT); // segment g
    pinMode(13, OUTPUT); // segment DP, also Arduino LED

    // turn LEDs "off"
    digitalWrite(2, HIGH); // digit 1 off
    digitalWrite(3, HIGH); // digit 2 off
    digitalWrite(4, HIGH); // digit 3 off
    digitalWrite(5, HIGH); // digit 4 off

    // set up 1 second interrupt on Timer/counter1
    TCCR1A = 0;
    TCCR1B = 1<<WGM13 | 1<<WGM12 | 1<<CS12 | 1<<CS10; // clock = F_CPU / 1024 = 15625 Hz
    ICR1 = 15625;
    bitSet(TIMSK1, ICIE1); // enable capture event interrupt

    // set up ~240Hz interrupt on Timer/Counter2
    TCCR2A = 0;
    TCCR2B = 6; // select CK/256
    bitSet(TIMSK2, TOIE2); // enable overflow interrupt
}

void loop() {
    // nothing happens here!
}

void drawSegment(byte index) {
    digitalWrite(6, numerals[index] & 0x01); // segment a
    digitalWrite(7, numerals[index] & 0x02); // segment b
    digitalWrite(8, numerals[index] & 0x04); // segment c
    digitalWrite(9, numerals[index] & 0x08); // segment d
    digitalWrite(10, numerals[index] & 0x10); // segment e
    digitalWrite(11, numerals[index] & 0x20); // segment f
    digitalWrite(12, numerals[index] & 0x40); // segment g
}

ISR(TIMER1_CAPT_vect) {

    // keep time:  this interrupt should happen once every second

    seconds_units++; // count seconds x 1
    if(seconds_units > 9) {
      seconds_units = 0; // reset seconds x 1
      seconds_tens++; // count seconds x 10
```

```
    if(seconds_tens > 5) {
      seconds_tens = 0; // reset seconds x 10
      minutes_units++; // count minutes x 1
      if(minutes_units > 9) {
        minutes_units = 0; // reset minutes x 1
        minutes_tens++; // count minutes x 10
        if(minutes_tens > 5) {
          minutes_tens = 0; // reset minutes x 10
          hours_units++; // count hours x 1
          if(hours_units > 9) {
            hours_units = 0; // reset hours x 1
            hours_tens++; // count hours x 10
          }
          if((hours_units == 3) && (hours_tens == 1)) {
            hours_units = 1;
            hours_tens = 0;
          }
        }
      }
    }
  }
}

ISR(TIMER2_OVF_vect) {

  // tell time:  this interrupt should happen 240 times a second

  static byte digit = 0;

  // turn on the correct digit 0-3

  switch(digit) {
    case 0:
      digitalWrite(13, HIGH); // turn off decimal point
      digitalWrite(5, HIGH); // digit 4 off
      drawSegment(minutes_units);
      digitalWrite(2, LOW); // digit 1 on
      break;
    case 1:
      digitalWrite(13, LOW); // turn on decimal point
      digitalWrite(2, HIGH); // digit 1 off
      drawSegment(minutes_tens);
      digitalWrite(3, LOW); // digit 2 on
      break;
    case 2:
      digitalWrite(13, LOW); // turn on decimal point
      digitalWrite(3, HIGH); // digit 2 off
      drawSegment(hours_units);
      digitalWrite(4, LOW); // digit 3 on
      break;
```

```
    case 3:
      digitalWrite(13, HIGH); // turn off decimal point
      digitalWrite(4, HIGH); // digit 2 off
      drawSegment(hours_tens);
      digitalWrite(5, LOW); // digit 3 on
      break;
  }

  digit++; // move on to the next digit
  if(digit > 3) digit = 0; // roll over
}
```

Some global variables are declared at the beginning of the sketch. These represent the individual digits that are displayed on the clock. It's easier to increment and test these single-digit values than to try to extract them later using integer division and bit masking.

The bit patterns for the segments are stored in a `const byte` array called `numerals[]`. Because the segments in the example clock circuit are active low, the segment binary values are specified with a tilde (~) prefix, indicating they should be inverted by the compiler. This could be done with a single instruction in the function that actually writes the segment values out to the pins, but why? It's constant data, and it's not going to change in the course of the sketch's execution. There's no reason to code it wrong and have the Arduino fix it at runtime.

The `setup()` function first initializes the direction of the output pin and then sets the digit-driver outputs `HIGH` to turn off all the LEDs at once. Remember that the signal levels in this circuit are all active low.

The `setup()` function then configures both Timer/Counter 1 and Timer/Counter 2 to generate periodic interrupts. Timer/Counter 1 is used to generate a 1-second time base, using the Input Capture Event interrupt. Timer/Counter 2 provides a ~240Hz interrupt that schedules the multiplexing of the display digits. Each time through the Timer/Counter 2 overflow interrupt, one digit is decoded and displayed. This is done by sending the numeric value to be displayed to the `drawSegment()` function, which looks up the correct bit pattern in the `numerals[]` array and sends it to the segment drivers. This ensures that the entire display is refreshed at 60Hz.

The actual timekeeping is done in the Timer/Counter 1 Input Capture Event interrupt. Each of the hours, minutes, and seconds values is broken down into the tens and units (ones) digits and maintained separately. The `seconds_units` variable is incremented each time the interrupt is triggered. When it passes the value of nine, it's reset, and the `seconds_tens` value is incremented. This process cascades all the way through the timekeeping variables.

A special case is invoked when the clock rolls over from 12:59 to 1:00. It would be easier to code a 24-hour clock, where 12:00 means 12 hours past midnight and 00:00 means midnight.

Notice that nothing at all happens in the `loop()` function. Everything is interrupt-driven in this example. This leaves lots of room to add new features, which are sorely needed.

This example works, but just barely. It could be the beginning of a really nice clock project, as previously stated. Let's take a look at some of the areas that need more work.

Accuracy

The first thing wrong with this clock is that it doesn't do the one thing you most (or only) expect from a time piece: it (probably) doesn't keep very good time. Its internal time base is derived from the Arduino system clock, which is only as accurate as the component driving it. If you have an Arduino that has a 16MHz quartz crystal, your clock is good for ±100ppm (parts per million). This means, in real-world terms, that your clock will gain or lose as much as 4 minutes in a 30-day period. That's not exactly *horrible*, but it's not good, either. This number will vary with temperature and the age of the crystal, as well.

If you have one of the newer Arduinos, your processor could be clocked by a ceramic resonator. If that is the case, the overall accuracy of the system oscillator is only ±1%, meaning you can gain or lose *over 7 hours* in the same 30-day period. This is certainly unacceptable in any real clock application. It's not even especially good for an egg timer.

What other time base can be used? On the Arduino Mega 2560, an external 32KHz watch crystal can be attached to TOSC1 and TOSC2, and Timer/Counter 2 can be clocked from it, asynchronously from the system clock. Even modestly priced watch crystals have much better tolerances than the typical quartz crystals used for microcontroller circuits.

An external time base is most definitely the way to go if long-term accuracy and stability are important design criteria in your next clock project. There are a wide variety of self-contained timer chips that can easily be added to your clock circuit. Some even include leap-year-aware calendars and alarm functions.

For the most accuracy for your money, you should look for a temperature-compensated crystal oscillator (TCXO). These circuits take into account a crystal's variance over temperature, which is the main source of error.

The 60Hz frequency of the main power grid in the US and other countries (50Hz elsewhere) isn't accurate in the short term, but it's exceedingly accurate over a long period of time. Most commercial digital clocks use this frequency standard to achieve timing accuracies that are better than one second per month.

A circuit to measure the frequency of the incoming power assumes access to AC voltages, which should be stepped down by a transformer first. The Arduino has a built-in voltage comparator available that you can use for the purpose, even generating an interrupt when the right time comes along.

If your Arduino is still feeding off the power from your PC, why not send it a time signal from a time server on the Internet? This could be done once per hour or even once per day, allowing the Arduino to freewheel the rest of the time, relying on its own, admittedly inaccurate time base in the between-times.

You have a couple of other solutions to the time-base problem. In the US, the WWV system transmits a radio signal that repeats every minute. You need a special radio receiver to decode this signal, but they're available. Most GPS receivers have a high-accuracy timing signal available, but not all of them wire this signal to the outside where it's easy to get at. You're looking for a 1PPS signal (one pulse per second) or something similar.

Finally, if you really don't want to rely on someone else for your timing, consider setting up your own *primary* timing reference, also known as an *atomic clock*. Many older cell-phone towers had their own rubidium-based atomic clocks, and a lot of these are finding their way into the surplus markets to be had for a mere fraction of their original cost. They generally require 24V and about half an hour to warm up, but once they do, they're *spot on*.

User Interface

There is no provision in this prototype for setting the time. This is a glaring omission, unless you can conveniently plug it in at either noon or midnight, in which case you're covered.

It might also be nice to momentarily look at the seconds portion of the time, or perhaps keep track of AM/PM or (gasp) maintain a calendar so you could know what day it was. All of these user interface functions could be handled using a state machine to keep track of the current mode.

Additional Features

An alarm function would be nice, as long as it's not *too* alarming. This would also present a user-interface design challenge. You could either go old school and make it work just like every other digital clock in the world, or you could come up with something new and interesting.

A battery backup would be really useful, in the event of a power outage. You only get so many "my alarm clock didn't go off" excuses, you know. Most of the external timekeeping chips have provisions for battery backup, so maybe this issue gets resolved when the time base is upgraded.

Real digital clocks, like the kind you buy at the store of $10 or less, automatically darken the LED display when the ambient lighting lowers. A light sensor can tell you how bright it is in the immediate vicinity, but how are you going to dim the display? Although the wiring in this example was arbitrarily chosen to make it easy to draw and to build on a breadboard, the sketch treats every wire as an individual and only wants to be told which wire goes where. There's nothing that says the digit drivers can't be connected to 4 of the 6 (or 16) PWM outputs. Just remember that the digit drivers are *active low*. Also remember that you've hijacked two of the three internal timers that are used for the PWM outputs.

A flashing colon might be a nice feature, or it might be plain annoying. Colons usually flash at 2Hz. How can you generate a 2Hz signal within this sketch? You don't actually have to do that. Just look at the value in the Timer/Counter 1 counter register and see if it's past the half-way mark on its way to a full second. If that condition is met, turn on the colon. If not, turn it off. Note that the example sketch turns on the colon within the display-update interrupt handler, but only in the cases where the inner two digits are being updated.

So there's your digital clock. Make something interesting out of it.

Summary

The Arduino and the LED: it's a love story that not everyone gets. But some people get it. Do you?

These are just a few of the many fun and exciting projects you can build with an Arduino and very little else. Let your creativity run wild, and be thinking of other cool LED projects that you can whip together over a weekend.

But enough of these basic topics. Let's get into the really hard-core design and implementation issues that you encounter with more complex projects.

Don't look directly at the LEDs!

CHAPTER 9

Project Management

You thought it would be easy. You imagined a simple device that performed a simple function. How hard could it be? Well, now you know. It started off simple enough, but you went and added *features* to it.

This chapter deals with the aftermath of your project, as well as some possible development issues should the project spill over to another programmer (or programmers), designers, makers, and users. You cover the vitally important topic of project documentation and how it can be of immense use to you even before the beginning, as well as during development and after deployment.

This chapter is all about communication: not bits and bytes between chips, but ideas and concepts between people. Every complex problem can be broken down into smaller, more *manageable* problems. It's the improved and enhanced management of these problems that is addressed here. Better communication makes this task easier.

You're going to need some help along the way. Maybe you'll only need a little help, like a suggestion about how to approach a problem, or the answer to a simple question. The good news is that you're not alone. Help is ready and waiting. A lot of excellent resources, mostly people, are here and willing to help. Learn about them, avail yourself to them, and soon it will be your turn to share, to help someone else, and all are thereby enriched.

Documentation

You have several very effective weapons with which to combat the increasing complexity of your design. The first and most effective weapon in your arsenal is *documentation*. Write it down. That's all it takes. It doesn't have to be fancy or even very detailed, but it does need to be accurate and as complete as you can make it.

Pretend that you're actually still going to be interested in this project in three months and may want to go back and understand "Just what was I thinking?" at some crucial point in the design process. You'll most certainly need more than some arcane program sketches and tangles of wire to figure this out.

Better yet, pretend that *someone else* will take an interest in your design. For all you know, they may even want to follow in your pioneering footsteps and re-create your clever invention for themselves. Show them the way. Leave a trail of breadcrumbs. Write it down.

■ **Note** If you don't write it down, it didn't happen.

Source-Code Comments

You already have one of the simplest yet most powerful tools at your disposal to help document your projects. Can you guess what it is? It's the code editor in the Arduino software.

If you type in the magical characters // (two forward slashes), you can type *anything you want* from there to the end of the line. The editor saves these program comments along with all the real code in your sketch, and even remembers to bring them back when you reopen the file in the future. Even more amazing, the compiler completely disregards these comments and properly and efficiently works on the real code only. You can write *anything* in these comments. You can wax poetical, describe your inner feelings, spin yarns about distant worlds … or ~~explain your ridiculously convoluted attempt at programming a computer~~ document your most elegant solution to the problem at hand.

There's no excuse *not* to properly document your code by using a bunch of single-line comments here and there. If you get really wordsome, you can use block comments, beginning with the /* character sequence and ending with the reverse, */. This latter method lets you span multiple lines of code without having to introduce each line with the double-slashes. See Listing 9-1.

Listing 9-1. Good Use of Program Comments

```
// filename.pde
// This is the main file in the "example" sketch
// Written by A. Programmer on 31 Dec 2099, email@example.com
// Placed in the Public Domain
// Based on examples found at arduino.cc
// version 1.1
```

...or...

```
/* filename.pde
   This is the main file in the "example" sketch
   Written by A. Programmer on 31 Dec 2099, email@example.com
   Placed in the Public Domain
   Based on examples found at arduino.cc
   version 1.1
*/
```

Here are some *general* guidelines to good commenting:

- Use comments generously.

- Put the most important information first, where it's easy to find when searching.

- Write for your audience: specifically humans, not machines.

- Be thinking of *who* is going to read these comments, *when*, and *why*.

- Explain, giving context, before defining.

- Cite your sources; give attribution where it is due, even if it's yourself.

- If your sketch has more than one file, list all those files on the first page.

- Always list any special dependencies or requirements (for example, libraries or hardware) in detail.

- Don't be cryptic or lazy; neither is helpful.

- Explain any clever or non-obvious bits in detail.

- Use more comments.

It's a good habit to practice. The more you practice, the better you'll get, and the easier it will be. The rewards are certainly worth the effort.

The examples in this book have had scandalously few comments inserted, in an effort to make the overall program listings less intimidating. It's a sad but true phenomenon that even creative and talented folk sometimes go all blurry-eyed when confronted with a big slab of code. This isn't true of everyone, of course, but it affects enough readers to warrant keeping the comments in the examples here to a minimum.

Whitespace

Claude Debussey is quoted as saying, "Music is the space between the notes." The *whitespace* in a program listing (that is, the spaces between words and lines of text) helps to visually separate and define the various elements involved. When this helps to communicate the meaning and intent of the programmer, it's a good thing.

The compiler ignores whitespace, for the most part. One of the first phases of the interpretation of the source code, long before it's resolved into ones and zeros, is the wholesale massacre of whitespace. The laws of syntax implicit in the grammar of the C language allow each and every individual *token*, or unique program element, to be identified without the presence of decorative whitespace, with only a few exceptions.

Whitespace, like source code, is for people. It makes things easier to read. It breaks up otherwise tedious or incomprehensible blobs of text, turning them into sentences, paragraphs, couplets, and verses.

Listing 9-2 is your old friend, the example sketch Blink, provided with the Arduino software. It's a good example of the use of both single-line and block comments, as well as whitespace. Comments are in light-gray. Compare it with Listing 9-3, which is, from a machine standpoint, identical. Which one would you rather read?

Listing 9-2. *The Blink Example Sketch*

```
/*
  Blink
  Turns on an LED on for one second, then off for one second, repeatedly.

  This example code is in the public domain.
*/

void setup() {
  // initialize the digital pin as an output.
  // Pin 13 has an LED connected on most Arduino boards:
  pinMode(13, OUTPUT);
}
```

```
void loop() {
  digitalWrite(13, HIGH);    // set the LED on
  delay(1000);               // wait for a second
  digitalWrite(13, LOW);     // set the LED off
  delay(1000);               // wait for a second
}
```

Listing 9-3. *The Blink Example Sketch as the Compiler Sees It*

```
void setup(){pinMode(13,OUTPUT);}
void loop(){digitalWrite(13,HIGH);delay(1000);digitalWrite(13,LOW);delay(1000);}
```

Both sketches compile to exactly the same size and perform identically. Which one would you rather maintain? Which one would you rather debug? Which one would you use to teach your children to program? To which one would you sign your name?

Note that a single space is still required after the return-type identified void. This is usually the case with any modifier, such as unsigned int or volatile byte. Otherwise, all that nice space evaporates away.

In this era of free gigabyte e-mail accounts and low-cost terabyte hard drives, the cost of whitespace is almost incalculable. Consider it free. Use it accordingly.

Code What You Mean, Mean What You Code

Use meaningful names in your code. Except for the setup(), loop(), and interrupt handler functions, you get to name everything, including functions, variable, and even filenames.

Every chance you get, be descriptive. It's OK to use i, j, and k as variable names when they're used as simple iterators. If they're going to hold any other values, take a minute and give those variables decent names that reflect their function and purpose in your sketch. Be concise, but please don't be afraid of typing a few more characters here and there. Future generations will thank you. The only names you *can't* use are the keywords of the compiler, such as if, while, continue, and so on.

When possible, use functions as subroutines to help reduce repetitive code. Breaking up the problem into smaller problems is the first step toward solving the overall problem. Breaking your code up into meaningful, abstract functions helps spell out your algorithmic intent. This has an overall space-saving advantage as well.

Functions should be well documented, both internally and externally. Internally, there should be at least some indication, in the form of a program comment, of why the function exists and what task it's expected to perform. Additionally, it's helpful if the parameters, if any, that are to be supplied by the caller are explained in detail, along with some interpretation of the return value, if any.

Data structures should also be carefully documented. Even scalar variables should have some clues associated with them as to their purpose, function, and usage. A good variable name is a good start, but a meaningful comment doesn't hurt, either.

These are all good suggestions for the documentation of your project that you can embed within the source code itself. Remember, however, that all the comments get thrown away by the compiler and don't get to go live with the executable code in the Great Upload in the Sky. Consider providing them a more permanent afterlife in the form of a user manual, or at least a theory of operation note attached to the source code.

Externally—that is, in a separate document—the overall operation as well as each of the functions should be documented with at least as much information as is presented in the source code (intended purpose, parameters, return value, and so on). Additionally, a diagram or description of the program's hierarchy, illustrating the relationships between the various modules, will help developers now and later to understand the context in which each element belongs—the big picture, so to speak.

This external user manual of the program's inner workings should also help paint a picture of the various algorithms and data structures that are being used in the sketch. Even the simplest example sketches like your favorite, Blink, can be categorized as a procedural algorithm: that is, do this, then do that, then do this other thing; repeat. If your sketch uses a loop within another loop, take the time to explain why. This is *not* always obvious to a third party. Be specific when you can.

One problem that often crops up in writing good documentation is that it sometimes lags behind changes in the code. Here is a common scenario: the code is written, tested, approved, and shipped. Meticulous detail was taken to document all the major aspects of its operation. Then a bug is reported from the field, a source code change is made to address it, and somehow this improvement fails to make it into the annals of history. Now the project and its documentation are out of sync. This can only lead to trouble when those tasked with maintaining the project's design rely on the documentation to provide a trustworthy source of internal information and insight.

Automated Documentation

There are several ways to help automate this documentation process, each with its own strengths and weaknesses. A good example is the documentation for the `avr-libc` library, which relies on the Doxygen documentation suite. The entire documentation package for this critically important piece of software is automatically generated from program comments contained in the source code for the library. As pointed out in Chapter 7, these comments aren't all correctly updated. This results in the downhill seep of error into the documentation. Even though the documentation process itself has been automated, it still doesn't work by magic. A saying as old as computers themselves states it succinctly: "Garbage in, garbage out."

This is no indictment of the Doxygen automated documentation software used to produce the `avr-libc` manual. It does its job. The problem goes back to the original source code, and simple errors made, usually when large changes are made to the code to accommodate new devices.

Doxygen works by using specially coded comments in the source code. This is similar to the Javadoc system that is available for Java programmers, as well as many other automated documentation systems. The C# language supports documentation comments but isn't well-supported by real-world products at this time.

The Arduino software supplies no automated documentation system, nor does it endorse any particular form of documentation.

Writing For Your Audience

Your source code has an audience. The audience is the compiler. The compiler is pretty specific about what it will accept. This helps narrow down the otherwise-unlimited array of potential sketches you might try to compile.

Although it's possible for humans to read your source code, they aren't the intended audience. The comments contained in your source code *are* intended for human consumption, however, so please write them accordingly.

For example: people like to detect patterns. They like to see relationships among various items. This is the beginning of understanding. People like to understand things, at least to the point that they can effectively utilize something to their benefit.

Anywhere from zero to a very large number of people will come into contact with your handiwork. Some of these people will want to see how it works, in the broadest possible sense, without delving into the actual implementation details. A good example is someone looking at your Arduino code and thinking about using the underlying algorithms and data structures on a different platform to accomplish something similar to what you've accomplished. Others will want to scrutinize every detail, looking for possible optimizations or vulnerabilities (and not always in a helpful way). Talk to these people in your writing, both in your code and in your other documentation. Let them know what you were thinking, what you intended to do, and potentially even why you discarded alternative approaches. This will help *you* most of all, if you ever get the chance to come back to this place in your history. It will most certainly help others following in your footsteps.

Some people coming across your creations will be interested in learning only enough to use it toward their own goals. This typically describes the largest part of your audience: the users. Maybe this is someone wanting to incorporate one of your useful libraries of functionality into their own projects: for example, a particularly well-optimized hardware driver for a special peripheral. Or perhaps it's the end user, the person or persons you originally intended to benefit from your work. Talk to these people as well. Get them going quickly, with enough information to accomplish their intentions, but not so much as to overburden them with needless implementation trivia.

Know your audience, anticipate their questions, and help them achieve something close to your state of enlightenment. You figured it out. Now your job is to pass that knowledge onward. A cryptic sketch and a tangle of wires are just not good enough. You can do better than that.

Hardware Documentation

Does your latest experiment involve some special hardware? If so, you need to document that, as well.

Even if you use common or popular hardware, please consider documenting how it's used in your project. What is common or popular today isn't always so. Just because the vendor of that handy Arduino shield posts a datasheet on its web site today, don't assume this will live on through the ages.

The best way to start with your hardware documentation is by drawing a block diagram and labeling all the major components. Do this first from a functional perspective. Show the inputs, the outputs, and that middle part. Show any special power supplies or connectors needed. Give every block item a name. Then go back and break down each block, describing *what it does* and only then *how it does it*. By disassociating the intention from the implementation, you can later come back and easily augment or improve your design as newer technologies emerge.

Once upon a time, a 20MB hard drive with a controller could cost over $1,000. Then you had the privilege of writing your own device driver for it. Today, multigigabyte SD cards cost less than a cup of fancy coffee. The hardware to interface it to your circuit is similarly inexpensive. Libraries to use the two together are free for the taking.

Don't assume that the solution you envision today is the only possible solution to the design problem at hand. By decoupling the *what* from the *how*, you can take advantage of the potential of others' work in the future.

Your block diagram can be as simple as "here is the Arduino" and "here is the shield" and "here are the things that plug into the shield." Start at a high level, and work your way downward. See Figure 9-1.

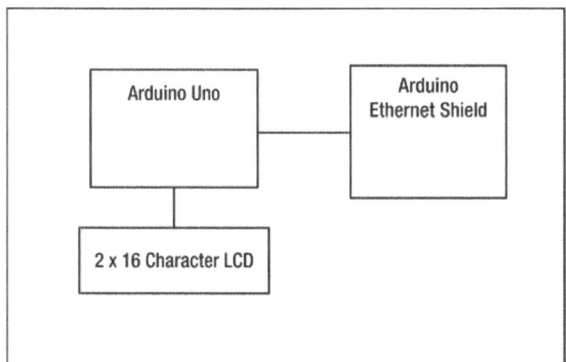

Figure 9-1. *A simple block diagram shows the high level organization of your project.*

You can later go into more detail about the individual components, as shown in Figure 9-2.

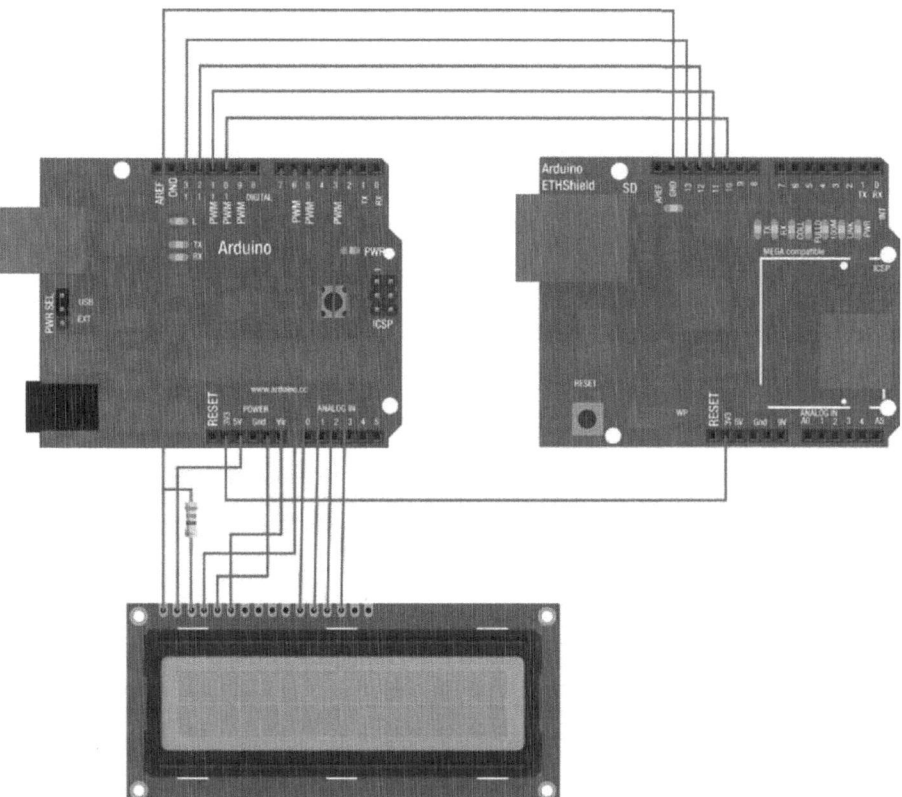

Figure 9-2. *A more detailed block diagram*

If you're designing your own circuit that will plug into your Arduino, you can go about documenting that circuit in a number of ways. The traditional approach has been to draw an electronic schematic, as described in Chapter 4. This isn't strictly required. It may be easier to simply take a picture of a prototype you've built, as long as enough information is visible to be able to understand what is going on in your circuit. Once you've gone past a very basic level of complexity, however, this solution won't serve you well enough.

If your intention is to show others how to re-create your design, a schematic is almost considered mandatory. Remember, a schematic is nothing more than a stylized representation of the essential elements of any system, along with indications of the relationships between those elements. In an electrical schematic, those elements are usually electronic components and connectors, and the relationships between them are usually wires. For a schematic diagram of this project, see Chapter 12.

Going Further

If you want to go past the prototype stage with your design, you need more documentation. The needs change depending on what you're inventing: hardware, software, or a combination of the two. It doesn't end there, however. Maybe you're designing decorative sleeves for your Arduino projects, or cool stickers to put on the project box. All of these things have to be written down, drawn up, and sent off to someone else, more than likely.

Software

The nice thing about software is that it usually doesn't weigh much. This makes it easier to distribute. Even so, it needs a nice box to travel in and perhaps a letter of introduction for when it arrives at its destination.

The Arduino software stores sketches in a file with an extension of `.ino`, as of the Arduino 1.0 release. Previous versions used the traditional Processing sketch extension, `.pde`. The software also organizes your sketches by putting each one in a folder by itself. That folder usually has the same name as your sketch. To share your sketch with someone else, you need only provide them with the sketch file itself. When the next user opens the sketch, the Arduino software offers to automatically create a proper folder for it to live in.

If your sketch is simple enough, you may get away with a well-written summary contained within the sketch in the form of succinct program comments. Anything that isn't obvious should be spelled out in detail, such as library usage or special hardware.

Beyond a very small range of trivial applications, you should seriously consider including a README file along with your sketch and other files. This is a good place to include an overview of the care and feeding of your creation. Also apropos would be contact information, should the user want to ask questions or suggest improvements.

Always include a revision number of some sort with each release, even if it's 0.00. Each time a change is made, *please* jot down a note about what changed and why, and then bump the revision level appropriately.

Have you decided how you want to license your valuable intellectual property? If so, do include a note to that effect in the project documentation. More on your licensing options later in this chapter.

Hardware

Hardware, the kind that is made of atoms and such, occupies space, costs money, and usually has a fixed shelf life. It almost certainly needs some sort of documentation attached, affixed, or associated with it.

Sometimes that's as simple as clearly labeling the power switch with ON and OFF markers. Please bear in mind that not everyone reads English. Iconography, however, sometimes leaves a lot to be desired. Consider the "e-mail or bacon" switch found in some cars, which was *supposed* to indicate a vent control.

As mentioned previously, if your hardware contains electronics, you should think about including a schematic diagram along with your other documentation. A schematic can serve several functions. It can be used to explain how the circuit works. It can serve as model for a detailed theory of operation. It can be used to assist in troubleshooting and diagnosing problems. It can also be the basis for a printed circuit board (PCB) design.

A PCB requires even more specialized documentation. Even if you're making your own PCBs at home, you still need to convert the boxes and squiggly lines of the schematic into actual pads and traces, representing the copper layer, along with an indication of the board's outline (sometimes called the *border* or *profile*) and where the holes, if any, need to be drilled. You learn more about PCBs and hardware design in Chapter 10.

Sometimes hardware is simply the hardware: the brackets, screws, covers, and other non-electrical components of your project. Whatever you envision, there's a kind of drawing (or *drafting*) specifically for that.

Are you using off-the-shelf parts in your design? Then tell where to get them, what they're called, and what users should expect to pay for them, if possible. Manufacturer names, part numbers, distributors, datasheets, and web sites are all good information to pass along. It will certainly also help *you* in the future when you come back to this project after a period of time.

Teamwork and Collaborative Development

Will you be working with others on this project? How will you coordinate and communicate your ideas and work product between design team members? Several methods are available for sharing the load.

Even if you're doing all the work yourself, there's still the possibility that you may want to ask for help in the future. Perhaps you'll want to share what you've done with your local club or the entire world. These are all good reasons to arrange your project so that it's easily accessible to others. Let's look at a few cheap or free tools at your disposal to achieve these goals.

Blogs

Once they were called web logs; online diaries; or journals of individuals' ideas, expressions, or whatever. People are awfully busy these days, so the name has been shortened to *blogs* to save time. You can share long or short essays, photos, videos, music or just about whatever you can think of using a blog. These are generally distinguished from other content-management systems (CMSs) by their journalistic format, wherein a single topic is contained in a single article, arranged by date or subject, and searchable by blogger-defined tags.

People often use their blogs to document their progress on development projects. This could be anything from an Arduino shield to building a treehouse or proposing to a fiancée. This list is limited only by the very human need to document things.

The Arduino Team keeps a blog at `http://arduino.cc/blog` and posts interesting Arduino projects and other Arduino news. The blog headlines are fused into the Arduino main page as well. As you might expect, you can find blogs dedicated to every conceivable interest, with a little searching. You have been warned.

You can easily create your own blog and post your own ideas, pictures, projects, and whatever else you want the world to see. This is a great way to get into the habit of documenting your projects. If your blogging platform allows reader comments, you can sometimes get a lot of great ideas, suggestions, and help from unexpected sources. People like to browse through other people's work and sometimes will offer helpful advice or constructive criticism. Of course, you can expect a certain number of soreheads and pranksters in the mix, so either set your reader comments to require approval (by you) or be prepared to regularly monitor what's going on. That's just the nature of things in this connected world.

You can get your own free blog from various providers, each with its own strengths and weaknesses. WordPress (http://wordpress.com) is a very popular and powerful system that has many other features besides blogging. There is a bit of a learning curve, due to the sheer number of features it provides.

Posterous (http://posterous.com) has to be the easiest blogging platform to use. It has the traditional web-based user interface as well as an e-mail–driven interface. You can e-mail your blog posts to the site, which automatically formats whatever content you send into a readable, searchable, attractive article format. This can include photos, documents, music, or just plain text. It's also possible to automatically forward all your posts through Posterous to social media sites such as Facebook, Twitter, and Flickr, so it looks like you're diligently updating multiple web sites when in reality you sent a single e-mail.

Forums

The Arduino Forum (http://arduino.cc/forum) should be your first stop for all Arduino-related questions. If you're pondering an Arduino-related conundrum, it's quite likely that several others in the past have similarly pondered similar conundrums, all of which is very often documented in detail in the forum. You must sign up for a free account to be able to post to the forum, but you can search and browse anonymously if you like.

It's always a good idea to search through a forum for your topic of interest before posting a question. The Arduino online community as a whole tends to be patient and helpful. Please perform your due diligence and at least do a cursory search for your topic before asking for help. Also, don't expect strangers from around the world to do your homework for you for free, just because you were either too lazy or waited until the last minute to turn something in. Show a little respect and appreciation and, you'll be rewarded.

Along the same lines, if you see a question on the forum and you have some relevant experience that might help, consider posting a helpful answer. Vague generalities and "I read about it somewhere so I think it should work…" aren't as useful as you may imagine.

The official/unofficial support forum for all things AVR (not just Arduino-related) is AVR Freaks (www.avrfreaks.net), the Nr.1 AVR Community. The site has a comprehensive collection of tutorials and projects documented online, as well as an enormous pool of AVR talent contributing to its support forums. Atmel officially endorses AVR Freaks for AVR support for hobbyists. It's a good place to ask questions, but again, be prepared to at least search the forums first before asking a question that you think may have cropped up before.

Wikis

A *wiki* is a user-editable collection of organized information, presented as a web page. The most famous wiki is Wikipedia, (http://en.wikipedia.org), whose aim is the sum of all human knowledge.

Several Arduino-themed wikis have popped up over the years, including the official Arduino Playground (http://arduino.cc/playground). A huge number of top-level categories exist, each containing dozens or hundreds of topics. The new Arduino Labs wiki (http://labs.arduino.cc) is also getting some interesting topics, including the Mega Android Development Kit (ADK) and GPRS Shield projects.

The good thing about wikis is that anyone can edit them. The bad thing about wikis is that anyone can edit them. It's certainly an interesting format. Depending on the user community, it can also be an interesting experiment in democracy and free speech.

Revision Control Systems

Keeping track of changes and revision to your project can be tricky, but it's very important. It's important to your sanity ("I'm *sure* I fixed that bug already!") and it's important to anyone else who may want to work on your project.

Revision control systems, also known as *version control systems*, assist in this endeavor. A perfectly acceptable system is to keep the master drawings locked in a drawer and allow only one person at a time to look at them or make any changes. In this day of electrical computing devices and robot memory banks, it's also possible to use various *software* systems to keep track of what's been done and when.

A good revision control system allows you and anyone you designate (perhaps even the whole world) to gain access to not only the most recent version of your work, but also any previous versions, if need be. A more useful system keeps track of the individual modifications made and can help keep a log of changes. The best systems are easy to use and unobtrusive, allowing designated individuals to check out a file, module, or some other subset of data; perform improvements on it; and then check in the results, leaving a note as to what was done for future reference. You can even get some systems to notify the proper folk when selected events occur.

There's always more to it, of course, but that's the basic idea. Revision control systems have been in place in one form or another since people stated writing things down, which was a long time ago. Today, word processors, wikis, and blogs often support some sort of version control system. Some operating systems employ a versioning file system that automatically keeps track of changes made to files contained in the system.

Different projects use different revision control systems for different reasons, not all of them *good* reasons. A lot of it has to do with a project's legacy or origins, as well as the preferences and skill sets of the developers making these decisions. Different project-hosting services offer various combinations of version control systems, and this very often dictates the facilities and functionality available to developers.

The Arduino code, for example, is hosted by Google Code (`http://code.google.com/p/arduino`) and stored as a Git repository on GitHub (`http://github.com/arduino/Arduino`).

A Note About Revision- or Version-Numbering

The terms *version* and *revision* both imply change of some sort, or at least the *possibility* of change. A *version* is one particular configuration of a system, whereas a *revision* describes a *change* (or a re-visioning) in the configuration of a system.

Unfortunately, these terms are often used interchangeably, even when their meanings differ subtly. The first one you make is Version 1, which used to be called the Mark I back when people still used roman numerals.

■ **Tip**   Don't use roman numerals. If you must, don't mix them with other numerals.

When you improve the Mark I enough to need to distinguish between the new! improved! version and the original version, you can call the latest version either the Mark II, Version 2, or Revision *1*. That's because this is the *first* revision or change.

So it's OK to call a new product Version 1.0, but it's a bit misleading to refer to it as Revision 1.0, because it has yet to be *revised* since it was released.

Feel free to use whatever version numbering scheme strikes your fancy. There is a trend toward increasing the major version number for major improvements, say from 1.0 to 2.0, and bumping the minor version number for intermediate or incremental changes, such as bug fixes, minor improvements, or other enhancements that don't affect the perceived usage of the system. Anything that fundamentally changes the operation of or interaction with the product should be considered a major enhancement. Again, you're free to use your best judgment in these cases.

Project-Hosting Web Sites

Let's say you've got a great idea for a project, and you want to share it with others. There are a lot of project-hosting web sites that would love for you to move on in and get to developing!

First you should look around and see if there's already a project similar or identical to the one you're presently imagining. Hey, it's possible. Try to find a group that already has some momentum, and you'll likely get farther with that idea of yours.

If not, then let's look at a few of the many popular project-hosting web sites.

Google Code: code.google.com

Open source projects can find a free home with lots of collaborative development tools at Google Code. The requirements are that you have a Google account, that you live in a country where Google is allowed to conduct business, and that your project be licensed as an open source project.

To create your own hosted project on Google Code, go to the Create Project page at `http://code.google.com/hosting/createProject`. You need to sign in using a Google account. If you don't already have one, you can create a new account right there.

Enter the name of your project (which should be unique). It has to be all lowercase. Then enter a short summary and a project description.

Now you get to pick what kind of version control system you would like to use with your project. Your choices are Git, Mercurial, and Subversion, which are all popular systems.

At this point you also get to select which license you want to use for your project. A specific list is provided, but it includes Other Open Source, allowing you to specify the exact license in one of your project files. Remember, to qualify for free project hosting from Google Code, your project *must* be open source. Google doesn't recommend placing your project in the public domain due to liability issues, but will consider it if you make a good case by entering an issue in their public issue-tracker at `http://code.google.com/p/support/issues/entry`.

Next, enter some project labels that will help others find your project. Sample labels are provided.

That's all it takes to complete the preliminary setup on Google Code. Now you can begin administering your project by adding other users, defining their roles within the project, and adding files.

Google Code offers wiki pages for your project, an issue tracker to keep up with bug reports and enhancement requests, as well as a wide variety of notifications for keeping everyone on your team up to date. Google doesn't place ads on project web sites.

The Arduino software is hosted by Google Code (`http://code.google.com/p/arduino`) as is Fritzing, the Sanguino, the LoL Shield, the BlinkM, the Meggy Jr, and an insane number of flying robots controlled by Arduinos.

Microsoft's CodePlex: www.codeplex.com

Microsoft also has an open source project hosting facility called CodePlex. Not surprisingly, it's largely dominated by Microsoft-related technologies, but because that covers a large an area of interests, it's not too terribly confining.

You can create your own project at CodePlex by visiting the Create Project page at `www.codeplex.com/site/project/create`. You can either use a Windows Live ID or register for a CodePlex-specific account. Registering for a CodePlex-specific account is fast and easy. You'll get an e-mail with a link to finalize the registration of your new account. Click that link, and you're ready to log in and create your project.

Enter the name of your project on the Create New Project web page. You also get to pick a URL for your project along the lines of `http://[your-project-name].codeplex.com` as long as *your-project-name* contains only letters and numbers.

Then pick the version control system you want to use for your project. Currently your choices are Mercurial or Team Foundation Server, which also speaks Subversion.

Describe your project briefly in the Summary area, letting the world know how wonderful your project is and how the world will be a better place because of it. Or be truthful—you decide.

CodePlex also offers you the opportunity to fund your project by placing an advertisement on your project pages. You can optionally elect to donate this ad revenue to Habitat for Humanity International (`http://habitat.org`). The ads and any resulting revenue are handled by Lake Quincy Media (`www.lakequincy.com`). You need to contact them directly to arrange payment.

You're asked to confirm your e-mail address to set up your project. You have 30 days to upload files and publish your project. Unpublished projects get deleted in 30 days.

You get an e-mail from CodePlex with all the important details about your project, including the publication deadline. Keep this e-mail handy because it contains a lot of good information about how to access your project.

You now have a place for your project to live: `http://your-project-here.codeplex.com`. You can create wiki pages, upload code and documentation, track issues, create releases, and add more participants to your project.

Launchpad: launchpad.net

Launchpad is the project hosting site provided by Canonical, Ltd. (`http://canonical.com`), the nice people who bring us Ubuntu. It's based on the Bazaar version control system (`https://launchpad.net/bzr`).

Most of the common project-hosting features are also found on Launchpad, including bug tracking, code hosting, version control, and mailing lists. Some of the unique features of Launchpad are crowd-sourced translation facilities and a contributor rating system called *karma*.

You need a Launchpad Login Service Account to use this project hosting site. Enter your name and e-mail address and pick a password to create a new account at `https://login.launchpad.net/t6tVJmZvgsVzGRRV/+new_account`. You must enter a strong password containing at least one number and an uppercase letter. The site then sends you a confirmation e-mail containing a six-digit confirmation code. Enter this code on the page where you requested a new account to continue the sign-up process.

Once you can log in to your Launchpad account, go to `https://launchpad.net/projects/+new` to create a new project. There you enter the name of the project as well as a URL in the form `https://launchpad.net/[your-project-here]`, a title, and a summary. Launchpad uses this information to search its database of existing projects. It lists anything similar on a page where you can either cancel or continue. You're brought back to the project-creation page and allowed to enter a more detailed description of the project, add a homepage URL, and select which license(s) you would like to use for this project.

Now you're set up to add other users, upload your code, track issues, and set up releases. Go nuts! Launchpad hosts some famous software projects, including Ubuntu, MySQL, and Inkscape.

GitHub: github.com

GitHub offers free hosting for open source projects, with unlimited public repositories and unlimited public collaborators. It also offers paid services for private repositories.

GitHub claims to be the most popular code host on Earth, with over two and a half million hosted repositories and close to a million developers. To create a free site for your project, sign up for a free personal account at `https://github.com/signup/free`. Enter a username and your e-mail address, and pick a password. That's all there is to it.

Now you can create repositories for your code and documentation. You'll probably want to get up to speed on how the Git version control system works and set up the required software on your computer (if it's not already there). The guide for Windows users is at `http://help.github.com/win-set-up-git`. Mac OS X users should look at `http://help.github.com/mac-set-up-git`, and Linux users go over to `http://help.github.com/linux-set-up-git`.

On Windows, the Git software will want to modify your system `PATH` statement. You should allow it to do so, because this will let you use the command-line versions of the tools from anywhere in your system.

You may have heard of some of GitHub's users: Twitter, Facebook, Digg, and Yahoo!, among others.

SourceForge: sourceforge.net

This is the grandmother of all open source project-hosting sites. It was open source before open source was cool.

To create a SourceForge account, go to `https://sourceforge.net/user/registration`. Enter your name as you would like it to be displayed, your e-mail address, your preference for a username (that you use to log in), and a password. You can also enter your preferred language, the country you live in as well as your time zone, and a security question to be used to regain your password should you lose track of it.

To create a new project, go to `https://sourceforge.net/p/add_project`. Enter a project name and URL (to be added to the end of `http://sourceforge.net/p/`) that is 3–15 characters long. Then select which options you want for your project: Git repository, SVN, or Mercurial version control; a blog; a download and stats page; a wiki; a ticket system for tracking issues; and a forum. That's a lot of stuff for free!

After you've created your project, you proceed to the Project Admin page where you can reign supreme.

Licensing Your Work

To share or not to share … that is *not* the question. The question is, *how* will you share your ideas?

Maybe you have no intention of sharing your ideas. Fine. Be that way.

Let's assume for the moment that you *do* intend to share your ideas, at least to some degree. You need to know what your options are and what's best for you, as the parental figure in your idea's growth and development, as well as what's in the best interest of your intended audience.

These are important decisions. Please take them seriously.

■ **Note** Ideas, like cats, are sponsored, not owned.

If you don't want to share, that's OK. Keep all your toys in your own yard, and don't let anyone else play with them. But consider for a moment what benefits you may enjoy if you consider sharing your ideas with others. Wealth, fame, honor, and immortality are, unfortunately, not guaranteed and, to be quite honest, are doubtful. Respect, appreciation, and a sense of satisfaction are much more likely.

■ **Note** Nothing in this book is to be considered legal advice of any kind. Double-check any statements made with the laws of your particular jurisdiction. Retain your own counsel when contemplating any legal issues.

Patents and Trademarks

The idea behind the modern patent system is to give inventors some legal protection for their ideas. This was supposed to encourage innovation. Sadly, for the most part, this is no longer true, especially in the rapidly changing areas of high technology, such as computers, chips, programming, and, well, Arduinos. Also, sadly, it's not helping the pharmaceutical world, either, which could really use some help.

A patent can be awarded for a *device* (usually called an *apparatus*), a *process*, or a *design*. Device and process patents are collectively referred to as *utility patents*. The exact rules vary from country to country. The basic patentable concept embodied in this new bit of shiny is supposed to be in some way new, useful, not derivative, and not obvious. It was once considered to be in society's best long-term interests to give an inventor a short-lived monopoly on the use of the product of their fertile imaginations, in order for it to gain traction in the marketplace and be profitable, without the inventor having to worry about others stealing the idea.

Many people seem to think that if you come up with a great idea, all you have to do is patent it, sit back, and wait for the riches to start pouring in. There are a few problems with that theory.

First, to obtain a patent, you must first apply (that is, submit a patent application): a potentially lengthy and expensive process that often involves lawyers. This doesn't guarantee that a patent will be granted.

Within the patent application, *everything* about the device, process, or design must be revealed in detail. Whether the patent is granted or not, this information then becomes publicly available. If you had a secret sauce that you thought was going to make you rich because you had it and no one else did, well, now they do.

■ **Note** A secret shared is a secret no more.

If your offering of brainwaves and bank notes is acceptable to the patent deities, you may eventually be granted a patent. Unfortunately, although you *do* get a fancy multidigit number and bragging rights, you do *not* get a magic bullet that kills evil, idea-stealing nogoodnicks dead in their evil, idea-stealing tracks. What you've earned for your trouble is a free pass to a local court of law, wherein you get to spend more money prosecuting those you suspect of using your ideas without properly compensating you. Of course, you have *right* on your side. Here's to hoping your pockets are deeper than your opponent's!

It gets worse. Because there is strength in numbers, many patent holders collectively pool their intellectual properties under a common flag. Often, hundreds or thousands of patents are owned by companies that do nothing with them other than to offer protection. This is seen by some to be the inevitable conclusion to such as system, similar to the heat death of the universe, where all matter eventually collects into black holes and disappears from view. This occurs because of the litigious and adversarial nature of the patent infrastructure.

But what about all those riches that were going to start flowing you-ward once your brilliant idea was patented? Again, unless you *do something* with the idea, it's just an idea, like Esperanto or the metric system.

Patents in the United States are administered by the US Patent and Trademark Office (`http://uspto.gov`), which has awarded over eight million patents in its 200+ year history. According to the web site, an inventor can expect to pay approximately $4,000 over the course of the lifetime of a patent.

Trademarks, on the other hand, are simply filed in a public registry of record. This is a way of memorializing a connection between product and owner, as long as a level of distinction and uniqueness can be demonstrated.

Copyright

Copyright means the right to copy. This right is owned by the copyright holder in a work and is protected by copyright laws. That work can be a book, a song, or just about anything that is an original work of an identifiable author.

Once upon a time, the very process of copying anything was tedious and cumbersome, requiring special skills and tools. Today, that remains the case in a few specialized areas, but not so much for the vast wealth of digital works that are available. Making a digital copy is now trivial.

Copyright laws vary from one place to the next. The level of protection granted by law also varies tremendously by jurisdiction. As with patents, the government won't go to bat for you in these areas, and the burden of identifying and successfully prosecuting violators lands squarely in the copyright holder's lap.

As a marketable right, copyright can be bought, sold, or licensed under various combinations of circumstances. It can get complicated. For example, you can buy an audio recording of a musical that you like and listen to it at home. You can't, however, play it over the public address system at your school; it's not licensed for that. Well, you *can*, but you're in violation of the contract that you entered into with the copyright holder (or their agents or assignees) when you purchased the recording.

This can have weird side effects. Since 1997, Canada has collected a blank media levy on all CD-Rs and other blank media and then passed those funds to the Canadian Private Copying Collective, which redistributes the booty to authors, publishers, and performers. The implication is that a certain percentage of blank media (high enough to warrant legislation) is used to illegally copy (pirate) copyrighted works, and someone's gotta pay. All European countries, with the exception of Luxembourg, have similar systems in place.

Even so-called *free software* has copyrights. The original authors may have wanted to share the product of their work with the world for free, and to make an effort to allow the software to remain free, but still wanted to retain control of the product and the terms of its usage. See? Complicated.

Copyrights are registered in the United States by the US Copyright Office (`http://copyright.gov`).

Open Source

The term *open source* means different things to different people. At its core is the concept of making the source code (in whatever form that may take) openly available to any interested party, especially users and potential developers. In its simplest sense, this is a great idea. It fosters ingenuity by sharing previous accomplishments and helps people "stand on the shoulders of giants," as famously stated by Isaac Newton.

Here is a simple example. Let's say you write a clever sketch for your Arduino and post the source code on your blog for all to see. You have made your source openly available. If you design a really nice paper-towel holder out of plywood and publish the layout and assembly instructions somewhere (not necessarily the Web), you have likewise participated in open source development. Good for you! Sharing is nice.

This openness begins to get confusing when you start to attach licensing issues to the matter. Just because you post the source code to your latest sketch online, perhaps either to invite help debugging a tricky problem or to share it because you think it could be useful, does that automatically convey a license to anyone within the sound of your online voice to use your valuable intellectual property for whatever purpose they want with no compensation or attribution paid to you? Some people seem to think so. However, the two issues of *publication* and *licensing* are completely separate. Revealing your secret sauce recipe *does* let the proverbial cat out of the bag, but does that then obligate you to be responsible for the success of anyone else's project that incorporates your ideas? How about updates? And how far should the openness extend? If you post a schematic, are you then obligated to also post a PCB layout and a bill of materials? In how many formats or languages? How long are you required to make this information available?

Then there comes the idea of restricting the use of your ideas. Some think this is important. Maybe you're happy to let others peek under the hood to get an idea of how your invention works, and you would even encourage (tolerate?) hobbyists repeating your experiments elsewhere (this is called *peer review* in some circles—a mandatory requirement for being taken seriously, it would seem) without wanting to allow others to financially benefit from your genius unless you're compensated (see CadSoft's EAGLE license for a freeware version). What if you want to limit the use of your technologies to peaceful applications and prohibit military applications? How can you do this?

You do this by carefully licensing your work. A multitude of licensing options are available today, some of which will actually stand up in a court of law. A *license* is a contract between you and someone else, specifically detailing the permitted use and scope of your idea or product, but only under certain circumstances. Some licenses are quite liberal, requiring only that the end user think good thoughts about the original developer, or perhaps buy them a pizza should the opportunity arise. Others are drastic and restrictive.

In all cases, the license dictates the relationship between two parties, both of which are supposed to be getting something of value out of the deal. Maybe you get paid, if that's the deal. The license should dictate how, when, and probably *how much* you'll get paid. Maybe you don't want to get paid, but you do want *attribution* (credit) for all that cleverness. Again, the license should spell out exactly how this attribution is to be worded and placed in any derivative works.

Someday, try reading the fine print you always click through when installing software. It was common in years gone past that you didn't even own the *media* through which the software was delivered (back when physical media were used); it remained the property of the seller and would be required back at some point in the future.

Even some open source licensing has lots of strings attached—the kind of strings that can land you in court. Everyone knows that Linux, for example, is free. You can install it on your computer and do all kinds of great things with it for no charge. You can even get the source code for it and make a whole new kind of gizmo that runs Linux. The licensing on some of the components of Linux, however, mandates that you make available any source code used in your product that was based on free software (the meaning of *free* here pertaining to liberty, not price), thus keeping the source code free. This has resulted in several lawsuits against companies that didn't abide by the fine print in these licenses. Because the intention of the original authors of these particular components was for the code to remain free forever, these conditions were included in the licensing.

Licensing, like patents, only buys you a ticket to your local court of law. If you feel strongly about who should be allowed to use your ideas, when, and in what circumstances, then by all means, please do spell out these concerns in your license.

If, on the other hand, you just want the world to be a better, richer place, and you think that sharing your ideas and solutions with others is the way to do that, then please read the next section.

The Open Source Initiative (`http://opensource.org`) maintains a list of open source licenses of all kinds.

The Public Domain

The public domain is a legal term, so it means different things in different places. The basic understanding is that anything that isn't copyrighted, or whose copyright or other intellectual property rights have been forfeited, abandoned, or specifically disclaimed, is in the public domain. This means it isn't owned by anyone. Another way of thinking about it is that this means it's now owned *by everyone*.

The Berne Convention, signed by most countries over the past century, imagines that an author automatically has a copyright on any fixed work without having to register or declare it. Therefore, to place something in the public domain requires the author to disclaim any rights in the work. Again, all these rules and regulations vary from one place to the next. Some countries don't recognize the concept of a public domain.

A work that is in the public domain is a gift that already belonged to you even before you knew it existed. An excellent example of a project whose source code has been placed in the public domain is SQLite (`http://sqlite.org`), a relational database library.

If you want to send your little thought-children out into the world with no strings attached, please consider placing your documentation in the public domain. The public, thereby enriched, thanks you.

There is a down side, of course. Depending on your particular situation (that is, jurisdiction), you may still be vulnerable to litigation from folk who use your idea and somehow feel injured by it. Without a specific disclaimer of liability or warranty, you *personally* can potentially be sued for damages arising from the use of your stuff, even though you gave it away and asked nothing in return for it. There are variations of liberally *permissive* licenses, such as the MIT license, that allow unfettered use of a copyrighted idea for any purpose but specifically allow you to distance yourself from any litigious wrath down the road. For more details, ask your attorney.

Summary

It started out as an idea. Then it took shape, growing and expanding and changing until it more closely resembled the solution you had in mind. Do everyone a favor and write it down, won't you?

Maybe it's just a series of blog posts on your progress (or lack of it). That's a great place to start, especially if you get some good feedback from your readers. Take some pictures of your work along the way. It's entirely possible that the idea you discard will be the perfect solution to someone else's dilemma.

If you don't write it down, it didn't happen. Make something happen today.

Now let's move on and look at the tools and techniques you need to design, build, test, and program your own Arduino creations.

CHAPTER 10

Hardware Design

If you want to extend the capabilities of your Arduino, and you find there's not a shield for that yet, don't give up hope. You *can* design and build your own Arduino hardware. Maybe you want to connect a new device to your Arduino, or maybe you need to completely design your Arduino from the ground up, including connections for the new things you absolutely *must have* and dropping all non-essential circuitry. Either way, you're going to have to deal with some aspects of *hardware design*.

Let's start modestly and proceed to greater things. You begin like a child, playing with toys and imitating others. Next you look at some more complex techniques for both documenting your ideas and turning them into realities. You look at some design tools for extending your Arduino's capabilities and then move on to designing your own stand-alone Arduino-compatible devices.

This chapter can't possibly teach you everything about modern electronic design, and it doesn't try. But the examples given here show you what is involved in replicating existing circuits and in dreaming up your own. Ideally this will inspire you to give it a shot, if you haven't before. If you already have, this chapter will spur you on to more ambitious hardware projects in the future.

The practical goal of this chapter is to give you a good understanding of what tools you need and what you need to know to build some simple add-ons for your Arduino, as well as to build an Arduino clone of your very own.

Learning About Hardware

The absolute best way to learn, and learn *quickly*, about electronic hardware in general and hardware design in particular is to get some and *play* with it. That's right: have fun. Make stuff. Break stuff. See what works and what doesn't with your own eyes, your own hands. These are lessons you *teach yourself*, and they will last a lifetime.

Basic electronic components today are so commonplace and produced in such huge quantities that they have become incredibly inexpensive. In fact, it doesn't take much looking to find a lot of parts for free. If you're lucky enough to live in or near a city that has an active hacker space or electronics club, you can probably find *lots* of surplus electronics with which to learn and play. Most of these organizations have a free box or collection of donations that can yield all manner of interesting bits. Kids, get permission first. Adults, get permission first.

Also, don't go too far. There's prudent stocking, which is certainly handy when you need that one special part in the middle of the night to complete your experiment. This can, unfortunately, lead to eccentric collecting that sometimes devolves into disorganized hoarding (see Figure 10-1). There is no good reason to house for extended periods of time parts that can be easily and inexpensively obtained with a phone call or a visit to a web site.

Figure 10-1. Combination electronics/photography/robotics laboratory in a secret, undisclosed location. No, those aren't some of the example projects from this book. Don't let this happen to you!

Even if you're not that lucky, it's still a good bet that you can find some discarded consumer electronic products in your vicinity. The older, the better. You want ~~junk~~ treasure that has individually removable components, and the most recent crops of gadgets are woefully lean in that department.

■ **Caution** Television sets with cathode ray tubes (you remember them, don't you?) are *strictly off limits* to novice harvesters. These commonplace appliances can contain *and* retain very high voltage charges for years—more than enough to kill or seriously damage you. Don't take chances! Leave those TVs on the side of the road. Don't open them!

Even if your immediate area suffers from a lack of discarded technology, don't give up hope. As mentioned previously, the basic components you want for experimenting with electronic design are ridiculously inexpensive to obtain if you do a bit of comparison shopping online.

Things You Must Have

You need a clean, well-lighted space. If you don't have the luxury of a dedicated laboratory, find a nice box to pack away your stuff when you relinquish the dining table. Fishing-tackle boxes are good because they have lots of nooks and crannies to organize small parts.

Keep your smallest parts separated and organized, and then be sure to put them back in the right place when you're done. Don't waste 45 minutes rooting through a pile of identical-looking resistors to find the right one (this will happen more often than you would like) when it would have taken you all of 20 seconds to put it in the right place to begin with.

Invest in (or borrow) some more-than-adequate lighting. It makes a big difference.

You'll be making a lot of electrical connections. Wire is really good for this. Smaller-diameter wire is better than the heavy stuff, at least to a point. There seems to be a lot of it hiding in old computer cables. You'll very quickly develop a preference as to what size and kind of wire you like for your projects.

You also need real wire cutters and, if possible, some good wire strippers. Don't use scissors or nail trimmers, and *please* don't use your teeth.

All great projects, even great *practice* projects, need documentation. Graph paper is good, and plain copier paper or notebook paper will do. If you've already mastered a computer-aided design (CAD) software package, you can use that. If not, please hold off on diving into that particular can o' worms for now. You've got enough on your plate as it is. There's no need for more distractions. Pencils (with big, fat erasers) and paper will work nicely for now.

What will hold your prototype circuits together? You can only twist so many wires and component leads together before something comes frustratingly undone by itself. You've already seen several examples of entire Arduino circuits built on solderless breadboards. They're relatively inexpensive, and you can cut and strip your own jumper wires at home. If you already know how to solder (more on this later, if you don't), you can use point-to-point wiring in a freeform arrangement of wires or thread the component leads through a perforated sheet of flat material, sometimes called *perfboard* or the trademarked Veroboard brand. As previously mentioned in Chapter 1, you can even breadboard your circuits on an actual bread *board*, using a hammer and small nails.

The main idea of experimenting with electronics and building prototypes is to learn what works and what doesn't. Find a method that you like that allows you to quickly try out new ideas without having to run to the store or wait for things to show up in the mail. Having a reasonable inventory of tools, wire, basic components, and connectors helps.

■ **Note**   Keep a first-aid kit handy. You're going to cut, scratch, or burn yourself eventually. When this happens, stop what you're doing and attend to your wounds promptly.

Things You Want

Eventually you'll want to memorialize your latest circuit doodling for posterity. This will most likely involve soldering. You want a small, pencil-style soldering iron in the 25–50 watt range. You do *not* want one of those big pistol-grip soldering irons. Those are for circus tents, zeppelins, and plumbing.

When you're first learning to solder or getting back in practice, it often helps to have an articulated vise or helping-hands device to hold your assembly at that special, weird angle needed to make that very last connection. These gadgets come in all sizes and with all manner of options. Start with something simple.

You don't have to solder to be able to design and build electronic circuits. But it helps. It also opens a lot of opportunities for you. If you don't already know how to solder, you're encouraged to learn. Mitch Altman publishes a great one-page cartoon-style "learn to solder" flyer that is free to download: www.tvbgone.com/cfe_mfaire.php.

Some test equipment will make your life easier, especially when your newest creation seems to develop a mind of its own. You get extra points for building your own gear.

A *continuity tester* is a simple device that indicates whether there is a conductive path between two points. You can make one out of an LED, a coin cell, a spring-loaded clothespin, and three pieces of wire (see Figure 10-2). Alternately, you can use a beeper for audible feedback, which is sometimes more useful when you need to keep your eyes on where you're probing. Always use a low-voltage power source for a continuity tester. The common lithium coin cell puts out 3V and has enough internal resistance to allow you to omit a current-limiting resistor in your circuit. You don't want to blow up a 5V circuit by probing it with a 9V battery!

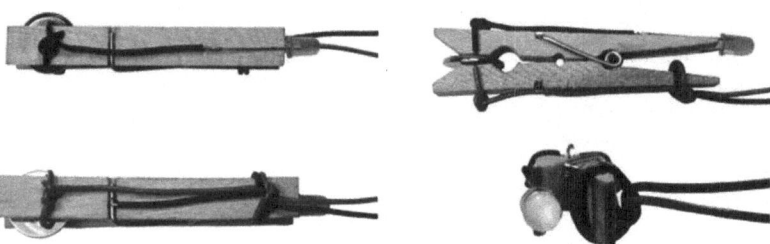

Figure 10-2. *A continuity tester made with a clothespin (no programming required). The long lead (anode) of the LED is wedged under the spring coil (upper right).*

In Figure 10-2, the short lead (cathode) is soldered to a wire, stripped, and looped across one jaw. The other jaw is similarly stripped and looped with a red wire, forming the positive test lead. The negative test lead is wrapped around the spring clip. A 3V lithium cell is held between the jaws. When the circuit is completed, the green LED lights. Also makes a good button-cell tester. A volt-ohm-amp meter (VOM) is great to have to take various electronic readings. For low-voltage readings of 5V and lower, you can use an Arduino (see Chapter 7). However, a standard meter or an Arduino is only really effective for reading direct current (DC) voltages or very slowly changing voltages. For higher frequencies, such as those found in audio circuits or more complex waveforms, an oscilloscope is required.

An oscilloscope is an excellent tool to have on your bench. These have traditionally been very expensive items. Luckily there are a lot of good deals to be had on used equipment, and the cost of new units is coming down, especially for some of the more humble models. This versatile instrument lets you measure voltage, frequency, duty cycle, and many other parameters by visualizing the signal on a display, so you can really see what is going on within your circuit.

Although a dedicated oscilloscope is an excellent addition to your collection of test equipment, it may not be within your budget, or you simply may not have room for any more equipment in your lab. USB-based oscilloscopes are available in all sizes and price ranges. They generally consist of a small box of electronics to house the front-end electronics and do most of the heavy lifting in software on your PC.

Infrared Proximity Sensor

As promised, you begin with a project that is straightforward and not too difficult. An *infrared (IR) proximity detector* is a combination of an infrared emitter and an infrared detector. The very simplest implementations of this circuit suffer from some pretty severe performance drawbacks, but they can still be used in certain controlled situations to accomplish noncontact proximity detection.

The emitter is usually an IR LED. It looks just like a visible-spectrum LED except you can't see it shining. These LEDs are usually packaged in clear resin, although you sometimes find them in various shades of gray, blue, or pink. An IR LED's forward voltage is much lower than a visible LED's, usually in the 1.2V–1.5V range. Ideally, for this type of circuit, you want to use an IR LED that was originally intended for use in a remote control. These IR LEDs are often rated at 100mA maximum current, which is four or five times higher than most visible LEDs.

There are several types of inexpensive IR detectors. You can use an IR phototransistor. These often look like regular LEDs, except they're encased in what looks like solid black resin. This coloration helps filter out any visible light and allow only the IR light to enter the package. Don't confuse this with the once-popular darkness emitting diode (DED), a very low-power device used for power-off indicators in the 1970s.

Infrared phototransistors are true transistors, but the base terminal usually isn't connected to an external lead because the light hitting the transistor die inside the package is what controls the amount of current flowing through the transistor. Therefore they have only two leads and look a lot like normal LEDs.

A more effective IR detector is the *photodiode*. It's also often packaged in a T13/4 or 5mm LED lead-frame, also with a dark resin to block non-infrared light from entering. These devices act like normal diodes in the dark, allowing current to flow in one direction but blocking the flow of current in the opposite direction.

There are several types of photodiodes. The PIN photodiode is similar to a normal diode with a PN semiconductor junction, but it has an extra layer of *undoped* or *intrinsic* semiconductor material between the P-region and the N-region. It also has some unique electrical characteristics when used in high-frequency circuits, but you focus on their optoelectronic applications for the moment. The long and correct explanation of how this works is Long Indeed. The short version is that if you hook up a PIN photodiode *backward* (that is, reverse-biased) it does *not* conduct electricity in the dark and it *does* conduct electricity when exposed to IR light. This is functionally identical to the operation of a phototransistor, except that a PIN photodiode has a much faster response time. For this reason, PIN photodiodes are often used as detectors in fiber-optic networks for sending lots of information really quickly. See Figure 10-3.

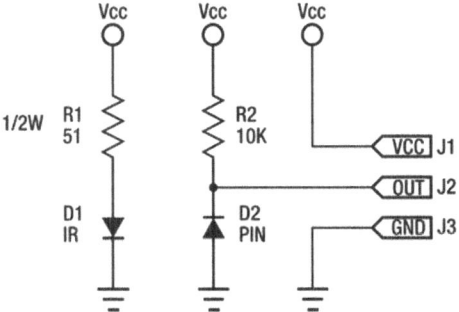

Figure 10-3. *A complete IR proximity-detector circuit, consisting of an IR emitter and IR detector. Note that R1 must be at least 1/2W if V_{cc} is 5V.*

The left side of the schematic in Figure 10-3 is the IR emitter circuit. As drawn, it's always on, emitting IR light as long as the power is applied. R1 is a 51Ω, 1/2W current-limiting resistor, and D1 is a 5mm IR LED, preferably with a peak output wavelength of 940nm and a *beam angle* (technically, the *half-angle*) of 20°. This makes for an invisible beam that is rather tightly focused.

If V_{cc} is 5V, then the current flowing through D1 and R1 is about 75mA. This is less than the maximum for most IR LEDs of this type, but because it's always on, you don't want to run it at 100%. The total power being dissipated by R1 is ~275mW, which is more than a common quarter-watt resistor can ever handle. You bump it up to a 1/2W resistor so things don't get too hot. Two 100Ω, 1/4W resistors in parallel will also suffice.

The PIN photodiode is located at D2. Note that it's reverse-biased. If you didn't know something technical and mysterious was going on, you'd assume that no current would flow from V_{cc} through R2 and D2 to ground, and you'd normally be right. This is the case when no IR light is falling on D2. In the presence of IR light, however, strange things happen with electrons and holes and carriers and such, and D2 begins to conduct. The amount of current flowing is related to the amount of light striking D2.

When D2 isn't conducting current to ground—that is, in the dark—the voltage on J2, the output, remains at V_{cc}. This is because R2 is acting as a pull-up resistor. However, if D2 begins to conduct, the voltage on J2 begins to drop. The output voltage can be converted to a number by the Arduino's analog-to-digital converter (ADC), and you can make decisions based on this reading.

Because very little current is ever expected to flow through R2, it can be a common quarter-watt resistor of anywhere from 10KΩ–100KΩ. The exact value of R2 determines the sensitivity of the circuit to IR light. A higher resistor value for R2 makes the circuit more sensitive, because it takes less current being conducted by D2 to drop the voltage. A lower resistance reduces the sensitivity of the detector, because it takes more IR light to achieve the same voltage drop.

A Modest Prototype

OK, now it's time to quit *talking* about this circuit and start *building* it. Let's start with a simple version and then make it much more complicated later. See Figure 10-4.

Figure 10-4. A prototype of the IR proximity sensor. The positive lead (anode) of a PIN photodiode is connected to one of the ground pins (GND) of the power expansion connector.

In Figure 10-4, the negative lead (cathode, indicated by the flat side at the base of the photodiode package) is attached to the first analog input, A0. The IR emitter is just an IR LED powered directly by a 3V lithium coin cell. The longer lead of the IR LED is the anode (positive lead), so it's placed next to the positive side of the battery. The coin cell has enough internal resistance to keep the IR LED from drawing too much current.

Besides an Arduino, you need an IR LED, a PIN photodiode or an IR phototransistor, and a 3V lithium coin cell. Do you see any resistors in this picture? No, you don't (the resistor networks on the Arduino don't count!). The lithium coin cell has more than enough internal resistance to safely limit the amount of current flowing through the IR LED, thus eliminating the need for R1. This trick works with most visible-spectrum LEDs as well. You use one of the available built-in pull-up resistors inside the AVR chip to replace R2.

If you don't have an IR LED or an extra coin cell floating around the lab, don't fret. You can use a remote control from just about any consumer appliance. A special provision in the testing software allows for this.

Let's test out this prototype hardware with a little prototype software. See Listing 10-1.

Listing 10-1. Detecting IR Light Using a Reverse-Biased Photodiode

```
void setup() {
  pinMode(13, OUTPUT); // LED pin
  digitalWrite(14, HIGH); // enable pullup on analog input A0/D14
}

void loop() {
  if(analogRead(0) < 900) {
    digitalWrite(13, HIGH); // LED on = IR detected
    delay(100); // stretch...
  } else {
    digitalWrite(13, LOW); // LED off = no IR detected
  }
}
```

This is a very simple sketch, but it performs a very important function. It proves that the IR detector circuit works. Compile and upload this sketch to your Arduino. Make sure you've got the photodiode installed in the correct direction. Also, make doubly sure you have the anode connected to GND and not the VIN pin. When you point the coin-cell-powered IR LED at the photodiode, the LED on your Arduino should light.

Bear in mind that both of these optical components are usually tightly focused. You need to shine the IR LED directly into the top of the photodiode for best results.

Now let's take a look at the sketch to see what's going in inside. The setup() function configures D13 as an output so that you can blink the built-in LED. Then it turns on the built-in pull-up resistor for the first analog input, A0, using the digitalWrite() function call and A0's alter ego, D14. Remember, all the analog inputs can also be used as plain-old digital inputs or outputs. As such, they have a built-in pull-up resistor that can be enabled or disabled by software control. This would normally skew a true analog voltage reading, but it's required in this experiment.

The loop() function takes a reading of A0's voltage, which corresponds with J2 in the schematic previously shown, using the analogRead() function. This value can range from 0 to 1,023. Due to the way you've arranged the components, a higher voltage means *less* IR light detected. As the amount of IR light increases, the voltage goes lower, approaching ground. In normal room lighting (not direct sunlight), the reading should stay above 1,000, because the optical properties of the photodiodes container block most ambient light.

The reading obtained using the analogRead() function call is compared to the hard-wired value 900. If the reading is less than 900—that is, some IR light is being detected—then the LED on D13 is turned on. If the value is 900 or above, then the LED is turned off, indicating that no IR light is currently being seen by the detector.

An additional delay() function call is made in the event that some IR light is detected. This allows you to get a good visual indication of detected IR light, even if it's just a short flash.

As previously mentioned, you can also use just about any IR remote control to test this detector circuit. The extra delay() function call helps stretch the positive test result long enough to make it visible to your slow, human eyes.

Now that you can get some visual feedback about the operation of the IR detector circuit, try seeing how far away and how far off angle you can get with the coin-cell-powered IR LED or the remote control. Assuming everything is working properly, you should quickly get a good sense of how well this simple circuit works and under what circumstances it fails. For example, even indirect sunlight can swamp your detector, because daylight contains an enormous amount of IR radiation. You can adjust the hard-wired 900 threshold in the prototype sketch to adjust the sensitivity of the circuit. With this configuration, a lower threshold *decreases* the sensitivity of the detector, because it takes more IR light to drive the output voltage that low. Experiment with different values and see what happens.

Some Modest Improvements

Let's add a few improvements to the circuit. You want to use this circuit as a *proximity detector* and not just an IR light detector. To accomplish this, you need to bounce the IR light off of a potential obstacle and detect how much light is reflected back at your sensor.

It takes a lot more IR light to bounce off a target and measure than it does when you can point the IR LED directly at the sensor. The typical coin cell has enough internal resistance to limit the current flowing through the IR LED to 30mA–40mA. This is less than half of its capacity, so you need *more power*.

You don't need the IR emitter to be blazing away at full power all the time, though. That's wasteful. You should turn it on just before you need to take a reading, give the PIN photodiode enough time to react to the light, take the reading, and then turn off the IR LED.

You can control the IR LED directly with a dedicated I/O line, but then you're limited to the 40mA-per-pin limit imposed by the silicon chip that forms your AVR. You need an LED driver. It would also be nice if there was some sort of visible indication that the IR emitter was enabled. You can use a regular LED for that purpose. It's always nice to have positive, visual confirmation that your sketch is behaving properly. Wasting time trying to figure out why the IR sensor isn't responding, only to find out that you weren't powering the right pin, is very aggravating. LEDs are cheap, so you add one to the driver circuit.

On the receiver side, it would also be nice to have a visual indication that something is happening. It would be even better if this indicator didn't depend on the proper operation of the sketch to work.

Additionally, let's add an adjustable threshold to the sketch, so you can tweak the trigger point in real time instead of having to adjust a constant in the sketch, recompile, upload, and so on. See Figure 10-5.

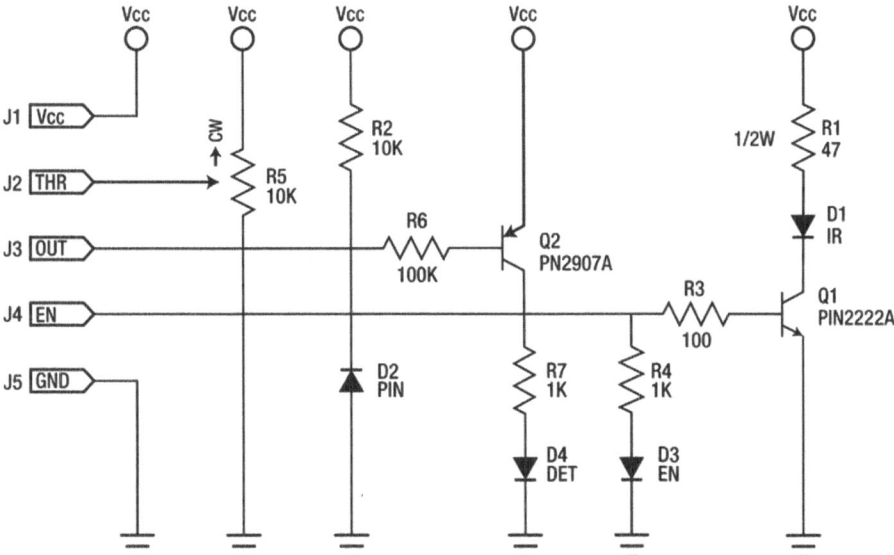

Figure 10-5. *A more complex proximity-detector circuit*

The emitter circuit is now on the far-right side of the schematic, with the detector circuit to its left. The addition of an NPN transistor allows you to drive almost as much current as you could ever want in the application. The current-limiting resistor R1 has been dropped to 47Ω, to accommodate the voltage drop across the transistor. Also, because you won't leave the IR LED on all the time (in theory), you can drive it closer to the maximum rating during those times that it's on.

R3 limits the current flowing from the AVR pin to the base of the transistor. Almost a volt drops across the base-emitter junction, so you use the figures 4V (V_{CC} = 5V less ~1V) and 40mA to arrive at 100Ω as the optimum value (E = I × R, so R = E ÷ I, according to Ohm's Law) for this resistor.

R4 is the current-limiting resistor for the IR emitter-enabled indicator. This is just an indicator LED, so you don't need to budget much current for it.

Don't try connecting both the LED D3 and the transistor Q1 through the same resistor. The voltage at the base of Q1 won't get much over 1V, so D3 will never be illuminated. Even a red LED needs closer to 2V to overcome its forward voltage requirement. Use two resistors, each one carefully selected for optimum performance in this circuit.

The adjustment circuit is a 10KΩ linear potentiometer connected as a voltage divider. The CW indication shows which way the wiper moves when the potentiometer's shaft is rotated clockwise. This increases the voltage as the knob is turned to the right.

The IR detector is fundamentally unchanged. A dedicated pull-up resistor, R2, is placed in the schematic, but you can omit it in the final circuit if the internal pull-up within the AVR is sufficient.

Added to the detector circuit is an indicator LED D4, with a PNP transistor driver. Because the *absence* of IR light leaves this point in the circuit at approximately 5V, the emitter-base junction of Q2 isn't forward biased, so no current flows through the LED and its associated current-limiting resistor, R7. Only when the voltage drops below ~4V does the transistor begin to turn on, lighting the LED, which indicates that IR light is being detected. This circuit gives a nice analog response, allowing you to gauge how effectively the sensor is responding.

The resistor connecting the photodiode to the transistor is relatively high in resistance at 100KΩ. This prevents excessive current from flowing back through the transistor to act as more of a pull-up on the signal. You can use lower resistor values, but they then prevent the signal voltage from dropping all the way down to ground.

This circuit can't easily be scaffolded up from the expansion connectors on a typical Arduino, although you're more than welcome to try. A more reasonable approach, or perhaps an approach with a more reasonable expectation of success or longevity, is to build the circuit on a solderless breadboard and then connect it to your Arduino. One way to do this is illustrated in Figure 10-6.

Figure 10-6. The improved proximity detector built on a solderless breadboard, atop the Maker Shield. The clear LED is the IR emitter, and the black LED is the PIN photodiode. The two small red LEDs are the associated indicator lights. Having these lights hard-wired to the circuit means they work even when your sketch doesn't. The Maker Shield has a built-in potentiometer that is used as the threshold adjustment.

Only a few changes are necessary in the prototype sketch. See Listing 10-2.

Listing 10-2. Slightly Improved Software for the Improved Proximity Detector Hardware

```
void setup() {
  pinMode(9, OUTPUT); // IR emitter enable
  pinMode(13, OUTPUT); // LED pin
  digitalWrite(14, HIGH); // enable pullup on analog input A0/D14
}

void loop() {
  int infrared; // how much infrared: 0=none, 1023= a lot
  int threshold; // adjustable comparison value

  digitalWrite(9, HIGH); // enable infrared emitter
  threshold = 1023 - analogRead(1); // get threshold value
  infrared = 1023 - analogRead(0); // convert voltage
  digitalWrite(9, LOW); // disable infrared emitter

  if(infrared > threshold) {
    digitalWrite(13, HIGH); // LED on = IR detected
  } else {
    digitalWrite(13, LOW); // LED off = no IR detected
  }
}
```

The setup() function adds a statement to configure D9 as an output enable signal. This allows the software to turn on the power-hungry emitter only when necessary. During the course of this example sketch, it seems to always be necessary, but your sketch will be smarter than this.

The loop() function declares a couple of ints to hold the IR light reading (infrared) as well as the adjustable threshold setting (threshold).

At the beginning of the loop() function, the emitter is enabled by writing a HIGH value to digital pin D9. To give the PIN photodiode time to react to the illumination, the threshold-setting conversion is now performed, and only then is the IR reading taken, both using the analogRead() function. After this, the IR emitter is disabled.

The values for both the infrared reading and the threshold setting are mathematically inverted by subtracting the actual conversion result from 1,023, the maximum reading. This effectively reverses the meaning of the magnitude of the values. Now a larger infrared reading means more IR, and the same applies for the threshold setting. Bear in mind that the threshold potentiometer could have been wired with the opposite polarity, with a lower voltage corresponding to a clockwise rotation of the shaft. This might save some precious bytes of program memory as your sketch nears 100% utilization some day.

Printed Circuit Boards

As mentioned in Chapter 1, there are several low-cost options to design and build your own printed circuit boards (PCBs). Later, this chapter covers a couple of software tools to help you design your board. Right now, let's review a bit about how PCBs are made, so you can start to wrap your head around the design process.

The most basic PCB typically starts out as a sheet of nonflammable, flat material with a layer of copper foil attached to one side. This will be a *single-sided* PCB when finished. This means the printed circuitry is only on one side. Components can be installed from either or both sides, although it's more common for the components to be on one side (the component side) and the circuitry and soldered connections on the other side (the solder side).

PCBs with through hole parts, as opposed to surface-mount devices, need lots of holes drilled, along with any mounting holes that are required. These holes are usually drilled by a computer numerical control (CNC) machine at very high speeds and with amazing accuracy. The blank boards are usually stacked and many boards (from three to ten) drilled at the same time with a single drill bit. The really big machines have multiple drill spindles running in parallel, each drilling its own stack of PCB panels.

Once upon a time, not so long ago, these drilling machines used paper tape to store the data for the drill sizes and hole locations. You still hear people refer to *drill files* and *drill tapes* interchangeably.

All the points on the PCB are electrically connected together at first, all being within the plane of the highly conductive copper foil on the blank PCB. To form the individual wires and connections between components, the unnecessary copper is removed, usually by a chemical etching process. A pattern of what should stay and what should go is produced at the end of the design process (you get to that in a bit), and this is called the *artwork* for the copper layer. Typically, this artwork is printed on large transparent sheets (still often called *plotted* or *photoplotted* because it was once done with plotters) and is used in a photographic process to allow some of the copper to be made insensitive to the chemical etch (that is, converted into *etch resist*) and the remainder to be left sensitive the etching process. This process generally takes many steps by itself. The board is then etched in acid, removing the vulnerable, untreated copper but leaving the protected, resistant areas.

On a single-sided PCB, it almost doesn't matter if the component holes are drilled before or after the copper has been etched. The production of *double-sided* PCBs, however, requires a plating process to connect the two sides where connections are necessary; and this must be done after the board is drilled but *before* the board is etched, because the electroplating process requires a conductive path. Because many PCB production facilities build both single- and double-sided PCBs, the order of the processes is determined by the physical layout of the machinery in the plant, which is often optimized for fastest production.

Once drilled and etched, a PCB can be stuffed with components and soldered together. In most cases, except for extremely cost-sensitive products, two additional manufacturing steps are performed. This first is to coat the board with a specific pattern of *solder mask*, or *solder resist*. This layer covers the entire PCB except the points specifically requiring solder, such as component holes and connectors. The solder mask layer helps separate tightly spaced component leads and prevent shorts and solder bridges from forming between parts. The solder mask is what typically gives common PCBs their green color. It can be any color you want, if your PCB supplier is willing to do this for you.

The final layer applied to a PCB is often the *silkscreen* or *parts legend*. This is a way of printing text such as reference designators and component values as well as part outlines and any explanatory information, such as part numbers. This layer is called a silkscreen because that is the usual method of applying the contrasting ink to the board. White ink on green solder mask is generally the cheapest combination, which accounts for its overwhelming popularity.

After all the additional layers have been applied, some form of final plating is done to the exposed copper; otherwise it would rapidly oxidize. A tin-lead mixture was until recently the most popular option, but this is being replaced because lead is being phased out of most electronic production facilities (what with it being poisonous and all). Gold is another popular choice, not only for its beautiful luster but also due to its excellent electrical properties and noble character. Gold is a member of the noble metals because it's naturally resistant to corrosion and oxidation and therefore makes an excellent plating for electrical contacts.

You can start to see that a lot of different kinds of artwork and design files are required in the traditional manufacture of PCBs. You can also hack away the copper from a blank panel with a Dremel tool or an X-ACTO knife and then drill all the holes by hand. It's tedious and time-consuming, but sometimes that's exactly what you want in a hobby. It also gives you the freedom to put the art back in artwork, if you so choose.

In earnest, there are a lot of excellent methods for producing small batches of PCBs yourself, and the results very often are more personally meaningful than what can be made by a machine.

PCB Layout Techniques

It doesn't matter what specific manufacturing technique you use to fabricate a PCB. It needs to be well-designed and follow a few simple rules to work effectively as a substrate for your circuit. This applies whether you're using state-of-the-art CAD software or masking tape with ferrous chloride. Let's review a few basic tenets and see some examples of how to apply them, using your IR proximity sensor as a test run.

First, give yourself some room. This applies both to your production area as well as your design. Yes, you can cram all the parts in as close as possible and do some tricky routing to get everything connected, but then you have a board that's hard to assemble and even harder to repair. Only when you begin getting into production quantities of PCBs does the cost of those precious square inches or millimeters outweigh the practical concerns of assembly, troubleshooting, and repair.

■ **Note**   *Please* design your inventions to be repairable. The world's oceans and landfills thank you.

Next, remember that although copper is an excellent conductor of electricity, the copper on your PCB is typically quite thin. One-ounce copper cladding is a very standard thickness of copper for printed circuit work. This means there is one ounce of copper for every square foot of surface area (take *that*, metric system!). This equates to a typical thickness of just 0.00134" to 0.00140" of copper in your connections. Make those connections, called *traces*, as fat and wide as you possibly can. If it still fits and it doesn't overlap another signal, it's not too fat. Two-ounce copper and half-ounce copper are also commonly available, with twice and half the copper thickness, respectively.

Back to room issues. Between those fat traces are the *spaces*, and these need to be as big as you can make them, too. The etch process isn't perfect, and sometimes it etches too much (*overetch*), eating away at your conducting wires; and sometimes it doesn't etch enough (*underetch*), possibly leaving visible or microscopic shorts between your signals. PCB houses will tell you up front what their minimum *traces and spaces* capabilities are. Don't push it to the limit everywhere all the time. Give yourself and your PCB design plenty of room.

PCB units are generally intended to measure pretty small things. Therefore, thousandths of an inch are called *mils*, which has *nothing* to do with the metric system. One mil = 0.001". Get used to thinking in terms of mils, unless you live in France. Millimeters are also used a lot.

Label everything possible on your board. If you're going to forego a proper silkscreen, you can still put text in the copper layer. If you're scratching out your boards by hand, consider typing up a label to stick on your board after it's assembled. Future generations will thank you.

Laying out a PCB takes time, patience, and, above all, practice. Don't be afraid to start over, perhaps many times. Using CAD tools makes this a lot easier.

One way to approach laying out your first few PCB designs is to imitate the layout of the schematic. It's not a *good* way, and it's far from ideal, but it's relatively easy and helps to get you started. Otherwise the translation from conceptual schematic to physical layout can be a hurdle too high for aspiring designers, and they quit. Don't quit! Don't be lazy! Don't be afraid to do it wrong a few times and then completely start from scratch and do it again.

Let's apply some of these ideas to your IR proximity sensor. It can certainly be laid out in a compact and efficient manner, but it would prove quite difficult to assemble by hand. In addition, the *routing* of all the connections becomes much more challenging as the available room diminishes. You begin with a blank PCB that is two inches on a side—more than enough room to effectively place the components and still have enough room between them to easily get everything connected.

A First Attempt

The components are placed on the PCB in sorta-kinda the same arrangement as the schematic. It's not an absolutely faithful copy, because the physical components aren't exactly the same size as their schematic symbols. A little nudging and playing around with the placement of the components result in the arrangement shown in Figure 10-7.

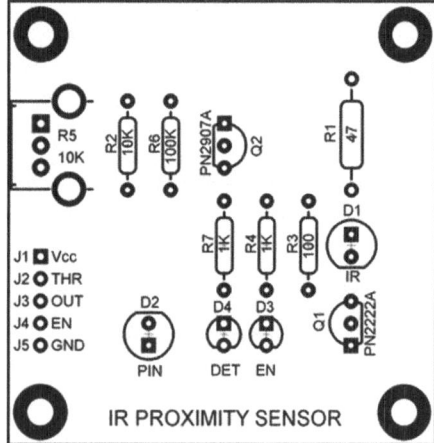 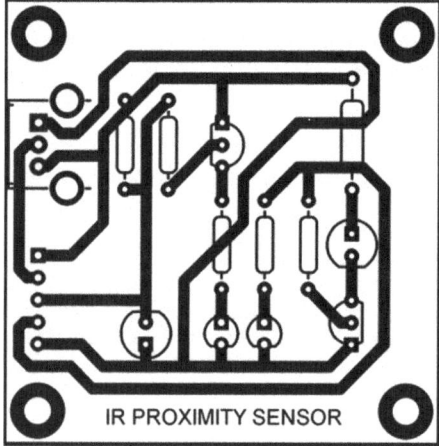

Figure 10-7. The first attempt at laying out the IR proximity sensor on a PCB. The image on the left contains the component pads, part outlines, reference designators, and component values, and is often called an assembly drawing, *because it can help in assembling the PCB. The image on the right shows the copper layer and component pads as well the parts outline for reference.*

Figure 10-7 shows two distinct views of the same PCB, each one offering different information about the board. These views are composites of several of the individual pieces of artwork that would be needed to actually build the PCB.

The view on the left shows a good approximation of what the blank PCB looks like before it's filled with parts and assembled. This is called an *assembly drawing* and can be used as an aid to constructing the final circuit.

Because this is a through-hole design, all the component leads are threaded through the board and soldered into place. The excess leads are then trimmed and discarded. Each of the component leads has a doughnut-shaped pad surrounding the hole. Most of the pads are round, but a few of them are square. The square holes are usually there to indicate something special, such as proper part orientation when it matters, or the numbering of pins in a series. A square pin usually indicates pin 1 in a series or group of similar pins, although this convention is, unfortunately, not universally adopted.

If this board was manufactured as a single-sided PCB, it would be possible to omit the pads from the top side (the component side), leaving only the pads on the bottom (the solder side). This is because all the soldering would be done on the bottom. It's generally cheaper to build a single-sided PCB than a double-side PCB, because there are fewer steps involved in the manufacturing process.

However, a double-sided PCB can have all the holes *plated* with metal using an electroplate process during manufacture. This provides an electrical connection between the two sides of the board, where appropriate. Also, the solder joint between a component lead and the PCB itself is much stronger, both mechanically and electrically, when you use a plated-through hole versus just a pad on one side of a single-sided PCB.

The component outlines, reference designators, and values are printed on the board using a silkscreen printing process. These assist in identifying the locations of the parts for assembly, testing, troubleshooting, and repair.

The border around the edge of the board defines the board's *profile*. This tells a machine, usually a high-speed CNC router, how to cut the individual PCB out of the panel from which it was produced. Alternately, it can show you approximately where to point your hacksaw.

The image on the right shows the same board outline, component pads, and outlines as well as the identifying label announcing IR PROXIMITY SENSOR. These items are shown only for reference; the main thing you need to look at in this image is the copper pattern. This pattern, in conjunction with the component pads, forms the traces and spaces of the circuitry that remain after the unneeded copper is removed in the etch process. The bulk of the traces will be covered by the solder mask layer, if applied, leaving only the component pads exposed. These component pads should be plated to prevent the inevitable oxidation of the copper material.

Here's an important concept to understand right now and never forget. The copper layer describes the bottom side of this particular PCB. However, you're *not* looking at the back side of the board. The convention with all PCB artwork is that you're looking *through* the PCB as if it were semitransparent. That way, when it comes time to plot the individual artwork layers, everyone is on the same page and can align everything properly.

■ **Note**   You're always looking *through* the PCB artwork, from the top to the bottom.

Because these components are spaced so far apart, and there is so much room between the component leads, it wasn't difficult to *route* all the traces on a single side of the PCB. On a tighter design, it might have been necessary to route some of the wires on the top as well as the bottom.

On especially tricky signals, it's sometimes necessary to start out on one side of the board but end up on another by travelling through a *via*, or extra plated-through hole added to facilitate a wiring connection. Once upon a time, and possibly even today, you would be charged extra for each hole or via contained in your design. Today, most PCBs are priced according to the number of layers and total surface area, excluding any special services you want, such as purple solder mask or gold plating.

Notice that all the traces are nice and fat (0.050" wide, or 50 mils, to be exact) with plenty of open spaces between traces and component pads. Because this layout mimics the schematic, most of the wiring connections are relatively short. This resulted, however, in all the best routes being taken early, leaving a couple of traces to have to wander all over the board to find their ways home.

Overall, this isn't a *bad* PCB layout. It could easily be manufactured at home or at a professional PCB fabrication facility. Being a little on the large side is a big *plus* when building prototypes. The only real drawback to this design is that the IR LED and the PIN photodiode aren't physically close to each other, which would normally be a desired arrangement. Of course, there's no reason the two optoelectronic parts couldn't be mounted *off-board* by extending the component leads with wires. Then you could place the two parts wherever you wanted in relation to each other.

A More Compact Version

Let's take a quick look at a slightly more compact version of the same circuit. See Figure 10-8.

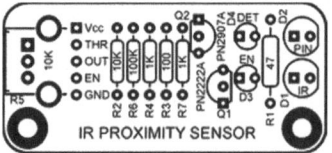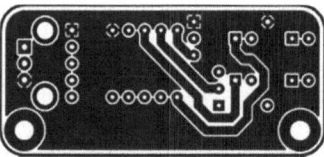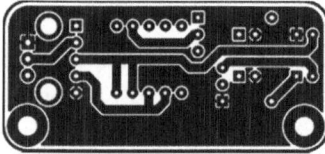

Figure 10-8. A more compact version of the IR proximity sensor, showing assembly drawing (left), top copper layer (center), and bottom copper layer (right)

Again you have an assembly drawing that shows the relative positions of the components along with their reference designators and component values. Due to the lack of wide-open spaces, some of the traces were routed on the top side and some were routed on the bottom side.

The power and ground connections are made using *copper floods* or ground planes. These are the dark areas in the artwork. The top ground plane is actually the V_{cc} signal. The ground plane on the bottom side is the ground signal. The component leads that attach to these two signals, or *nets*, are connected with up to four small traces, radiating from the center of the pad. The extra space around the pad is called a *thermal relief*. If the pads became part of the larger plane, it would be very difficult to solder, because the ground plane is made of copper, which is an excellent *thermal* conductor as well as an electrical conductor. The pads that do *not* attach to the ground planes have a small relief around them as well to electrically isolate them from the copper flood.

All signals on a PCB are called *nets*, even if they connect only two points. A *net list* is a listing of all the connections between all the components on a PCB.

This more compact version of the IR proximity sensor is less than half the size of the previous version (2.00" × 0.90" to be precise) and could be made even smaller by using surface-mount devices instead of through-hole components. Two mounting holes have been eliminated, but they would most likely not be needed for such a small board. All the part labels and identifying marks are retained. The profile of the PCB now uses rounded corners.

The main difference, besides the size shrinkage, is that the IR LED and photodiode are now side by side at the end of the PCB. In actual usage, there could be IR light leakage between the two, when you want to measure the *reflected* IR returning from an obstacle or target. This can be minimized by inserting an opaque barrier between the two devices or installing a shroud of black heat-shrink tubing around one component or the other.

Also note that the compact version of the PCB bears little resemblance to the original schematic, as far as the placement of the components is concerned. That's OK. The two designs express the same ideas but with different intentions and applications.

Making the Connection

How do you connect this sensor to an Arduino? No specific connector is identified in either the schematic or the PCB designs. Right now it's just a line of holes in the PCB, with each hole spaced 1/10" (100 mils) from the next. Pin 1 is indicated by the square pad, and the rest have round pads.

You could solder in a female header, similar to the expansion connectors on the Arduino. Then you could install jumper wires between the module and the Arduino.

You could just as easily solder wires directly to the board and then stuff the other ends of those wires into your Arduino's expansion connectors. That would work until anything moved.

Another option is to rearrange the interface pins to directly correspond with the expansion connectors on your Arduino. This could be the basis for an entire Arduino shield or a *wing*; that is, a module that plugs into only one or two of the expansion connectors and doesn't entirely cover (or *shield*) the Arduino I/O Board. Such a design in presented in Figure 10-9.

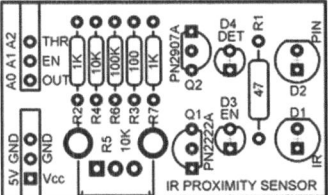 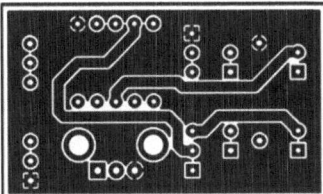 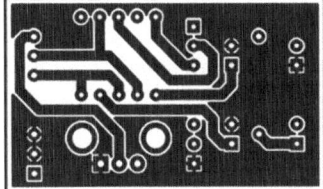

Figure 10-9. An Arduino wing that holds the IR proximity sensor. The assembly drawing is on the left, illustrating the component layout. The top copper layer is in the center. The bottom copper layer is on the right.

Again you have an assembly drawing, showing the relative positions of all the components. The center image is the top copper layer, again with a copper flood that constitutes the V_{cc} net. The image on the right is the bottom copper layer with its ground plane. Header pins can be soldered to the bottom of this wing design, allowing the board to be directly installed on the bottom two expansion connectors (POWER and ANALOG) of the Arduino I/O Board.

Analog pin A0 is the analog voltage input that inversely corresponds to the amount of IR light detected. Analog pin A1 must now be used as a digital output and becomes the IR emitter enable output. Analog input A2 can serve as the threshold setting input.

A partial connector outline on the silkscreen layer helps the user align the wing properly when plugging it into the Arduino. All the components are labeled with their reference designators and values.

An entire Arduino shield devoted to a single IR proximity sensor might be considered overkill, but it's certainly possible. A six-channel IR proximity sensor, on the other hand, might be useful for a mobile robot that needs to see in several directions at the same time.

You come back to this simple circuit later in the book.

Your Own Custom Arduino

It's not a big jump to go from designing your own Arduino shield to designing your own Arduino I/O Board. There's a lot of flexibility in what can properly be called an Arduino-compatible device. Pick the processor you want to use, slap on the parts it needs, and then decide what other ingredients you want on your ~~pizza~~ Arduino.

You need to make several design decisions along the way. These include compatibility with existing Arduinos and shields, power-supply options, processor selection, and additional circuitry. Let's look at each of these areas in a little detail, so you can get on your way to making your own Arduino.

Compatibility with Existing Arduinos and Shields

You should think about this topic first, because it will affect how you begin your design. You're completely free to go in your own direction when building an Arduino-compatible device, but having some initial design goals helps in the decision-making process down the road. Also, a clear set of design goals lets you know when you're finished, which can get somewhat blurry as projects roll on and on.

Hardware Compatibility

If you want to maintain even a modest amount of physical compatibility with the Arduino family, then you can use the existing design files made available by the Arduino Team. Go to the Arduino Hardware web page (http://arduino.cc/en/Main/Hardware) and pick which Arduino model you'd like to emulate, or the one that best suits your needs. You can even take a trip into the past and choose from one of the older Arduino models, if that more closely resembles your design target. Look at the Arduino Hardware Index at http://arduino.cc/en/Main/Boards, and download the schematics and EAGLE files. You cover the EAGLE CAD software later in this chapter.

If you start with one of the existing Arduino designs, try to keep the expansion connectors and mounting holes in the same location. Leaving the board profile intact also makes your PCB more readily identifiable as an Arduino-compatible device. This ensures at least physical compatibility for the wide variety of shields that are already out there. If you know positively that you won't want to add any shields to your board, then you can eliminate the expansion connectors and mounting holes.

The locations of the USB connector and the power jack are problematic. These two components are taller than the expansion headers and protrude vertically from the PCB. The standard full-size B connector on official Arduino I/O Boards has a metal case that will short against any circuitry on an installed shield. Most shield designers know about this and leave that area free of exposed circuitry. If you move your USB connector (assuming you're using a USB connector), you may possibly run into this problem in the future.

Software Compatibility

In addition to mechanical and form-factor compatibility, there are also issues of software compatibility. Will your new Arduino be programmable using the standard Arduino software? If so, you need to make provision for a bootloader. This includes not only being able to program the bootloader into a blank AVR, but also the circuitry required to activate and talk to the bootloader during normal operation.

The traditional Arduino bootloader operates over the serial port. It uses the TX and RX pins to communicate back and forth between the host PC, where the sketch is being written, debugged, and compiled, and the target device, which is the processor on board your Arduino I/O Board. It also uses one of the traditional serial-port handshaking lines, data terminal ready (DTR) to induce a reset pulse on the AVR chip. The DTR signal is normally *capacitively coupled* to the -RESET line so that only changes in the DTR line cause a reset, thus preventing the DTR line from keeping the AVR chip held in a reset state. This restarts the chip, which is supposed to be configured to automatically start running the bootloader code. At this point, the host PC and the target device should have a nice little conversation, usually about uploading a new sketch. If no conversation ensues, the chip begins executing the previously uploaded sketch, if any.

All the serial interface lines—TX, RX, and DTR—must be at TTL-compatible voltage levels by the time they arrive at the AVR chip. This is taken care of automatically when using the traditional FTDI USB-TTL interface chip or the recently adopted Atmel ATmega8U2 microcontroller with USB interface.

You can omit the serial or USB interface on your design if you provide some other method of talking to the bootloader. One popular solution is to leave the actual USB interface entirely off-board and only make provision for a programming header on the board. This allows the USB circuitry to be planted on a removable cable and installed only when needed, thus saving the cost and PCB real estate that would otherwise be committed to each Arduino-compatible controller.

Power Supply Options

All electronic devices need power. You have to make some provision for getting this power to your board, and making sure it's of the right flavor and color. Not only do you have to provide more than enough power for the processor and related circuitry, but you also need to make some allowance for any devices that may attach to your Arduino.

If you don't know exactly how you want to power your new design, then copy the existing Arduino power-supply circuit. It's OK. You already have the company's blessing to do so. The existing Arduino power-supply design has evolved over several generations of Arduino models. In fact, it could very well be the *most* evolved aspect of the entire Arduino project. It has multiple input-connector options and gracefully handles both regulated and unregulated voltage supplies. It even handles itself well under bad circumstances, utilizing components that intentionally shut themselves down under adverse conditions.

If you already have a good idea of what your power-supply options are, then go ahead and design them into your board. It's always a good idea, however, to allow for a potential Plan B scenario, even if it's just an extra set of power terminals somewhere in the mix.

Both the ATmega328 and the ATmega2560 microcontrollers require a regulated 5V supply to run at or near their maximum clock rates. A good design practice is to place one or more large filter capacitors somewhere either near the on-board voltage regulator (if used) or near where the power enters the PCB. A 47µF capacitor is deemed sufficient by the Arduino Team for their boards, but a little more won't hurt and probably won't cost most, either. Also place at least one smaller capacitor, 0.1µF or so, near each of the power pins of the microcontroller device and any other component that uses or switches any significant amount of current. This will prevent spurious glitches on your supply busses that could lead to erratic behavior. It's also a good idea to add some of these smaller capacitors at any point where power *exits* your board.

Processor Selection

You can use any microcontroller you want—really you can. If you choose one of the microcontrollers that have already been used in one of the official Arduino I/O Boards, then you can use the existing bootloader firmware and library cores that have already been written and tested.

Nobody says you have to use an Atmel AVR. That's been the trend out of Italy, but then again they're consensus builders and are working hard to make it easier for everyone to get up and running with the Arduino. If you're a rebel and want to drop a Socket 7 processor into the mix, go ahead. Blaze that trail! Be a dear and drop you a note when you get there.

Generally speaking, your processor selection is mostly determined by your required pin count. Every member of the AVR family is based on the same CPU core, from the teeniest ATtiny to the most monstrous ATmega.

Atmel also manufactures a broad line of ARM-based, 32-bit microcontrollers. The Netduino is produced by Secret Labs LLC (www.netduino.com) and features the AT91SAM7X, a 48MHz microcontroller with 128KB of program memory and 60KB of SRAM. The Netduino is compatible with the .NET Micro Framework, which means you can develop applications for it in C# using Microsoft's Visual C# Express 2010. So don't think you're fenced in by the selection of available AVR devices.

After pin count, available program space is most likely the next major criterion in processor selection. The original Arduinos had the ATmega8 processor and its 8KB of program memory, and many interesting and exciting projects were launched with it. The 32KB program memory of the current

ATmega328 device is ample for most small applications, but it's certainly possible to use it all up once your project develops a few features.

The monster ATmega2560 installed on the Arduino Mega 2560 has both the largest program memory (256KB) and the largest pin count at 100 pins. If you need more than that, you have to look elsewhere.

You should give serious consideration to providing an In-System Programming (ISP) header for the main processor on your board, assuming you're staying within the AVR family of devices. Doing so allows you to program blank, factory-fresh processors using the correct device-programming hardware. This step isn't optional unless you're planning to either buy the parts already programmed and properly configured or have some other mechanism in place for programming the parts before installing them in your new board. Even if you don't think you need an ISP header for the traditional reasons (bootloader burning and so on), it can also serve as a debug port if you happen to have the right hardware (AVR Dragon, JTAGICE mkII) and software (AVR Studio, avarice), allowing you to both program and debug your application with access to individual registers and memory locations at runtime. You can even *single-step* your program through the source code or machine-language instructions, checking that it's meticulously doing your bidding at every step. Include that little six-pin header in your design even if you don't think you'll ever use it. You don't have to actually install the pins, but it's nice to know you can.

Anything Else?

What makes *your* Arduino special? Why are you going to the trouble and expense of designing your own? Here is the best part about designing your own Arduino from scratch: it can literally be anything you want it to be.

It can be spartanly simple or bizarrely complex. For the utmost in simplicity, strip out everything nonessential and stick to the bare minimum. See Figure 10-10.

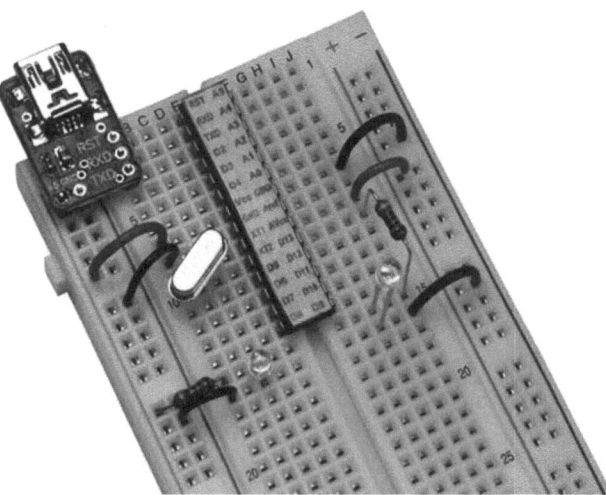

Figure 10-10. A breadboard Arduino circuit with removable USB adapter. This is perhaps the least of all possible Arduinos, but someone will probably find a way to do it with less.

Bear in mind that you can design a very complex circuit but then only populate the parts you need at the time. See Figure 10-11.

Figure 10-11. *A partially populated Arduino Duemilanove PCB with only the minimal parts required for USB support. This prototype was used in the digital clock example project in Chapter 7.*

There's an old saying that some hold to be true: never build what you can buy. Or was it the other way around?

Design Software

You don't have to use a computer and software to design electronic devices, but it does make it more challenging to do so. The tools at your disposal are a very personal choice. Use what works for you. On the other hand, keep an open mind when it comes to the tools you select for a task. Invest some time in learning more about the tools you already have, and don't be afraid to try new tools as well. Sometimes seeing how others fail is a great motivator.

There are more computer-aided design (CAD) tools available for designing PCBs than there are pages in this book, with more popping up every day. Let's look at just one of them, which has a special link to the Arduino project. Feel free to try this and many other tools on your journey.

CadSoft EAGLE

The Arduino was designed and documented using the popular electronic design automation (EDA) software EAGLE from CadSoft (www.cadsoftusa.com). EAGLE is an acronym meaning Easily Applicable Graphical Layout Editor, so technically it should always be written using capital letters.

EAGLE is proprietary software available for Microsoft Windows, Linux, and Mac. CadSoft offers a variety of end-user licenses, ranging from a free, limited version (the EAGLE Light Edition) for nonprofit or evaluation purposes to full Professional licenses with various numbers of users.

All versions of EAGLE have three main modules. The Schematic module lets you draw your circuit and make a very nice-looking document to share. The Layout Editor module lets you convert your schematic to a PCB layout and generate the industry-standard files necessary to have your PCBs manufactured. There is a back-and-forth connection between the schematic and the PCB layout editor, allowing you to back annotate your design from either program. The Autorouter module attempts to connect all the parts in your circuit using wires on the PCB layout, which is very interesting to watch. You can also *route* the traces (wires) on your PCB by hand.

Parts are defined using a library editor to define both the schematic symbol and the PCB footprint, as well as the relationship between the two. The standard EAGLE library comes with thousands of predefined parts. You can also define your own parts and share your library with other EAGLE users.

EAGLE also supports its own scripting language, which can automate many tasks. An example of what you can do with the scripting language is EAGLE3D (`www.matwei.de/doku.php?id=en:eagle3d:eagle3d`) by Matthias Weißer, a three-dimensional rendering script that takes your PCB layout and generates a script that can be interpreted by the open source program Persistence of Vision Raytracer (POV-Ray, `www.povray.org`), also available for Windows, Mac OS/Mac OS X, and i86 Linux. Really nice images can be generated. See Matthias's web site for several good examples.

EAGLE has a bit of a learning curve, but it isn't too terribly difficult. There are, at last count, a bajillion tutorials available online for learning EAGLE.

EAGLE Tips

The free-of-cost version of EAGLE limits you to a single sheet for drawing (what the industry calls *capturing*) the schematic diagram of your circuit. Luckily, you can make this one sheet as big as you want.

Try to keep your schematics logically organized. Feel free to add notes to remind yourself of any interesting or non-obvious aspects of your design. Just as with the PCB layout, don't try to cram everything as close together as possible. Use some of that whitespace.

You can name everything on your schematic, both the parts and the connections between them. You can make these labels visible or not. Every component can also have a value. For some components, this doesn't make sense; and for others, a single value isn't enough. You can always add additional text to the schematic, but it won't be associated with any particular part as the name and value are.

When you move a part, the name and value move with it. You can adjust the placement of the name and value, but only after you smash the part. The name and value still move with the part if the part is subsequently moved.

Parts in EAGLE come from a parts library. Thousands of parts are included, grouped into distinct libraries, and many more are available online. You're strongly encouraged to learn to make your own parts from scratch.

To make your own parts, you must understand the relationship between a schematic symbol, a physical package, and the possible connections between them. Many components are available in different packages, and EAGLE accommodates this well. Again, you're encouraged to master the creation of new parts from scratch, because doing so liberates you from the limitations of the existing libraries. There's always one part you need that's either not available or not up to your standards.

EAGLE offers direct-to-PDF printing options, making it easy to share your designs across many platforms. You can also create image files directly from the screen. Always create your distributable content in monochrome (black and white). It's much easier to read both on a computer screen and in print.

You can use EAGLE to generate artwork directly on a printer, using either toner-transfer paper or transparency material.

To have your PCB professionally produced, EAGLE also has a very sophisticated facility for exporting industry-standard production files. The best way to learn how to do this is to contact your PCB fab and ask what formats it can accept. Generally these are Gerber files for the layer artwork and Excellon drill files for the holes. Each PCB house has its own preferences for how these files should be formatted and named. Some services accept EAGLE files directly, which saves you time and perhaps helps avoid file-translation problems.

Summary

Just enough to get you interested, but not enough to do it for you: that was the goal of this chapter. Designing your own circuits (or borrowing them from others) is a wonderfully engaging activity. It pulls in several different parts of your brain and makes them cooperate to achieve the goal. This gives some people headaches. Other people get great ideas.

A circuit can be as simple or as complex as you need it to be. Start simple, prove what works, and try to understand why. *Then* move on to more complex designs. And repeat. Always repeat. Build your skill set, and you build yourself.

Now that you've got a good idea about the hard stuff, let's dive deep into some of that soft stuff in the next chapter. How hard could it be?

CHAPTER 11

Software Design

By now you've developed an appreciation of how much software is involved in the Arduino phenomenon. It's everywhere! Let's take a quick look at some of the more advanced things you can do with the existing Arduino software, such as creating your own Arduino libraries and targeting alternate cores (that is, something other than the ATmega328 or the ATmega2560). Then you look at some of the tools you can use to augment or replace the Arduino software infrastructure.

Advanced Topics Within Arduino

The first part of this chapter is devoted to a couple of semiadvanced software topics that fit squarely within the Arduino software's domain.

You can develop very modularized code with Arduino by utilizing its version of a library system. You design your software widget to perform a particular task or range of tasks, conceal all the "how" deep inside your library, and expose only the high-level functions needed to interact with the library's functionality.

If you'd like to use the Arduino software environment with an AVR chip that hasn't traditionally been supported, you can certainly do so, by writing your own core files to support it. This chapter examines in detail an example of how to write programs for the diminutive and inexpensive ATtiny13A using the Arduino environment.

Writing Arduino Libraries

Arduino libraries are distributed in a different format than, say, the `avr-libc` library. Arduino libraries consist of uncompiled source code and header files, with optional keyword definitions and example sketches. Let's go through the process of setting up a simple Arduino library. Once installed in the correct location, your new library and associated examples should be accessible from within the Arduino IDE.

Arduino libraries often implement *objects*, using C++ techniques. For those seasoned C++ developers out there, this makes perfect sense, and there will be murmurs of "but of course" and "how else?" For the rest of the C-loving world, and those still learning C++, this can serve as a *very* limited introduction to *object-oriented programming* (OOP). If the deep, dark secrets of C++ don't interest you, you can skip the explanations, but you still need to comply with the methodology outlined if you want to create or even effectively use Arduino libraries.

In case you're wondering, everything else you've been doing so far in these example sketches falls under the category of *procedural programming*. You've been instructing the Arduino to 1) do this, 2) do that, and 3) do this other thing, outlining a *procedure* for manipulating data and performing predefined actions. It's certainly easier to follow and understand, and makes for better example sketches. Real-life applications, however, may be different.

OOP, on the other hand, focuses on *objects*, which are abstract collections of associated data and functions. There are some decided advantages to the object paradigm, including encapsulation, inheritance, and possibly polymorphism, but you don't need to get into all that right now. Here you approach the writing of Arduino libraries and its brush with OOP in the traditional, time-tested Arduino way: by blinking an LED.

A Trivial Example Arduino Library: LED

A few words about how the Arduino software provides support for libraries are in order. Within the file folder hierarchy of the Arduino software installation is a folder called `libraries`. In this file folder, also known as a *subdirectory*, is a collection of even more folders. These folders bear a striking resemblance to the menu items found in the Arduino software, specifically the Sketch ➤ Import Library menu item. You should also find the same list at the bottom of the File ➤ Examples menu. Your new LED library will appear in these places as well, after you've placed the files for the library in the right place.

You'll call your new library LED. Create a file folder named `LED` in the `libraries` folder of the Arduino installation. When you restart the Arduino software, this new library appears in the Sketch ➤ Import Library menu but, oddly enough, *not* in the File ➤ Examples menu. You can even click the LED menu item in the Sketch ➤ Import Library menu item, but nothing happens, because there is no header file to import (yet).

At a minimum, you need to create two new files for your library. The first file is the source code for the actual implementation of the library functions. This file *must* have the specific C++ source file extension `.cpp`. You can't use the old `.pde` or the new `.ino` file extension used for sketches. Make sure your editor doesn't automatically append an extension for you, such as `.txt`. You can't use the Arduino code editor to write these files, because it wants to protect you from making file-naming errors, such as using the `.cpp` extension.

The Library Header File LED.h

The other file you need to create is a header file with a `.h` file extension. The header file is where you store the definitions needed to use the library in your sketches. For the purposes of this admittedly brief introduction, call the header file `LED.h`. In reality, you can name your header file anything you want. The Sketch ➤ Import Library menu item adds references to *all* header files contained in the library folder you choose.

Your library's header file should, in turn, include the `Arduino.h` header file. This header file defines all the built-in Arduino-specific functions that are normally needed in a sketch. The Arduino software includes this file for you automatically when compiling a regular sketch, but not for a library.

In previous versions of the Arduino software, the `Arduino.h` file was called `WProgram.h`. It was inherited, as were many Arduino details, from the Wiring project. This change in header file names will cause a problem for users of your library who are running Arduino 0022 or older. To support users who haven't yet transitioned to the Arduino 1.0 software, you can include a conditional preprocessor directive that examines the `ARDUINO` symbol that is included on the command line sent to the compiler. It ends up looking something like this:

```
#if ARDUINO < 100
#include <WProgram.h>
#else
#include <Arduino.h>
#endif
```

If the Arduino software version is less than 100 (supposedly indicating 1.00; older releases such as 0022 were assigned a value of 22), then the older WProgram.h file is included. If the software is version 1.0 or later, the newer Arduino.h file is included. If you plan to release or share your libraries with others, at least for the next year or so (not everyone upgrades as soon as a new version is released), then please consider adding this workaround to your library header files.

You can also use this type of check in the future if you want your code to be able to tell what version of the Arduino software is being used. This can come in handy when you want to use a new feature or need to provide a workaround solution as just outlined.

After this, add the definition of the library's object *class*. A C++ class is similar, in a very broad way, to a compound data type that can hold both functions, known as *methods*, and data, referred to as *members*.

The class definition can have both *public* and *private* parts. The public parts are visible to all parts of your sketch. You want the principle methods to be public, for example, while hiding the internal variables by declaring them of private scope. Or the exact opposite—it depends on your object's purpose. Let's outline a simple class to start; feel free to go crazy with it later.

The first items listed in a class definition are private by default. You can add an additional private: heading later in the definition if you need to mix the private and public parts.

As mentioned, a class can contain methods that are peculiar to it. One special method is called a *constructor*. If defined, it's called when a new instance of a class is created. You can have more than one constructor for a class as long as they all have a different signature—that is, a different combination of parameters or types of parameters. For example, you could have a constructor that took no parameters as well as one that took a byte parameter. The compiler can tell them apart by the number or type of parameters given, and you can define different methods depending on how the constructor gets called.

Let's take a stab at defining your class now. It looks something like this:

```
class LED {
            byte _pin; // the pin number
            byte _state; // the state of the LED:  HIGH or LOW
        public:
            LED(byte pin); // the constructor
            void on();
            void off();
            void toggle();
            byte state();
};
```

In the public section of the class definition, you see prototypes of five functions. The first function is considered a constructor because it shares the name of the class, LED. You declare only one type of constructor in this example, but you can create as many as you like, as long as they all have different numbers or types of parameters. The constructor function is special in that it doesn't specify a return type.

The other functions define code that you'll write in the implementation phase, which properly belong in the LED.cpp file. You can probably guess what they do.

You wrap up the header file by enclosing it within a conditional compiler directive to prevent recursive inclusion. Wow, that's a mouthful; say that three times fast. You do this by checking to see if a compiler symbol named LED_h has *already* been defined. The #ifndef is super-short for "if not defined." It shouldn't be, unless this header file has been included somewhere upstream. It shouldn't be, and by making this check you prevent it from being duplicated.

If the symbol *hasn't* been defined, then you define it: #define LED_h. Then comes the actual class definition, and then the close of the compiler conditional statement, #endif. There's not that much to the library header file at this point. Listing 11-1 shows what it ought to look like, unless you've already started taking liberties.

Listing 11-1. LED Example Library Header File, LED.h

```
// LED.h - Example library for manipulating LEDs - public domain

#ifndef LED_h
#define LED_h

#if ARDUINO < 100
#include <WProgram.h>
#else
#include <Arduino.h>
#endif

class LED {
            byte _pin; // the pin number
            byte _state; // the state of the LED:  HIGH=on, LOW=off
      public:
            LED(byte pin); // the constructor
            void on(); // turn the LED on
            void off(); // turn the LED off
            void toggle(); // toggle the LED
            byte state(); // return the current state of the LED
};

#endif
```

The Library Implementation File LED.cpp

The implementation source code file is where all the code lives. Again, name this example file LED.cpp to keep things simple. You start out with the library's own header file, LED.h. Note that the Arduino.h file is surrounded by angle brackets (in the library header file) whereas the library header file LED.h gets double quotes in the implementation file. The angle brackets tell the compiler to look in the designated location for system header files, and the double quotes tell it to look in the same subdirectory as the current source file.

Because the library implementation file includes the library header file, and the library header file includes the Arduino.h file, you can use the built-in Arduino functions in the implementation file without having to explicitly include the Arduino.h file.

Now you can define all of your class's methods, and you're finished. Listing 11-2 shows what a first version of the LED library's source code might look like.

Listing 11-2. Implementation File (Source Code) for the Example LED Library

```
// LED.cpp - Example library to manipulate LEDs - public domain

#include "LED.h"

// the constructor

LED::LED(byte pin) {
        _pin = pin; // save the pin number
        pinMode(pin, OUTPUT); // configure pin as output
}

// the public methods

void LED::on() {
        digitalWrite(_pin, HIGH); // turn on LED
        _state = HIGH;
}

void LED::off() {
        digitalWrite(_pin, LOW); // turn off LED
        _state = LOW;
}

void LED::toggle() {
        if(_state) {
                off();
        } else {
                on();
        }
}

byte LED::state() {
        return _state;
}
```

Let's begin by looking at the constructor. As you can see, class constructors in C++ classes don't have return values, so you skip that part of the definition. In a standard C program (not C++), you would always specify a return value, even if it was void.

Your constructor is called LED::LED(). The first part is the name of the class (LED), the middle part (double colons) is the scope-resolution operator, and the last part is the name of the function. Because the name of the function is the same as the name of the class, this tells the compiler that this is the class's constructor. As mentioned previously, there can be zero or more constructors, depending on how many different ways you need to be able to create these objects and what needs to happen when they're created.

In your example constructor, a single byte parameter named pin is passed to the function, indicating the pin that is connected to the LED you want to control. In this constructor, you stash the value of the incoming parameter into a *private* variable named _pin. Prefixing private members with an underscore is a convention to help you remember who can see what, and when. The pin in question then gets configured to be an OUTPUT using the pinMode() function, although by now you may know some other ways to do this.

The remainder of the functions in the class definition are public in scope, meaning they can all be called directly from your sketches.

Using the LED Library

Let's rewrite your good friend Blink to use this new LED library. See Listing 11-3.

Listing 11-3. Blink Example Sketch,Rewritten to Use the LED Library

```
#include <LED.h>

LED led(13); // assign digital pin 13 to an LED

void setup() {
}

void loop() {
  led.on();
  delay(1000);
  led.off();
  delay(1000);
}
```

The first thing you have to do, in order to use the new LED library, is to add the #include <LED.h> compiler directive to the beginning of your sketch. You can either type this by hand or choose Sketch ➤ Import Library ➤ LED. If you've placed at least the LED.h file in the LED subdirectory of the Arduino libraries folder, the menu item method should work. If you've done that, but the LED library doesn't appear in the menu, you must restart the Arduino software.

To *instantiate* (that is, create an instance of) an LED object, you declare it like any other data type. The data type of your LED class is LED, and you declare an object of type LED with the statement LED led(13);. This prompts the compiler to insert a call to the class constructor. You've defined only one, and it takes a single byte parameter to indicate which pin to use. This parameter is passed to the constructor, and the code in the constructor is executed. In this simple example, all it does is configure the indicated pin as an output and remember the pin number by storing it in a private variable.

Here are some interesting facts about how classes are handled in C++. First, because your object declaration is global in scope (that is, not in any particular function), the object is created even before the setup() function is called. If you had declared the LED object in the setup() function, for example, it wouldn't have been visible in the loop() function. Additionally, you can declare more than one LED object and assign different pins to them. You need to give them different names, of course. Each object automatically has memory allocated for all the private variables, but only one copy of each method is generated.

The setup() function is empty because all the initialization you need for this sketch is performed by the class constructor, which is called when you instantiated the class.

In the loop() function, you see the syntax used for invoking the object's methods. In this simple example, you see the LED being turned on by the led.on(); statement and turned off again by the led.off(); statement.

You don't have to tell it which pin to use, because the object knows best and remembers which pin you specified when it was constructed. The object name is led, the period is the member of operator, and both on() and off() are public methods defined in the class. You already know how the delay() function works.

You can also make things a little fancier by using that toggle() function and changing the delay times based on the state of the LED. See Listing 11-4.

Listing 11-4. Slightly More Complex Version of Blink, Using the LED Library

```
#include <LED.h>

LED led(13); // assign digital pin 13 to an LED

void setup() {
}

void loop() {
  led.toggle();
  if(led.state()) {
    delay(1000);
  } else {
    delay(250);
  }
}
```

The library header file remains included, as does the object declaration. The setup() function remains empty. It's only in the loop() function that you see any changes.

First, notice that neither the led.on() nor the led.off() method is called. Instead, you use a single led.toggle() method call to invert the present state of the LED. The toggle() function uses the private _state variable to decide whether to turn on or turn off the LED. The _state variable is updated whenever the state changes, which for now is only when either the on() or off() method is invoked.

The led.state() function returns the present state of the LED, either HIGH or LOW. Because HIGH corresponds to a one and LOW corresponds to a zero, you can use C's true/false mechanism in a conditional statement to direct the flow of the program. The condensed if(led.state()) is equivalent to if(led.state() == HIGH). In this example, if the LED is on, then a one-second delay is stated. If the LED is off, only a quarter-second delay is performed.

You can just as easily define functions named led.isOn() and led.isOff() for the LED library if you think that reads better. Each would return a true value if its named condition applied.

Obviously, you could apply many optimizations to this trivial example. For example, the state of the LED could easily be determined by inspecting the appropriate bit in the I/O port assigned to the LED; this approach wouldn't require a _state variable to be allocated and maintained. You also know a better way to toggle I/O lines (see Chapter 6). The pinMode(), digitalWrite(), and digitalRead() functions can all be replaced with smaller, faster alternatives. And the list goes on.

Providing Sample Sketches for Your Library

If you'd like to include some sample sketches, illustrating the use of your shiny new library, you can include them in an examples folder in the libraries folder. If you do so, they appear in the File ➤ Examples menu. It's always a good idea to provide simple examples that show how to use a library or at least get started.

Recognizing New Library Keywords

To fully integrate your library into the Arduino environment, you can also supply an optional `keywords.txt` file that describes the new words your library adds to the Arduino's vocabulary. You see this reflected in the color-coded syntax highlighting done by the Arduino code editor.

The code editor differentiates words it recognizes, such as data types, functions, and constants, with different colors and the use of **bold** fonts. You specify these items, one per line, in a plain-text file called `keywords.txt` that resides in the same folder as your library header and implementation files. Listing 11-5 shows an example of what your `keywords.txt` file should look like.

Listing 11-5. keywords.txt File

```
LED        KEYWORD1
on         KEYWORD2
off        KEYWORD2
toggle      KEYWORD2
state       KEYWORD2
```

Each line defines a single keyword. The line starts with the keyword, then a tab (not spaces), and then either `KEYWORD1` for user-defined data types and classes, `KEYWORD2` for methods and functions, or `LITERAL` for constants defined in the class. Your example `LED` library doesn't use any unique literals, whereas the built-in Arduino functions like `pinMode()`, for example, use `INPUT` and `OUTPUT` as literals.

Alternate Cores

Since Arduino release 0018, it has been possible to add support for alternate cores in the Arduino software. This allows developers to use microcontroller chips other than the ones that have been traditionally supported in the Arduino ecosystem: that is, the ATmega8, its successors, and the ATmega2560.

Here is an example showing how to use the Arduino software to write programs for a much smaller device, the ATtiny13A. The ATtiny13A sports 1KB of program memory, 64 bytes of SRAM, a single 8-bit timer/counter with two PWM channels, and a 4-channel analog-to-digital converter (ADC), and runs at up to 20MHz. It's available in an eight-pin package in both surface-mount variations and the traditional dual-inline package (DIP), making it breadboard friendly. Another nice thing about this chip is that the price is about one dollar, even in small quantities.

On the other hand, this little device is, well, little. Quite little. It has a *total* of eight pins, and two of them are V_{cc} and ground, leaving only six. And one of those remaining pins can be either an I/O pin or the RESET pin, and for your purposes it needs to be the RESET pin, so you're left with a grand total of five general-purpose I/O lines.

It's true that the ATtiny13A is also available in a 10- and 20-pin surface-mount package, but those additional pins aren't connected to anything. You don't get the bonus extra ADC inputs as you do with the surface-mount version of the ATmega328. Still, let's see what you can do with five I/O lines.

To convince the Arduino software that you really want to work with a new kind of Arduino board, you need to create at least three new files and some new subdirectories.

First you must identify your Arduino sketches folder on your PC. Select File ➤ Preferences, and look at the first item in the resulting dialog box. It should be Sketchbook Location.

In this folder, you must create a new folder called `hardware`, if it doesn't already exist. This is where the Arduino software looks for information about additional boards, bootloaders, cores, and programmers. In this basic example, you add only one new board and one new core for that board. You see the bootloader and programmer options shortly.

A New Arduino Board: tinyCylon

In this (possibly) new `hardware` folder, you need to create a file called `boards.txt` that contains a brief description of your new board. You're going to build a board that has an ATtiny13A processor and five LEDs that scan back and forth, called the *tinyCylon*. The Arduino software has its own `boards.txt` file in another location that describes all the boards you see in the Tools ➤ Board menu. Your `boards.txt` file (even though it contains only a single board) should look like Listing 11-6.

Listing 11-6. `boards.txt` File for Your New Board, the tinyCylon

```
### boards.txt

# tinyCylon

tinyCylon.name=tinyCylon

tinyCylon.build.mcu=attiny13
tinyCylon.build.f_cpu=1200000L
tinyCylon.build.core=ATtiny13A

tinyCylon.upload.maximum_size=1024
tinyCylon.upload.using=arduino.ArduinoISP
```

That's all you need for right now. Each line in this file describes one piece of information needed to compile and upload a sketch for this particular board. The general format is `board.setting=value`.

Lines beginning with # are considered comments and ignored. The first comment line identifies the file itself. The next comment identifies the following block of board-related definitions. You can have more than one board in the `boards.txt` file, so it helps to be able to clearly see where one definition ends and the next one begins.

You'll eventually add more definitions to this file, but for now this is enough.

The first definition in the file assigns the name *tinyCylon* to this board type. This is the text the Arduino software uses in the board-selection menu. It's a coincidence that this is the same name used as the board descriptor in this file. When you expand the file later in this chapter, it should be a little clearer.

The next line identifies the processor used. This is the parameter passed to both the `avr-gcc` compiler as well as `avrdude` to compile the program and upload it to the chip. The ATtiny13 (with no -A suffix) has been obsoleted by Atmel and has been replaced with the ATtiny13A, which is mostly the same but adds some new power-saving features. The software, however, hasn't quite caught up with the hardware in this case; so you tell it that you're using an ATtiny13 instead of an ATtiny13A, and it still works fine. The *signature bytes* or device identifiers in the two chips are identical.

The clock speed of the processor is defined on the next line. The ATtiny13A has three built-in oscillators running at 9.6MHz, 4.8MHz, and 128KHz. It can also be driven by an external oscillator, but it lacks the built-in oscillator circuit needed to use a quartz crystal.

The default clock option is the internal 9.6MHz oscillator. So why are you using 1.2MHz? Another default value in a brand-new, factory-fresh ATtiny13A is that the `CKDIV8` configuration fuse is programmed, dividing the internal oscillator by a factor of eight. This results in the 1.2MHz effective clock rate, which is represented as `1200000L`. The L on the end tells the compiler to treat this number as a long integer. It works without the L, but why invite ambiguity?

Anything having to do with setting the configuration fuses has to wait until you get to the bootloaders part of the story, but there's plenty of fun to be had in the meantime. You'll get there. Unless, of course, you already know how to do all that stuff, in which case, please, go nuts.

This clock rate is also made available in any code written for this board, defined as the compiler symbol F_CPU. This symbol was used previously in calculating the baud-rate divisor in Chapter 6. You don't have to worry about that for now, because the ATtiny13A doesn't have a hardware USART peripheral.

The core to be used for this board is defined in the next line. The ATtiny13A isn't covered by the current or legacy cores made available by the Arduino software. That means you get to write them. This process is described shortly; stay tuned.

The next section of the boards.txt file describes the upload mechanism needed for your new board. This simplistic, illustrative example doesn't use a bootloader. In this way, you can devote the entire program memory space to your sketch. This is a good thing, because there's just not that much space to go around.

The maximum upload size (in bytes) is specified in the next line. You set it to 1,024 in this example because that's the maximum amount you can squeeze into the ATtiny13A's program memory.

Finally, you must indicate the proper upload mechanism. Because you aren't using a bootloader in the traditional Arduino fashion, you specify the use of the ArduinoISP In-System Programmer (ISP). The ArduinoISP is made out of an Arduino and some wires. The complete procedure for getting all this arranged correctly is detailed shortly. You have a few more files to generate before you can upload anything.

Defining a New Arduino Core

Create another subfolder in your hardware/tinyCylon folder, and name it cores. In the new cores subdirectory, create yet another subfolder called ATtiny13A. This is the location of the core files needed by the Arduino software to properly compile your sketches for boards utilizing this core.

At a minimum, you need only two files in this folder: main.cpp and Arduino.h. The Arduino software uses main.cpp to wrap up the canonical Arduino setup() and loop() functions. You place calls to these functions in a more traditional main() function after including your very own Arduino.h file, which you also get to write.

The main.cpp file contains your main() function, which is where all C programs *appear* to begin execution. In reality, the compiler automatically inserts a little housekeeping and initialization code. Because you're adding *yet another* layer to this structure, you'll eventually add your own initialization code to the main.cpp file, but you skip that right now in the interest of simplifying this example. You complicate it enough later.

A working main.cpp file is shown in Listing 11-7.

Listing 11-7. Bare Minimum main.cpp File Needed to Implement a New Arduino Core

```
#include "Arduino.h"

int main(void) {
  setup();
    while(1) {
      loop();
    }
  return 0; // this never happens
}
```

Your main.cpp program file begins with a compiler directive to include the contents of your Arduino.h file, which you shall compose anon. Note that the header file name is enclosed in double quotes and not angle brackets. This tells the compiler to use the file by that name *in the current subdirectory* instead of the system-wide include path specification. You want to use *your* Arduino.h and not the Arduino version.

Following the header file, you have a very simple main() function that calls the setup() function *once* and then calls the loop() function repeatedly from within an endless while() loop.

To prevent compiler warning messages, you add a completely gratuitous return 0; statement. Your forebears thought that the main() function should be invoked by an operating system of some sort and that it might be useful to find out under what circumstances the main() function returned. Therefore, the typical main() function is always expected to return a signed integer value upon return. Even today, compilers insist on honoring this convention unless you specifically tell them otherwise. With the avr-gcc compiler, this can be done by adding the -ffreestanding compiler option to the command line. This isn't, however, an easy thing to do in the Arduino environment at this time.

You'll eventually add your own init() function to the main.cpp file and include a call to it in the main() function just before the call to the user-supplied setup() function. That can wait for a bit and is implemented shortly.

You have one more file to create: Arduino.h. The good news is that not much is needed in this file at the moment. Listing 11-8 shows how little you need to get started with an example application.

Listing 11-8. Bare Minimum Arduino.h File Needed to Implement a New Arduino Core

```
#ifndef Arduino_h
#define Arduino_h

#include <avr/io.h>

void setup(void);
void loop(void);

#endif
```

The include guard mechanism, which you may remember from the previous section on writing Arduino libraries, begins your short include file. The only other additions you need to make are an #include directive of your own and function prototypes for your user-supplied setup() and loop() functions.

You really do need to include a *lot* more here, if you want anything resembling expected Arduino functionality in your sketches. You start with the bare minimum, which is to include the header file <avr/io.h> from the avr-libc library that defines the names of the internal registers and bits you need for your sample sketch.

The function prototypes are needed to tell the compiler what to expect from the user-supplied setup() and loop() functions. The number and type of parameters as well as the return type have to be known to the compiler to properly stitch everything together. This is necessary only because you're *referring* to those two function in your main() function, without having defined them previously. If all these functions were in the same source file, and the function definitions preceded the references to them, the prototypes wouldn't be required.

The compiler otherwise assumes, in the absence of function prototypes, that all functions take no parameters and return a signed integer value. Because that is *not* the case with your user-supplied setup() and loop() functions, you must spell out how they're to be used.

That's all you need in your Arduino.h file—at a minimum. You add more to it shortly.

■ **Note**   Remember to completely exit and restart the Arduino software for these changes to take effect.

Writing the tinyCylon Sketch

Let's write a short sketch to demonstrate what you can do with this new core. Remember that your board is called a tinyCylon and has five LEDs that are illuminated in a back-and-forth scanning motion. This is often called a *Larson Scanner*, in tribute to Glen Larson, who developed both the *Battlestar Galactica* and *Knight Rider* TV shows. These shows feature the iconic scanner effect.

Your LED scanner is a bit more humble. If you wire an LED and a 120Ω resistor to each of the available I/O pins and arrange the LEDs in a straight line, you can achieve the basic scanner effect using the sketch in Listing 11-9.

Listing 11-9. Larson Scanner Sketch Using the New ATtiny13A Core

```
void setup() {
  DDRB = 0b00011111;
}

void delay(volatile unsigned long int i) {
  while(i) i--;
}

void loop() {
  for(PORTB = 1; PORTB < 32; PORTB<<=1) {
    delay(100000);
  }
  for(PORTB = 8; PORTB > 1; PORTB>>=1) {
    delay(100000);
  }
}
```

You start out in the typical Arduino fashion with a `setup()` function. This function performs only a single initialization step, and that is to configure the lower five pins of the Port B data direction register (DDRB) to be outputs. Remember that a one makes an output and a zero makes an input, and all the pins are inputs at startup.

You don't use the `pinMode()` function because it doesn't exist yet in your core implementation. Also, your core wouldn't know what an OUTPUT or an INPUT was, anyway. You haven't defined those in your `Arduino.h` file yet. In truth, they're just numbers (OUTPUT is a one, and INPUT is a zero, not coincidentally), but you have to define them using the compiler directive #define to associate the word with the value.

You don't need to do that yet, because you already know how to manipulate the I/O lines by writing to and reading from the hardware registers directly (see Chapters 6 and 7 if you need a reminder). This works in your new sketch because you *did* take the time to include the `<avr/io.h>` header file, which gives names to all the registers and their constituent bits.

Next in your tinyCylon sketch you find a `delay()` function defined. Why? You know why. Because you didn't already define one within your skeletal core definition. At this point, your sketch has access to all the functionality of the C and C++ programming languages, as well as an in-depth knowledge of and access to the inner workings of the AVR hardware. That's a lot. Yet it has *none* of the Arduino-specific capabilities of even the most humble Arduino sketch (that is, a sketch written for one of the *supported* cores). These include all the bit-manipulation functions like `digitalRead()` and `digitalWrite()`, the analog input and PWM output functions `analogRead()` and `analogWrite()`, and the delay functions like `delay()`, `delayMicroseconds()`, and `millis()`.

The `delay()` function you supply here counts down from a number that the caller supplies, and then returns. The number is declared as a `volatile unsigned long int` primarily so that the compiler doesn't make assumptions about the usage (or non-usage) of this parameter and optimize your function out of existence. Secondarily, it needs to be a large number (unsigned long integers are 32-bit numbers according to the `avr-gcc` compiler) because even at a leisurely 1.2MHz clock rate, this chip is still screaming fast, and smaller numbers would produce really short delays that result in LEDs flashing too fast to see.

The `loop()` function performs a single back-and-forth sweep of the LEDs by shifting a 1 from the lowest bit in the PORTB hardware register to the fifth position and then shifting it back down again. This is accomplished using two `for()` loops, one to shift up and the other to shift down. A call to your own `delay()` function is included in each of the `for()` loops to maintain the right speed.

Bringing It All Together

You have everything you need to compile a sketch for your newly defined core, along with a pretty good idea of what it will and won't do for you at this point.

Be sure to select the tinyCylon option in the Tools ➤ Board menu. Otherwise, the Arduino software will compile your new tinyCylon sketch for whatever board you were working with most recently. A good indication that this is the problem is if you get error messages complaining about "multiple definitions of 'delay.'" Choose the correct board, compile the sketch, and see what happens. Cross your fingers!

You *should* be greeted with a status line that says "Done compiling." The text area below the status line should indicate "Binary sketch size: 174 bytes (of a 1024 byte maximum)," if all goes well.

That message tells you three important things. First, it works. Yip! Second, sketches written for your new core are tiny! One hundred and seventy four bytes is about a third of the smallest sketches you were able to shrink in Chapter 6. The third thing is that the compiler is definitely using your new core files, as revealed by the "1024 byte maximum" part of the message.

Now all you have to do is get those ones and zeros into an ATtiny13A!

Uploading a Sketch Without a Bootloader

As mentioned previously, you aren't implementing a bootloader in your new core. Why not? It's entirely *possible*, because the ATtiny13A has the ability to rewrite its own program memory. However, to do this, it would have to emulate the programming protocol supported by the STK500 development system. This is what the bootloaders in the existing Arduino boards have emulated. The new Optiboot shipping in the current Arduino Uno and Arduino Mega 2560 is considered tiny by bootloader standards but would occupy half the available program space of the miniscule ATtiny13A (not including the extra software needed to emulate the missing USART peripheral). You leave the enticing prospect of an ATtiny13A-based bootloader as a Project for Future Reference.

Don't despair! No bootloader doesn't mean no uploading of sketches. You can still get there, but you need some help, in the form of a device programmer, or ISP. Luckily for you, as mentioned earlier, there's an example sketch for that: ArduinoISP. This Arduino-supplied example sketch turns your Arduino into an ISP. Well, almost. You need to make one small (but nonpermanent) addition to the Arduino Uno to make this sketch work properly.

First, load the ArduinoISP sketch in the code editor, compile it, and upload it in the normal fashion to your Arduino Uno or equivalent. This procedure works quite well with breadboard Arduinos as well.

After successfully programming the ArduinoISP sketch into your Arduino of choice, remove the USB or power cable from it. Now install a 10μF capacitor across the RESET line and the GND connection brought out to the power expansion connector, or wherever they happen to be on your particular Arduino. If your capacitor is polarized, be sure to put the negative striped lead in the GND connection and the positive lead in the RESET connection.

This capacitor effectively filters out the incoming reset pulses that come from your PC when the Arduino software starts to program your part. Because you want to program a part further downstream, you filter the reset pulses coming into the Arduino. Otherwise, you'd invoke the Arduino's bootloader and program *that* Arduino, and that's not what you want at all.

You also need to make six more connections between your Arduino-as-ISP and the target device, the ATtiny13A chip. They're summarized in Table 11-1.

Table 11-1. *Connections Needed to Use the Arduino as an ISP for an ATtiny13A*

Signal Name	Arduino Pin	ATtiny13A Pin
RESET	10	1
MOSI	11	5
MISO	12	6
SCK	13	7
V_{cc}	+5	8
GND	GND	4

This technique, in theory, will work on any Atmel AVR that supports in-system programming. You need to check with the datasheet to find out which pins are used for ISP-mode programming on different devices.

Figure 11-1 shows this wiring arrangement on a solderless breadboard. The green LED on the bottom half of the breadboard is a power-on indicator. The red LED on the top half shows programming activity, and the green LED on top fades up and down in brightness to indicate a *heartbeat*, meaning your Arduino-as-ISP is still alive.

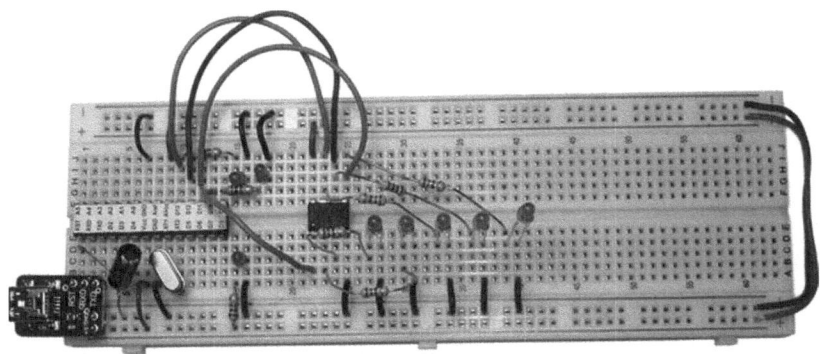

Figure 11-1. *A breadboard Arduino being used as an ISP with an ATtiny13A connected as a tinyCylon LED scanner. Note the extra 10µF capacitor installed on the RESET line (lower left).*

Recall that in the `boards.txt` file you created for your new tinyCylon board, on the very last line, you designated the upload process to be performed using the ArduinoISP. Other programmers are also available, and you're encouraged to try them and see what works and what doesn't. The assumption in this book has been that you have (or have access to) and Arduino Uno or equivalent. If you have additional hardware, that's great, too! If not, you don't have to feel left out, nor must you immediately go out and spend a lot more money.

However, because you've already set everything up to use the ArduinoISP automatically, you can now click the Upload button, and your tinyCylon sketch should be programmed into the ATtiny13A chip. Alternately, you can choose File ➤ Upload Using Programmer, as long as you select the correct programmer from Tools ➤ Programmer.

The Arduino software, ever vigilant, recompiles your sketch and proceeds to the uploading part. Lights flash, time passes, and then you should be rewarded with a mesmerizing LED scanner.

You'll probably get a warning message from `avrdude` to this effect: "avrdude: please define PAGEL and BS2 signals in the configuration file for part ATtiny13." You can safely ignore this warning.

Setting the Configuration Fuses

There are several ways that you can program the fuses on your new ATtiny13A chip, should you want to. Most of them, however, require you to read *and decipher* the relevant bit combinations from the data sheet and then use `avrdude` to actually do the fuse programming.

Although these configuration fuses are *nonvolatile* (that is, they retain their settings even after power has been removed), they aren't fuses in the sense that they can only be blown once and then never again altered. They can be set and reset many times. The problem with fuses arises from the fact that several possible combinations of fuse settings will render your AVR chip completely inaccessible.

The best possible way to program the configuration fuses is from within a program that offers *smart fuse warnings*: that is, the program alerts you to possibly irrevocable fuse combinations before programming them for you. AVR Studio and the AVR Plugin for Eclipse both offer this safety feature and are described in detail later in this chapter.

Fuse Settings the Hard Way

You can manually set the fuses using the avrdude utility from the command line. This is as tedious and error-prone as it sounds. However, if you have the Arduino software, you already have the avrdude software installed. Whether or not you can get to it is another matter.

The short version of the story is that you must have your operating system's path variable set to point to the subdirectory or folder where the avrdude utility has been installed. The Arduino software gets around this requirement by specifying a fully qualified pathname prefixing the avrdude command every time it's used.

Open a command-line window, and try typing avrdude and pressing Enter to see what happens. When invoked with no command-line options like this, avrdude patiently lists all of its possible options, without actually doing anything. This is a good test to see if avrdude is presently in your system's path. If it's not, you either need to add it to the path or copy both the avrdude executable and its accompanying configuration file, avrdude.conf, into a subdirectory that *is* included in your systems' path variable. These steps obviously vary from one operating system to another. Assuming you can execute the avrdude utility from a command line, let's proceed.

From the command line, issue the following command:

```
avrdude -p attiny13 -c stk500v1 -b 19200 -P \\.\com15 -q -q -U hfuse:r:-:h -U lfuse:r:-:h
```

The avrdude utility and its colorful command-line options are described in Chapter 2. Briefly reviewing, -p is the part (device), -c is the programmer protocol, -b is the baud rate (required to work properly with the ArduinoISP), -P is the serial port to use (your port is probably different), and -q is for *quell* or *quiet* (and, yes, there *are* two of them, telling it to be doubly quiet). Then comes some gibberish that reads out the values of the two eight-bit fuses on the ATtiny13A: the high fuse and the low fuse.

You get the standard complaint from avrdude regarding PAGEL and BS2. Either fix the configuration file already, or ignore. It's your choice.

After this warning, and because of the double-hush-hush, you should get just two lines printed out on the console:

```
0xff
0x6a
```

This is assuming you're using a brand-new, factory-fresh ATtiny13A chip.

■ **Note** Make a note of your fuse settings while your circuit still works.

Brand-new, factory-fresh ATtiny13A chips have their high fuses set to 0xFF and their low fuses set to 0x6A. A confusing Atmel standard is that fuses are considered *programmed* when their value is 0 and considered *unprogrammed* when their value is 1. This happens to correspond with the typical behavior of EPROMS, which were what Atmel was successfully manufacturing before it started making microcontrollers. Old habits die hard.

You can safely change the CKDIV8 configuration fuse from a zero to a one, thus *disabling* the default system clock prescaler and allowing the chip to run full-bore at 9.6MHz. The CKDIV8 configuration bit is located in bit 4 of the low-fuse byte. This changes the composite value of the low-fuse byte from 0x6A to 0x7A. It's just hexadecimal math with a weird industry convention thrown in.

To write this new value to your ATtiny13A chip, issue the following command:

```
avrdude -p attiny13 -c stk500v1 -b 19200 -P \\.\com15 -q -q -U lfuse:w:0x7A:m
```

Most of the command-line parameters are identical. You omit the first of the -U clauses and modify the remaining one. Instead of doing an r for *read* on the low-fuse byte, you're now performing a w for *write*. Instead of the - (dash), which *everyone knows* is a reference to stdout or *console* (the standard output device), you specify the exact value of 0x7A, with the trailing format signifier changed from h for *hexadecimal* to m for *manual*.

Well, *that's* something no one wants to have to do twice. Let's figure out what fuse settings you want once and for all, write them down, and then let the machine handle it from here.

Fuse Settings the Not-As-Hard Way

To be able to change the fuse settings from within the Arduino environment, you have to resort, again, to trickery. One of the options available is Burn Bootloader, one of the options in the Tools menu.

The burning of the bootloader is a task that involves not just the writing of the bootloader image file to the chip, but also a slew of other, ancillary operations. First, the avrdude utility is instructed to erase the chip, reset the program memory-lock bits to allow writing, and then write the high and low fuse bytes, in that order. If this works, a second avrdude command is issued, this time writing the bootloader file and then resetting lock bits.

So that's the mechanism you use to set the fuse bytes. It's a bit of a winding road, but you'll get there.

Bear in mind that each of these individual actions is composed of a write and an accompanying verification step before proceeding to the next item in the list. That may explain why it takes approximately ten seconds or longer to write a new bootloader.

The details of the bootloader-burning process are specified in the boards.txt file. You need to add a few lines to your new boards.txt file to convince the Arduino software to update the bootloader for you. See Listing 11-10.

Listing 11-10. Additional Lines to Add to boards.txt

```
tinyCylon.bootloader.low_fuses=0x7A
tinyCylon.bootloader.high_fuses=0xFF
tinyCylon.bootloader.unlock_bits=0x3F
tinyCylon.bootloader.lock_bits=0x3F
tinyCylon.bootloader.path=ATtiny13A
tinyCylon.bootloader.file=zero-length.hex
```

The first two lines are really the only ones you care about, because they're concerned with the values you want to use as the low and high fuse bytes, respectively. In a more perfect world, you'd be finished. But you're a pioneer, blazing trails, and so on. You specify the lock bits and the unlock bits to be the same, which happens to be the setting for no memory protection. You would normally *want* memory protection if you were actually writing a bootloader here, but you're not, so you don't.

Fun fact: the datasheet for the ATtiny13A says that the default value for the lock bits is 0xFF. It's not. It's 0x3F. The top two bits, for some reason, aren't ones. If you specify lock bits of 0xFF, avrdude tries mightily to program them for you. As becomes its faithful nature, it also then valiantly attempts to verify that said write took place, effectively by reading back the programmed value and comparing it to the value that was intended to be written. Because the chip reads back 0x3F, it thinks it failed, and it cancels the remaining bootloader-update process with a blast of lengthy error messages. In there, somewhere, is the "verify failed" message.

Next you come the most deceitful part of your plan: the fake bootloader file. The Arduino software insists that there be a file, and that it be written, and that it be verified. So you give it one. You specify the path to be ATtiny13A and the file name to be zero-length.hex. This new file needs to be in a subdirectory called ATtiny13A (the path) inside a subdirectory called bootloaders in your new board's folder, which in this example is tinyCylon.

It's a file, true enough. It's properly encoded in the correct format, specifically the Intel HEX format. It contains a description of a binary image that is exactly zero bytes long.

This isn't a problem for either avrdude or the Arduino software. The file gets written, it gets read back out again, the two are compared (somehow?), and the results are a success. The process continues.

You need the file to make this particular trick work. It's a plain-text file, but all those zeros need to be exactly as you see them in Listing 11-11.

Listing 11-11. Fake Bootloader File zero-length.hex *in Intel HEX Format*

```
:0000000000
:00000001FF
```

In reality, you can put anything you want in that file. The chip will be erased in any case.

This technique pays off when you craft several different boards in your boards.txt file, each with the same core but with different bootloader options specified. Then you can change the configuration fuses on the fly by selecting a different board from the menu and then instructing the Arduino software to Burn Bootloader.

■ **Note** Be sure to select Arduino as ISP from the Tools ➤ Programmers menu before burning the bootloader.

Here is what your resulting file hierarchy looks like when you're finished:

```
<Arduino sketchbook location>
        <hardware>
                <tinyCylon>
                        <bootloaders>
                                <ATtiny13A>
                                        zero-length.hex
                        <cores>
                                <ATtiny13A>
                                        Arduino.h
                                        main.cpp
                        boards.txt
        <tinyCylon>
                tinyCylon.ino
```

Expanding the Core

You have just enough functionality in your baby core to flash some LEDs, and not much else. Any of the Arduino-specific features you would like to have available must be added by you.

A good place to start looking for inspiration (that is, stuff worth stealing) is the Arduino.h header file supplied by the Arduino software. Don't try dropping the whole thing in your core folder. It won't work.

The official `Arduino.h` file relies on a lot of other files being in place for it to compile properly. However, there *is* a lot you can borrow that costs nothing in terms of code space but offers a *slightly* more Arduino-esque user experience.

For example, if you copy the official `Arduino.h` file into your core folder and then remove *all* the file-include directives, along with all the mega-specific doodlings, you can use a lot of the built-in macro functions, predefined constant values, and function prototypes as a checklist of coding you need to do to complete this core.

Starting a new core is a straightforward process. Finishing one is a challenge.

And Without Arduino

The Arduino folk are quick to point out that you can use any tools you want with your Arduino I/O Board. Again, as plainly stated in the official Arduino FAQ, "It's an AVR development board."

Now that you know what an AVR is, let's apply that knowledge toward learning about some other methods that have become popular, not just with Arduinos and the eight-bit AVRs, but with embedded development projects of every kind.

One of the tremendous advantages of the Arduino-supplied software is its platform independence. Virtually the same software runs on Windows, Linux, or Mac. That's quite an accomplishment! Unfortunately, that can't necessarily be said for most of the alternative programming environments available for the Arduino. The majority of them seem to have a preference for supporting Microsoft's popular operating systems. This obstacle can sometimes be overcome with emulators, but this certainly isn't guaranteed in all situations.

The Bare Metal, Revisited

In Chapter 2, you looked at a method for writing a simple program in C to blink an LED. Once the source code was written, it was just a matter of executing three command-line instructions and *voilà*, the LED blinked.

As promised in Chapter 2, a better way of invoking the compiler and so on to program the chip can be realized using *makefiles* and the make utility. The Arduino software for Windows includes a copy of the GNU make utility, contained in the `<Arduino installation directory>/hardware/tools/avr/utils/bin` folder. You need to adjust your system `path` variable to be able to access it from the command line. Linux and Mac OS X have their own native versions of the make utility available.

The make utility uses a *makefile* to specify a set of rules. These rules indicate what should be done, and when. The make utility can tell when a file has been modified and can then perform all the necessary actions to bring the entire project up to date.

In the simplest scenario, you have a single source file. When the compiler crunches this file, it produces an object file. You extract the binary image required for downloading to the chip from this object file. This binary image file, often formatted as an Intel HEX file, is then uploaded to the AVR chip using the `avrdude` utility.

At each step along this path, your operating system updates files at your request and places a timestamp on them, sometimes known as a *time of update*. So when you edit a file and then save your changes, the time of update for that file is changed. The make utility uses this information to tell when your project needs its internal files updated. If the time of update for your source file is *newer* than the object file, it recompiles the source file for you. If the object file is then newer than the binary file, and so on, this produces a cascade of activity until everything is properly updated.

The makefile is a specially formatted text file that lists all the rules for this updating process. In make parlance, there are *targets* and there are *dependencies*. A target is a file that needs to be built by the compiler or some other utility. The dependencies are the files that govern when a new target needs to be built. An example illustrates this more succinctly.

To automate the compilation and upload process for your Blink in C project, you begin with the source code, `blink.c`, and a makefile, outlined in Listing 11-12.

Listing 11-12. Makefile for the Simple Blink in C Project

```
# makefile for blink

all: blink.hex

blink.hex: blink.o
        avr-objcopy -O ihex blink.o blink.hex

blink.o: blink.c
        avr-gcc -mmcu=atmega328p blink.c -o blink.o

prog: blink.hex
        avrdude -p atmega328p -c arduino -P \\\.\COM11 -U flash:w:blink.hex:i↵
-C D:\Progra~1\arduino-1.0-beta1/hardware/tools/avr/etc/avrdude.conf

clean:
        rm blink.o
        rm blink.hex
```

The first line is a comment, as indicated by the leading #. It's always a good idea to use comments liberally when you can.

The next line is a phony target that you name `all`. All the rules begin with a target. Targets always begin in the very first column of a new line and are followed by a colon. Sometimes the target is the name of a file, and sometimes it serves another purpose. Because these other targets don't point to real files, they're described as *phony*.

Phony targets can be very useful, however. The `clean` target instructs the `make` utility to clean up all the intermediate and final forms of your code, using the `rm` (remove) command. This subsequently forces a complete recompile when the `make` utility is activated again.

You also use a phony `prog` target to invoke the `avrdude` utility to upload your sketch.

For rules that only need to run when something is out of date, you add the *dependency* (or dependencies) on the same line, after the target. If a target has no dependencies, it always executes when called. It can have one or more dependencies, which are usually the files that have changed, thus requiring the targets to be updated.

The next part of the rule is the *action* to be performed if the rule is satisfied. The action is written on the next line, following the rule, and is always indented using exactly one tab character. Actions are command-line instructions that are executed when the rule needs to be enforced.

The default target for the `make` utility is either `all` or the first rule encountered in the makefile. You define a dependency for `all` in your makefile: the file `blink.hex`. The `make` utility looks for a rule for the `blink.hex` file and finds it (it's the very next rule). The `blink.hex` file *depends* on the `blink.o` file, which, if you peek ahead a bit, depends on the `blink.c` file, which is your original source file.

The phony target `prog` also depends on the `blink.hex` file being up to date. If it isn't, the whole process to make sure `blink.hex` is current is enacted.

You start this process by typing `make` at a command-line prompt from within the subdirectory where your files are contained. If you give the `make` utility no command-line arguments, it assumes the target is `all` and proceeds. You can also type `make prog` or `make clean`.

To produce the object file (`blink.o`), the compiler is invoked with all the appropriate command-line options. To produce the binary image file, the `avr-objcopy` utility is used to extract the image and store it in the `blink.hex` file. You should start to be able to see how this is arranged in the structure of the makefile.

This is a simple makefile. The `make` utility has a lot of additional capabilities you're not using here. It does only a few things for you, but it's certainly easier to use than typing out all the steps to compile and upload the sketch by hand.

The main point of the `make` utility, however, is to *intelligently* update only the necessary files without wasting time on any steps that need not be taken. This becomes tremendously advantageous when your project contains many files spread across multiple folders.

Note that some weirdness is going on in the `avrdude` command line. First, the selected serial port to be used (COM11 in this example; yours is probably different) is preceded by several backslashes and a period, like this: `\\\.\COM11`. This is a Windows-specific requirement for COM ports with more than a single-digit number. You have to add an extra slash to the madness to get the `make` utility to send the proper sequence (which ought to be `\\.\COM11`, with two slashes, a period, and then another slash).

You can use the `-c arduino` option if you're using an Arduino Uno. If you're using a Duemilanove, you need to add the `-b 57600` baud-rate option to make it work.

The `make` utility uses the backward-slash character to *escape* special characters. You actually *want* a literal slash here (several, in fact), so you add a preceding slash to the mix, and it works fine.

Also note that you must specify the location of the `avrdude.conf` configuration file on the command line, using the `-C` command-line option. The `avrdude` utility doesn't understand file names with spaces in them. Normally you would enclose the entire path and filename in double quotes, but the combination of `make` and `avrdude` doesn't like that, either. You resort to a very old Microsoft workaround, replacing the `Program Files (x86)` folder name with `Progra~1`. This workaround emerged when most of the world broke free of the previous 8.3 file-naming convention (eight characters for the file name and three characters for the file extension, separated by a period).

Also note that some of the slashes in the path to the `avrdude.conf` file are backslashes and some are forward slashes. Fun! This is actually how the Arduino software invokes the `avrdude` utility from within whatever constitutes its automatic build intelligence.

You can bypass this configuration file madness by placing a copy of the `avrdude.conf` file in the same directory as the `avrdude` executable file. Technically, they don't belong in the same place (executables and data files are a bad mix), but it makes invoking the `avrdude` command *much* simpler for you. Or you can use the Atmel AVR toolchain, described in the next section, instead. It keeps the two files together.

Please feel encouraged to not only use simple makefiles for projects like these, but also invest in learning a little more about how `make` and other handy utilities can help you spend less time typing and more time writing.

On the other hand, sometimes a batch file *is* easier.

Other Development Environments

Nobody says you have to use the Arduino software to program your Arduino. Many alternative environments are available, both open source and commercial.

This section looks at a couple of the most popular alternative development environments (IDEs) available for the AVR family.

Atmel's AVR Studio

AVR Studio is the official development environment for AVR devices. It's provided free of charge from Atmel, although the source code is proprietary. See the Atmel website (`www.atmel.com`) to download the Windows-only software. You need to register, but the registration is free.

Note that this is a really big download (>600MB), and it also requires additional large downloads from Microsoft. Start these downloads early, and make sure your laptop is plugged into the wall.

It's not really fair to call AVR Studio an alternative to the Arduino environment. The Arduino concept from the beginning was to hide as much of the complexity of embedded design from the user as possible, to help promote faster learning curves and wider adoption among nontechnical users. As such, the *Arduino* software is really the alternative here.

The most recent version of AVR Studio is Version 5, which is based on the Microsoft Visual Studio Shell. For those of you familiar with other Microsoft programming environments, this will look quite familiar (see Figure 11-2).

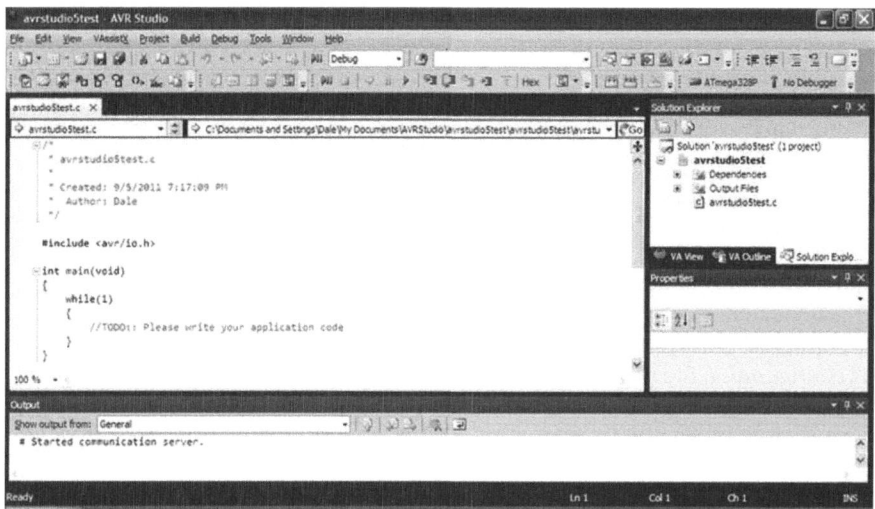

Figure 11-2. A screenshot from Atmel's AVR Studio 5, showing a freshly created project using the Project Wizard

Even though Version 5 is the latest and greatest, it's still so new that not all of Atmel's extensive portfolio of devices are fully supported. For this and other reasons (mostly because some people resist change), the previous version, Version 4, remains popular with hobbyists and professionals alike. See Figure 11-3.

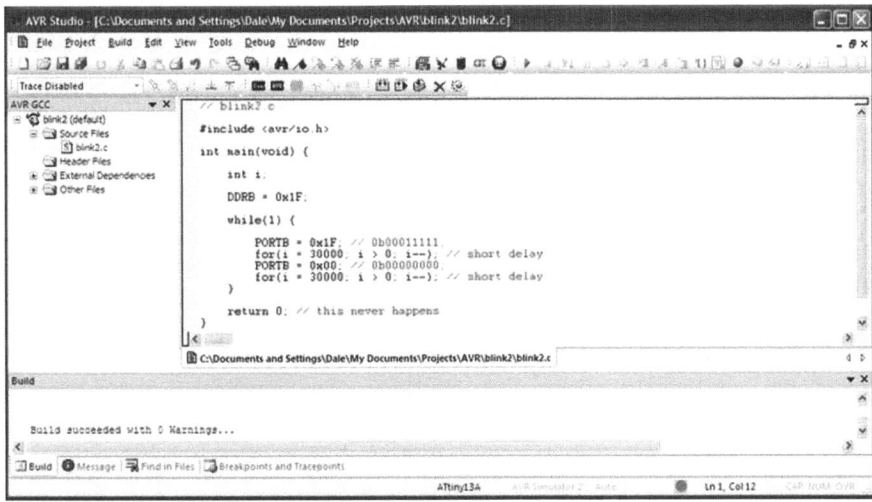

Figure 11-3. A screenshot from Atmel's AVR Studio 4, in development mode

Again, nothing earth-shattering or unconventional here. If you're familiar with other development environments, you begin to see a trend. There are several panes in the enclosing window, each having a different function. Along the top you see some icons in a toolbar. On the left is a hierarchical listing of all the elements of the project, including the source file(s), dependencies, and so on. The main pane is devoted to the code editor, which highlights syntax by color. You can configure the colors and font used however you like. Multiple source code files can be edited at once, and the tabs along the bottom of the editor window let you flip back and forth among them. At the bottom is the build-results window, showing the results from the last build attempt.

AVR Studio supports both assembly language programs as well as programs written for the GNU Compiler Collection (GCC). This just happens to be the same family of compilers used by the Arduino software.

The GCC programs aren't included with AVR Studio. You must download them and install them yourself. For a good, long while, the best Windows port of the AVR port of the GCC (`avr-gcc`) was the WinAVR package managed by Eric Weddington and available from SourceForge (`http://winavr.sourceforge.net`). The Arduino Team borrowed heavily from this distribution for the Windows version of the Arduino software.

The combination of WinAVR and AVR Studio still works great and will continue to work for years to come. The only problems you'll run into are mainly related to support for new devices as they become available.

To get the latest officially supported version of the `avr-gcc` toolchain, you can also use the Atmel AVR Toolchain for Windows (also available for Linux). AVR Studio 4 works well with this toolchain, as well as the WinAVR package.

The main advantage of using AVR Studio 4 instead of the Arduino environment is the tight integration of device programming and debugging tools. These tools allow you to write, program, and debug your program all in the same software framework.

Eclipse

The Eclipse project was originally developed within IBM as a modular, extensible development environment. IBM decided to make it an open source project and formed an industry consortium. The Eclipse Foundation eventually emerged as a not-for-profit corporation to oversee the future of Eclipse.

Originally targeted at Java development, Eclipse still sees its greatest strengths in this area. The C Developers Toolkit (CDT) is a version of Eclipse specifically designed for C and C++ programming. See Figure 11-4.

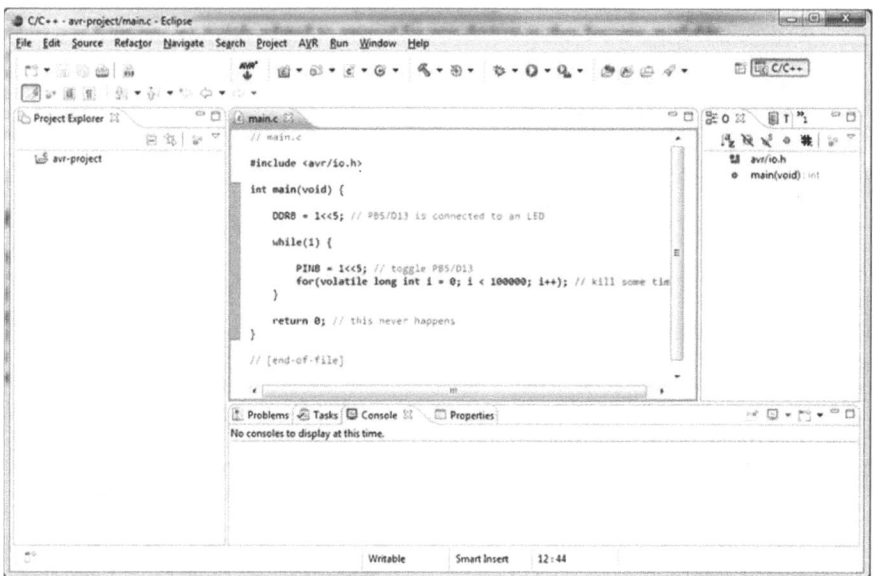

Figure 11-4. *The Eclipse workbench showing the development perspective. Note the AVR icon and menu item added via the AVR Eclipse Plugin.*

You can download a version for Windows, Mac OS X, or Linux from the Eclipse download page at `www.eclipse.org/downloads`.

Like the Arduino software, Eclipse doesn't require an installation, per se. Instead, you download a large archive file and unpack it in the location of your choice. In the primary `eclipse` folder, there should be an executable file that you can click to start up Eclipse.

Eclipse organizes your projects with a *workspace*. This is a designated folder in your computer's file system. Eclipse prompts you for your desired location for this workspace when it first starts. It even suggests what it thinks is a reasonable location for you.

After this, Eclipse begins to load its workbench. This takes quite a while the first time Eclipse is run on your machine. Eclipse actually starts up on another screen with just a handful of icons. On the right is an icon to take you to the workbench; click that icon to open the development perspective.

To work effectively with AVR devices, you need to extend the capabilities of Eclipse via a plug-in. This is one of the major design elements of Eclipse, allowing new features to be added incrementally without having to rebuild the entire system.

One Eclipse plug-in that works well is called the AVR Eclipse Plugin, available from `http://avr-eclipse.sourceforge.net`. However, it's easier to download the plug-in from within Eclipse. In the Eclipse workbench, select Help ➤ Install New Software. This brings up the Install dialog box. The first item in this dialog box is the Work With text box. Type in the URL `http://avr-eclipse.sourceforge.net/updatesite/`, and click the Add button. This, in turn, brings up the Add Repository dialog box, which gives you the opportunity to add a descriptive name to this web address. Type anything you want, and click OK.

The Install dialog box momentarily populates the list in the middle of the screen with a single option: CDT Optional Features. Select the check box to the left of this item, and then click Next. Some dependency checks are made, and you're presented with a list of items to be installed. There should be two items listed: one for the AVR Eclipse Plugin and another for the sources. Click Next again to proceed to the licensing page.

You must review and accept the licenses presented. The AVR Eclipse Plugin is released under the GNU General Public License. If you accept these terms, click the appropriate radio button at the bottom of the dialog box, and then click Finish.

Eclipse begins to download and install the plugin for you. It warns you that it's unsigned content and asks you to verify that you want to continue. If you do continue, then when complete, it notifies you that Eclipse should be restarted. Allow it to restart; when it does, you have yet another icon on your Eclipse workbench toolbar, as well as a new AVR menu.

Creating a New AVR Project in Eclipse

From the Eclipse workbench, choose File ➤ New ➤ C Project. This brings up the C Project dialog box. Type an appropriate project name, and then select Empty Project from the AVR Cross Target Application group. Click Next to get to the Select Configurations dialog box.

You can click the Advanced settings button to bring up the project properties, allowing you to specify the device type, programmers used, and so forth. You can always return to this area and make more changes to the development environment by right-clicking the project name in the Project Explorer pane on the left, or by selecting Project ➤ Properties.

You need to create a programmer profile. The `avrdude` utility is well known to this plug-in, so it's easy to configure the necessary options. You no longer have to memorize or look up all the parameters and their possible values. Instead, pick from the available options in the dialog boxes, and you're all set.

Once you've written your program and successfully compiled it, all it takes is a click of the AVR icon to download (you're downloading now, instead of uploading in the Arduino world) your program to the AVR chip.

Summary

The Arduino software environment is a great place to start learning about microcontrollers, programming, and even hardware. To take it to the next level, you can add your own Arduino libraries and create your own Arduino cores for unsupported AVR devices.

Beyond that is a world of more powerful tools waiting for you. Both the AVR Studio and the Eclipse packages support more than just the eight-bit AVR world, so this could very well be your launching point into … who knows what? The sky is the limit. Newer and more powerful (but cheaper!) microcontrollers are being introduced all the time. Keeping up with them is a full-time job.

Let's march forward and put this new information to good use. In the final chapter, you design and build a number of small, interrelated circuits and devices that come together to be a completely autonomous robot. Don't be alarmed. The Crush! Kill! Destroy! option hasn't been implemented.

And no, that isn't a personal challenge.

CHAPTER 12

Networking

One Arduino can do a lot. More than one Arduino can do more. There's an old saying: "Many hands make light work." Arduinos are also known for working and playing well with others. The "others" may be other Arduinos, or they can be devices of a different stripe entirely.

To work together, they have to talk to each other. A certain amount of cooperation is necessary in order for a meaningful exchange of information to take place. Who will be involved in this conversation? Where will it take place? What are you going to talk about? Who goes first? After these questions are answered, the conversation can follow.

Let's look at some of the ways you can use both the built-in networking capabilities of the Arduino and some low-cost add-ons that can literally let your Arduino talk to the world.

Point-to-Point Networking

The Arduino has several communication interfaces already built in, and it's trivially easy and relatively inexpensive to add communication capabilities these days. First you look at the built-in options, and then you reach out a bit and hook up some more linkages to the outside world.

Talking Over the Serial Port

You've already worked extensively with the Arduino's built-in serial port. You've given it ho-hum tasks like uploading sketches and mindlessly reciting "Hello, world!" Wouldn't it be nice if you could transcend the mundane shuffle of bits back and forth and have a meaningful conversation?

The Arduino's serial port is often hard-wired to the USB interface, making it difficult to apply it to other tasks. On the Arduino Mega 2560, of course, this is no problem, because you have three more USARTs available for such tasks. All isn't lost with the Arduino Uno, however, because you can also use any pair of digital I/O lines to communicate serially using either the `SoftSerial` or `NewSoftSerial` library.

An excellent example of networking you can do with your Arduino right out of the box is to use the Firmata communication protocol to control your Arduino from your PC. Load the Arduino-supplied example sketch by choosing File ➤ Examples ➤ Firmata ➤ StandardFirmata. Compile and upload to your Arduino board.

Now download the Firmata test software appropriate for your operating system (Linux 32-bit, Mac OS X, or Windows) from the Firmata web site: `http://firmata.org`. This test program runs on your PC and communicates over the serial port where your Arduino is connected.

Select the correct port, and the software begins to talk back and forth over the serial link. You can use the user interface to control the settings of all the I/O pins on your Arduino. See Figure 12-1.

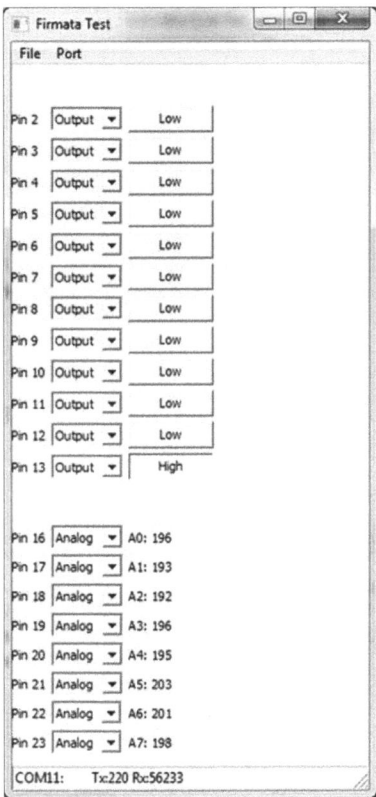

Figure 12-1. *The Firmata test software. You can configure and control each of the I/O pins on your Arduino from your PC.*

You can configure any of the digital pins to be Input, Output, PWM, or Servo. The analog input pins can likewise be configured as Input, Output, Analog, or PWM.

When configured as an Input, each pin's state is reported as either High or Low. Change the setting to Output, and you can toggle the pin's state using a pushbutton that alternates between High and Low.

The PWM setting replaces the pushbutton with a slider, allowing you to smoothly adjust the PWM value on the pins—assuming they're PWM-capable outputs. If not, they respond like any other digital output pins when addressed with the analogWrite() function, having a High level when the PWM value is 128 or larger and a Low value otherwise.

The Servo configuration also reveals a user-adjustable slider control. Adjusting this control causes a servo-compatible control signal to be generated, repeating at 50Hz. The lower limit is 560μs, and the upper limit is 2,400μs.

All this remote-control magic is brought to you by the miracle of an agreed-upon command-and control-system, implemented over the serial port.

There's more to the Firmata protocol than you can see from the simple user interface example program. The latest version also supports communication with shift registers, limited MIDI support, and I²C peripherals. The protocol is designed to be easily extendible, so feel free to think up new things for it to talk about.

Arduino to Arduino

Talking to a PC is almost a no brainer for the Arduino. It's like it was born to do that kind of thing. What else can the Arduino's USART talk to? How about another Arduino?

You can easily make up your own conversation for two Arduinos. Just decide what needs to be said. Break these ideas down into discrete symbols that can be easily emitted by one Arduino and just as easily understood by another Arduino. The implementation details differ, depending on your circumstances, but the basic idea is always the same.

The Doorbell Example

For example, you can build a doorbell using an Arduino. Yes, it's overkill, but it's an imaginary example at this point, isn't it? Once upon a time, a doorbell was a bell attached to a door. Then people started stealing the bells. So the bell was mounted on the *inside* of the door and tied to a string that went through a hole in the door. Visitors announcing themselves would tug on the string, thus ringing the bell. But why leave something simple and reliable when you can make it more complicated? That was the motivation behind the electric doorbell. See Figure 12-2.

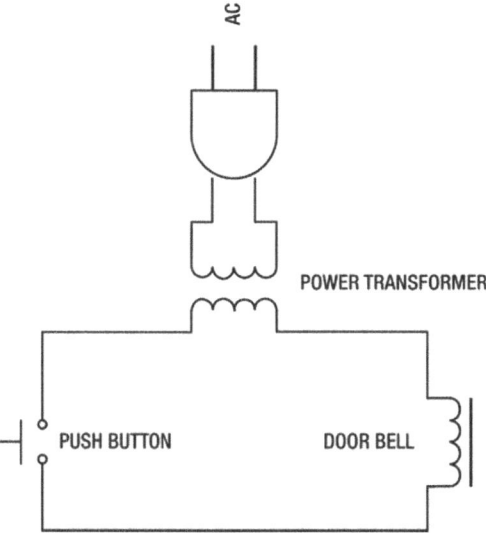

Figure 12-2. A basic doorbell circuit

When the pushbutton is pressed, it completes a circuit, engaging an electromechanical bell of some sort. A transformer is usually used to reduce the working voltage to typically 24VAC. One of the nice features of this arrangement is that the bell and the button can be separated by quite a long distance, if necessary. This can also be done with a long bit of string, but it starts to get complicated.

Now replace the pushbutton with an Arduino, and then replace the doorbell with another Arduino. You, umm, also need to attach a pushbutton to the first Arduino, as well as a bell to the second Arduino. But let's continue.

This doorbell Arduino illustrated in Figure 12-3 has a momentary-contact pushbutton attached to it, and the appropriate sketch is running that can tell (or be interrupted) when the doorbell button is pressed. The use of the button is traditional; any appropriate sensor (or combination of sensors) will do. This button press initiates the transmission of a "ding dong" message to another Arduino inside your house, via the serial port.

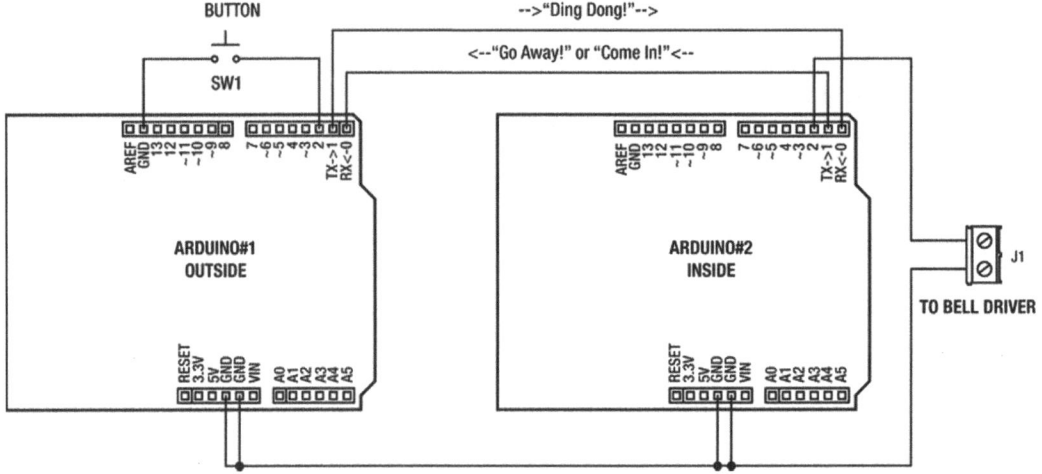

Figure 12-3. Using two Arduinos to build an improved doorbell network

■ **Note** Please note that the TX line of the outside Arduino is connected to the RX line of the inside Arduino, and vice versa. Also, the GND lines must be connected between the two Arduinos for this to work.

The inside Arduino receives the "ding dong" message and decides what to do with it. In the old days, there wasn't a lot of thought put into this decision. The button was pressed, therefore the bell was struck. This behavior was programmed using a length of wire. You don't need two Arduinos and several wires to do what a single loop of wire can easily do.

But your inside Arduino has a tiny amount of intelligence. It can make decisions. A "ding dong" message was received; let's *decide* what to do about that. Maybe you go ahead and either strike a mechanical bell using a solenoid and an appropriate driver circuit, or play a short note or notes on a speaker. That's the traditional approach.

Alternately, you can ring the bell *and* play a short tune on the speaker *and* light up a flashing indicator light *and* mute the TV (or pause, depending) *and* make a note in the doorbell log.

If the inside Arduino has some idea of the time of day, perhaps further thought can be put into choosing the correct response. Perhaps you don't want to be disturbed after bedtime or during naptime, or you want a different bell or chime to sound at different times of the day. Lots of options exist when your doorbell is smarter than a length of copper wire.

Here's another possible scenario: the doorbell Arduino (the one outside that has the pushbutton) sends the "ding dong" message in response to a button press. The inside Arduino, with its fancy brain, decides what to do, and sends a message back to the doorbell Arduino. This message can be a command to either say "Who's there?" over a speaker or display the message on an LCD. Maybe it says "Go away." Let your imagination take over from here, as far as Space Age doorbell systems are concerned.

The important concept is that you have two things talking to each other. You now know the answers to the who, where, and what questions concerning the conversation. Who: two Arduinos. Where: one outside with a button, the other inside with a bell. What: button-press events and possible responses.

A Two-Node Dimmer Network

Consider two Arduinos connected as in the doorbell example from the previous section. Each Arduino has a dimmable LED attached to PWM output D11, as well as four individual pushbuttons. The respective USARTs are properly cross connected: that is, the TX of one goes to the RX of the other, and so on. They share a common ground. See Figure 12-4.

Figure 12-4. A two-node Arduino network, built on a solderless breadboard. Chip labels with the Arduino pin numbers assist in rapid prototyping. Each Arduino has its own reset button along with four programmable pushbuttons. The red LEDs are the dimmable LEDs mentioned in the example sketch. Pressing the buttons on either unit controls the brightness of both LEDs. Not shown is the removable USB-to-TTL adapter used to upload the sketches to the individual Arduinos.

You want to use the four pushbuttons to control the brightness of the LED. You assign the functions On, Off, Bright, and Dim to these buttons. Press the On button, and the LED comes on at full intensity. You can imagine the rest. See Listing 12-1.

Listing 12-1. *Sketch for a Two-Node LED Dimmer Network*

```
void setup() {
  // pin directions
  pinMode(11, OUTPUT); // LED on PWM pin D11
  pinMode(5, INPUT); // D5 = button 1 (up)
  pinMode(6, INPUT); // D6 = button 2 (bright)
  pinMode(7, INPUT); // D7 = button 3 (dim)
  pinMode(8, INPUT); // D8 = button 4 (off)
  // initial settings
  analogWrite(11, 0); // LED off
  digitalWrite(5, HIGH); // enable pullup
  digitalWrite(6, HIGH); // enable pullup
  digitalWrite(7, HIGH); // enable pullup
  digitalWrite(8, HIGH); // enable pullup
  // serial port
  Serial.begin(9600);
  Serial.write(byte(0)); // turn off all the other LEDs
}

void loop() {

  static int brightness = 0; // the brightness of the LED: 0=off, 255=on
  static int previous_brightness = 0; // the previous brightness

  previous_brightness = brightness; // remember for later

  // check buttons
  if(digitalRead(5) == LOW) brightness = 255; // full on
  if(digitalRead(6) == LOW) brightness++; // brighter
  if(digitalRead(7) == LOW) brightness--; // dimmer
  if(digitalRead(8) == LOW) brightness = 0; // off

  if(brightness < 0) brightness = 0; // lower limit
  if(brightness > 255) brightness = 255; // upper limit

  if(brightness != previous_brightness) {
    // the brightness has changed
    Serial.write(brightness); // broadcast the new brightness
  }

  // any news from the network?
  if(Serial.available()) {
    brightness = Serial.read(); // fetch new brightness level
  }

  analogWrite(11, brightness); // update LED
  delay(10); // a short delay
}
```

The setup() function configures the PWM output D11 as an output and uses the analogWrite() function to turn off the LED. Technically, you could omit this particular pinMode() function call, because this happens automatically when using the analogWrite() function.

The input pins attached to the pushbuttons are configured as inputs, and their associated pullup resistors are enabled using the digitalWrite() function. This is necessary because the momentary-contact switches used are connected to ground, but only when they're pressed. When not pressed, the input pins are floating, and there's no telling what they might report. Enabling the built-in pullup resistors solves this problem without having to add more hardware. Again, the pin-direction statements can be omitted because INPUT is the default state after the chip is reset. The calls to digitalWrite() to enable the pullup resistors, however, are required, unless you install actual resistors between the input lines and V_{cc}.

The setup() function finishes by initializing the serial port to run at 9,600 baud and sending out a binary 0. The reason for this initial transmission is explained shortly. The parameter passed to the Serial.write() function has to be qualified using the byte() *typecast*. The Serial.write() function is *so smart* that it can't figure out what to do if you tell it to send a zero value, like this: Serial.write(0);. The compiler reports "call of overloaded 'write(int)' is ambiguous." No, *you're* ambiguous.

An *overloaded* function is one that has been defined in more than one way, depending on the number and type of parameters passed to it. This is very useful for handling different scenarios with a generic function that knows how to deal with all sorts of different combinations of data. Serial.write() is a good example. However, in this instance, you have to give the compiler a clue as to what kind of a zero you want it to send. Because you want to send a little eight-bit zero for now, you *cast* the constant value into a particular data type by surrounding it with the word *byte* and some parentheses, like this: Serial.write(byte(0));.

That's all there is for the setup() function. Now let's move on to the loop() function.

The loop() function starts out with a couple of static int declarations for brightness and previous_brightness. You use brightness to represent the variable level of brightness you want to emit with your big LED on each node. This technically only needs to be an eight-bit value, because that is the default resolution of the PWM functions you're using in this sketch. However, by declaring it as a signed, integer value (an int), you can do some tricks with it that make coding the sketch a little more straightforward.

These two variables wouldn't have to be declared as static if you declared them outside the scope of the loop() function, thereby making them *global* variables. For now, however, they're only used within the loop() function, so technically speaking they're *local* to the loop() function and there they stay.

At the beginning of the loop() function, you note the present value of the brightness variable by assigning it to the previous_brightness variable. If the value of the brightness variable changes by the end of the function, you can tell by performing a comparison between these two variables. This lets you know if anything needs to happen. In this example, if nothing changes, then nothing needs to be done about that.

Next, you check the state of each of the pushbuttons. Because the pushbuttons are normally open, they aren't connected to ground if they aren't being pressed at the time you check them. Also, because of the pullup resistors you enabled on each of the pushbutton inputs, the logic level on each pin is High if the button isn't pressed. Conversely, if the button *is* pressed, the logic level of the input pin is Low; you can read this using the digitalRead() function.

Each button is evaluated in turn. If the button is currently being pressed, a button-specific action is taken with regard to the brightness variable. If the On button is being pressed, the brightness level is set to the maximum: 255. If the Off button is being pressed, the brightness level is set to the minimum: 0. Alternately, if the Bright button is being pressed, the brightness level is increased by incrementing the value of the brightness variable. The Dim button, when pressed, causes the brightness level to be decreased by decrementing the value of the brightness variable.

If the LED was already off (the `brightness` variable was zero) and the Dim button was pressed, what would happen? The brightness variable would be decremented, resulting in a *negative* brightness level. Oops.

Similarly, if the LED was already on full-tilt and the Bright button was pressed, what would happen? You guessed it: the value of the brightness variable would be 256, which is no longer within the valid range of PWM duty-cycle settings.

These specific conditions are tested, and the value of the variable is limited to the proper values. This is why you declare the brightness variable to be of type `int` (a signed, integer number). It's OK if it goes negative or exceeds the eight-bit range of the PWM hardware. You can fix it in software before proceeding.

An alternate approach to value clipping or constraint is to make the appropriate test *before* the adjustment of the value. For example, you could have written the code for handing the Bright and Dim buttons as follows:

```
if((digitalRead(6) == LOW) && (brightness < 255)) brightness++; // brighter
if((digitalRead(7) == LOW) && (brightness > 0)) brightness--; // dimmer
```

Either way, a comparison is performed. In this overly simplistic example, either one works as well as the other. In real-life applications, it's always more complicated. You need to use your good judgment to decide which is a more appropriate approach. Try to lean toward cleaner code with fewer exceptions and boundary conditions, if possible.

If this wasn't a networking example sketch, you'd be done already. Set the PWM duty cycle using the `analogWrite()` function, and repeat from the beginning. Done and done.

However, this *is* a networking example sketch, so you have to do some networking. First, you need to define and describe your network. Right now it's two Arduinos with their USARTs cross-connected. If one Arduino detects a change in the desired brightness level, it reports this new setting to the other Arduino. It makes this report by sending the new brightness level as a single byte of information over the serial port. There's no handshaking, no error-checking, and no verification.

Your sketch now has the responsibility to report changes in the desired lighting level to the other node. If the brightness level has been altered by the local user (that is, the presser of buttons), you can detect that using a couple of different methods. One popular method is to set a flag whenever a button has been pressed and then check to see if that flag has been set by the end of the function. Remember to reset any such flags after they have been processed; this requires a separate flag variable to be declared.

Your example sketch is so simple that you can use the value of the `brightness` variable as your flag by comparing it with its previous value, cleverly hidden in a variable named `previous_brightness`. If the variables have the same value, then nothing happened. You can assume (in this example only) this means that no buttons were pressed. It the two variables have diverged in value, then something happened to cause this. A good assumption is a button press or other event. If it's determined that a change did occur, it's reported by sending the new value out the serial port to the other Arduino.

The sketch also has to respond to changes in lighting-level brightness as reported by the other node. You can check this by looking to see if anything has been received via the serial port. The `Serial.available()` function returns the number of bytes that have been received by the USART and stored in a buffer. The only two values in which you have interest are *some* and *none*. You really don't care about the exact number of bytes received in this example. This allows you to use C's built-in true/false evaluation mechanism to determine if anything needs to be done. False evaluates to a value of zero, and true is anything else (any nonzero value). Therefore, if even a single byte is waiting in the `Serial` library's buffer (remember, the AVR's USART has only a single byte-receive buffer; any other buffering is done in software), then the `Serial.available()` function is evaluated as true (nonzero) in a conditional statement, such as used in the example sketch. If there are no bytes waiting in the buffer, `Serial.available()` is evaluated as a false statement. This makes for shorter and clearer coding.

If a byte has been received via the serial port, it's read and interpreted as the new brightness level. Again, no testing or verification is done in this trivial example. In real-world applications, you would always check to make sure that incoming settings or commands make sense or are valid within the context used.

Now comes the long-awaited explanation of the zero sent on startup. Other than button presses, one other event can cause the two LEDs to lose synchronization: this happens when one or the other Arduino loses power or is otherwise reset.

In a more well-mannered network, provision is made for a network-status request of some sort that allows newly arrived nodes to inquire, "What's going on?" and respond accordingly. Your network message space is completely full, due to the adoption of an overly simplistic network protocol that encompasses a one-byte status message. Think about the implications of this decision for a moment.

Node synchronization is maintained by forced updates after *any* status change. The practical upshot of this is that if an Arduino gets unplugged or reset, everyone is plunged into inky darkness—at least, until someone can get to one of the pushbuttons and turn the lights back on. An alternative is to omit the reset scenario and allow a node to remain out of synchronization (gasp!) until either another (ahem, *the* other) node updates it or it's adjusted locally. You get to decide these things when you invent networks.

Expanding the Network

Connecting two Arduinos is certainly fun, and there may even be some useful applications for this new technology. Can this little network be expanded? How would that work?

Let's add two more Arduinos to the mix, for a total of four. They can no longer simply be cross-connected without adding more circuitry to prevent the respective transmitters from stepping on each other. Let's link them up in a loop, with the TX of the first one going to the RX of the second, then the TX of the second one going to the RX of the third, and so on. Finally, the TX of the last Arduino goes back to the RX of the first Arduino, completing the loop. See Figure 12-5.

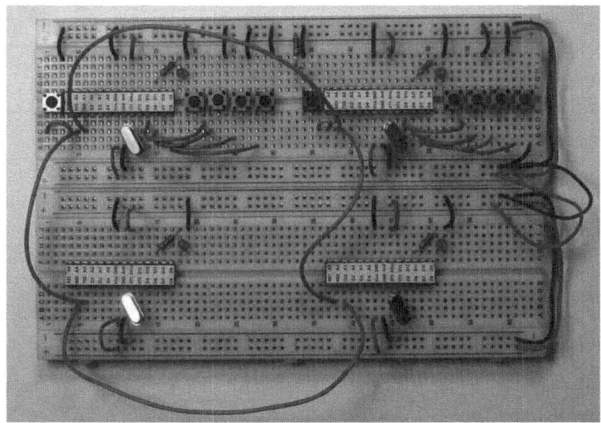

Figure 12-5. A more ambitious four-node network of breadboarded Arduinos. The USARTs are laced together in a loop this time, forming a circle. The pushbuttons on the third and fourth Arduinos have been omitted, but they still have the dimmable LED that responds to network updates from the other two Arduinos.

You only have to make subtle changes in the sketch. The `setup()` function remains intact. The bulk of the `loop()` function remains unaltered. You only need to address the two network sections of the code: the duty-to-report-changes section and the duty-to-conform section. Let's start with the second one and then come back to the first.

The only change in the duty-to-conform section is to echo the incoming status message back out the serial port, thus sending it further along the loop. You have to again outwit the clever `Serial.write()` function by camouflaging the `brightness` variable as a `byte` with a typecast. Otherwise, it would correctly deduce that the `brightness` variable is a signed integer (it really is) that is 16 bits in length and send it as 2 consecutive bytes, which is *not* what you want. The updated section should look like this:

```
// any other news from the network?
if(Serial.available()) {
  brightness = Serial.read(); // fetch new brightness level
  Serial.write(byte(brightness)); // send it along
}
```

So every time you receive a byte, you send it back out? Won't that cause a cascade effect when the status word gets all the way around the loop (which could theoretically be as quickly as 4 milliseconds, if the `Serial` library were a little more optimized)? Yes, it most certainly would, if you didn't handle that very possibility within the duty-to-report-changes section.

This section works exactly the same way as before, detecting changes by comparing the present brightness level with what it was previously. If detected, the same report is made to the network by transmitting the new brightness level as a single byte.

The only addition you need to make to this code is to wait for the status message to make its way around the loop and then eat it up when it arrives. Problem solved, unless two nodes try to send different update messages simultaneously. The updated code looks like this:

```
if(brightness != previous_brightness) {
  // the brightness has changed
  Serial.write(brightness); // broadcast the new brightness
  while(Serial.available() == 0); // wait for it to come back around
  Serial.read(); // gobble it up; do not re-transmit
}
```

The only problem with this network methodology (technically, a *ring network*) is that it's intolerant of any node faults. If even a single Arduino goes offline or loses power, the circle is broken. To overcome this limitation, you should implement a different network topology (arrangement).

Other Network Topologies

A *star network*, such as the popular Universal Serial Bus (USB), connects all endpoints to a central hub. The functions of the hub and of the nodes are very different and require different hardware and software.

A *bus network* connects all the nodes together with a single medium. Nodes then have to take turns talking or risk collisions on the network. Advanced protocols have been developed to handle these potential train wrecks.

A *fully connected network* has a unique connection between every node in the network. The charlieplexed LEDs covered in Chapter 8 are an example of a fully connected electrical network.

A *mesh network* allows nodes to act as relays for other nodes, passing information back and forth among themselves and figuring out how to get from point A to point B, right now, based on available routes.

The nice thing about the simple examples so far is that they have used *identical* sketches on all the nodes. There is no concept of *addressing* or any distinction made between nodes. The idea has been to get you thinking about how networks actually work, instead of relegating all that wondrous technology to vague ideas about a cloud somewhere.

You come back to the more complicated networks (such as the Internet) later. Now, let's take a look at some of the real-world issues you encounter when dealing with networks of devices, even if that network has a population of two.

Making the Connection

You now turn to some practical aspects of this little conversation between Arduinos. First, there has to be a proper connection between these two aspiring conversationalists. One answer is to hard-wire the two devices together electrically. For the most basic serial-port connection, this requires a minimum of three wires. One wire carries a signal from the first device (the talker) to the second device (the listener). Another wire makes the opposite connection, allowing the second unit to talk back to the first unit. A common ground connection must be made between these two devices, and that is the purpose of the third wire.

That may sound like the simplest and easiest way to get these two parties talking, but it's fraught with peril. The low voltages involved, coupled with the relatively high resistance of thin wires of any appreciable length, mean that no discernable signal may be able to bridge the gap betwixt the two. It works fine on a desk with the two units sitting a meter or two apart. After being wired up through the walls and over the ceiling or under the floor, it may not work. Or, most frustratingly of all, it may work *sometimes.*

RS-232

One possible solution is to translate those low voltages into higher voltages so they carry farther. This is the idea behind the RS-232 standard. A high voltage on the TTL-level TX or RX pins of your Arduino measures in the range of 3V–5V and is called a *mark* condition. A *space* is a low voltage, something closer to ground or 0V. The TX line stays in the mark condition while idle and then squirts out a carefully timed series of marks and spaces to signify a data transmission. After the transmission is complete, the TX line returns to the mark condition.

Forcing the data line to a space condition and holding it longer than normal for a legal data transmission is called a *break* condition and is sometimes used to get the attention of the other end of the line when other handshaking methods have failed or aren't available.

Once translated to RS-232 levels, a mark condition, instead of being a High logic level, is now a *negative* voltage in the range of -3V to -15V, and possibly as low as -25V. Anything in this range qualifies as a mark, according to the RS-232 specification. Similarly, a space is translated from a Low logic level to a positive voltage in the range of +3V to +15V. Most PCs and RS-232-to-TTL adapters work with voltages between ±5V and ±10V, typically.

Some PCs fudge a bit and accept 0V and 5V signals, but they're still of opposite polarity from the TTL-level serial signals on your Arduino. Voltages above 6V can permanently damage the AVR chip on your Arduino. Always use an RS-232-to-TTL adapter when interfacing with RS-232 signals.

Converting RS-232 levels to TTL levels isn't hard. You can do this with a transistor, a diode, and two resistors. Because one of those resistors is acting as a pullup on the received signal, it can be replaced by the built-in pullup resistor available on the AVR's I/O line, bringing the component count down to a manageable three. See Figure 12-6.

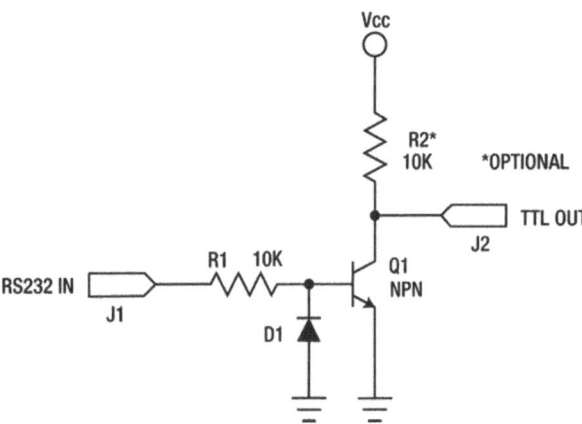

Figure 12-6. *An RS-232-to-TTL receiver circuit. This circuit limits the voltage swing of the incoming signal to TTL levels (0–5V) and provides the necessary logical inversion.*

Looking at the circuit schematic in Figure 12-6, you see the RS-232 input going straight into R1, a 10KΩ resistor. The purpose of R1 is to limit the amount of current flowing to the base of Q1. Yes, in theory, it should be a mild-mannered RS-232 signal, always between the mandated voltage of ±15V. But it may not be. This is by far the most common point of failure in any electronic circuit: the connection to the Outside World. All kinds of terrible things are lurking out there, waiting to zap your tender creation. Static electricity, being plugged in backward, being plugged into the wrong device—these are just a few of the possible scenarios. You don't need to go crazy adding protection circuitry to every node in your invention. You *do* need to know where to look for the most commonly occurring failure points when things start acting strangely. The connections to the Outside World are the usual suspects and a good place to start.

Diode D1 also offers some protection for Q1 by keeping the base from going *too negative* with respect to the emitter. Bipolar junction transistors (actually, most semiconductors) have a failure mode called *reverse voltage breakdown*. Even a beefy small-signal transistor like the PN2222A, which was used to drive loads up to 1.0A back when you were blinking LEDs, has a teeny-tiny emitter-base breakdown voltage ($BV_{(BR)EBO}$) of only 6.0V. That means if the base becomes more negative than the emitter by as little as 6.0V, the transistor fails.

You prevent this particular failure by keeping the voltage at the base within a volt or so of ground, by clamping the base to ground via the diode, D1. D1 can be any small rectifier diode, such as the 1N4148 or 1N914.

The collector of Q1 is connected through a pullup resistor to V_{cc}. This keeps it at a logic High level until the transistor starts to conduct.

When the input voltage of the RS-232 input goes high (a space condition), this causes a small amount of current to flow through R1 and into the base of Q1. Q1 becomes forward biased enough to begin to conduct current from its collector to its emitter. This causes the voltage on the collector to drop to very close (but not all the way) to ground. This produces a logic Low level on the output pin.

When the input voltage of the RS-232 signal is ground or negative, very little or no current flows through R1, Q1 remains unbiased, and the output remains High. This is the mark condition, indicating that the data line is either idle or disconnected.

The transistor effectively *inverts* the logic level of the incoming signal, which is exactly what you need it to do. It also *attenuates* (reduces the amplitude of) the signal in the process, assuming that V_{cc} is lower than the incoming RS-232 signal, which it most likely is.

Listing 12-2 shows a short example sketch for an Arduino Mega 2560. One of the extra serial port inputs (RX3) is tied to the output of the circuit in Figure 12-4. An RS-232 signal is attached from a PC, and serial data is transmitted from the PC through its serial port to the RS-232-to-TTL adapter circuit and then received on the Arduino Mega 2560. The received data is then sent back to the PC via the Serial Monitor in the Arduino software.

Listing 12-2. Example Sketch to Test an RS-232-to-TTL Adapter Circuit

```
void setup() {
  Serial.begin(9600);   // serial monitor
  Serial3.begin(115200); // from PC
  digitalWrite(15, HIGH); // turn on pullup resistor on RX3/D15 * required
}

void loop() {
  if(Serial3.available()) {
    Serial.write(Serial3.read());
  }
}
```

Note that using the built-in pullup resistor works up to 115,200 baud but only for very short distances. For longer distances or higher communication rates, please use a real pullup resistor of 10KΩ or so. This decreases the rise-time on the TTL signal coming from the adapter circuit. Resistors are cheap.

Converting from TTL to RS-232 levels is a little more complicated. You can use a circuit similar to the one presented in Figure 12-7. It steals the negative voltage required to comply with the RS-232 standard from the incoming TXD signal and stores it in C1.

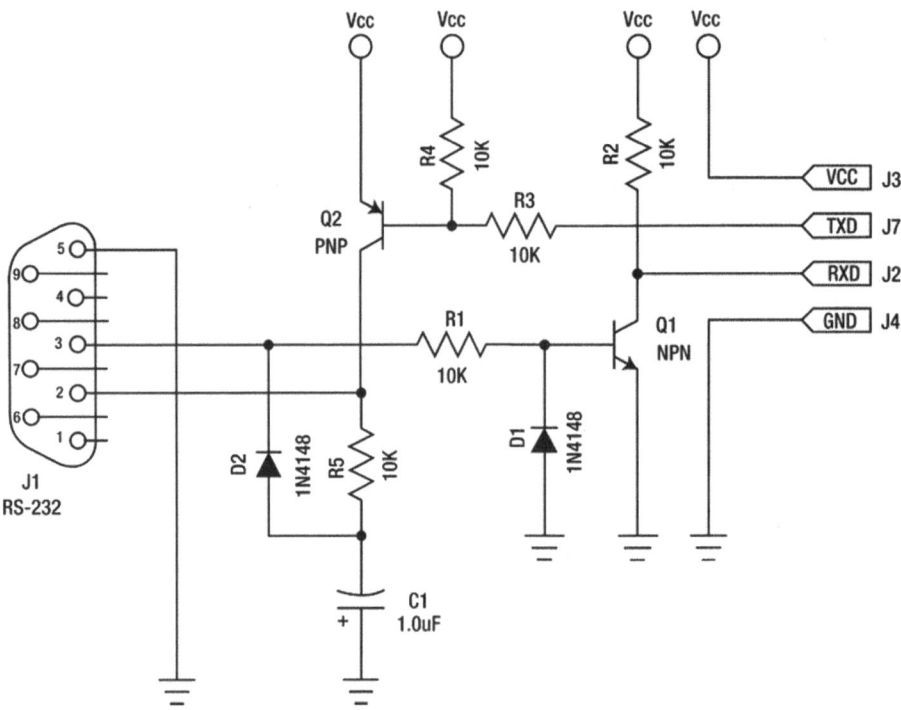

Figure 12-7. A bidirectional RS-232-to-TTL converter

A circuit very similar to the one in Figure 12-7 was used on the original AVRISP from Atmel, which used an RS-232 port for communication with the PC. The more recent AVRISP mkII (ah, Roman numerals) uses the more recent USB-type connection.

If your eyeballs are starting to cross from looking at this schematic, have no fear. There's a chip for that. It was originally designed and manufactured by Maxim IC (www.maxim-ic.com) and called the MAX232. Several other manufacturers also produce a similar part today. It's much better in almost every way when compared with the circuit in Figure 12-7. Have a look at the schematic in Figure 12-8.

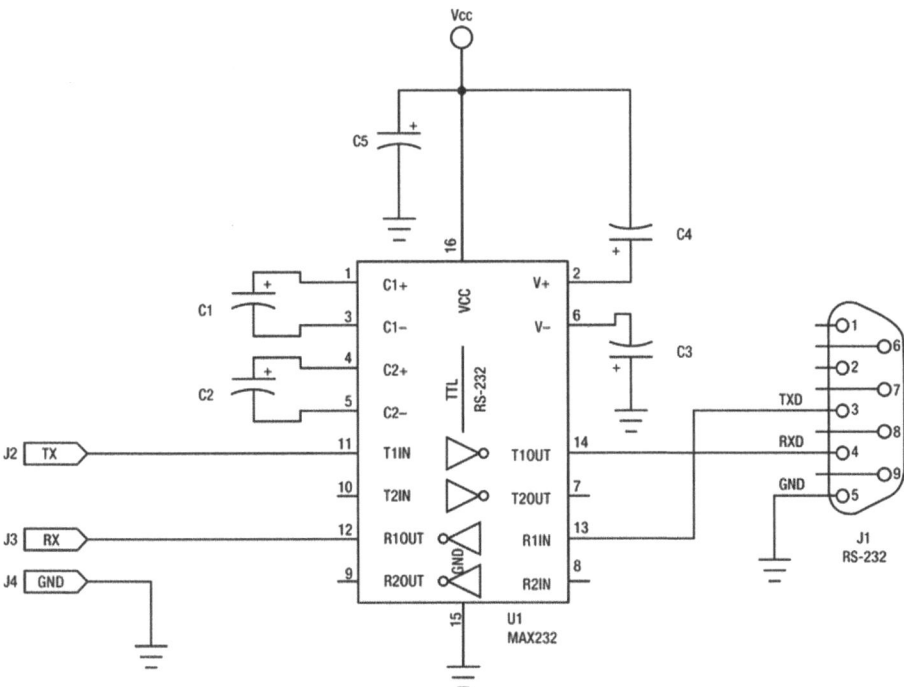

Figure 12-8. *The MAX232 chip makes RS-232 interfaces simpler and more reliable, while only requiring a single 5V supply.*

The MAX232 does several things. It contains a pair of RS-232-to-TTL receivers and a pair of TTL-to-RS-232 transmitters. It also contains a voltage doubler and a voltage inverter. The doubler converts the 5V input voltage to ~10V. The inverter takes the ~10V and converts it to -10V. This ±10V supply is then used to drive the RS-232 transmitters. The MAX232 also offers 15KV of isolation, protecting your sensitive circuits from the harsh world.

The capacitors surrounding the chip are required. C1 is used in the voltage-doubler circuit. C2 is used in the inverter circuit. C3 and C4 are the filter capacitors for these ±10V supplies. C5 decouples the input power supply, reducing the electrical noise generated by the internal oscillators.

For the original MAX232 device, C1–C4 should be 1.0μF capacitors. For the improved MAX232A, the capacitors can be much smaller, only 0.1μF. The MAX233 incorporates the capacitors C1–C4 internally.

Many variations are available with different numbers of transmitters and receivers.

RS-485 and Others

RS-232 still suffers from voltage drops when long line lengths are involved. Another alternative is the RS-485 standard, where a *differential balanced line* is used instead of a voltage-only interface. This arrangement allows a signal to travel much further and is also more immune to environmental noise. There are several possible configurations for serial communication using the RS-485 standard, including *multipoint* arrangements in which more than two devices communicate over the line. The AVR at the heart of your Arduino already supports some of the more common conventions, which sometimes require nine data bits to transmit data and address information over the bus.

An Example Library

Bill Porter's `EasyTransfer` library for Arduino makes it really easy and fast to communicate between two Arduinos. See Bill's web page at `www.billporter.info/easytransfer-arduino-library/` for more information and to download the latest version.

The big advantage of the `EasyTransfer` library is that all communication is done in binary, which makes it a lot faster than if the data was being sent back and forth using ASCII codes. It also supports using both the hardware USARTs as well as the other kind using the `NewSoftSerial` library.

MIDI: Musical Instrument Digital Interface

The MIDI standard has been around since the early 1980s. At that time, electronic musical instruments were increasing in popularity, but it was difficult or impossible to connect them together. The MIDI standard solves this problem using a simple serial connection. The standard was once freely available on the Web but has since been improved and can be purchased from the MIDI Manufacturers' Association (`www.midi.org`).

A MIDI connection sends control and event information over a digital serial port. It doesn't transmit sounds or audio. For example, let's say you have a nice MIDI keyboard that you've practiced on for a long time, so you're really familiar with it. Other keyboards are OK, but they don't play as well as yours. The problem is that the built-in instruments and sounds are getting a bit dated, and you want some new stuff. You buy a shiny new MIDI module that has a few buttons and knobs on it, but no keyboard. You plug a MIDI cable (and there is only one kind of MIDI cable, but different colors and lengths) from the MIDI OUT port of your keyboard to the MIDI IN port of your new module. Plug your headphones into the new module, turn everything on, and jam out to the latest sounds. That's all there is to it. It was designed so that even musicians could use it.

In reality, a lot of thought went into making MIDI easy and reliable for everyone, not just musicians. It was literally plug-and-play before anything else was.

The MIDI hardware interface is simple but effective. The underlying communication protocol has a simple, basic structure; but like everything else, it has been improved over the ages and now includes all kinds of stuff.

The keyboard *describes* what and how you play by sending messages to the module. To reiterate, it does *not* send audio or sound signals of any kind. If you play a note by pressing a single key, it sends a single Note On message, describing which key was played (note number) and how hard you struck it (velocity information). When you release the key, the keyboard then transmits a Note Off event, also naming the key involved and, oddly enough, describing how hard you released the key. True story.

If you play a chord, the keyboard sends a series of Note On messages, one for each of the keys in the chord. They aren't all sent at the same time exactly, but fast enough that it's almost impossible to detect any delay.

A MIDI port and a serial port both communicate by sending one bit at a time over a channel. Whereas the Arduino and PCs use a voltage interface, MIDI uses a current loop. This dramatically lowers the amount of noise on the line. Why don't PCs use current loops? The old-style Teletypes did, and the very first serial interfaces available for the IBM PC had a current loop option.

Current flowing through the loop is perceived as a logical 0. No current flowing is a digital 1. That is all.

Also a wee bit different from your familiar serial ports, MIDI always uses the same communication rate of 31,250 bits per second. This is perhaps more easily remembered as $1\text{MHz} \div 32$. The framing format is 8N1, or eight data bits, no parity, and one stop bit. This makes it easy to set up using the Arduino software: `Serial.begin(31250);`.

The hardware interface is likewise easy to build. The MIDI example sketch provided with the Arduino software describes a simple hardware MIDI transmitter circuit, but it isn't in strict compliance with the official MIDI specification. It lacks only a single resistor to be fully MIDI-compliant. To paraphrase and correct:

- Connect digital pin 1 (TX) through a 220Ω resistor to MIDI pin 5.

- Connect MIDI pin 2 to ground.

- Connect MIDI pin 4 through another 220Ω resistor to +5V.

Let's take a look at this MIDI connector. It's a 5-pin DIN modular connector with a 180° pin spread, sometimes known as a 5/180°. These were once used as shielded audio cables. You might also remember them from such all-time favorites as the original IBM PC keyboard cord. MIDI cables always have male connectors on both ends, and all MIDI equipment has female sockets. See Figure 12-9.

Figure 12-9. *The business end of a MIDI cable. The pins are numbered, left to right: 1, 4, 2, 5, 3. There is an alignment notch in the bottom half of the shield.*

If you can't find a proper MIDI socket for your experimental purposes, you can always chop a MIDI cable in half. There can be as few as two wires and a shield inside, or all five pins may be connected. The pins are wired straight across: pin 1 goes to pin 1, and so on.

The shielding within the cable is connected to pin 2 (the center pin) on both ends of all MIDI cables. The MIDI OUT port should connect pin 2 to the local ground. To eliminate the possibility of ground loops, the other end of the cable (the MIDI IN port) does *not* connect pin 2 to ground. It isn't required to complete an electrical connection, as you did previously using TTL serial communication. It only serves to shield the pair of wires inside. This is sometimes referred to as a *telescoping ground.*

The two other pins, 4 and 5, form the two legs of the current loop. By connecting the MIDI cable to your Arduino as outlined earlier (the Arduino MIDI example sketch omits the 220Ω in series with the TX pin for some reason), when the TTL level of the USART goes to zero (logical Low), then current flows through the loop. When the TTL level rises to +5V, there is no difference in potential, and no current flows through the loop.

On the receiving end, the two wires are connected to the LED portion of an opto-isolator. Well, they're supposed to be. Some vendors cut corners and don't isolate the signal on the receiving end. This violates the MIDI specification and most likely adds a terrible amount of noise to the system.

An opto-isolator works by having two isolated circuits in close proximity to each other, and cut off from ambient lighting. Inside these little chips is a small cavity with an LED on one side and a phototransistor on the other. They aren't electrically connected in any way. They're *optically coupled*, meaning that when the LED comes on (that is, when current flows through it), the emitted light forward-biases the phototransistor, causing it to conduct more current than in the dark condition. That makes these devices perfect for current-loop applications.

The phototransistor side of the circuit then typically pulls a signal down to ground when activated. The signal floats back up when no signal is present due to a pullup resistor connecting it to V_{cc}. You work with the receiver part shortly. For now, let's make some MIDI noises using an Arduino.

The Arduino example MIDI sketch is a good starting point: File ➤ Examples ➤ 4.Communication ➤ MIDI. However, it gets old quickly. Try the sketch found in Listing 12-3.

Listing 12-3. Arduino MIDI Keyboard

```
#define KEYS 8

volatile byte previous_state[KEYS];
volatile byte state[KEYS];
volatile byte changes[KEYS];
const byte key_pins[KEYS] = { 5, 6, 7, 8, 9, 10, 11, 12 };
const byte notes[KEYS] = { 60, 62, 64, 65, 67, 69, 71, 72 }; // middle C and up

void setup() {
  for(byte i = 0; i < KEYS; i++) digitalWrite(key_pins[i], HIGH); // pullups on!
  Serial.begin(31250); // MIDI special baud rate
  TCCR2B = 0<<WGM22 | 1<<CS22 | 1<<CS21 | 1<<CS20; // CK/1024
  TIMSK2 = 1<<TOIE2; // enable overflow interrupt
}

void loop() {

  byte i;

  for(i = 0; i < KEYS; i++) {
    if(changes[i]) {
      Serial.write(state[i] ? 0x90 : 0x80); // Note On or Note Off, channel 1
      Serial.write(notes[i]); // the MIDI note number
      Serial.write(0x64); // medium velocity
      changes[i] = 0; // done!
    }
  }
}
```

```
ISR(TIMER2_OVF_vect) {
  byte i;
  // scan the buttons
  for(i = 0; i < KEYS; i++) {
    previous_state[i] = state[i]; // save previous state
    state[i] = digitalRead(key_pins[i]) ? 0 : 1; // record present state
    changes[i] = state[i] ^ previous_state[i]; // any changes?
  }
}
```

You need to add some pushbuttons to digital pins 5–12. See Figure 12-10.

Figure 12-10. An Arduino MIDI keyboard, using a harvested MIDI cable (lower left)

The sketch looks surprisingly simple, but it's doing some interesting things on the inside. Let's take a look at what's going on.

You #define a constant, KEYS, for the number of keys you want to use. In this case, it's eight. This number crops up several times in the sketch, and it would be cumbersome to change them all if you decided to add or take away a few keys.

Next are some volatile byte array declarations. You use those to keep track of the states of the ~~buttons~~ musical instrument keys. You declare them as volatile because they're manipulated by an interrupt handler, and you don't want the compiler making any sort of assumptions about their contents, which it would otherwise do.

After that, you have a couple of look-up tables in the form of const byte arrays. The first one, key_pins[], tells you the pin numbers associated with each of the keys. Similarly, the notes[] table assigns a MIDI note number to each of the keys. MIDI note numbers can range from 0 to 127, with middle C being number 60. You assign the white keys from middle C and up an octave to the little keyboard.

The setup() function first turns on all the built-in pullup resistors that are connected to the buttons. It does this in a compact for() loop that iterates through all the items in the key_pins[] look-up table, using the digitalWrite() function to set the outputs to a HIGH level if they were outputs. But they're not outputs; they remain inputs because you didn't specify otherwise.

The `Serial.begin(31250)` function call is the only MIDI-specific hardware configuration you need to perform. Everything else goes toward learning to speak MIDI properly and scanning the keyboard.

Timer/Counter 2 is used to generate a periodic interrupt. You set the prescaler to divide by 1,024, giving the 8-bit counter a 15,625Hz clock. Because Timer/Counter 2 remains mostly configured for PWM service by the low-level Arduino code, this results in an overflow about 30 times per second. You enable the overflow interrupt by setting the `TOIE2` bit in the `TIMSK2` register. Global interrupts have already been enabled for you.

You define an interrupt handler for the Timer/Counter 2 overflow interrupt using the mandated vector name `TIMER2_OVF_vect`. In this interrupt handler, you again iterate through the keys. First, the present state (pressed or not pressed) of each of the keys is copied to a `previous_state[]` array. This helps you decide what, if anything, has happened.

Then the state of each of the keys is interrogated using the `digitalRead()` function, by using the key-to-pin look-up table. Additionally, the `HIGH` and `LOW` values returned by the `digitalRead()` function aren't really what you want, although they would certainly do if you wanted to keep track of them that way. Instead, you use the return value (`HIGH` or `LOW`) from the `digitalWrite()` function as a true/false test, using the C conditional operator `? :`. The first value following the `?` is returned if the condition is true; otherwise the value following the `:` is returned. This lets you arbitrarily assign a value of one in the `state[]` array if the key is currently being pressed and zero otherwise.

Next the present state and the previous state are compared using the exclusive-or function. If they're the same (still pressed or still released, you don't care which), this returns a value of zero to the `changes[]` array for this key. Only if the state has changed (again, you don't care which way) does the `changes[]` array indicate that something happened.

This keyboard scan happens just over 30 times per second.

The `loop()` function continuously looks through the `changes[]` array to see if a key has been either pressed or released. These are the only things MIDI cares about, at least as far as this simple example goes.

If a key has recently changed status, you send a MIDI message to a MIDI synthesizer of some sort to play the actual musical parts. MIDI messages are made up of one or more eight-bit transmissions. The first byte is the *status byte*. It has bit 7 set to indicate that it's a status byte. All other bytes following the status byte must have their bit 7 cleared. This limits many MIDI variables to a 0–127 range, such as note number, mentioned earlier.

If the key was just pressed, you want to send a Note On message. This message has a status byte starting with 9 and ending with the MIDI channel number, assuming hexadecimal notation.

There are 16 available MIDI channels that can be addressed over a single MIDI cable. Although the channel numbers are shown as 1 through 16 to the human types, inside the computer parts the channel numbers are 0–15. To send a Note On message on MIDI channel 1, the correct status byte is 0x90.

After the properly formatted Note On status byte has been sent, the MIDI module expects both a note number and a velocity report. The *velocity* is a measure of how hard the note was struck. This only applies to dynamically expressive instruments, but that is most of them.

Your sketch sends either a Note On or Note Off message, depending on the state of the key in question. It then transmits the appropriate note number, having looked it up from the table. A fixed velocity of 0x64 is sent along to complete the message. At this point, the MIDI module receiving this message (which could be your PC if you have a MIDI adapter available) should start or cease to play the note, depending.

Alternately, you can send the equivalent of a Note Off message by sending a Note On message with a velocity of zero.

Because the `loop()` function is in no way synchronized with the background keyboard scan, it goes ahead and clears the flag in the `changes[]` array to prevent it from acting on it in its next iteration.

Now you have an Arduino that thinks it's a keyboard. This keyboard-scanning technique can be used in a lot of user-interface applications.

The Internet

As delivered, your Arduino isn't ready for Internet connectivity. It's not far off, though. Believe it or not, you're only an Ethernet adapter away from surfing the World Wide Web or serving up your own web pages with your humble little chip. There are two popular ways to go about this.

The standard Ethernet Shield for Arduino is based on the WIZnet 5100 chip. It plugs into the Arduino Uno like any other shield and has an Ethernet jack on one edge. The standard Ethernet library, as supplied by the Arduino software, has several example sketches, including both a WebClient and a WebServer application. So plug, plug, click, upload, and you're in the web business. Not complicated at all, and almost a little *too* easy.

To make it more interesting, let's use a different Ethernet adapter, the Microchip ENC28J60. This is a single-chip driver that connects directly to an Ethernet jack (the kind that already has the isolation magnetics built in) and comes as either a shield or as a separate module. The module is the least expensive route and can be had for as little as $10–$35, which is less expensive than the WIZnet-based solution.

For some reason, although the Microchip part number of this chip is ENC28J60, several vendors refer to their Ethernet adapter modules as EN28J60, without the C. This carries over to the documentation and into the driver software, as well.

One of the simple reasons that the ENC28J60 device is less expensive is that it does less. The WIZnet device implements the UDP and TCP protocols on-chip, relieving the Arduino from handling those tasks, which are moderately complex. However, never fear: the Arduino community of generous and clever folk to the rescue! Several Arduino libraries are available to talk to the ENC28J60 chip. You can use one of these and pick and choose what you require from the feature set. Listing 12-4 shows an example sketch that presents a static web page on a fixed IP address.

Listing 12-4. Arduino Web Server Example Sketch, Boiled Down to a Bare Minimum

```
#include "EtherShield.h"

EtherShield es; // the EtherShield "object"

// please change these numbers!
byte mac_address[] = { 0x04, 0x07, 0x01, 0x09, 0x06, 0x03 };
byte ip_address[] = { 192, 168, 0, 99 };

#define BUFFER_SIZE 1000 // make it 500 for '168-based Arduinos
byte page_buffer[BUFFER_SIZE];

const char webpage_contents[] PROGMEM =
"HTTP/1.0 200 OK\r\nContent-Type: text/html\r\n\r\n"
"<html><head><title>Arduino EN28J60 Web Server</title></head><body>"
"<h1>Arduino EN28J60 Web Server</h1>"
"<p>Yup, it works.</p>"
"<p>Simply amazing!</p>"
"<hr />"
"</body></html>"; // The End. This line must have a semicolon ";" at the end of it
```

```
void setup() {
  es = EtherShield(); // create the EtherShield 'object'
  es.ES_enc28j60Init(mac_address); // initialize EN28J60
  es.ES_init_ip_arp_udp_tcp(mac_address, ip_address, 80); // use port 80
}

void loop() {
  if(es.ES_packetloop_icmp_tcp(page_buffer, es.ES_enc28j60PacketReceive(BUFFER_SIZE,
page_buffer))) {
    // send web page contents if HTTP request received
    es.ES_www_server_reply(page_buffer, es.ES_fill_tcp_data_p(page_buffer, 0,
webpage_contents));
  }
}
```

This example sketch is derived from the web-server example provided with the EtherShield 1.6 library, available from http://blog.thiseldo.co.uk. The EtherShield.h header file is included in the sketch, which defines the functions available. The es variable is declared as an instance of an EtherShield object and created in the setup() function. After that, the EN28J60 chip is initialized with its MAC address, and the library is configured to perform a variety of web-related tasks, implementing several of the underlying protocols necessary for web pages to be served.

A buffer is reserved for both sending information to and receiving it from the Internet. This buffer can be as large as 1,000 bytes on the Arduino Uno, but it should work better at around 500 bytes for ATmega168-based Arduinos.

A const char array of bytes is placed in program memory using the PROGMEM keyword. This array holds the contents of the web page to be delivered upon request from someone's web browser. You use a little C coding trickery here. Notice that each of the lines of HTML code is contained within matching double quotation marks, but no connecting punctuation is used between them. The compiler concatenates these strings together into one big string. Just remember to put a semicolon at the end.

If you're familiar with HTML, the contents of the web-page definition should look pretty predictable. The only additional items are the HTTP headers at the beginning. These are transmitted back to the requester (usually a web browser) as part of the data negotiation that takes place every time you look at a web page. If you're *not* yet familiar with HTML, now is a good time to get started.

The rest of the web page is the bare minimum required for a well-formed HTML document. A <head> is defined, where the page title is stored. The <body> of the web page contains a single <h1> or first-level heading, again repeating the page's title. A couple of short <p> paragraphs follow, ending with a <hr /> horizontal rule, or line. Feel free to replace the contents of this example page with whatever wonderful prose you like. You could even link to a funny cat video, in keeping with the original purpose and traditions of the Internet.

The real magic happens in the deceptively-short loop() function. A call to a library function waits for an Ethernet packet to arrive. This packet's content is then examined. If it's an Internet Control Message Protocol (ICMP) or control packet, such as a ping request, it's handled. If the packet contains an HTTP GET request, then the page buffer is filled with the contents of the static web page (preceded by the HTTP headers, of course) and shipped back out the Ethernet port. Deceptively simple, yes?

The reality is that there are many, many layers of protocols hidden beneath this simple loop. The EtherShield library is handling the uppermost layers, and the Ethernet module is handling the lower-level stuff. All this in a sketch that is only about 6KB. That leaves quite a bit of room for more fun stuff!

Wiring up the web server is pretty simple. If you build or buy the EN28J60 Ethernet adapter in Arduino shield form, all you have to do is mate it to your Arduino, and the wiring is finished. Connect the RJ-45 jack to your router with an Ethernet cable, and you're all set.

If you're using the smaller EN28J60 adapter module, it's still pretty easy to wire it to your Arduino Uno. See Figure 12-11 (schematic) and Figure 12-12 (photo). Only six wires are required.

Note that this only works reliably with the Arduino Uno and later boards that can supply 150mA of current on the 3.3V line. The earlier FTDI-based Arduino boards are much more limited in their ability to provide regulated 3.3V, which is what the EN28J60 module requires.For those older boards, or derivatives that lack a 3.3V regulator, an external 3.3V regulator is required.

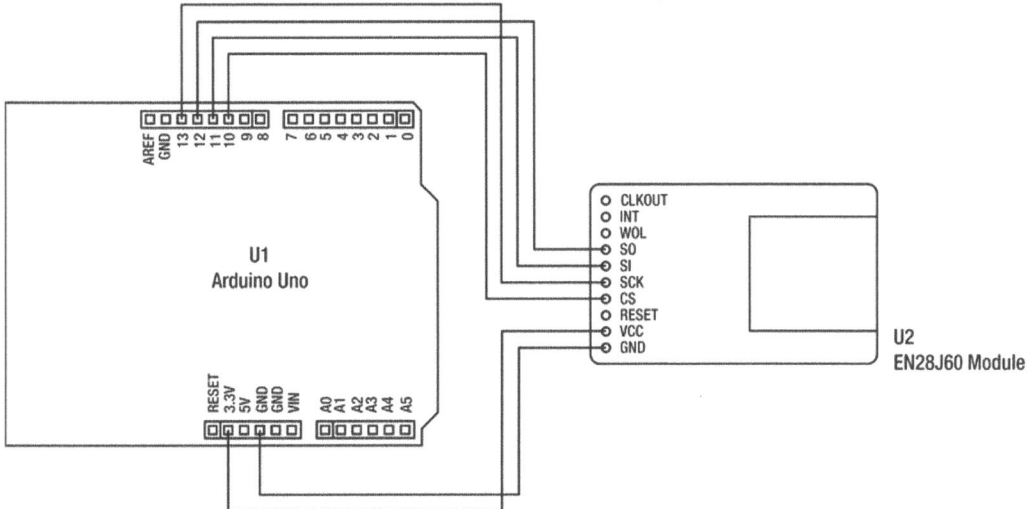

Figure 12-11. *The schematic diagram of the Arduino web server, using the inexpensive EN28J60 Ethernet module. Only six wires are required.*

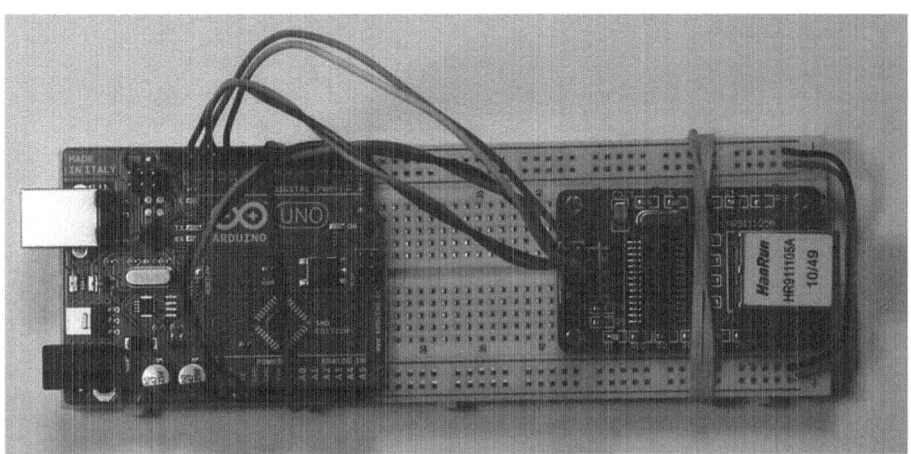

Figure 12-12. *The Arduino web-server prototype, with high-tech mounting option*

Figure 12-13 shows the mostly unimpressive output of all this tinkering.

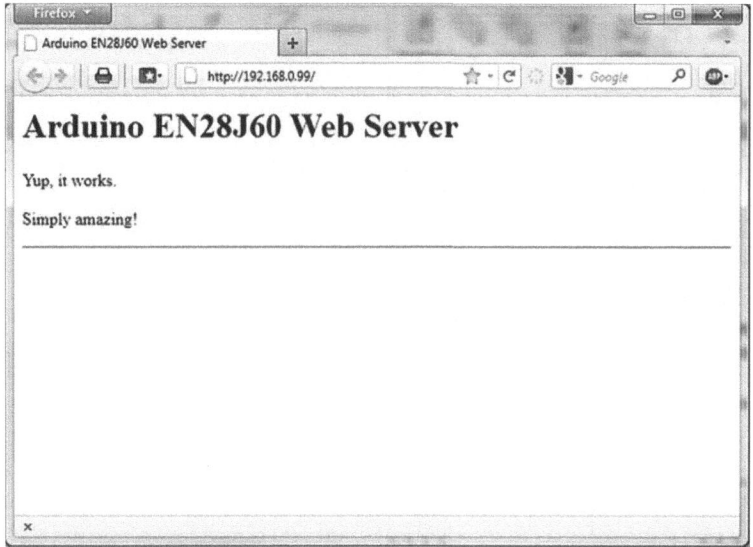

Figure 12-13. The web page delivered by the Arduino web server. Not much, but a good start.

Summary

An Arduino that doesn't get to talk to someone gets bored. It could be another Arduino sitting on the table right next to it, or it could an Arduino on another planet. For all you know, it could be some (gasp!) non-Arduino computer that wants to hold a conversation. Anything is possible with the proper networking. Just decide what you want to talk about, and get to talking.

This chapter covered only a few of the really basic ideas involved with networking. Space limitations preclude including all the great projects that can easily use the Arduino's various communication peripherals. This gives you some ideas about how to get more than one computer to communicate and maybe even cooperate toward accomplishing a task.

Bear in mind that when the now-popular World Wide Web was first getting started in the early 1990s, it was mostly connecting a bunch of Intel 386, 486, and first-generation Pentium processors that were running between 16MHz and 60MHz. With high-speed broadband Internet access spreading across the world at an ever-increasing pace, it seems inevitable that all things electronic will soon be able to talk to each other, creating an Internet of things. You have the opportunity to help decide what these things can and should do. How will your next Arduino networking project affect the world?

CHAPTER 13

More Example Projects

So here we are in the very last chapter of the book. Let's take something you've learned from each of the previous chapters and build a little Arduino-based project out of it all. What shall you build?

How about a robot? Robots are an excellent *second* Arduino project because they usually involve more than one active, working system. This involves a certain amount of planning ahead of time, as well as having a good idea when one of the subprojects is working well enough to be able to move on to the next subproject.

Like any other complex idea or task, designing and building a robot of your own can be divided into many smaller projects. Each of the mini projects in this chapter has application in other areas, and not just in personal robotics. This is one of the excellent benefits of robotic engineering, both as a hobby and as a profession. It forces you to approach the problem as a whole with a multidisciplinary viewpoint, requiring proficiency in several arts and crafts and a keen sense of how all the various parts will come together as a single, working unit.

Many topics and lots of interesting tidbits are covered in the briefest and shortest manner possible. One chapter in a book won't teach you everything you need to know about designing and building successful robots. The intention is to whet your appetite and spark your enthusiasm, while showing some actual robot designs that you can use as a launching point.

An Autonomous Robot

What defines an autonomous robot? It's a robot that can interact with its environment independently, with little or no human control required. Let's stop just shy of giving it complete free will, emotions, and flame throwers for now and see what kind of problem-solving skills you need to get something going.

As previously mentioned, there are several interrelated systems working together within even the simplest robot design. An autonomous robot, if it's to operate independently and without tethers, cables, or trailing wires, must have its own power supply. This power supply must meet the immediate needs of the robot, must permit lengthy periods of activity, and should be replenishable, ideally under the robot's control. It needs a motive system and perhaps some additional articulation. A *sensorium* of various detectors and sensors should provide the robot with data about its immediate environment. All of these systems must be coordinated by an internal control system that should at all times remain compliant to your wishes.

OK, let's get started! How hard could it be? You look at each of the major subsystems in a little detail and then move on to an iterative process of experiment and refinement.

Power Supply

Several types of power can be utilized in a robot structure. The first that may come to mind is electrical power, to run the computer chips and electric motors. Many small-scale robots rely entirely on electrical power. Compressed air, hydraulics, fuel cells, solar panels, steam, tightly wound springs, and gravity can also be used, depending on your facility with these technologies.

Because it's completely predictable that you're going to use an Arduino of some sort along the way, you should make at least preliminary plans for providing electrical power in the robot.

The typical Arduino Uno or similar circuit requires a steady stream of regulated electrical power to operate reliably. The on-board voltage regulator on most store-bought Arduinos permits you a certain amount of latitude when it comes to the specific characteristics of your supply. Anything between 6V and 12V should do nicely. Only a small amount of current is required for the microcontroller and supporting circuitry. The large-scale power consumers are typically the sensors and electric motors.

For anything except the teensiest, tiniest motors, you're *strongly* encouraged to implement a separate power supply for use by electric motors. These devices characteristically draw wildly varying amounts of current, depending on the demand placed on them. Maintaining a particular motor speed requires surprisingly little current, but *getting* to that speed requires a correspondingly large amount of current.

The principal symptom you encounter that indicates it's time to move to separate, dedicated power supplies is when your Arduino begins to act even more erratically than normal. This is most likely caused by giant current surges from the motors attempting to accelerate, which produces a corresponding drop in supply voltage to the AVR. Below a certain point, the AVR goes into a self-imposed reset state to prevent unreliable operation, and it remains there until the supply voltage returns to a safer level.

To run at the full clock rate of 16MHz, both the ATmega328 and the ATmega2560 require from 4.5V–5.5V of well-regulated power. The voltage requirement drops substantially with lower clock frequencies. To achieve lower frequency operation, you have several choices. You can swap the quartz crystal or ceramic resonator for a component of a different value, which can be tricky. Alternately, it's possible to change the fuses to use either the internal 8.0MHz RC oscillator or the 128KHz RC oscillator, although neither of these internal oscillators is particularly accurate. Another option is to program the CKDIV8 fuse to divide the 16MHz quartz crystal oscillator down to 2MHz. Finally, and least intrusively, you can leave the clock hardware alone and reduce the system clock using the system clock prescaler, which offers divisors between 1 and 256.

Lowering the clock rate lowers the minimum voltage requirement. You can then entertain the idea of running the electronics directly from a battery, such as a single lithium cell (3.7V) or a bank of between two and four nickel cadmium (NiCD) or nickel-metal hydride (NiMH) rechargeable cells (2.4V–4.8V).

For very preliminary designs, you can depend on a very small amount of power being made available via the USB connection to your PC. With the right interface circuitry, the power from your USB connection can be used to recharge the robot's battery, assuming it's a small one. Remember, there are only 2.5 watts of juice coming through that cord. That may sound like a lot, but it's really not.

Power-supply design for any mobile platform is a study in both robustness and efficiency. Milliwatts saved equate to extended runtimes. A reliable power supply eliminates one of the variables when attempting to diagnose robot behavioral oddities and eccentricities.

Motion Control

You can use a couple of small electric motors to scoot a little robot around on the floor, and maybe throw in one or two more to operate a primitive gripper or arm-like mechanism. On the other end of the spectrum, you can design and build arrays of powerful servos that fully emulate a humanoid. Your first robotic experiments ought to be somewhere in between. To guarantee that you build your skill set rapidly and effectively, it's recommended that you move from one successful project to the next. Now to do *that*, it's best to start out with baby steps, learn from your mistakes what works and what doesn't work, and then apply that hard-won expertise in the next design challenge.

As you might expect by now, there are several technologies available to imbue a robot with movement. This decision is based on requirements, cost, and physics. Does your robot want the ability to move itself around freely, or can it stay mostly in one place and manipulate objects within its reach? A *mobile* robot is much more challenging to design and build than a stationary one. A wheeled robot is, in turn, easier to design and build than a walking one. Flying robots are becoming more prevalent among the hobbyist community, showing surprising dexterity, accuracy, and robustness. Many of the smaller flying robots are controlled with a single AVR processor, such as quad copters.

Before you fly, you must crawl. Even crawling requires controlled motion, and not random flailing.

The key point in *motion control* isn't motion but control. All robot motions must be controlled. This implies several important ideas that many, many books would lack the space to cover in their entirety, but you explore a few of the major ones:

- It's never too early to start thinking about safety.

- There should be a well-defined *intent* associated with every robot motion.

- Any motion performed should be measurable, or at least verifiable.

- Limits to motion may be required and must be respected, when implemented.

- Finally, it's never too early to start thinking about safety.

Electric Motors and Actuators

Let's look at a few of the many available types of electric motors and actuators that you can use in a small robot project. Each has its own unique qualities, abilities, requirements, and drawbacks.

These are only introductory comments about the following motors and actuators. Excellent references exist for the asking that describe the underlying theories as well as practical applications. The hope is to expose you to enough information to help you make a better-informed decision when you decide to invest in a particular technology.

DC Motors

The modern DC motor is a marvel of engineering. It turns direct current (DC) voltage into rotary motion. It does this efficiently and relentlessly. How does it perform these apparent miracles? Just like any other trickster: with the clever use of magnets.

There are many kinds of DC motors, but by far the most common these days is the *permanent magnet* variety. This is the kind of motor you find in inexpensive toys, so they're often referred to as *toy motors*.

In the most basic type of permanent magnet DC motor, there are two magnets that are fixed in place. A rotating shaft spins between the two magnets. On the shaft is a coil that is typically wound around some soft iron plates. When a current flows through this coil, it becomes an electromagnet, which causes the freely rotating shaft to turn, trying to align the poles of the electromagnet with the poles of the fixed permanent magnets. If it were not for a bit of mischievous electrical wiring in the motor, the coil would line up with the magnet and stick there. The trick is that the wiring to the coil is threaded around the shaft, making contact with the spinning shaft through a pair of spring-loaded, conductive brushes. As the shaft rotates, the brushes lose contact with the coil momentarily and then are reconnected, but this time in reverse. This causes the electromagnetic field to reverse polarity, now causing the electromagnet to *repel* away from the fixed permanent magnet. Because of the inertia previously imparted on the shaft from the previous magnetic attraction, the shaft continues spinning in the same direction, which brings it around to the opposite side of the motor from whence it started. Then the whole process repeats, as the current is again reversed by the clever arrangement of the brushes and the coil wiring.

This process of alternating the currents and magnetic fields is called *commutation*. It's done with a clever combination of mechanical and electrical components in the motor, so all the user has to do is apply a DC voltage and the motor spins. Remove the voltage, and the motor coasts to a halt. Reverse the current, and the motor spins in the opposite direction. It couldn't be simpler to use.

Because even the smallest commonly available DC motors requires dozens or hundreds of milliamps of current to operate, they can't be directly connected to the I/O pins of a microcontroller. A driver circuit of some sort must be used.

The most basic control circuit turns the motor on or off, in effect operating as an on/off switch. When the switch is on, the motor spins. When the switch is off, the motor coasts to a stop. The motor spins only in a given direction. Reversing the motor requires a more complex wiring arrangement.

One such arrangement is the addition of a double-pole, double throw (DPDT) relay that reverses the current going to the motor. With the use of the basic on/off switch and this direction-control relay, the motor can be run forward or in reverse, as well as brought to a halt. This requires two I/O lines: one for the on/off switch and another to control the relay, which will also most likely require a driver circuit to operate.

By pulsing the on/off switch quickly, a la pulse-width-modulation (PWM), you can achieve variable speed control of the motor. This is because the speed of the motor is controlled by the applied voltage, whereas the *torque*, or twisting force, is controlled by the current flowing through the motor. Because the *average* voltage across the motor can be manipulated with PWM, you can use this as a way of controlling the motor's speed.

One additional driver that can be used to give a wide range of control over a DC motor is an H-*bridge circuit*. It's called this because the motor is attached between two half H-bridges and the resulting wiring diagram resembles a capital letter *H*.

A half H-bridge circuit has a switch, relay, or transistor to connect to a positive voltage and another such switch to connect to a more negative voltage. This allows a low-power signal such as can be generated by a microcontroller to switch one terminal of the DC motor to either a high voltage or a low voltage. By placing another such half H-bridge circuit on the other side of the motor, you can achieve both forward and reverse spin of the motor. By modulating some or all of the control signals to the H-bridge, you can accomplish variable speed and bidirectional control of the motor.

If both terminals of the motor are connected to the same voltage, the motor is effectively braked. It's not locked rock-solid, but it's more difficult to spin the shaft under these conditions.

It's also quite possible to program an H-bridge circuit to self-destruct if appropriate precautions aren't taken. This happens when both the upper and lower portions of one half H-bridge are engaged at the same time, causing a condition known as *shoot through*. These combinations are often humorously labeled *fuse test*.

You can also use any number of possible combinations of these techniques effectively to control the speed and direction of a DC motor. The selection will mostly depend on your familiarity with the different options as well as the availability of the proper components to build the required controller circuits.

DC motors often spin at a rate of several thousand revolutions per minute (RPM). This makes them unsuited for vehicular motive applications unless an intermediate gear reduction is introduced. Typical wheel rotational velocities are in the 25 to 250 RPM range. The actual land speed is then dependent on the wheel diameter.

Brushless DC Motors

The limiting factor in the life expectancy of a typical DC motor is the inevitable wear on the brushes. These components must both carry electrical current (intermittently, with possible arcing) and bear up under constant friction as the motor shafts spin. Higher-quality DC motors have replaceable brushes, but these are by far in the minority.

To solve the problem of the brushes, a *brushless* motor design is used. This type of motor is inherently more reliable in operation and subject only to the ravages of time in the form of thermal abuse (overheating) and mechanical wear of the internal bearings.

The disadvantage of this simpler design is that the required commutation must be performed externally to the motor itself. This can be done mechanically, but it's much more commonly accomplished electronically, with a specially designed motor-driver circuit.

A simple brushless motor has three or more independent coils. The coils are typically wired across three terminals, forming a triangle. An H-bridge driver circuit is connected to each motor terminal, and a sequence of pulses is sent to the motor from a controller. The specific sequence determines the direction of rotation.

Some brushless controllers require rotation sensors to be mounted to the motor to provide the necessary feedback. Other controllers measure the back-EMF (electromagnetic force) generated by the idle coil to determine speed and direction.

The controller logic involved can become quite complex, especially in high-performance designs. Luckily, the popularity of DC brushless motors in the model car and airplane hobbies has resulted in very reasonably priced electronic speed control (ESC) drivers that respond to a simple pulse control, similar to the hobby servo motors described shortly. This makes them very easy to interface with microcontrollers, and they're finding their way into more autonomous vehicles every day, of both the rolling and the flying varieties.

Stepper Motors

A *stepper motor* is very similar to a DC motor but lacks a commutator. Although a seemingly infinite variety of stepper-motor technologies exist, the basic theory of operation is similar.

As mentioned in the section on DC motors, without the trickery of a commutator in the circuit, the shaft would rotate to a point where the magnetic poles were aligned and then stick. This is exactly what a stepper motor does. It moves in discrete steps, with each step representing only a small angle of rotation. The number of steps per revolution of the motor shaft is determined by the geometry and manufacture of the motor. Typical values run from 24 to hundreds of steps per revolution.

There are generally two or more coils involved in a typical stepper motor. The most commonly used varieties among hobbyists are referred to as *unipolar* or *bipolar* steppers.

A typical unipolar stepper motor has four coils. One lead of each of the four coils is ties to a common terminal. The other ends of the four coils are brought out of the motor separately. Most but not all steppers with five wires are unipolar stepper motors.

By applying a positive voltage to the common terminal, the motor shaft can be stepped by selectively grounding the other leads of the coils in a particular sequence. Reversing the sequence reverses the direction of the steps. You can also perform half-stepping by energizing two coils at once in between the single coil steps. Microstepping of a stepper motor can be accomplished by varying the current through the various coils, although this starts to get a little complicated and is mostly suited for precision placement devices, such as computer numerical control (CNC) machines.

The primary advantage of unipolar steppers is that they're easy to interface. A single transistor per coil is typically all that is required. The disadvantage is that because current only ever flows in a single direction with a given coil, twice as many coils are needed, and at least two of the four coils (in a four-coil stepper) are always inactive.

A bipolar stepper can have as few as two coils, which are electrically isolated from each other—that is, they have no common terminals. A bipolar stepper with two coils requires an H-bridge circuit on each coil. This allows the motor-controller logic to drive current in either direction (or not at all) through both coils at once. Again, a specific sequence of coil excitations is required for stepping in one direction, and reversing the sequence causes the steps to go in the opposite direction. Most but not all four-wire steppers are bipolar stepper motors.

The most critical electrical characteristic of a stepper motor is its maximum current-handling capability per coil. Each coil also has a characteristic impedance. If a voltage rating is stated, it's the product of the current and impedance, and not a maximum value. You can use more volts than are printed on the label of a stepper motor (nice when they do that!) or stated in the manufacturer's datasheet, but you *cannot* exceed the current rating.

The Arduino software comes with a `Stepper` library that works with either unipolar or bipolar steppers. Example sketches are also provided, along with connection diagrams in the embedded reference material that accompanies the software distribution.

Servo Motors

Technically, almost any kind of motor with a built-in *feedback* control can be termed a *servo motor*, being a particular type of *servomechanism*. This means you give the motor an instruction, so to speak, indicating what speed, acceleration, or position (among many possible things) you desire it to obtain, and it knows how to do that. Servos are excellent choices for positioning systems and other high-precision applications.

As mentioned, a servomechanism of any sort uses feedback to correct its behavior. A motor, for example, can be configured to maintain a constant speed, even under varying loads, by measuring its own speed and comparing it to a *set point*, which is the desired speed. The difference between the actual speed and desired speed is the *error*. The amount and polarity of the error (too much? too little?) is used to adjust the speed control of the motor automatically.

Servo motors come in all sizes and configurations. Again, thanks to the popularity of model cars, boats, and aircraft, small but powerful servo motors are available for relatively reasonable prices. An additional bonus derived from their popularity is a standardized convention for controlling these motors, no matter what their intended application.

The typical hobby or RC (which stands for either remote control or radio control, depending on who you ask) servo motor contains a small DC motor, a gear-reduction mechanism, and some built-in electronics to control the whole thing. Due to the gear-reduction added to the small DC motor, the output of the servo motor has a great deal of torque for its small size. Also, the total rotation of the output shaft is generally constrained to between 90° and 180° of mechanical movement. This is more than adequate to steer model cars or boat rudders, or to adjust the control surfaces on a model airplane.

The output shaft is internally attached to a potentiometer that is used to report the present angle of the output shaft to the controlling electronics. The built-in controller compares this position with the desired position or *set point* indicated by its input controller. If there is a difference between these two values (the *error term*), the controller spins the DC motor in the correct direction to bring the two values into alignment.

The standardized control input is a pulse of varying width that is repeated at a given interval. A typical servo motor twists the output shaft to the far right (as viewed when looking at the face of the motor) if it receives a pulse 1.0 millisecond in length. A 2.0-millisecond pulse twists the shaft to the other extreme on the far left. Any position between these two limits can be represented by a pulse width of the proper ratio. For example, to center the output shaft, a 1.5ms pulse is sent.

The 1.0–2.0ms pulses are typically characterized to move a servo's output shaft 90°. A standard servo has hard, mechanical limits built into the final reduction gear, limiting the overall sweep to 180° or less. These extreme points can be reached with proportionally over- or under-sized pulses (<1.0ms or >2.0ms) but are executed at the peril of the output drive train. Pushing servos past their mechanical limits causes them to bind, stalling the internal DC motor, which then draws what seems like (or *is*, for larger servos) an enormous amount of current, possibly overheating the servo or permanently stripping the gears.

These pulses are expected to be repeated approximately 50 times per second, or once every 20 milliseconds. The exact update rate isn't critical. An update frequency that is too low allows the servo to periodically go slack, causing it to yield its position to an applied force. Too fast an update rate can cause servos to chatter. No pulse at all causes the servo to de-energize the motor and make no adjustments.

Normally, the splined shaft is attached to one of several types of interchangeable servo *horns* and secured by a screw or bolt. These horns usually extend away from the center of the shaft and have several small holes in them for connecting to pushrods and other linkages. By connecting your linkage farther away from the center of the shaft, you increase the throw as the shaft rotates but decrease the force behind it. Similarly, a placement closer to the center of the shaft produces a shorter throw with much more persuasion.

Hobby servos are excellent choices for robotic arm and hand applications, due to their small size, tremendous torque, and simple interface. If you already have a model car, boat, or airplane that uses hobby servos, you can use the radio transmitter and receiver for quick tests of motion.

Most hobby servos can be modified to remove the hard-stop and permit continuous rotation. The procedure varies from one model to another, but the basic steps are as follows:

1. Carefully open the servo body by removing the four screws from the back.

2. Remove the final output gear, which is often molded to the output shaft.

3. Cut or file off the stop tabs (don't get any particles in the gear's teeth).

4. Drill out the center of the output shaft that engages the position-sensing potentiometer.

5. Center the shaft of the potentiometer (if power is applied to the servo, adjust the pot until the motor stops spinning).

6. Reassemble the gear train, without disturbing the position of the potentiometer.

7. Close the servo body by replacing the cover and tightening the screws.

The centering of the position-sensing potentiometer is critical in this process. Some guides suggest removing the potentiometer completely and replacing it with a pair of matching, fixed-value resistors, to simulate the centered pot without the possibility of it accidentally getting readjusted.

The setting of this internal pot determines the null or center position of the servo in its new role as a continuous rotation gear-motor. A modified servo behaves in a number of different ways to varying control inputs when compared to a nonmodified servo. First, and perhaps most important, it should now have the mechanical freedom to rotate continuously in either direction. Second, because the position sensor is no longer directly connected to the output shaft, the motor responds differently to the input pulses.

Instead of seeking a leftward position, the motor spins to the left indefinitely. This is because the error term—that is, the difference between the desired position and the actual position—isn't decreasing over time. The same is true for rightward motion, with the motor endlessly spinning to the right and never seeming to be able to catch up.

If the now-detached potentiometer is properly and exactly centered, then when a pulse of exactly 1.5ms duration is received, the motor will stop. This is the only time the inner control system feels that it has done its job properly. That is why the adjustment of this pot, even though mechanically isolated from the remainder of the mechanism, still plays an important part in the operation of the servo.

Some servo layouts permit an access hole to be drilled in the case of the servo so the potentiometer can be adjusted even when the servo is fully assembled. In some cases, the potentiometer shaft can be accessed via the center hole in the output shaft when the servo horn is removed. There's no reason you can't physically remove the potentiometer from the unit entirely, extending the wires from it back to the control board, and mount the pot anywhere that is convenient for you.

Because the servo's null point varies by a few (or maybe several) microseconds over voltage and temperature, there's not a lot of value in going overboard with the hardware side of things, because you can make the same adjustment just as easily in software (adjusting the pulse width to match the hardware, instead of the other way around), with the exception of really severe misalignments.

Modified servos make excellent digitally controlled motors for small, wheeled robots. You get a DC motor with gear-reduction, a standardized package, and shaft and control electronics all in a single compact and lightweight device.

Solenoids

The simplest variation of an electromagnetic motion transducer is a *solenoid*. It converts electric current into linear or rotary motion, depending on the solenoid's configuration. It's basically a coil of wire (the *electromagnet*) and a metal slug or plunger, which is technically the *armature*. When the coil is energized, a magnetic field surrounds the solenoid, and the plunger is drawn into it.

Plungers can either be free or captive. There may or may not be a bottom to the solenoid. If not, it's open at both ends.

The linear motion of a solenoid is quite nonlinear in behavior. Close to the bottom of the stroke of a closed, linear solenoid, the force exerted on the plunger is enormous. As it moves farther away from the body of the solenoid, the force diminishes rapidly.

Solenoids are usually specified for a certain effective stroke length. They also have a maximum current capacity (rated in amps or milliamps) and a characteristic impedance (in ohms).

Sensors

Your robot can have as many or more senses than you have, or it can wear blinders and focus entirely on a small trickle of data from a rudimentary sensorium. The ultimate deciding factor lies in your expectations for each of the robot projects that you design.

Light Sensors

If you look at insects closely, they have fascinating, multifaceted *compound* eyes. The world must look interesting to them!

But look a little more closely, and you also see some *simple* eyes, which resemble little black dots. OK, now back up a little; you're making that bug nervous. The difference between simple and compound eyes lies in the number of lenses involved, and not in the inner complexity of the underlying photoreceptors and neural systems. Because the simple eyes of insects lack a more sophisticated lens system than human eyes, they aren't able to resolve images. They are, however, quite good at determining light levels and due to their more streamlined connections directly into insect brains, are considered faster than compound eyes at detecting motion. The celebrated compound eye of the insect is much more effective at more complex tasks such as edge-detection.

The human eye, no matter how much more complex than Spidey's seventh or eighth eye, is still considered a simple eye. Don't let the word *simple* fool you!

So you want to give your robot some eyes? It's very easy. You can even use an LED as a low-resolution light sensor. It's low resolution in the sense that it doesn't resolve images like the insect's simple eye, as well as by the fact that it only gives a rough idea of the ambient lighting levels. It's not hard to add a simple transistor amplifier circuit to the LED-as-light-sensor to give it a much larger range of readings.

A single light sensor such as this one can report on the ambient light levels in a room, perhaps turning on a nightlight when the sun goes down. Beware of the endless loop this can create! Light level goes down, LED comes on, increasing the light level, which turns off the LED … you get the idea.

This type of oscillation is certainly unwanted and can result any time some sort of amplification is used in the feedback loop. You can add *hysteresis* to the circuit, either in hardware or in software, to compensate for the affected readings. This means moving the trigger point *up* or *down* after you've done something that's going to propagate back to the beginning of your feedback loop.

You can use the different values reported by *two* light sensors to determine the direction of the light. This allows you to play follow-the-leader with a flashlight.

Another vision application is line-following. A robot that can follow a line on the ground sounds easy to build but has some interesting design challenges. An array of infrared emitters and detectors is used to see the line on the ground. The robot can change its heading based on the relative position of the line. There are several clever algorithms for successfully following a line, and you look at a couple of them shortly.

A derivative of the line-following sensor is the cliff sensor, which can let your robot know when the floor ends and that first really big step begins.

Photo-sensitive resistors, also known by many other names, such as *photo cells*, *light-dependent resistors*, and CdS (cadmium sulfide) cells, act like a variable resistor, exhibiting high resistance in the dark but lower resistance when exposed to light. CdS cells, specifically, were once quite common in anything that needed to react to changes in lighting, such as street light controllers, alarm clocks, automatic nightlights, and so on. Because cadmium is a toxic substance, other materials are being used these days in their manufacture.

Phototransistors and photodiodes can also give your robot an idea of what the world looks like. Typical phototransistors and photodiodes, however, are usually optimized for use in the near-infrared region of the spectrum. This is handy when you want to detect infrared light, but not so good otherwise.

An array of light sensors, even a small one, can give your robot the ability to resolve very simple images. Coupled with some clever programming, you can then detect motion and edges.

You can even add a color video camera with object-tracking capabilities. This is possible if you can find or build an AVRcam, an open source alternative to the CMUcam. These units are from *way back* in 2004; they used a couple of AVRs to read the output from a digital VGA camera module and had the ability to track objects of a defined color. Even though the AVRcam is no longer available for sale, you can still download the schematic and source code from the creator's web site: `www.jrobot.net/Download.html`. Isn't open source great?

Touch Sensors

Technically referred to as *tactile sensors*, touch sensors are anything that reports a physical touch to the robot. This can be as simple as a microswitch or two built into a bumper or as complex as a capacitive touchpad for user input. Atmel publishes a set of functions for its AVR products that implement several kinds of touch sensors, including button, sliders, and wheels, called the QTouch library. See the Atmel web site (`www.atmel.com`) for more information.

Several models of microswitches have extended levers attached to the body of the switch, and some even have rollers on the end of the levers. These are often attached to panels on electronic modules to deactivate high-voltage circuits when a user opens an access panel. They have many other uses, of course, and you can use them as bumper switches on your robots. They look like blunt antennae and serve a similar purpose.

If you place two switches, left and right, past the front edge of your robot, you can tell if your robot bumps into an obstacle (not *every* obstacle, but it's a start); plus you can determine if it hit something on the left, the right, or spang in the middle, if both switches are activated at the same time. This can give your robot a clue as to what to do next. If you're intending it to *avoid* obstacles, you can stop, back up, and turn in the appropriate direction. If, instead, you wish your robot to *engage* obstacles, like a bulldozer, you have a good idea of what to do then, as well.

By pointing the levers of the switches downward, you can implement a different kind of cliff sensor. Just be careful not to orient them in such as way such that the levers form barbs, preventing your robot from backing away from the edge.

Noncontact Sensors

Although I earlier spoke of line-following sensors as vision sensors, you can also use a very similar circuit, but with a slightly different hardware orientation, to act as a proximity sensor (see Chapter 10 for a basic version of the IR proximity sensor). This type of proximity sensor depends on the reflectivity of the obstacle in the near infrared (IR) band.

A more sophisticated approach is to use software to measure the IR detector reading with the IR emitters on and then again with them *off*. The difference is then used to determine if an obstacle is reflecting the emitted light or if the sensor is picking up ambient infrared in the vicinity.

An even more sophisticated and often more reliable approach is employed when modulated IR light is emitted and a tuned receiver is used as a detector. This is identical to the IR remote-control example project in Chapter 8. The only difference is that the signal output by the IR LED is a modulated carrier wave and contains no remote-control codes.

It's difficult to extract precise measurement information from the IR proximity detector, however. There are too many uncontrolled factors governing the amount of infrared light that is reflected back to the sensor.

Another solution is to use sonar. The speed of sound in air is known and depends on temperature and air pressure. You can emit a coded burst of sound and measure the amount of time it takes to make a round trip. Half of this time is the time it took the sound waves to strike the *first* obstacle and return. There are almost always secondary obstacles, whose sonar profile returns later. More complex sonar devices report not only the closest obstacle, but also a number of subsequent echoes.

Simple sonar modules are now quite inexpensive, compact, and reliable. Their radiated sound cone is tailored for several different applications, so you can pick the one that is right for your robot.

The simplest method for interfacing with a sonar module to is to trigger a ping and measure the time it takes for the echo signal to arrive. Using the timer/counter peripheral on the AVR, you can measure distances with very good accuracy and high resolution.

Many sonar modules have a dead spot immediately in front of their transducers, preventing them from measuring the distance to targets that are very close. One solution is to mount the sonar module at the rear of the robot and pointing forward, where it won't accidentally pick up echoes from part of the robot body.

However, if you already know the distance to a particular part of the robot, and either the sonar module or an articulated member can be correctly aligned, then you can measure the temperature or air density, depending on which one is less likely to remain stable.

Laser range-finders are generally much more sophisticated sensors, with the associated price tag. But bargains pop up from time to time, especially in the electronic surplus markets. These sensors can scan an entire room in a fraction of a second and give accurate measurements to each reflective point within millimeters. They do tend, however, to be quite large, heavy, and power-hungry, when compared with other available sensors.

A laser range-finder typically uses an IR laser and a spinning mirror to distribute the modulated laser beam. A high-speed sensor is used to measure any returning reflections, and an on-board computer calculates the range and angle.

Audio Sensors

Measuring sound tends to be tricky using an Arduino because of the short durations of most sounds. A microphone with the proper preamplification circuit can easily be attached to an analog-to-digital converter (ADC) input, but the Arduino either needs to be listening at *exactly* the right time or it needs to be continuously sampling the incoming audio at a very high rate as well as constantly analyzing the incoming data for patterns of interest.

Self-contained speech-recognition modules are becoming more affordable and robust. The simplest type of speech recognition is termed *speaker-dependent* and must be trained by the intended speaker. This training is performed by repeatedly saying predetermined phrases into a microphone. The module then analyzes these samples and calculates an average profile that it uses to match incoming voice commands.

Responding to single-word commands is one thing; *continuous* speech recognition is quite another. Be prepared to speak slowly, clearly, and *patiently* to your robot. Involuntary stress reactions may alter your voice characteristics enough to push them outside the acceptable recognition parameters. Yelling doesn't help.

Speaker-independent voice recognition is much more complex, because it must account for natural variations in pitch and intonation from various speakers.

If you're willing to put the power of your PC into the loop, there are many free as well as low-cost speech-recognition programs available that can effectively utilize those larger computing resources.

Indicators, Controls, and Other Forms of Communication

Your robot needs blinking lights (so many lights) and possibly the occasional beep or chirp. The lights are mesmerizing, but the noises are annoying after a while.

Here are a few suggestions for making the ideal, well-behaved robot. Don't assume that other people are going to intuitively know how to operate your robot. It's up to you to make it safe and robust. People *like* to interact with robots, so try to make it an entertaining experience. For example, don't put the Initiate Dance Sequence button right next to the Deploy Bee Cannon button.

Your robot certainly needs some visual indicators to let you know what's going on at a glance. Some number of controls also need to be available, which, in conjunction with the indicators, form the local user interface. A remote user interface can also be implemented.

If your robot uses any form of stored energy, such as batteries, for safety reasons it's necessary to implement a quick-disconnect for local power. This is sometimes called a *kill switch* and should be readily accessible and prominently marked.

For a robot that can scoot faster than you, the switch can be implemented using a tether or lanyard. When installed, the robot operates normally, but when pulled or completely detached, the robot shuts down. This type of mechanism is sometimes used on personal watercraft, where the lanyard is attached to the user's life jacket. If the user for some reason leaves the vicinity of the vehicle, the motor is automatically killed, preventing it from getting too far away.

The robot should also have a primary power switch for normal usage. This switch should be prominently labeled. In the immediate vicinity of this power switch should be some sort of visual indicator, such as a green or blue LED. Save the red, orange, and possibly yellow LEDs for warning indicators.

Beyond these basic tenets, the design of your local user interface is governed by the robot's intended function. Is it a multipurpose robot, able to address a wide array of tasks? It might need a fairly complex user interface, involving one or more graphic displays and user inputs. Does it have a single purpose? Then it should have specialized controls precisely adapted to its function.

Buttons are good. People like to press buttons. Mount your robot's buttons so they're easily accessible when the robot is in its normal environment. Match the button's tactile force (the amount of force necessary to activate the button) with the size and shape of your robot. Don't use a button that's so stiff that pushing the button slides the robot away from you.

If possible, place some sort of label *above* the button, so the function of the button isn't obscured by the pressing finger. It's also nice to have visual, audible, or tactile feedback that the button-press has been received by the robot's control system.

Toggle switches are also good as long as they're properly labeled. Don't make people guess which way is "on." Again, some sort of additional feedback to indicate that the robot has noticed the change in the state of a toggle switch is always welcome.

Dials and knobs are also very useful but can be problematic on a mobile robot. Vibration and accidental contact with obstacles can upset a carefully adjusted setting in no time.

Would your robot benefit from having its own voice? Beeps and blips are all within the traditional robot milieu, but a synthesized (or recorded) human voice is handy in certain circumstances. Digitized sound samples tend to take up a lot of room, storage-wise, but this becomes a non-problem with the addition of an SD card interface to your Arduino (yes, there's a shield for that). Self-contained speech synthesizers are even less expensive than speech-recognition modules these days. Again, if you want to include your PC in the robot-control loop, text-to-speech (TTS) software is freely available.

Exactly how autonomous do you want your robot to be, anyway? If you envision a completely self-contained system that automatically performs its intended function with no interaction with you, then the user-interface part of the design process can be very straightforward. If you want to interact with your robot on a regular or even frequent basis, a more complex and well-thought-out user interface is required. There's no problem if this takes a while and must be adapted over several iterations.

Even if you don't envision spending a lot of time chatting with your robot, it's always a good idea to implement some sort of command-and-control protocol. This can be as simple as a text menu system over a serial port or as complex as you want to imagine. You need to be able to query the robot as to its present status, possibly including battery level, present location, or any other runtime variables you may need to know. You also need to be able to alter or direct the robot's behavior as you see fit. Again, these design decisions are driven directly by your goals and aspirations for a particular robot.

This command-and-control protocol should be implemented using whatever robust communication channels are available to your robot. Do you want to tether the robot to your PC with a USB cable? That's great for starting out, as you try later in this chapter. How about a wireless link? This can be a radio connection of many different types or a modulated IR remote control. Bear in mind that ideally you have two-way communication with your robot. A backup plan is good to have, as well.

Control Systems

An entire subfield of mathematics and engineering is devoted to the subject of *control theory*. The central idea is that a system, which has a measurable output and a controlling input, can be stabilized with the use of negative feedback.

You can use an Arduino to perform several of these functions for you in a robot. You already know that the Arduino is good at doing simple things quite rapidly. It can measure voltages, count accurately, and control external circuitry with the appropriate driver circuits. These abilities make it especially well-qualified to use as a starting point in building a robot-controller circuit.

Open-Loop Systems

When you blink an LED using an Arduino, you verify the output with your eyes and then make any needed adjustments to your sketch until you get the correct behavior. This is an example of two different control loops in action: both *open* and *closed* loops. Let's look at each one in turn.

The Arduino and its associated LED form an *open-loop* system. The Arduino raises the voltage on an I/O pin and then makes several, possibly faulty, assumptions. The first assumption is that there is an LED properly wired with the correct polarity to this particular pin. The second is that the LED then turns on. The Arduino takes no steps to verify success or to correct any problems.

Yet the LED still blinks. It's not hard to connect an LED to an Arduino; but there were enough bad possible combinations present in the solution space that the Arduino Team wisely decided to go ahead and plumb one directly on the board, eliminating any possibility of failure at this introductory level. That was an unquestionably good decision on their part. People like to experience positive results early in a new adventure.

Now the Arduino can issue a command to the LED, and the LED will comply. There is no need for any sort of confirmation. This is an open-loop system because there is no feedback loop connecting the output of the system with the controller that is in charge of the input.

In many situations, no feedback is necessary for proper operation. You don't need to attach a microphone to every speaker to verify that beeps are being emitted. You can assume they're being emitted and continue. Likewise, hobby servos can be directed to align with an indicated angle by sending a variable-width pulse, without having to measure the rotation and adjust the input signal. This is because the servo is implementing *its own* closed-loop feedback system, comparing the output shaft angle with the requested input and making changes accordingly. From the Arduino's perspective, the servo motor just works.

When you add yourself to the loop, you provide the necessary feedback to ensure success by using your high-level detectors to validate proper behavior. When you detect error, you then take measures to correct the error. In the case of blinking the LED, you first check that the LED is attached in the necessary configuration and then verify that it isn't on fire.

■ **Note**   If it's not on fire, it's a software problem.

Once you've ruled out hardware problems, you look to the software involved. Did you get the I/O port's direction bit correctly using the `pinMode()` function? Are you addressing the right pin number? Are the delays long enough to prevent the blinking from blurring into, um, well … non-blinking?

You try *this* and then you try *that*, and eventually you get the LED blinking. In this example, the programmer forms the feedback loop, adjusting the input parameters until the error is *zeroed out*—that is, the output corresponds with your expectations.

Closed-Loop Systems

When the system being controlled gets more complicated than a single LED or simple actuator, you should start looking at closed-loop control systems. This requires a feedback path that can measure the output and compare it to the desired *reference*, or set point. The difference in these two quantities is the *error term*. The error term is used to adjust the input that controls the system, and the loop repeats.

Sometimes a closed loop system can be very simple. If a robot needs to go from Point A to Point B, assuming it can keep up with its own position, then the only question it has to ask is, "Am I there yet?" It does this by comparing its present position with its target position, which is Point B. If the distance from the target is increasing, the robot must turn around. If the distance is decreasing, the robot must continue until the distance (the error) is zero. At this point, it needs to stop, as far as achieving its goal of arriving at Point B.

Other examples of simple closed-loop systems are heating elements. Suppose you want to raise the temperature of a process oven to a particular temperature and then keep it there for a specified period of time. A temperature probe provides the present temperature in the oven, and some sort of adjustable heater control is manipulated by the controller. This control can be as simple as an on/off switch. If the temperature is too low, turn on the heater. If the temperature is too high, turn off the heater. Assuming the heater element is capable of achieving the desired temperature, the closed-loop controller will ensure that it gets to the right temperature and stays there.

Now here is where it starts to get interesting. Heater applications are a really good example because they're never as simple to control as it would seem. First, the heater element doesn't go up to infinity instantly. It takes a certain amount of time. This varies with the element's present temperature, the temperature of the ambient air, and the amount of current that can be supplied to the heater (assuming it's an electric heater), among other things. All these factors affect how quickly the temperature rises. Also, the time it takes for the oven to cool off enough to trigger the heater again varies according to its own unique set of parameters.

These factors contribute to *lag* in the system. An adjustment to the input is made, but the output hasn't quite gotten there … yet. Also, the actual temperature in the oven and the reading reported by the thermometer may not be exactly in synchronization either. In most practical applications, many more factors affect the system's response time.

Several problems can result from too much lag in the control loop. One is *overshoot*, where the system output continues to rise even after the control input has been adjusted downward. This is *very* common in thermal-management systems, because heat takes its sweet time spreading through some materials yet flows like water through others. The corresponding symptom of *undershoot* is equally problematic.

Both overshoot and undershoot can be mitigated by having more subtle adjustment capabilities than on and off. If you can reduce the amount of correction to the input as the error approaches zero, a very smooth transition can take place from the warming-up stage to the maintaining-temperature stage.

This is called *proportional control*, where the input control is slewed at a rate proportional to the error. In the case of a large error, a great deal of input is requested. If only a little error exists, then only a nudge is made to the control input. This error is also called the *present* or *instantaneous* error term.

Because the application of proportional control usually involves an *amplification* of the error signal, the possibility of oscillation exists. This behavior either can result in hunting back and forth near the reference point, without actually achieving equilibrium, or in worse cases can cause damaging full-scale swings, slamming the control input from the top of its range to the bottom repeatedly. This second scenario is exactly what happens when a microphone gets too close to a public-address speaker, and ear-splitting feedback takes over the system.

The error is typically not fed directly back into the control input, because it may or may not directly correspond with the sensitivity of the control input. Instead, a fraction (or multiple) of the error is combined back to the input. This *proportional factor* must be tuned for each system. Too large a factor produces instability and the possibility of oscillation. Too small a factor increases the response time, causing it to only slowly adjust to changes in the desired input. Typically you start with a factor of 1.0 and see how it goes. The proportional term generally contributes the most to the total correction, and you can calculate a couple of other error terms that will also be of value.

Adding up all the error terms over time gives you the *integral* error term. Ideally, the errors should eventually all cancel out, returning this value to near zero over time. By adding this term to the proportional term, the controller input can more accurately correct for *drift* (or *steady-state* error), which can happen when a large change is made to the desired set point. The integral term should also have its own factor, which, like the proportional factor, must be tuned for each application. The integral factor, however, is often much smaller than the proportional factor, because it should only contribute additional correction when the error has been significant over a period of time and the proportional correction just isn't getting the job done quickly enough.

The possibility exists, on the other hand, that the integral error term quickly spirals out of control, because the system hasn't come back into compliance soon enough. Because it's a cumulative record of all errors ever, it can take some time for it to get back to a usable value, yet still be skewing the control input in the process. Applying an integral windup limit can help prevent this from happening.

You can make one further adjustment to the control loop to predict the future and help smooth out any bumps. The rate of change in the error term, or *derivative*, is a good predictor of where the error is headed. This can be elaborately defined using calculus, or it can be approximated by subtracting the previous error term calculated from the present term.

The derivative error term helps reduce the rate of change of the control input, helping to slow things down and smooth things out. This helps to reduce overshoot and undershoot when the set point changes. It can also have the undesired effect of reducing the system's sensitivity to change and overall responsiveness. Like the integral factor, the derivative factor is usually quite small when compared to the proportional factor.

These three calculated error terms are usually abbreviated *P*, *I*, and *D*. You often see references to PID filters and PID control loops when reading about speed controls and other automation topics. The associated factors for each of the terms are generally referred to as K_P, K_I, and K_D.

Using just the proportional term is often sufficient to get good closed-loop control of a system. Sometimes only the P and I terms are needed, and this is called a *PI controller*. If only the P and D terms are used, it's a *PD controller*.

Example Robot Projects

Here are some really simple robots that you can build using an Arduino and a minimum of other parts. They aren't especially good at anything, except perhaps helping you learn how things work inside a robot.

You start with a simple group of projects based around a mobile robot that never seems to get anywhere. Then you move on to a mobile robot that has a good but not infallible idea of where it is. Finally, you start to think about what you would like to have in your ultimate robot. What will that be?

Each robot project is a collection of smaller subprojects. It won't do you much good to skip ahead here, because each project builds on the results of the previous ones. Remember, the robot as a whole succeeds or fails based on the collective cooperation of its constituent components.

Although most robotics tutorials give interesting or at least descriptive names to their project robots (usually ending in *bot*), that particular aspect of creativity is left as an exercise for you.

A Practice Robot

Let's start with a very simple robot that you can use to practice your budding robotics techniques. You build an Arduino-compatible circuit (Duemilanove class, to be exact) on a solderless breadboard, then attach a pair of servo motors with plastic wheels mounted to them. Next you add a pair of potentiometers to be able to adjust parameters in real time, and finally you add a pair of bumper switches to the front of the robot.

There is a *lot* of latitude left in the exact execution of this robot. You're free to place the components anywhere you see fit, or where you find them to be most convenient. Using a standard 830-tie-point breadboard, plenty of room is left over for more experimental circuitry. Feel free to improvise. See Figure 13-1.

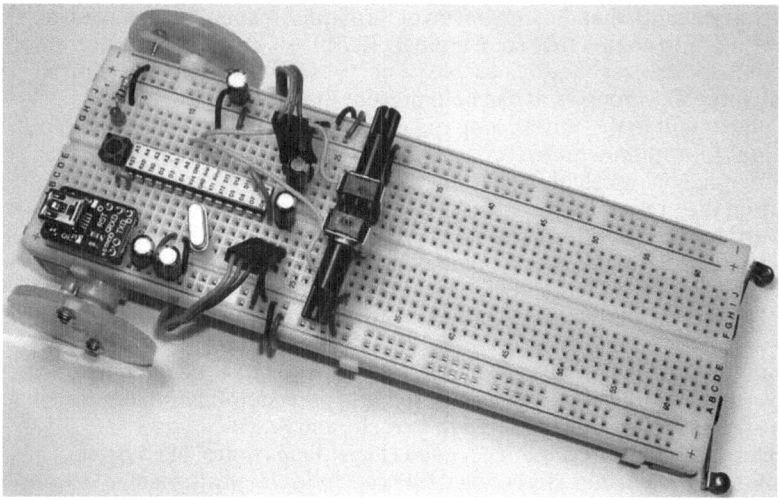

Figure 13-1. An Arduino robot built on a solderless breadboard

The Control Circuit

The basic construction of the Arduino circuit is very straightforward. An ATmega328 chip, preprogrammed with the Arduino bootloader and bearing a handy pin label, is the heart of the circuit. Power and ground connections are made on both sides of the chip, and a 10μF capacitor is placed at each location to help minimize the effects of power surges. In fact, anywhere in the circuit where power enters or leaves, a 10μF capacitor is placed across the power lines. The circuit uses a 16MHz quartz crystal as the system clock. The main processor section of the circuit also contains a reset pushbutton (just in case) and a power-on LED indicator.

Two potentiometers are placed back-to-back on the breadboard and configured as voltage dividers between V_{cc} and GND. The wiper contacts, being now a user-variable voltage between 0–5V, are connected to analog inputs A0 and A1.

Two three-pin headers are installed in the breadboard to form connectors for the two servo motors that will be used as drive motors. These connectors are connected to V_{cc} and GND, and each has its own 10μF capacitor to help supply sudden current demands made by the motors.

The motor-control signals are connected to digital pins D9 and D10 for the left and right wheel motors, respectively. Not coincidentally, these pins correspond to AVR I/O pins PB1 and PB2, which also serve as PWM output pins for Timer/Counter 1, OC1A, and OC1B.

The Wheel Motors

The motors are mounted to the bottom of the breadboard using the double-sided foam tape provided with the breadboards. Only a small portion of the protective backing is removed, just the size of the side of the servo motors. See Figure 13-2.

Figure 13-2. Mount the servo motors to the bottom of the breadboard using double-sided foam tape.

The servo motors are 10-gram analog micro servos from Hobby King (www.hobbyking.com), part number HK 15178. They're cheap and easy to modify for continuous rotation, assuming you've got the tiny screwdriver needed to take out those tiny screws. Once you're inside, it's not hard to make the alteration.

Use the supplied servo horns to mount a plastic disc to be used as a wheel. The screws that are provided for mounting the servos to a frame are repurposed for mounting the horn to the wheels. Note the center hole in the wheel, which allows you to remove the horn and wheel as an assembly from the servo without having to remove the wheel from the horn.

Larger servos can certainly be used. Feel free to substitute parts as you find them available. The nice thing about really small servos is that they don't draw much current. Just don't try stalling them, because then they *will* draw that much current, and maybe a little more.

The wheels aren't very good. That, believe it or not, is by design. This robot isn't really supposed to go anywhere. You want the wheels to spin, but you don't want the robot to run off the edge of the desk. You can also put the robot on a little stand or, better yet, mount a collapsible kickstand near the back wheels. Save that for a later project—you still need to get the wheels spinning before you consider solutions to unintended consequences.

And The Rest

The bumper switches on the front of the robot are mounted in a similar manner, using the double-sided foam tape on the underside of the breadboard.

For power, at least during the very initial stages of bringing this robot to life, you use the regulated +5V provided by the USB interface.

Drive Configurations

Note the configuration of the servos. They're mounted as mirror images of each other. This allows the output shafts to emerge from opposite sides of the robot carapace without requiring any extra gears or linkages. This drive arrangement is often referred to as *differential steering*, which isn't exactly the same thing as the differential drive commonly used in an automobile, although they share some common principles. Think of it more in the way you can navigate while sitting in a wheelchair.

If both wheels roll in the same direction and at the same speed, the robot goes either forward or backward in a straight line. If one wheel travels in the opposite direction of the other, but they still rotate at the same speed, then the robot turns in place, pivoting about a center point. By varying the velocity of the wheels with respect to each other, any straight or curved path can be travelled, and at any point along the way the robot can stop and swivel into any other heading and continue travelling. That's a lot of flexibility in what could possibly be the simplest mechanical arrangement.

There are many more possible configurations for wheeled robots. Each has its own relative merits, although some are *much* more complicated than your practice robot's system and others are *exceedingly* more complicated. The choice is yours.

Motor Math

You knew it was coming.

First you need to exert some control over the speed and direction of each wheel independently. Technically, *speed* combined with a *direction* is *velocity*. The direction can be up or down, right or left, clockwise or counterclockwise, or even positive or negative.

If you're having a hard time understanding the difference, perhaps They Might Be Giants can help. See their entertaining and instructional video on YouTube: `www.youtube.com/watch?v=DRb5PSxJerM`.

When you speak of the rotation of a motor, the convention is to refer to the apparent motion when viewing the motor's face, with the shaft emerging from its face and pointing at yours. Let's start spinning those motors already.

To begin, let's check how closely your servos are calibrated by sending a precise 1.5ms pulse to each of the motors and seeing if they spin. Alternately, you can use this sketch as a timing reference for calibrating your servos, if you're still in the process. See Listing 13-1.

Listing 13-1. Creating Precise 1.5ms Pulses to Calibrate or Verify Modified Servos

```
#include <Servo.h>

Servo leftServo, rightServo;
```

```
void setup() {
  leftServo.attach(9); // D9 is connected to the left servo
  rightServo.attach(10); // D10 is connected to the right servo
  leftServo.writeMicroseconds(1500); // centering pulse
  rightServo.writeMicroseconds(1500); // centering pulse
}

void loop() {
}
```

You include the header file for the Arduino-supplied Servo library, Servo.h. This gives you access to some convenient functions for working with servo motors, both standard and modified.

In this case, everything is performed in the sketch's setup() function. The loop() function is empty but required. A pair of Servo objects is instantiated in the global scope (that is, outside of any function), named leftServo and rightServo. In the setup() function, you attach them to the PWM output pins with the Servo.attach() method.

The Servo library's write() method takes a parameter expressed in degrees and converts that into the appropriate number of microseconds for the PWM outputs. You want to bypass that and express your desired setting in microseconds, and the Servo library accommodates that with the Servo.writeMicroseconds() method. You set both the left and right servo objects to 1,500 microseconds, which should cause the wheels to be energized (that is, you shouldn't be able to turn them, or at least should feel a good bit of resistance) but *not* moving. If they *are* moving (and they most probably are), then you have an excellent opportunity to calibrate them to what your Arduino thinks is a 1.5ms centering pulse. Remember, this calibration is done by adjusting the internal position-sensing pot of the servo, which should no longer be mechanically attached to the output shaft.

As a side note, it really doesn't matter that much how accurate your Arduino's clock is at this point, as long as you can calibrate everything according to its standard. The real problems come into play when the voltage and temperature begin to drift, because these are the chief components of clock error.

OK, so the first fact of motor math is that 1,500 microseconds is supposed to be the middle of the range, at which point the wheel is spinning neither clockwise nor counterclockwise. Got it? It comes up a lot when dealing with servo motors, so you might was well understand it instead of blindly accepting it and committing it to memory.

Next up are the endpoints to this range. They're easy enough to remember: 1.0ms and 2.0ms. But which one spins which way? Let's find out. See Listing 13-2.

Listing 13-2. Experimenting with Servo Direction and Speed

```
#include <Servo.h>

Servo leftServo, rightServo;

void setup() {
  leftServo.attach(9); // pin D9 is connected to the left servo
  rightServo.attach(10); // pin D10 is connected to the right servo
}

void loop() {
  int leftAdjust, rightAdjust;
```

```
leftAdjust = analogRead(0); // read left servo adjust
rightAdjust = analogRead(1); // read right servo adjust

leftServo.writeMicroseconds(leftAdjust + 1500 - 512);
rightServo.writeMicroseconds(rightAdjust + 1500 - 512);

delay(20);
}
```

Again you include the Servo.h header file because you're still using the Servo library. The same leftServo and rightServo objects are instantiated and then attached to the correct PWM output pins in the setup() function using the Servo.attach() method.

The real fun begins in the loop() function, which actually has something in it this time. Two adjustment variables, leftAdjust and rightAdjust, are declared as signed integers (remember, all scalar variables in C are *signed* values unless you specifically indicate they aren't with the unsigned qualifier—except for char, which is implementation dependent for some reason). You want these values to be signed because they may or may not stay within the realm of positive numbers. In this example sketch they do, but you may find other uses for them soon enough.

The two potentiometers are read using the analogRead() function, and the results are stored in the leftAdjust and rightAdjust variables. If you recall, the results from these analog-to-digital conversions will be in the range of 0 to 1,023, with 0 representing voltages closer to ground and the high end of the scale corresponding to a voltage at or near V_{cc}. Because the potentiometers are wired up as voltage dividers across V_{cc} and ground, they should provide a full range of these values as you adjust the dials.

Now a little tricky math comes into play. You really want the two adjustment values to be positive or negative offsets, centered about zero. You could subtract 512 from both values, which would shift (technically, *translate*) their values from 0–1,023 to a more balanced range of -512 to +511, giving you a lot of latitude in both directions, so to speak. But let's wait a second, because you're about to do add another constant value into the mix; and by doing all of them at once in the same formula, the compiler can do most of the math for you, saving calculation time and program memory for your little Arduino.

You have a good range of adjustment values, in theory, because if you consider these leftAdjust and rightAdjust values to be numbers that represent microseconds, you can use them, with a suitable offset, as the parameters for the Servo.writeMicroseconds() method. That suitable offset happens to be 1,500, the number of microseconds that constitutes a centering pulse for a modified servo. If you add 1,500 to the adjustment values, you get a number that varies across a good range of numbers with 1,500 right in the middle.

I could have just said, "Now add 988 to that number, and you're done," and it would have worked (and that's *exactly* what the compiler is going to do anyway), but it makes no sense. It's what is known as a *magic number*. It works, but nobody knows how or why. You should avoid magic numbers at every opportunity.

■ **Caution** Avoid magic numbers and special cases.

So now you look at the long train of numbers in the formula, and you can see numbers that you understand. The adjustment variable is a number in the range of 0 to 1,023; 1,500 is the center of the desired range; and 512 is the midpoint (half of the maximum) of the adjustment variables' range. Oh, it gets better. Much better.

When you run the sketch, you should be able to adjust the velocity of both motors independently. You should even be able to get the motors to stop rotating completely. You may notice that after some time, the motors start to creep slowly in one direction or the other. This is the inevitable *null creep* that beleaguers robots with modified servos until you implement some sort of velocity feedback, which you do in the next section of this chapter.

Now, back to the original question, which is, "Which way does the motor go?" It helps if you have (or have access to) an oscilloscope to view the actual pulse waveforms on a screen. You can still figure out this puzzle without the use of such gizmos if you walk through the steps methodically.

If you've wired up the potentiometers so that a clockwise turn *increases* the voltage going to the Arduino's analog inputs, then you can assume (correctly) that the value of the adjustment variable correspondingly increases. This, in turn, *increases* the width of the pulse going to the servo. You should be able to observe that this causes a more *counterclockwise* spin to the motor. Conversely, turning the adjustment down results in a more clockwise spin of the motor.

To reiterate: the further away from the center (1,500 microseconds) and toward the lower endpoint (1,000 microseconds), the more clockwise the spin of the motor will be, and vice versa.

Also note that the speed of the motor can be finely adjusted when it's near the middle of the range, down to a very slow crawl. It would be really convenient if this response was linear across the entire 1.0–2.0ms range!

Sadly, it's not. Some hobby servos have an extremely narrow range near the midpoint that allows any sort of speed control. Sometimes this band can be as narrow as 0.2ms, with pulse widths of 1.4ms and 1.6ms producing full-tilt rotation in either direction.

The HK 15178s used in this particular experiment show surprisingly *good* range under no-load conditions, not reaching their maximum speeds until approaching the endpoints.

Now you know how to spin the motor full tilt in either direction with no problems, but getting it to stop is iffy at best. There is another way that removes all doubt as to its effectiveness, and that's exactly what you need for as long as this remains an open-loop system. All you have to do is stop sending pulses.

You would reasonably think that a call to `Servo.writeMicroseconds()` with a parameter of zero would work, but it doesn't. The `Servo` library's method constrains the range of permissible value to various ranges depending on what version of the `Servo` library you're using, usually between 0 and either 180 or 200 degrees, depending.

There is an overloaded `Servo.attach()` method that not only permits you to specify the pin number, but also lets you use an overriding minimum and maximum pulse width value. This also doesn't work properly, because the library fudges the actual values with a `TRIM_DURATION` offset to account for interrupt latency. Several other layers of cleverness in this library will ultimately make it unsuitable for your uses, but for these first, simple steps, it's adequate.

You *can* stop the wheels with the `Servo.detach()` method. It's a bit heavy-handed, because you have to re-`attach()` it later with the right pin number to get the motors to spin again.

To be fair to the `Servo` library, most of the layers of complexity it has developed are to serve two important purposes. The first is to hide the math-terror of microseconds and pulse widths from new users, substituting settings in degrees instead, and the second is to help prevent inadvertent settings beyond the mechanical limits of most commonly available hobby servos. You'll soon be in a position to take the training wheels off your robot and craft your own servo functions.

Forward, Reverse, and Stop

You can now write some really simple control functions for your servos, if all you need is three speeds. Let's use the bumper switches as your local user interface for initial testing. The left bumper switch is connected between digital pin D2 and ground, and the right bumper switch is connected between digital pin D3 and ground. If you enable the built-in pullup resistors on both of those pins, then the inputs should be HIGH when the bumper switch is *not* engaged and LOW when the switch has been activated. See Listing 13-3.

Listing 13-3. Testing the Three Speeds of a Servo: Forward, Reverse, and Stop

```
#include <Servo.h>

Servo leftServo;

void setup() {
  digitalWrite(2, HIGH); // enable pullup on left bumper switch
  digitalWrite(3, HIGH); // enable pullup on right bumper switch
}

void loop() {
  leftServo.attach(9); // left wheel
  if(digitalRead(2) == LOW) {
    leftServo.writeMicroseconds(1000); // clockwise
  } else if(digitalRead(3) == LOW) {
    leftServo.writeMicroseconds(2000); // anti-clockwise
  } else {
    leftServo.detach(); // stop
  }
}
```

This test uses only one servo motor, the left one. The setup() function enables the built-in pullup resistors on the two digital pins, D2 and D3, which default to being inputs after a reset.

You attach() the servo to the PWM pin every time the loop() function is called, because you may or may not need to detach() it in order to stop the servo rotation.

If the left bumper switch attached to digital pin D2 is LOW, that means the left bumper switch is being pressed, so you start turning the left servo clockwise. Then you check digital pin D3 in a similar manner, except here you induce a counterclockwise turning. If neither switch is registering, then the servo is disabled using the detach() method.

Notice that if you press *both* switches at the same time, the wheel spins clockwise. Why is this? If you follow the logic in the sketch, you see that if the first test succeeds (the left bumper switch is pressed), then the remainder of the tests are skipped, and they have no chance of acting on the rotation of the wheels.

This behavior is acceptable in your trivial test sketch, but give some consideration to the undesirable effects this could have in a real-world application. There are other ways to evaluate sensor inputs and take actions appropriate to them, and you cover a few of them briefly in the next section of this chapter.

Let's rewrite this sketch to factor out some of the common elements, placing them in specialized functions. See Listing 13-4.

Listing 13-4. Using Servo Smart Functions to Hide the Implementation Details of Spinning a Wheel

```
#include <Servo.h>

Servo leftServo;

void setup() {
  digitalWrite(2, HIGH); // enable pullup
  digitalWrite(3, HIGH); // enable pullup
}

#define leftBumper() (digitalRead(2) == LOW)
#define rightBumper() (digitalRead(3) == LOW)

void leftServoClockwise() {
  leftServo.attach(9);
  leftServo.writeMicroseconds(1000); // clockwise
}

void leftServoAntiClockwise() {
  leftServo.attach(9);
  leftServo.writeMicroseconds(2000); // anti-clockwise
}

void leftServoStop() {
  leftServo.detach(); // stop
}

void loop() {
  if(leftBumper()) {
    leftServoClockwise();
  } else if(rightBumper()) {
    leftServoAntiClockwise();
  } else {
    leftServoStop();
  }
}
```

First you #define some macros that replace the bumper tests with simulated functions, leftBumper() and rightBumper(). These functions return TRUE or FALSE depending on the pressed state of the switch.

Next are three function definitions for explicitly setting the direction of the left wheel: leftServoClockwise(), leftServoAntiClockwise(), and leftServoStop(). These functions dictate the motion of the wheel by adjusting or omitting the pulse signal going to the servo motor. The loop() function becomes much less cluttered with implementation-specific information regarding servos and their peculiarities, and looks more like a high-level program that is only interested in results.

You can, however, do a little bit better than this and pass a single parameter to a single function and have that function figure out what to do. See Listing 13-5.

Listing 13-5. A Single Function to Control the Velocity of a Servo-Driven Wheel

```
#include <Servo.h>

Servo leftServo;

void setup() {
  digitalWrite(2, HIGH); // enable pullup
  digitalWrite(3, HIGH); // enable pullup
}

#define leftBumper() (digitalRead(2) == LOW)
#define rightBumper() (digitalRead(3) == LOW)

#define leftServoClockwise() leftServoVelocity(1)
#define leftServoAntiClockwise() leftServoVelocity(-1)
#define leftServoStop() leftServoVelocity(0)

void leftServoVelocity(signed char velocity) {
  switch (velocity) {
    case 1: // clockwise
      leftServo.attach(9);
      leftServo.writeMicroseconds(1000); // clockwise
      break;
    case 0: // stop
      leftServo.detach(); // stop
      break;
    case -1: // anti-clockwise
      leftServo.attach(9);
      leftServo.writeMicroseconds(2000); // anti-clockwise
      break;
  }
}

void loop() {
  if(leftBumper()) {
    leftServoVelocity(1); // clockwise
  } else if(rightBumper()) {
    leftServoVelocity(-1); // anti-clockwise
  } else {
    leftServoVelocity(0); // stop
  }
}
```

You've replaced the three separate functions with a single function, `leftServoVelocity()`, that takes a `signed char` parameter indicating the direction desired, with +1 for clockwise, -1 for counterclockwise, and 0 for stop. The original functions can still be used, because new #defines are created for each one with the appropriate parameter passed to the new function. These values are arbitrary and will be subsequently altered, as explained shortly.

In the `leftServoVelocity()` function, a `switch` statement is used to select the appropriate course of action, depending on the value of the `velocity` parameter. It's exactly the same code you've been using all along, just wrapped in a different format.

If all you need is to be able to start and stop the servos and control their direction, but you *don't* require fine control of the speed, then this is all you need to get started. A little creative programming should produce an obstacle-avoiding robot that can bounce around the walls of a confined arena.

When the novelty wears off, please come back and go a little further.

Normalization of Velocity Parameters

Well, you certainly don't want to have to mess with microseconds and offsets and null-compensation factors and all that forever. Let's wrap up some of these calculations into useful functions so you can concentrate on higher-level tasks, like driving forward or turning.

An additional benefit of abstracting these low-level control functions is that you can then focus on what you want done and not how to do it. By using these abstraction techniques, you can replace the servo motors with an entirely different kind of motor, such as plain DC motors or steppers, write *their* low-level control function *once*, and be able to continue writing higher-level code to control the motion of the robot as a whole, and not as a pair of motors.

So now you need to forget that a 2ms pulse spins the wheel counterclockwise, that a 1ms pulse spins it clockwise, and that it slows down and stops somewhere in between. Instead, let's imagine a `velocity()` function that takes a single meaningful parameter to indicate both speed and direction. You use the arbitrary range of -1.0 to +1.0, using floating-point numbers to represent the fractional continuum between the endpoints. These abstract values are now considered normalized because they have been stretched or shrunk to fit, but they apply to any type of rotary motion.

Floating-point mathematical functions take longer to calculate and require more program space to do so. Even so, they're quite well optimized and work well.

You can obviously craft a range of parameter values that makes sense to you and doesn't require the use of floating-point math, if you like. How about -100% to +100%? Or -1,000,000 to +1,000,000? Anything works, as long as you have sufficient *granularity* to accomplish your desired goals: that is, your range allows sufficiently fine adjustment of the wheel's velocity.

Using your adopted (arbitrary and artificial) range, a velocity of 0.0 represents no motion. That makes sense, doesn't it? A velocity of +1.0 is full-speed forward, and a velocity of -1.0 is full speed in reverse. These values should be easy to remember. If they aren't, feel free to substitute values of your own choosing. Using these simple values makes the inevitable mathematics much easier to understand.

But which way is *forward* and which way is *reverse*? Again, that depends on your preferences. It really doesn't matter, as long as you *consistently* apply the same methodology in your calculations.

There would seem to be only two possible combinations, and they have both been implemented by respected professionals in the past. The first is that *counterclockwise* rotation is considered *positive* rotation. This is the view taken by mathematicians, scientists, and non-civil engineers (not rude engineers, but those practicing in fields other than civil engineering). Consider the unit circle in trigonometry as an example.

The second and opposite convention is that *clockwise* rotation represents positive rotation. This is practiced by navigators, cartographers, and those ever-so-polite practitioners of civil engineering. A good example is the dial surrounding a magnetic compass.

Again, pick one and stick to it. The $300 million+ Mars Climate Orbiter went missing in 1999 due to a *metric mixup*, where ground-based software computed trajectories in English pound-force units instead of metric Newton units. Oops.

Even if your robotic budget is less than that, take extra care to standardize your units, possibly even documenting them. You may not be out $300 million, but you risk losing time and enthusiasm, which is much, much worse.

For now, you use the mathematical model where positive angles move in a counterclockwise manner. This eliminates the need to convert to real-world coordinates for the time being. When your

GPS-equipped robot is ready to leave the laboratory and travel the world, you can convert to whatever units you like.

This results in the conventions regarding wheel velocities shown in Table 13-1.

Table 13-1. *Relationship Between Wheel Velocity Parameters and Servo Motor Behavior*

Description	Velocity	Speed	Direction	Pulse Width
Forward	+1.0	Full	Counterclockwise	2ms
Stop	0.0	Zero	None	1.5ms/omitted
Reverse	-1.0	Full	Clockwise	1ms

Because the actual wheel speeds have yet to be characterized with any accuracy, you refer to them as *full* or *stop*. The response curve isn't expected to be perfectly linear, so half speed is more likely to be closer to the center point than either of the endpoints. The HK 15178 servos appear to rotate at approximately 100 revolutions per minute (RPM) in either direction, with no load, when signaled to run at full speed.

You can collect this implementation-specific code for handling variable-speed servos in a function, similar to what you did previously, but accepting a floating-point argument instead of a signed integer. Assuming an ideal servo that properly slows down and comes to a complete stop when its control pulse width is exactly 1,500 microseconds long, you can write that function very simply. See Listing 13-6.

Listing 13-6. *Servo Velocity Function That Accepts Normalized (-1.0 … +1.0) Parameters*

```
#include <Servo.h>

Servo leftServo;

#define leftBumper() (digitalRead(2) == LOW)
#define rightBumper() (digitalRead(3) == LOW)

void setup() {
  digitalWrite(2, HIGH); // left bumper pullup
  digitalWrite(3, HIGH); // right bumper pullup
  leftServo.attach(9); // left wheel
}

void servoVelocity(Servo servo, float velocity) {
  int pulseWidth; // in microseconds
  pulseWidth = velocity * 500; // +/- 500 microseconds from center position
  pulseWidth += 1500; // center position offset
  servo.writeMicroseconds(pulseWidth);
}
```

```
void loop() {
  static float leftVelocity = 0.0;
  if(leftBumper()) {
    leftVelocity += 0.01; // more anti-clockwise
  } else if(rightBumper()) {
    leftVelocity -= 0.01; // less anti-clockwise, or more clockwise
  }
  servoVelocity(leftServo, leftVelocity); // set velocity
  delay(20);
}
```

This sketch again uses the bumper switches to jog the servo speed, but this time it uses very small increments instead of the all-or-nothing approach you saw previously.

A `static float` variable declaration for the test velocity begins the `loop()` function. It must be declared `static` or the adjusted value is lost when the `loop()` function terminates.

The `servoVelocity()` function is where the action is. It takes a `Servo` object and a velocity as parameters. In the function, an integer variable (`int pulseWidth`) is declared to incubate the desired pulse width in microseconds.

The first manipulation is to multiply the velocity parameter by 500 microseconds. This is half of the range of the possible pulse widths, the full range being 1.0ms wide (from 1.0ms to 2.0ms). If the requested velocity is -1.0, then `pulseWidth` starts out as -500 microseconds. If the velocity is to be +1.0, then `pulseWidth` starts out as +500 microseconds. You add a constant value of 1,500 microseconds to this intermediate calculation to obtain the ideal pulse width for the given velocity. This results in a translation of a velocity of -1.0 to 1ms (clockwise motion) and of +1.0 to 2ms (counterclockwise motion), with the input value of 0.0 producing a result of 1.5ms: the *ideal* pulse width for stopping the motion of the servo.

You need to add one more adjustment to this algorithm: the null-point offset, also known as the *dead band*.

Open-Loop Servo Null Compensation

To be able to finely control the speed of the servo motors, you need to be able to zero in on the actual dead band or null point of each servo. This adjustment is bound to vary over time, temperature, and voltage conditions. Also, each of the two motors has its own, unique way of going off center. You need a way, short of actually measuring the wheel velocity (which you do in the next section of this chapter), to compensate for this variable that is beyond your control.

Ideal servos, however, only exist in your imagination. Each of the real servos on this robot has its own idea of what should be the center point, and that idea will change in a little while. You need a compensation factor to handle this discrepancy. An optimistic design assumption is that this factor will change slowly over time, and a one-time offset should be sufficient for short runs. You can run with this optimistic idea and cancel out the null error using the two potentiometers at the beginning of a task, and hope they don't drift *too* far before the task can be completed.

Don't bother hard-coding a null offset into your sketches. That works once or twice, but you eventually have to nudge the correction values continuously to keep things starting and stopping precisely. A robot that is *supposed* to be sitting still but nevertheless begins to creep away in a slow arc isn't good.

Let's run a short calibration routine at the beginning of the remainder of your open-loop projects. This routine begins when the robot controller is reprogrammed, reset, or initially powered. You begin by emitting two perfectly synchronized centering pulses, one to each servo motor, and then you use the two potentiometers to adjust the respective pulse widths. Once the motors are properly adjusted (that is, they stop spinning), you can click one of the bumper switches to let the robot know it's safe to continue to the next stage. The adjusted pulse-width values are then used to calculate the offset from ideal to actual null point. You can use that calculated offset in the final version of the servoVelocity() function, which should then be ready for showtime. See Listing 13-7.

Listing 13-7. Servo Calibration Routine Run Before the Main Robot Behaviors Take Over

```
#include <Servo.h>

Servo leftServo, rightServo;

int leftServoNull, rightServoNull;

#define leftBumper() (digitalRead(2) == LOW)
#define rightBumper() (digitalRead(3) == LOW)

void servoNullCalibration() {
  while(!leftBumper()) {
    leftServoNull = analogRead(0) - 512;
    rightServoNull = analogRead(1) - 512;
    leftServo.writeMicroseconds(1500 + leftServoNull);
    rightServo.writeMicroseconds(1500 + rightServoNull);
    delay(20);
  }
}

void setup() {
  digitalWrite(2, HIGH); // left bumper pullup
  digitalWrite(3, HIGH); // right bumper pullup
  leftServo.attach(9); // left wheel
  rightServo.attach(10); // right wheel
  servoNullCalibration(); // calibrate those servos
}

void servoVelocity(Servo servo, float velocity, int nullOffset) {
  int pulseWidth; // in microseconds
  pulseWidth = velocity * 500; // +/- 500 microseconds from center position
  pulseWidth += 1500; // center position offset
  pulseWidth += nullOffset;
  servo.writeMicroseconds(pulseWidth);
}
```

```
void loop() {
  static float leftVelocity = 0.0;
  if(leftBumper()) {
    leftVelocity += 0.01; // more clockwise
  } else if(rightBumper()) {
    leftVelocity -= 0.01; // less clockwise
  }
  servoVelocity(leftServo, leftVelocity, leftServoNull); // set velocity
  delay(20);
}
```

When the sketch starts, the setup() function is called, and it proceeds to its normal initialization tasks of enabling pullup resistors and attaching servos to PWM pins. Then it calls the new servoNullCalibration() function, which allows the robot operator to adjust the potentiometers until the wheels stop spinning. A press of the left bumper switch terminates the calibration routine.

After the calibration routine has been successfully performed, the global variables leftServoNull and rightServoNull contain the proper offsets necessary to align the calculated pulse widths with recently taken samples. Note the additional third parameter of the servoVelocity() function, along with the corresponding additional calculation.

It would be nice to tie those calibration numbers to the servos themselves, but the present Servo library hasn't implemented any convenient way to refer to attached servos. You *could* iterate through the global servos[] array, looking though the entries and attempting to find your servos' entry based on the pin number assigned; but it's much simpler to say goodbye to the Servo library and write your own, which is what you're going to do now.

Life Without the Servo Library

The complexities of the present Servo library are overkill for your application. This is mainly due to the fact that the Servo library can provide software PWM signals on pins that lack PWM hardware, up to 12 on the Arduino Uno and up to 48 (!) on the Arduino Mega 2560. You only need two for right now, and writing directly to the hardware is straightforward. Once properly configured, the two PWM channels associated with Timer/Counter 1 (the only 16-bit timer/counter on the Arduino Uno) are more than adequate for generating your 1ms–2ms pulses. The eight-bit timer/counters lack the granularity you require, without resorting to complex programming algorithms. Using Timer/Counter 1, you can literally write the desired microsecond value once to a single register (OCR1A or OCR1B), and the PWM hardware handles the rest.

The only complex part of this transition is the initialization of the timer/counter hardware. The remainder of the new additions are mostly organizational tidbits that help you keep track of things later, when it starts to get *really* interesting. See Listing 13-8.

Listing 13-8. Talking Directly to the PWM Hardware Instead of Using the Arduino Servo Library

```
#define leftBumper() (digitalRead(2) == LOW)
#define rightBumper() (digitalRead(3) == LOW)
```

```c
typedef struct {
  int nullOffset; // in microseconds
  float velocity; // -1.0 to +1.0
  int pulseWidth; // adjusted pulse width (1000us to 2000us)
} ServoMotor;

enum {
  LEFT_SERVO_MOTOR,
  RIGHT_SERVO_MOTOR,
  MAX_MOTOR
};

ServoMotor servos[MAX_MOTOR]; // 0=left, 1=right

#define leftServo servos[LEFT_SERVO_MOTOR]
#define rightServo servos[RIGHT_SERVO_MOTOR]

void servoCalibrate() {
  while(!leftBumper()) {
    leftServo.nullOffset = analogRead(0) - 512; // left offset
    rightServo.nullOffset = analogRead(1) - 512; // right offset
    OCR1A = 1500 + leftServo.nullOffset; // left servo
    OCR1B = 1500 + rightServo.nullOffset; // right servo
    delay(20);
  }
}

void servoVelocity(char servoIndex, float velocity) {
  if((servoIndex == LEFT_SERVO_MOTOR) || (servoIndex == RIGHT_SERVO_MOTOR)) {
    velocity = constrain(velocity, -1.0, +1.0); // constrain parameter from -1.0 to +1.0
    servos[servoIndex].velocity = velocity; // save velocity parameter
    if(velocity == 0.0) {
      servos[servoIndex].pulseWidth = 0; // quit sending pulses
    } else {
      // translate normalized velocity to pulse width in microseconds
      servos[servoIndex].pulseWidth = velocity * 500; // +/- 500 microseconds variation
      servos[servoIndex].pulseWidth += 1500; // mid-point pulse width
      servos[servoIndex].pulseWidth += servos[servoIndex].nullOffset; // null adjust
      // constrain pulse width from 0 to 2500 microseconds
      servos[servoIndex].pulseWidth = constrain(servos[servoIndex].pulseWidth, 0, 2500);
    }
    switch(servoIndex) {
      case LEFT_SERVO_MOTOR:
        OCR1A = servos[servoIndex].pulseWidth;
        break;
      case RIGHT_SERVO_MOTOR:
        OCR1B = servos[servoIndex].pulseWidth;
        break;
    }
  }
}
```

```
void setup() {
  digitalWrite(2, HIGH); // left bumper switch pull up enable
  digitalWrite(3, HIGH); // right bumper switch pull up enable
  pinMode(9, OUTPUT); // PWM output for left wheel servo
  pinMode(10, OUTPUT); // PWM output for right wheel servo
  // initialize phase & frequency correct PWM outputs
  TCCR1A = 1<<COM1A1 | 0<<COM1A0 | 1<<COM1B1 | 0<<COM1B0 | 0<<WGM11 | 0<<WGM10;
  // timer clock = F_CPU/16, for 1us resolution
  TCCR1B = 1<<WGM13 | 0<<WGM12 | 0<<CS12 | 1<<CS11 | 0<<CS10;
  ICR1 = 20000; // period = 20ms
  servoCalibrate(); // calibrate those servos
}

void loop() {
  servoVelocity(LEFT_SERVO_MOTOR, 0.0);
  servoVelocity(RIGHT_SERVO_MOTOR, 0.0);
}
```

This sketch contains a few new features. First, the `typedef struct` wording creates a new data type based on a structure called `ServoMotor`. This structure contains the bits of information you need to track when using servo motors, including the null-point offset in microseconds, the specified velocity (if one has been given), and the derived pulse width, again in microseconds.

Following this is an enumeration, which automatically gives sequential index values to the terms `LEFT_SERVO_MOTOR` (0), `RIGHT_SERVO_MOTOR` (1), and `MAX_MOTOR` (2). The first two are indices into the upcoming `servos[]` array, which is an array of `ServoMotor` structures. You can then use these values as constants in the program without having to `#define` each one of them separately. The `enum` construct also handles the numbering, so you don't get duplicated or skipped values when the edits start flying.

Next you `#define` some shortcuts (`leftServo` and `rightServo`) for referring to the individual servos in the array. It's a bit of a time-saver, typing-wise, but it also makes for easier reading when trying to understand the code.

The `servoCalibrate()` function remains recognizable. The main change is that now you write directly to the PWM hardware registers instead of calling the `Servo.writeMicroseconds()` method, which was protecting you a little too much toward the end. Note the use of the `leftServo` and `rightServo` macros in the offset assignments—much clearer.

The `servoVelocity()` function is much more structured as well. It takes an index into the global `servos[]` array as its first parameter and the desired `velocity` as the second. The very first line in the function is an overarching test for correct values of the servo index. It *should* only be `LEFT_SERVO_MOTOR` or `RIGHT_SERVO_MOTOR`, but who can tell? It's best to check.

Next, the `velocity` parameter is constrained to a range of -1.0 to +1.0. Values outside this range are truncated to these maximum values. The verified new setting is stored in the servo information structure in case it's needed in the future. You're not using it now, but it might be handy to be able to call it back up if you need it.

A special case for zero velocity turns off the servo motor by the simple expedient of writing a zero to the PWM register. This forces the PWM hardware to quit sending pulses, which makes the servo coast to a stop.

Any other values are translated into valid pulse widths in a three-step process: you rescale the values, then add in the fixed-centering pulse value and null offsets obtained during the calibration step, and finally constrain the resulting pulse width to reasonable values, which in your case are 0 to 2,500 microseconds.

The very last thing to do is to take this translated and double-checked pulse width and write it directly to the PWM hardware. Because the configuration of the timer/counter peripheral (handled in the setup() function for now) permits a duty-cycle resolution of exactly one microsecond, there is a one-to-one relationship between the desired pulse width in microseconds and the binary number written to the PWM hardware. That was convenient!

Note that none of this works right if the system clock isn't exactly 16MHz! That's considered *brittle design*, where even the minor alteration of a single characteristic causes the entire system to fail. When you move on to your next robot, later in this chapter, you look at some ways to overcome this particular sensitivity to clock speed.

The fun stuff happens in the setup() and servoCalibrate() functions in this sketch. When you get to the loop() function, all that happens is that the velocity for both servos is set to zero, which turns off the motors.

However, you've successfully moved away from the Arduino Servo library, substituted your own functions to replace it, and factored out many (but not all) of the servo-specific functionality in your sketch. It shouldn't take much more thought or coding to extract all of the servo-specific code and dump it in a ModifiedServo library of your very own. You do a little more cleaning up here and there in the next section; but most of it has to wait until you get to the closed-loop robot design, which is *much* more interesting in many ways.

When you run this sketch, the robot enters servo-calibration mode. The potentiometers adjust the null offset for each servo motor, and then the left bumper switch is pressed and the motors come to a complete halt. Another approach would be to take a reading of the potentiometers once at the beginning of the calibration routine and use any difference measured in subsequent readings to use as the servo null offset. This would allow the robot user to perform a hardware calibration on the robot, instead of a software compensation. As it is, the pulse width is already contaminated due to the fact that it's being used as an absolute reference instead of a relative one. There's no predicting where the pots will be set at any given time, and it's not reasonable to expect them to be in the exact center of their travel, which may or may not correspond with the midpoint of their output as a voltage divider. Also, it wouldn't hurt to have some sort of mode indicator that lets the operator know that the robot is in servo-calibration mode. This could be done with an alphanumeric LCD or even a single LED with a label on it. These design decisions are what make robotics so interesting and hopelessly time-consuming—which, when coupled with the almost unlimited amounts of money you could spend, makes it the perfect hobby.

Wheel Motion into Robot Motion

You can control the speed of the motors with a certain amount of authority at this point, but where are they taking the robot? In the case of the little robot you saw in Figure 13-1, not very far. Its tiny wheels were made to be slippery and not gain much traction on the desktop. But let's imagine that it had proper wheels and that when those wheels turned, this little robot *went* places. It is hard to imagine, but try.

If you set both wheels to roll forward at full speed, will the robot move forward? No, it will spin in place. That's because one of the motors is mounted in the exact opposite orientation, so its wheel is spinning *backward* with respect to the other wheel. You need to figure out what combination of clockwise and counterclockwise translates into forward and backward for your robot.

Some quick thinking leads to the conclusion that one of the wheels needs to go the other way. The actual mathematical answer is that the rotation needs to be multiplied by a factor that is the cosine of the angle of the axle with respect to the centerline of the robot body. If you pick one motor, say the left one, to be the reference vector endpoint, with the other endpoint being the center of bodily rotation, then its axle's angle is zero radians. The other motor, the right one in this example, forms another vector with an angle of π radians. You adjust both rotational velocities by the cosines of their axle angles, and the problem is solved.

You can further derive some mathematical Ha! Got you there. The correct answer is that one goes the other way, because the cosine of 0 is 1.0 and the $\cos(\pi)$ is -1.0, so you reverse the right motor and all is well. Technically, the long-winded version is also correct and yields the proper adjustment factors even when you have more than two motors and they're not mounted symmetrically. But for your purposes, you flip the sign of the velocity for one motor and are done. Some robot builders further simplify the problem by reversing the polarity on one of their (DC) motors and leaving all the signs in place. This doesn't work as well with servos, so you fix it in software.

Straight-Line Motion

This works splendidly for forward and backward motion in a straight line. Well, let's call that *pretty straight*, because there is slight (or large) variation in actual wheel velocities under load, even with identical drive signals, which results in a little (or a lot) of curving in this straight-line motion. Wheel diameter also comes into play, with even slight variations supplying cumulative error.

Forward at full speed entails the left wheel spinning counterclockwise (+1.0) and the right wheel spinning clockwise (-1.0). Full speed in reverse implies just the opposite: left clockwise and right counterclockwise. A pair of quick and dirty straight-line functions can be as simple as the new functions and the new `loop()` function in Listing 13-9. All the other parts of the sketch remain the same as in the previous section (Listing 13-8).

Listing 13-9. Simple Forward, Reverse, and Stop Functions

```
void goForward() {
  servoVelocity(LEFT_SERVO_MOTOR, 1.0);
  servoVelocity(RIGHT_SERVO_MOTOR, -1.0);
}

void goBackward() {
  servoVelocity(LEFT_SERVO_MOTOR, -1.0);
  servoVelocity(RIGHT_SERVO_MOTOR, 1.0);
}

void allStop() {
  servoVelocity(LEFT_SERVO_MOTOR, 0.0);
  servoVelocity(RIGHT_SERVO_MOTOR, 0.0);
}

void loop() {
  if(leftBumper()) {
    goForward();
  } else if(rightBumper()) {
    goBackward();
  } else {
    allStop();
  }
  delay(20);
}
```

These functions work, but it's trivial to replace them with a single more generalized function that takes a velocity parameter. See Listing 13-10.

Listing 13-10. *Generalized Straight-Line Function*

```
void straightLine(float velocity) {
  servoVelocity(LEFT_SERVO_MOTOR, velocity);
  servoVelocity(RIGHT_SERVO_MOTOR, -velocity);
}

void loop() {
  if(leftBumper()) {
    straightLine(0.1); // slow ahead
  } else if(rightBumper()) {
    straightLine(-0.1); // slow reverse
  } else {
    straightLine(0.0); // stop
  }
  delay(20);
}
```

The `straightLine()` function takes a single parameter describing the desired speed and direction. If the sign is positive, the robot moves forward, and if the sign of the velocity is negative, the robot travels backward.

Experimenting with different velocities in this sketch gives you a good idea of how accurately matched your servos are when mounted in opposition to each other: that is, not very. Again, this *will not matter* when the loop is closed and the robot automatically adjusts the power to the motors to provide consistent and reliable performance.

Turning

You tell the robot to drive in a straight line, and it curves. If you tell it to curve, will it drive in a straight line? Oh, probably not. Let's think about how it *ought* to curve, swerve, pivot, slalom, and swivel for you.

The mathematical analysis of this drive arrangement appears pretty intimidating, even to roboticists of a mathematical bent. The issue is that there are many, many different ways of looking at the problem. You can accurately describe a straight line as an arc with infinite radius. True, but not helpful. Albert Einstein, internationally recognized smart person, is credited with many famous sayings, several of which were famous before he was born. One such quote is, "A clever person solves a problem. A wise person avoids it." Let's take his sage advice and avoid allowing the problem to tell you how to solve it.

There is at least one simple way to measure the motion of a robot that uses a drive system similar to your example robot. It's to break down the motion of the robot as a whole into *linear* and *angular* components. For example, if the robot is rolling along merrily in a forward direction, it has a measurable positive *linear* velocity and zero *angular* velocity. It's moving in a straight line (ergo linear) but isn't turning. If, on the other hand, the robot is spinning merrily in place, it has zero linear velocity but a measurable *angular* velocity. It's certainly moving, but it's not going anywhere. Driving in an arc or spinning about one wheel are examples of combinations of both linear and angular motion.

The Measuring of Things

So far you haven't *measured* anything. You told the wheel to spin, and it spun. With this, you were satisfied. That's the beauty of open-loop systems. But now it's time to talk of measuring many things.

You need some conventions to which you should stick, and some units from which you shall not wander. Both of these things are entirely matters of choice, but some work better than others.

Imagine a flat stage populated by prop robots and random obstacles. Now imagine that nothing is moving, and that nothing is *going* to move. If you remove all *motion*, then the only thing you can measure is *position*. You can measure position *absolutely*, by comparing the positions of all the objects on the stage with some designated *reference point*, or you can measure all of the objects *relatively*, with respect to the positions of all of the other objects on the same stage. As long as nothing changes, the only thing you can measure is position.

You measure things to assign a number to something that is *not* a number, such as a physical characteristic when compared to a standardized unit of measure. It doesn't matter if you use inches or millimeters, furlongs or light-years to measure distances. They're all expressions of exactly the same concept: distance or length.

You can measure to your heart's content all the sizes and placements and densities of objects on your imaginary stage. Nothing ever changes, nothing moves, so all you need to know is position. You begin with position.

Measuring positions is a very useful thing to be able to do, and you continue to find reasons to do so. However, your stage is a bit too artificial and lacking in real-world qualities, mostly because you have excluded motion to simplify your measurements. Let's be bold and allow a single one of the robots to move. Now you have many more things to measure!

Again, you constrain the experiment to as few variables (preferably one) as possible. Stipulate that the robot moved exactly three feet, then stopped. Sounds very simple, doesn't it? But it had to have taken some measureable amount of time to move those three feet. How much time elapsed? Let's say it took 36 seconds. That's a pretty slow crawl for anything except the tiniest of robots. Now you have a *duration*, which is a measure of time, and the units you're using are seconds. Three feet is (again, not coincidentally) the same as 36 inches, so although you could say that the *speed* of the robot was 3 feet in 36 seconds, you could just as easily say it was 1 inch per second, if you see the equivalence. If you don't, it's time to break out the calculator.

One inch per second is a speed and not a *velocity* because you haven't decided which *direction* it went yet. If you suddenly decide that it went three feet in a positive direction, then you can go ahead and call it a measure of velocity, but only then.

Here's where it's going to get all scary and mathy. You have to deal with (gulp) fractions. Anytime you hear the word *per*, it means a fraction is involved. *Per* means this many divided by that many, or this over that, or this upon that, depending on where you went to school. Inches per second is a measure of velocity, as long as those inches represent a value with a direction, so there is such a thing as negative velocity (which looks a lot like going backward).

Velocity is distance over time. Distance is velocity multiplied by time. Time is distance divided by velocity. The relationships between these three things are fixed by their definitions, just as voltage, resistance, and current are related and expressed by Ohm's Law. It's important that you understand the relationships that exist among these concepts, because they affect the way you approach solutions to the design challenges you face.

Your imaginary robot moved at a velocity of 1 inch per second for 36 seconds. You should quickly deduce that it moved a total of 36 inches, because you now understand the relationship between time, distance, and velocity (velocity is distance over time).

But did it actually travel at exactly that velocity for the entire trip? Impossible! Before it began to move, its velocity was zero. It was moving zero inches in (whatever amount of time, doesn't matter, still equals zero, because anything multiplied by zero is zero), so its initial velocity was zero. Because it stopped when it finished its short trip, its terminal velocity was also zero. This poses a problem.

You changed the position of the robot. The *rate* of this change in position was measured as a velocity. A rate is always a measure of the *change* in a measurable quantity over a specified period of time. In this case, it was the measure of a change of 3 feet of distance over the period of 36 seconds. Distance over time is velocity.

Velocity is the *derivative*, or rate of change, of position. The derivative of velocity is *acceleration*. Acceleration is the change in velocity over time. Your robot *did not* accelerate from a velocity of zero to a velocity of one inch per second in no time at all. It may have been a *short* time, but it was a measureable amount of time.

This leads to the conclusion that although the robot began with a velocity of zero, it had to accelerate at some finite rate until it achieved an average velocity of one inch per second, and then it decelerated at some other, negative rate until it stopped with a velocity of zero again.

If it maintained a fairly steady pace during the middle part of its journey, then that rate had to be slightly *above* the average of one inch per second, to make up for the acceleration and deceleration phases of the trip, which were included in the total travel time.

Oh, dear. All you wanted to do was turn the robot. What happened? Physics and mathematics happened, and they very well could happen again, so you need to be prepared!

Turning, for Real This Time

Linear motion is measured using distance or displacement. You can use whatever units are handy (*cough*, $300 million, *cough*). *Linear velocity* is measured in units of distance over units of time. *Linear acceleration* is measured as distance over time squared, because there are two time periods involved. The first is the time period associated with the distance that is changing (the velocity), and the second is the period of time associated with the acceleration itself. You sometimes hear acceleration due to gravity as being "32 feet per second per second." This can also be expressed as $32 \text{ ft}/\text{sec}^2$ or 32ft·s^{-2}.

Angular displacement is measured in degrees or preferably radians. Even if you're more familiar with using degrees for angular measurement, you should consider using radians. Here you use radians exclusively in the calculations, with only a minimal number of readings in degrees.

Angular velocity is the equivalent to linear velocity, being the measurement of angular displacement over time. Radians per second is the typical unit you use. The symbol for angular velocity is the lowercase Greek letter omega, ω. It looks a little like a loopy, lowercase cursive *w*, and you sometimes have to resort to that in code. You know what it means.

Angular acceleration is exactly the same kind of thing as linear acceleration, except spinning about an axis instead of rolling down the road.

You don't need to worry about exact velocities of either the linear or angular variety at the moment. All you need to do is indicate in your conventional terms how much of the motor's oomph you want to put behind those velocities. You use the same -1.0 to +1.0 range for specifying both the linear and angular velocities.

If you give your robot both a linear velocity and an angular velocity, it can take those two quantities, do some serious math, and figure out exactly how it should spin those two motors to give you what you want. That's amazing! The only problem is that you have to *tell* it how to do those amazing things first. Ready? Let's go!

OK, it's not as hard as it sounds … really it's not. See Listing 13-11.

Listing 13-11. Combining Linear and Angular Velocities to Calculate Left and Right Wheel Velocities

```
void move(float linearVelocity, float angularVelocity) {
  servoVelocity(LEFT_SERVO_MOTOR, angularVelocity + linearVelocity);
  servoVelocity(RIGHT_SERVO_MOTOR, angularVelocity - linearVelocity);
}
```

```
void loop() {
  if(leftBumper()) {
    if(rightBumper()) { // both bumpers engaged
      move(-0.1, 0.0); // straight back, slowly
    } else { // just the left one
      move(0.0, 0.1); // turn left/anti-clockwise
    }
  } else if(rightBumper()) {
    move(0.0, -0.1); // turn right/clockwise
  } else {
    move(0.1, 0.0); // straight ahead slow
  }
  delay(20);
}
```

That's all there is to it. The move() function takes two floating-point parameters: a linear velocity and an angular velocity. A linear velocity of +1.0 is forward, and a value of -1.0 is backward. The angular velocity is counterclockwise for positive values, when viewed from above, and clockwise for negative values. These correspond with angles in trigonometry, not with maps.

The move() function combines these terms in the appropriate manner for both motors. As you can see, it uses the higher-level mathematical operations of addition and subtraction to do so. This is one of those situations in math where everything works out with simple formulas, which is mostly due to everything being at right angles to each other. It also helps that you've consistently used the same conventions throughout this exercise.

Practice Robot Summary

There was a lot to learn to get to this point, and your little practice robot has certainly helped you along the way. Being able to make programming and logic mistakes with a robot that weighs four ounces is much less stressful and more prone to encouraging further exploration than with one that is larger, faster, and heavier than you are.

You've got a long way to go, and it's going to be a lot of fun. Keep your little practice robot around in case you need to try out some new algorithms for the basic drive mechanism.

The Next Robot

You explore techniques for working with closed-loop systems with your next robot. This allows you to pretty much ignore the whole servo null compensation business, because this will be monitored and corrected automatically by the robot, leaving you free to think of more important topics, such as where you want to go next.

But first, let's try a couple of simpler experiments in closed-loop motion control, using a small fan. This way, you can concentrate on one thing at a time instead of being overwhelmed by all the possibilities that a robot offers. This happens more often that you might think.

Measuring a Fan's Speed

You use a common 80mm computer cooling fan in these experiments. They're usually not hard to find and offer many features that make them an excellent starting point in closed-loop motion control. Make sure you get the kind with three wires. The third wire is the tachometer output and makes the measuring part a *lot* easier. See Figure 13-3.

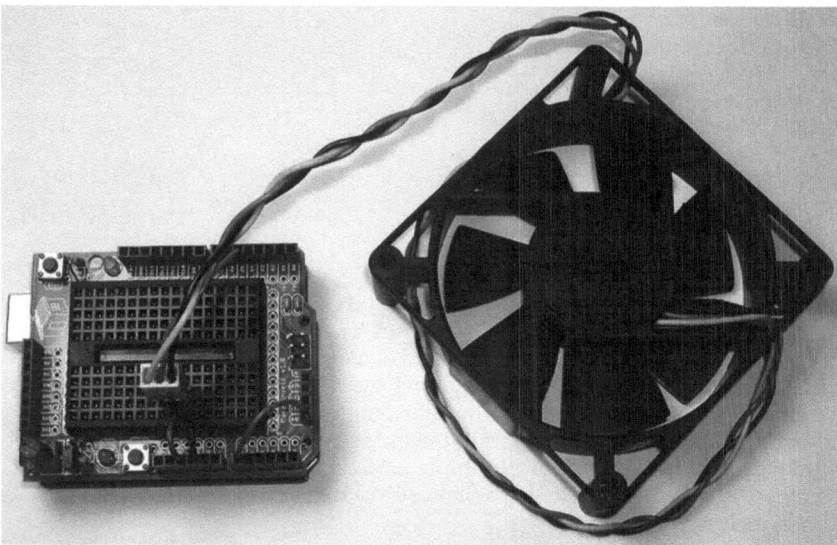

Figure 13-3. An 80mm cooling fan has a built-in brushless DC motor, a controller, and a tachometer output for measuring the fan speed, making it an excellent tool for studying closed-loop motion-control designs.

For your first experiment, you measure the fan's speed and not try to control it. The fan selected for this purpose is intended to run on 12V but still spins, albeit at a much more leisurely pace, when powered from only 5V. Some 12V fans won't even start to spin at 5V, but a lot of them will.

To begin, you supply +5V to the red wire and connect the black wire to ground. Not all fans have the same color scheme when it comes to wiring, but it shouldn't be hard to figure out. When the Arduino is powered up, the fan begins to spin, if everything is connected properly.

The yellow wire is the open-collector tachometer output, and it needs a pullup resistor. Luckily, you know how to do that. Connect the yellow wire to digital pin D5. This pin was selected because it can be used as the clock input for Timer/Counter 1, if properly configured.

You let Timer/Counter 1 count the number of pulses coming from the fan's tachometer. You then use Timer/Counter 2 to give you a precise time base to use for your measurements. See Listing 13-12.

Listing 13-12. Measuring the Speed of a Fan by Counting the Tachometer Ticks in One Second, Over and Over Again

```
void setup() {
  digitalWrite(5, HIGH); // enable pullup resistor for D5/PD5/T1 for tachometer input
  // timer/counter1 counts fan tachometer pulses on rising edge of T1, 2 per revolution
  TCCR1A = 0<<WGM11 | 0<<WGM10;
  TCCR1B = 0<<WGM13 | 0<<WGM12 | 1<<CS12 | 1<<CS11 | 1<<CS10;
  // timer/counter2 provides 125 interrupts per second
```

```
  TCCR2A = 1<<WGM21 | 0<<WGM20;
  TCCR2B = 0<<WGM22 | 1<<CS22 | 1<<CS21 | 1<<CS20;
  OCR2A = 124; // n-1
  TIMSK2 = 1<<OCIE2A; // enable compare match interrupt
  Serial.begin(9600);
  Serial.println("Fan Speed in RPM");
}

unsigned int fan_odometer = 0; // count of fan tachometer ticks
volatile byte update_flag = 0; // used to signal update of odometer reading

void loop() {
  static unsigned int previous_fan_odometer = 0;
  while(update_flag == 0); // wait for update to occur
  update_flag = 0; // reset update flag
  Serial.println(((fan_odometer - previous_fan_odometer) * 60) / 2); // in RPM
  previous_fan_odometer = fan_odometer;
}

ISR(TIMER2_COMPA_vect) {
  static byte prescaler;
  if(prescaler) {
    prescaler--;
  } else {
    prescaler = 125; // reset prescaler
    fan_odometer = TCNT1; // capture odometer reading
    update_flag = 1; // set flag
  }
}
```

The setup() function turns on the pullup resistor on digital pin D5, which is connected to the open-collector tachometer output. The tachometer output changes state for every 90° of fan rotation. This produces two full cycles, or *ticks*, for every complete rotation of the fan blade.

Timer/Counter 1 is configured to operate in normal mode with no PWM duties. You set the prescaler to advance the counter on every rising edge of T1 (instead of using a derivative of the system clock), which happens to be PD5 in AVR-speak, and which is known in Arduino Land as digital pin D5. Timer/Counter 1 is a 16-bit counter and now acts as the fan's *odometer*, recording the total number of tachometer ticks that you receive via T1.

The odometer will eventually overflow, starting back over at zero, but due to the peculiarities of unsigned integer math, you'll never notice. You're only interested in the difference between one odometer reading and the next one, and not the cumulative figure.

Setting up Timer/Counter 1 to be your fan odometer is straightforward. Setting up Timer/Counter 2 to be your precise one-second time base is a little trickier. This is because Timer/Counter 2 has only an 8-bit counter at its disposal, and even with the maximum system clock prescaler (divide by 1,024), you still get a timer clock of 15,625Hz. You divide that frequency further by using a software prescaler in the interrupt handler.

To obtain an *exact* one-second time base, you break up 15,625 into two, smaller numbers. By a happy coincidence, the square root of 15,625 is 125, which works out great for an 8-bit hardware counter (being less than 255).

It's often helpful when dealing with integer multipliers and prescalers to look at these big numbers in terms of their prime factors. The number 15,625 has only a single prime factor: 5. Five to the sixth power (5^6) = 15,625.

You set up Timer/Counter 2 to operate in Clear Timer on Compare Match (CTC) mode, tell it to count up to 124 and then start over (making the total count equal to 125, because you get to count 0 as one of the steps), and enable an interrupt to occur when the match is detected.

Note that this triggers the Compare Match A interrupt, *not* the Overflow interrupt. It's in the datasheet.

Looking ahead to the interrupt handler, you see a `static byte prescaler;` declaration. This is your secondary, software-based prescaler to lengthen your sample times all the way out to one second exactly. If the prescaler is *not zero*, it's decremented, and the interrupt handler exits. One down, 124 more to go. When the `prescaler` variable *does* get decremented all the way down to zero, a different path is taken, because exactly one second has elapsed.

Right away, the `prescaler` variable is reset to 125. The present odometer count in Timer/Counter 1's TCNT1 register is captured and stored in the global unsigned integer variable `fan_odometer`. Another global variable, `update_flag`, is set to 1 to tell the foreground task executing in the `loop()` function that a new odometer reading has taken place.

The `loop()` function spends most of its time waiting for the `update_flag` to be set. Note that this variable *must* have the `volatile` attribute or the compiler will fail to understand how it could ever change value in the `loop()` function and ultimately optimize away most of the interesting parts of your sketch.

As soon as the flag is set, the empty `while()` loop exits and the flag is reset, ready for the next update.

The newly captured fan odometer reading is compared to the most recent odometer reading, and the difference tells you how many tachometer ticks have occurred in the previous second. This raw tick-count is converted into RPM by accounting for the 2-ticks-per-revolution characteristic of this particular sensor and the fact that there are 60 seconds in one minute. You *could* have gathered data for a full minute, which would have been more accurate, but who wants to wait that long for data to appear?

The computed *rotational velocity* (full rotations, a measure of *angular displacement*, over a time period of one second) is reported via the serial port every second. The first reading is generally not reliable.

The newly captured odometer reading is saved for future reference by copying it to the `static` variable `previous_odometer_reading`. If it weren't specifically qualified as a `static` variable, it would disappear when the `loop()` function went out of scope.

And that's one way of measuring the rotational velocity of a fan. It's by no means the only way. You could measure the time between rising edges of the tachometer signal (the *period*) and calculate the velocity from your understanding of the relationship between a signal's period and its frequency (pssst … they're reciprocals).

Controlling a Fan's Speed

The first step to control is measurement. The first exercise illustrated one method that can be used for measuring a single data point (the velocity of a fan). The process was complicated by the need to measure a velocity, which actually involves measuring *two* things: displacement (or distance) and time.

Now that you can *measure* the result, let's try your hand at *affecting* the process. You're still a little way from *controlling* the process, but you'll get there.

You can control the amount of power going to the fan by adjusting the average supply voltage using the same PWM techniques you used in Chapter 8 to control high-power LEDs. You use a small signal transistor to drive the fan motor. They don't require much current, but it's certainly more than you can expect from a single AVR I/O line. A bipolar-junction transistor such as the PN2222A or 2N3904 works splendidly. A 1KΩ 1/4W resistor is used to limit the amount of current flowing from the I/O pin into the base of the transistor. See Figure 13-4.

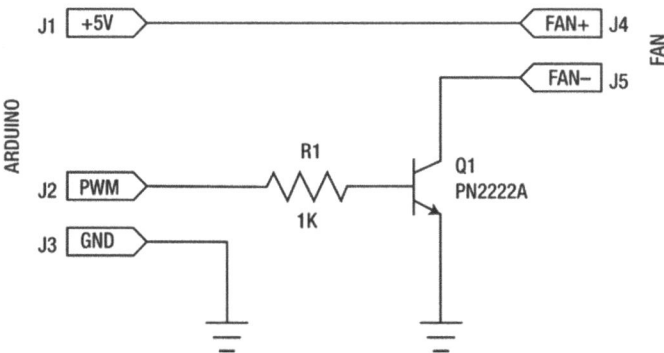

Figure 13-4. *The schematic of the fan power-driver circuit*

All of this can easily be assembled on a small solderless breadboard and connected to your Arduino. Using the Maker Shield is especially convenient because it brings all the pins right up to the breadboard and also offers a built-in potentiometer for making real-time adjustments. See Figure 13-5.

Figure 13-5. *The fan power-driver circuit built on top of an Arduino Uno, using the Maker Shield and a solderless breadboard*

The sketch to control the power going to the fan is almost trivial. Note that this *does not* yet control the fan velocity—only the power going to the fan. See Listing 13-13.

Listing 13-13. Controlling the Power Going to the Fan by Adjusting the PWM Duty Cycle to the Driver Circuit

```
void setup() {
}

void loop() {
  unsigned int adjust;
  adjust = analogRead(0); // read potentiometer setting
  adjust = map(adjust, 0, 1023, 0, 255); // scale for PWM output
  analogWrite(3, adjust); // set PWM duty cycle
  delay(50);
}
```

Nothing fun needs to happen in the setup() function. The loop() function reads the value of the potentiometer using the analogRead() function. It then scales it appropriately for use with the PWM output by mapping the values using the map() function. You could have also shifted the bits, but that's not always obvious in its intent, even if it accomplishes exactly the same thing.

The scaled adjustment value is used to control the duty cycle of the PWM output (D3) that is being used to signal the fan-driver circuit, using the analogWrite() function. You should know how to do this in your sleep by now.

The sketch, when executed, should allow you to adjust the relative speed of the fan by permitting more or less power to go to the fan. You still have no accurate control of the speed of the fan, even though it may seem like it.

You should spend a little time playing with this sketch. It gives you a *great* deal of insight into how the physics of the system interact. How long does it take the fan to accelerate from zero to full speed? It may take several seconds, depending on the agility and responsiveness of the fan you're using. How long does it take to coast to a halt? What is the minimum setting that allows the fan blades to continue to rotate? How far up does the power setting have to go to get the fan to start rotating from a complete halt? Does changing the orientation of the fan affect the velocity? At what power levels is it most sensitive to orientation changes?

Note that if you place your thumb on the hub of the fan, the blades slow down.

■ **Caution** Don't try this with a fully powered fan. Your voltage-starved test subject shouldn't pose much of a mutilation threat.

The same amount of power does *not* guarantee a steady velocity under varying loads. Keep playing with the sketch and try to get a good felling for what the hardware can do before you go making assumptions about what the software can do. If you can't do it with your big brain and complete control over the hardware, how can you expect a little Arduino to do any better?

Closing the Loop

You can measure the output of the system, which in this case is the velocity of a fan. You can adjust the power being supplied to the fan, which directly (but nonlinearly) affects the velocity of the fan. To close the loop, you need to pick a *reference* velocity or set point at which you want the fan to rotate. Then you use *feedback* from the fan (the tachometer signal) to help automatically adjust the amount of power being sent to the fan, thus stabilizing the system and *controlling* the velocity of the fan to be exactly what you want it to be—assuming the fan is capable of achieving the velocity you desire in the first place.

Of course it's not as simple as that. When you pulse the power to the fan, you're turning on and off the power supply for the tachometer sensor as well. This causes the PWM frequency to be impressed on the incoming tachometer signal, rendering it useless for counting purposes.

The information is still in the signal, and with the right techniques you could coax it out; but that gets somewhat complicated in short order, and this was intended to be a *gentle* introduction to motion control. Other techniques such as *pulse-stretching* can be used, where the PWM duty cycle is momentarily pegged at 100% for long enough to obtain a single cycle of tachometer information, but the slow speed of your underpowered fan has conspired against you in this case. You know how to take a measurement, and you know how to adjust power to both fans and servo motors, so let's jump ahead and start controlling the velocity of a robot.

Your next test subject is a larger robot with actual wheels. See Figure 13-6.

Figure 13-6. *The next robot you use is an example of differential drive that actually goes somewhere.*

The robot is built on a chassis from Budget Robotics and is similar to the current model called ArdBot, for Arduino Robot (`www.budgetrobotics.com/item/ArdBot-Chassis-Kit-340`). This is a very affordable and high-quality product designed by noted robotics author and columnist Gordon McComb.

In the center area of the robot is an Arduino Uno with the ever-faithful Maker Shield atop it. Custom wheels with O-ring tires are mounted to modified servos of the standard size, instead of the micro servos used previously. Rolling on the top of each wheel are spring-loaded shaft encoders for measuring wheel rotation.

Along the front edge of the robot are three sets of IR LEDs and photodiodes for line following. There is an IR demodulator on the top of the robot for receiving remote-control commands.

The robot is powered by a seven-cell nickel metal-hydride (NiMH) battery. The control panel on the rear of the robot contains a fuse holder, a power button with indicator light, as well as a battery-charging jack with its own indicator light.

An additional deck, not shown, can be stacked on top of the existing base, increasing the available area for more gear when it becomes necessary. And it *always* becomes necessary.

Quadrature Encoders

One of many ways to measure rotational velocity is with a *shaft encoder* that has *quadrature* outputs. A shaft encoder often looks like a potentiometer but can be packaged in a number of different styles. A quadrature signal usually consists of two square waves, typically referred to as A and B, and very similar to the tachometer pulses you were using on the fan but exhibiting a 90° *phase shift* between the two signals. This means one square wave leads or lags behind the other one by a quarter (hence *quadrature*) of a rotation. A sine wave and a cosine wave are a good example of a quadrature signal, except with sinus waves instead of square waves.

Whereas the single pulse train coming from the fan's tachometer indicates the fan speed, a quadrature output can indicate both speed and direction. There are several methods you can use to decode the quadrature outputs of a shaft encoder. Look at Listing 13-14.

Listing 13-14. Decoding Shaft Encoders with Quadrature Outputs

```
volatile unsigned int left_odometer = 0, right_odometer = 0;

void setup() {
  pinMode(9, OUTPUT); // left servo PWM output
  pinMode(10, OUTPUT); // right servo PWM output
  Serial.begin(115200);
  Serial.println("*** Robot initializing ***");
  // timer/counter1 is used for servo PWM (mode 8) and system heartbeat
  TCCR1A = 1<<COM1A1 | 0<<COM1A0 | 1<<COM1B1 | 0<<COM1B0 | 0<<WGM11 | 0<<WGM10;
  TCCR1B = 1<<WGM13 | 0<<WGM12 | 0<<CS12 | 1<<CS11 | 0<<CS10;
  ICR1 = 20000; // period = 20ms
  TIMSK1 = 1<<ICIE1; // interrupt at TOP count
  // INT0 = left shaft encoder, INT1 = right shaft encoder
  EICRA = 0<<ISC11 | 1<<ISC10 | 0<<ISC01 | 1<<ISC00; // both edges
  EIMSK = 1<<INT1 | 1<<INT0; // enable external interrupts
}

void loop() {
  int left_offset, right_offset;
  left_offset = analogRead(0) - 512; // left offset
  right_offset = analogRead(1) - 512; // right offset
  OCR1A = 1500 + left_offset; // left servo
  OCR1B = 1500 + right_offset; // right servo
  delay(20);
}

// system heartbeat interrupt handler: 50 Hz
```

```
ISR(TIMER1_CAPT_vect) {
  static byte prescaler = 50;
  if(prescaler) {
    prescaler--; // decrement prescaler
  } else {
    prescaler = 50; // reset prescaler
    Serial.print("Odometer reports L=");
    Serial.print(left_odometer);
    Serial.print(", R=");
    Serial.println(right_odometer);
  }
}

// left shaft encoder interrupt

ISR(INT0_vect) {
  if(bit_is_clear(PIND, PIND2) ^ bit_is_clear(PIND, PIND4)) {
    left_odometer++; // anti-clockwise rotation
  } else {
    left_odometer--; // clockwise rotation
  }
}

// right shaft encoder interrupt

ISR(INT1_vect) {
  if(bit_is_clear(PIND, PIND3) ^ bit_is_clear(PIND, PIND7)) {
    right_odometer++; // anti-clockwise rotation
  } else {
    right_odometer--; // clockwise rotation
  }
}
```

To ensure prompt response and accurate counting, you tie phase A of each of the wheel's shaft encoders to the two available external interrupt inputs on the Arduino Uno. The left wheel encoder A signal goes to digital pin D2, which is the INT0 (external interrupt 0) input. The right wheel encoder A signal goes to digital pin D2, which is the INT1 (external interrupt 1) input.

In the setup() function, you have the usual suspects. You configure digital pins D9 and D10 to be your PWM servo outputs, as before. Then you configure the serial port for *really fast* transmission speed (115,200 bits per second) because you might need that much bandwidth before it's over. Remember to adjust the baud rate on the Serial Monitor to be able to correctly receive the robot's reports.

Timer/Counter 1 is again selected to generate your PWM signals. You also use its Input Capture Event interrupt as a system *heart-beat*. This lets you perform all your magic motion-control activities in the background.

The external interrupts are configured to fire on *any change* detected on the interrupt input pin. This means that instead of only looking for either rising or falling edges of the incoming signal, you look for *both* of them. This effectively doubles the resolution of your encoders. You can also double-up again by generating an interrupt using the B phases, but you stick with this method for now.

The external interrupts must be explicitly enabled to allow them to operate, so you do this by setting the INT1 and INT0 bits of the EIMSK register.

Your loop() function is the servo-calibration routine from your previous robot. Instead of using it to find the null points of the servos, you just want to be able to control the rotation of the wheels and see what's happening with the wheel odometers.

You define three different interrupt handlers for this sketch. The first is the heartbeat interrupt, where you periodically report the odometer values. You use the same software-prescaler technique as the fan-speed-measuring sketch, so that even though the interrupt triggers 50 times per second, you only want a report sent *once* every second. Otherwise, your Serial Monitor window starts to become a blur, and it's hard to tell what's going on.

The other two interrupt handlers are for the external interrupts. They're activated when the phase A outputs from the respective shaft encoders change state. In each interrupt handler, the current state of the two phases is compared. This comparison is performed using the exclusive OR operator and the bit_is_clear() macro.

The phase B signals for the left and right encoders have been attached to digital pins D4 and D7, respectively. If the two phases of the encoder aren't equal, the odometer is incremented, representing counterclockwise rotation. Alternately, the odometer is decremented, which indicates clockwise rotation.

If you're following along at home and have replicated a robot similar to the one described here, run the sketch and open the Serial Monitor window. Then adjust the two potentiometers until the servo motors stop spinning. Note the respective odometer readings being reported by the robot once a second.

If the wheels have stopped spinning, the odometer readings should remain steady. Try adjusting the relative speed of the motors using the potentiometers, and verify that the odometers *increase* in value with counterclockwise rotation and similarly *decrease* with clockwise rotation.

If your values seem to go in the wrong direction, you can swap the A and B phases to correct this.

Measuring Wheel Velocity

Now that you can accurately count encoder ticks of both the *up* and the *down* variety, you can calculate the wheel velocities. The odometer readings represent *angular displacement* expressed in encoder ticks, unlike the odometers typically found in cars, which express cumulative miles or kilometers traveled.

Each encoder tick also represents a *linear displacement*, because this robot moves when the wheels spin. This distance can be calculated if you know the number of encoder ticks per full revolution of the wheel as well as the wheel's exact circumference.

For now, you concentrate on calculating the wheel's velocity in terms of odometer counts per timer tick. You know that the heartbeat interrupt occurs 50 times per second, so the interval between timer ticks is 20 milliseconds. So now you have a time, and once you have a distance, you'll have a velocity.

To avoid rounding errors, stick to integer numbers for as long as you can, and only convert into real-world units of measure at the very end of the process. Odometer counts per timer tick is a perfectly valid velocity, as long as you can define what those units mean.

To calculate the wheel velocities, you look for changes in the odometer readings. To do this, you maintain a copy of the previous odometer reading for each wheel and then compare it to the current reading. This is done 50 times per second in the Timer/Counter 1 interrupt handler.

Two new global variables are declared at the beginning of the sketch:

```
volatile int left_velocity, right_velocity;
```

The remainder of the sketch remains intact, with only a few changes (in **bold**) made to the timer interrupt handler. See Listing 13-15.

Listing 13-15. Updated Interrupt Handler That Now Calculates Velocity for Each Wheel and Reports Once per Second

```
ISR(TIMER1_CAPT_vect) {
  static byte prescaler = 50;
  static unsigned int previous_left_odometer, previous_right_odometer;
  if(prescaler) {
    prescaler--; // decrement prescaler
  } else {
    prescaler = 50; // reset prescaler
    Serial.print("Velocity reports L=");
    Serial.print(left_velocity);
    Serial.print(", R=");
    Serial.println(right_velocity);
  }
  // calculate wheel velocities
  left_velocity = left_odometer - previous_left_odometer;
  right_velocity = right_odometer - previous_right_odometer;
  previous_left_odometer = left_odometer; // remember...
  previous_right_odometer = right_odometer; // ...for next time
}
```

You should see left- and right-wheel velocities being reported in the Serial Monitor window. These numbers can be either positive or negative, depending on the direction of rotation.

Run the motors up to full speed in both directions, and note the velocities reported. If your shaft encoders provide many, many ticks per revolution, you should see relatively large numbers: from dozens to hundreds or even more. These values determine the granularity of your speed control. For example, if you see numbers ranging from +20 to -20, these are the possible values to which you can set the speed of your motors.

If, on the other hand, your velocity numbers span only a small range, such as +3 to -4, you can double-up the encoder ticks using the B phases and pin-change interrupts. You could also sample the odometer readings less frequently by using another software prescaler in the interrupt handler routine or setting up Timer/Counter 2 to interrupt at, say, 10Hz or so. The velocity calculations need to happen several times per second, but the exact number depends on your robot's physical properties. The popular Segway personal transporter, for example, runs its update loop at 100Hz.

As promised, it's time to let the robot figure out the servo motors' null point. You use a very primitive feedback loop that lacks subtlety but actually works. See Listing 13-16.

Listing 13-16. Primitive Feedback Loop That Prevents the Motors from Spinning

```
volatile unsigned int left_odometer = 0, right_odometer = 0; // in encoder ticks
volatile int left_velocity, right_velocity; // velocities in encoder ticks per period
int left_wheel, right_wheel; // wheel velocity set points

void setup() {
  pinMode(9, OUTPUT); // left servo PWM output
  pinMode(10, OUTPUT); // right servo PWM output
  Serial.begin(115200);
  Serial.println("*** Robot initializing ***");
  // timer/counter1 is used for servo PWM (mode 8) and system heartbeat
  TCCR1A = 1<<COM1A1 | 0<<COM1A0 | 1<<COM1B1 | 0<<COM1B0 | 0<<WGM11 | 0<<WGM10;
```

```
    TCCR1B = 1<<WGM13 | 0<<WGM12 | 0<<CS12 | 1<<CS11 | 0<<CS10;
    OCR1A = 1500; // ideal servo null point in microseconds
    OCR1B = 1500; // ideal servo null point in microseconds
    ICR1 = 20000; // period = 20ms
    TIMSK1 = 1<<ICIE1; // interrupt at TOP count
    // INT0 = left shaft encoder, INT1 = right shaft encoder
    EICRA = 0<<ISC11 | 1<<ISC10 | 0<<ISC01 | 1<<ISC00; // both edges
    EIMSK = 1<<INT1 | 1<<INT0; // enable external interrupts
}

void loop() {
    left_wheel = 0; // stop
    right_wheel = 0; // stop
}

// system heartbeat interrupt handler: 50 Hz

ISR(TIMER1_CAPT_vect) {
    static byte prescaler = 50;
    static unsigned int previous_left_odometer, previous_right_odometer;
    int left_error, right_error;
    if(prescaler) {
        prescaler--; // decrement prescaler
    } else {
        prescaler = 50; // reset prescaler
        Serial.print("Power reports L=");
        Serial.print(OCR1A);
        Serial.print(", R=");
        Serial.println(OCR1B);
    }
    // calculate wheel velocities
    left_velocity = left_odometer - previous_left_odometer;
    right_velocity = right_odometer - previous_right_odometer;
    previous_left_odometer = left_odometer; // remember...
    previous_right_odometer = right_odometer; // ...for next time
    // calculate errors
    left_error = left_wheel - left_velocity; // set point - reading
    right_error = right_wheel - right_velocity;
    // adjust power settings
    OCR1A += left_error;
    OCR1B += right_error;
}

// left shaft encoder interrupt
```

```
ISR(INT0_vect) {
  if(bit_is_clear(PIND, PIND2) ^ bit_is_clear(PIND, PIND4)) {
    left_odometer++; // anti-clockwise rotation
  } else {
    left_odometer--; // clockwise rotation
  }
}

// right shaft encoder interrupt

ISR(INT1_vect) {
  if(bit_is_clear(PIND, PIND3) ^ bit_is_clear(PIND, PIND7)) {
    right_odometer++; // anti-clockwise rotation
  } else {
    right_odometer--; // clockwise rotation
  }
}
```

You add `left_wheel` and `right_wheel` velocity set points as global variables at the start of the sketch. These are used as the targets for the wheel velocities. These values are expressed in encoder ticks per sample period for now.

The `setup()` function remains largely the same, with the introduction of some preliminary settings of the PWM duty cycles. The registers `OCR1A` and `OCR1B` are set to 1,500 for the left and right servo motors, respectively; this is the ideal servo null point in microseconds. It doesn't matter if they're exactly right when compared with your actual (as opposed to the ideal) servos. They will be corrected in time.

You drop the user-interface code that was once in the `loop()` function and replace it with simple assignment statements to the `left_wheel` and `right_wheel` set-point values.

The heartbeat interrupt handler now reports the power settings of each servo motor, expressed as the pulse width of the servo control signal. This is adjusted by the following (primitive) code.

After the wheel-velocity calculations have taken place, the errors are computed. Here the errors are the differences between the set points and the measured velocities. A positive error means that the measured velocity is less than the set point.

So instead of doing any fancy PID algorithms or filters, you add the errors to the PWM registers. If the error is positive, meaning that the wheel *lacks* the velocity you desire it to have, then the pulse width of the servo signal is increased *proportionally*. This causes the servo to rotate in a more counterclockwise manner.

If the wheel is going too fast already, then the error is negative, and the pulse width is reduced, producing a more clockwise rotation.

Surprisingly enough, this works. It may even work on your robot, unless your encoders report an unduly number of ticks. The motors may spin a bit, but then they settle down, and you can see the pulse widths being emitted by looking at the Serial Monitor. This tells you the actual null points for your two servo motors at this particular moment.

You can even set the values in the `loop()` function to other numbers, as long as they exist in the range of achievable velocities for your motors. This is where you see the deficiencies of this primitive feedback loop, because the motors erratically try to maintain a steady velocity. That's where some refinement, in the form a proper feedback filter, will prove its worth.

In the meantime, marvel at the not-spinning motors of your robot. Try to move them yourself, and see what happens. They should try to undo any alterations you make to their position, however erratically.

Feedback Filter

First let's investigate the *proportional* error and how it affects the stability of your controlled process. In the previous example sketch, the proportional error was added to the control signal. It was happy chance alone that pushed the servo motors in the right direction, with an increased pulse width resulting from a positive error term. It could have just as easily worked against you, had you adopted a different convention for describing either the error or the motion of the wheels.

Your feedback loop should react well to variations in the desired set points as well as steady states. Let's have the foreground `loop()` function serve up a series of settings, so you can evaluate how well your filter is responding to changing demands. Replace the `loop()` function from the previous sketch with this one:

```
void loop() {
  int set_point;
  for(set_point = -10; set_point < 11; set_point++) {
    Serial.print("Set point = ");
    Serial.println(set_point);
    left_wheel = set_point;
    right_wheel = set_point;
    delay(2500);
  }
}
```

Change the endpoints of the range to whatever is appropriate to your robot. Also, if your range of achievable velocities is quite large, you should increase the step value used in the `for()` loop to something more suitable.

Define a proportional constant KP somewhere in your sketch (for example, `#define Kp 5`), and modify the power adjustment code to look like this:

```
OCR1A += left_error * Kp;
OCR1B += right_error * Kp;
```

Now experiment with these integer factors and see how this affects the responsiveness of the motor-control function. Too high a value results in unwanted oscillation. This is a test best performed with your robot up on blocks.

To proceed to the integral and derivative errors, you need to restructure the code a bit. The integral error needs to have a static variable that keeps track of the sum of all errors over time. You might consider it the *unforgiving* term. The derivative has a much shorter memory and only wants to know the magnitude of the previous error. It's also time to normalize these power settings so you can more easily keep track of them.

Let's calculate the various error terms and see what effect they have on loop stability. See Listing 13-17.

Listing 13-17. Basic PID Filter Placed in the Feedback Loop

```
#define Kp 25 // proportional factor
#define Ki 0.1 // integral factor
#define Kd 0.5 // derivative factor

volatile unsigned int left_odometer = 0, right_odometer = 0; // in encoder ticks
volatile int left_velocity, right_velocity; // wheel velocities in encoder ticks per sample
period
```

```
int left_wheel, right_wheel; // wheel velocity set points
float left_wheel_power, right_wheel_power; // -1.0 to +1.0

unsigned int servoPower(float power) {
  int pulse_width = 1500;
  power = constrain(power, -1.0, +1.0); // limits
  pulse_width += power * 500; // +/-500 microseconds
  return pulse_width;
}

void setup() {
  pinMode(9, OUTPUT); // left servo PWM output
  pinMode(10, OUTPUT); // right servo PWM output
  Serial.begin(115200);
  Serial.println("*** Robot initializing ***");
  // timer/counter1 is used for servo PWM (mode 8) and system heartbeat
  TCCR1A = 1<<COM1A1 | 0<<COM1A0 | 1<<COM1B1 | 0<<COM1B0 | 0<<WGM11 | 0<<WGM10;
  TCCR1B = 1<<WGM13 | 0<<WGM12 | 0<<CS12 | 1<<CS11 | 0<<CS10;
  OCR1A = 1500; // ideal servo null point in microseconds
  OCR1B = 1500; // ideal servo null point in microseconds
  ICR1 = 20000; // period = 20ms
  TIMSK1 = 1<<ICIE1; // interrupt at TOP count
  // INT0 = left shaft encoder, INT1 = right shaft encoder
  EICRA = 0<<ISC11 | 1<<ISC10 | 0<<ISC01 | 1<<ISC00; // both edges
  EIMSK = 1<<INT1 | 1<<INT0; // enable external interrupts
}

void loop() {
  int set_point;

  for(set_point = -5; set_point < 6; set_point++) {
    Serial.print("Set point = ");
    Serial.println(set_point);
    left_wheel = set_point;
    right_wheel = set_point;
    delay(2500);
  }
}

// system heartbeat interrupt handler: 50 Hz

ISR(TIMER1_CAPT_vect) {
  static byte prescaler = 50;
  static unsigned int previous_left_odometer, previous_right_odometer;
  int left_error, right_error;
  int left_proportional_error, right_proportional_error;
  static int left_integral_error, right_integral_error;
  int left_derivative_error, right_derivative_error;
  static int left_previous_error, right_previous_error;
  if(prescaler) {
    prescaler--; // decrement prescaler
  } else {
```

```
    prescaler = 50; // reset prescaler
    Serial.print("Power reports L=");
    Serial.print(OCR1A);
    Serial.print(", R=");
    Serial.println(OCR1B);
  }
  // calculate wheel velocities
  left_velocity = left_odometer - previous_left_odometer;
  right_velocity = right_odometer - previous_right_odometer;
  previous_left_odometer = left_odometer; // remember...
  previous_right_odometer = right_odometer; // ...for next time
  // calculate errors
  left_error = left_wheel - left_velocity; // set point - reading
  right_error = right_wheel - right_velocity; // set point - reading
  left_proportional_error = left_error * Kp;
  right_proportional_error = right_error * Kp;
  left_integral_error += (left_error * Ki); // integrate
  right_integral_error += (right_error * Ki); // integrate
  left_derivative_error = (left_previous_error * Kd); // from last time
  right_derivative_error = (right_previous_error * Kd); // from last time
  left_error = left_proportional_error + left_integral_error - left_derivative_error;
  right_error = right_proportional_error + right_integral_error - right_derivative_error;
  // adjust power settings
  left_wheel_power += (left_error / 1000.0); // scale
  right_wheel_power += (right_error / 1000.0); // scale
  OCR1A = servoPower(left_wheel_power);
  OCR1B = servoPower(right_wheel_power);
  left_previous_error = left_error; // remember...
  right_previous_error = right_error; // ...for next time
}

// left shaft encoder interrupt

ISR(INT0_vect) {
  if(bit_is_clear(PIND, PIND2) ^ bit_is_clear(PIND, PIND4)) {
    left_odometer++; // anti-clockwise rotation
  } else {
    left_odometer--; // clockwise rotation
  }
}

// right shaft encoder interrupt

ISR(INT1_vect) {
  if(bit_is_clear(PIND, PIND3) ^ bit_is_clear(PIND, PIND7)) {
    right_odometer++; // anti-clockwise rotation
  } else {
    right_odometer--; // clockwise rotation
  }
}
```

The PID constants are defined at the beginning of the sketch. These *will* have to be tuned for your robot, but you can start with these factors.

You create some wheel power settings to be controlled by the feedback loop, called `left_wheel_power` and `right_wheel_power`. These floating-point numbers range from -1.0 for clockwise motion to +1.0 for counterclockwise motion. You pass these normalized values to the new `servoPower()` function, which returns the appropriate pulse width to be assigned to the PWM registers. You're already familiar with how that transformation works.

All the new calculations are contained in the timer interrupt handler. Each of the error terms is calculated, and then all the terms are combined and scaled to adjust the wheel power settings. The PWM registers are then updated. The rest of the sketch remains the same.

You can apply the same techniques for converting whole-robot linear and angular velocity to individual motor speed controls as you used with the first practice robot. The principles are identical in both cases, because the drive arrangement is the same.

Where Am I?

Keeping track of a robot's current position is a tricky prospect. *Odometry* is often used to perform dead reckoning to convert the incremental motion of the wheels at every sample period into Cartesian coordinates.

This conversion does require your little Arduino to perform some trigonometry, which it can easily and accurately do. The basic premise of odometry is to repeatedly calculate the distance traveled, if any, by either or both wheels. If no movement has taken place, it's a good idea to skip the remaining calculations. This calculation would normally be performed during the update loop, where you have been implementing all of the motion control algorithms.

The left and right wheel velocities must be converted from angular displacement to linear displacement, using the number of encoder ticks per revolution and the circumference of the wheel. It's a good idea to have a variable for *each* of the wheel's circumferences, because no two wheels are of identical size, and even small errors add up fast.

The effective linear velocity of the robot as a whole is then calculated as half the difference of the left velocity and the right velocity, or in other words, the average of the two. The distance just traveled is this calculated velocity divided by the sample time.

The present angle or heading of the robot is calculated by dividing the difference of the two odometers (once converted into real-world linear units such as inches or millimeters) by the distance between the two wheels, often referred to as the *wheelbase*. This gives the robot's heading in radians, with east representing zero and positive rotation being seen as counterclockwise from above.

The robot's x and y coordinates are then incremented by the cosine and sine, respectively, of the heading, multiplied by the distance just traveled. It's really not as hard as it sounds! Like many complex problems, it usually takes longer to explain it than it does to actually *do* it.

Note that any form of dead reckoning suffers from accumulated error over time. Should you need to know the robot's actual location and heading with any accuracy, you most certainly want to add in several other methods and not depend on odometry alone.

Your Ultimate Robot

Now you can move a simple robot around and exert a pretty impressive range of control over its motion. For some tasks, such as line following, this is already overkill. Just being able to turn left, turn right, and go forward as usually enough to accomplish this successfully.

To craft a robot that performs its tasks with grace and rock-solid reliability, you have to think in terms of worst case scenarios. What would happen if a sensor failed? What if a motor suddenly could only move forward and not in reverse? These things happen, and the ability to function with less-than-perfect hardware is the mark of excellent design and execution.

What will *your* ultimate robot look like? Will it be small enough to fit in a pocket? Or will it have to stoop to enter a doorway? The choices are up to you.

Summary

You've covered a *lot* of material in this chapter, but you haven't exhausted any of the topics presented. Perhaps you've gained some perspective on what it takes to design and deploy a successful robot project. And maybe robots just aren't your thing. Any of the particular problems addressed in this robotics-oriented chapter can also be used in numerous other fields and other, non-robotic projects. Either way, it's good to know the sorts of amazing things you can do with your simple Arduino, once you've had a chance to take a look at its internals.

Good luck with your Arduino projects! Remember to have some fun along the way.

Index

A

Analog reference (AREF) pin, 45

Arduino Bootloader, 33

Arduino Diecimila, 18

Arduino Duemilanove, 18

Arduino Forum, 222

Arduino hardware, 1, 71

    Arduino Extreme, 18

    Arduino Nuova Generazione, 18

    Arduino Uno, 2

    breadboard, 22

    classic LED blinker circuit

        astable multivibrator, 72

        component values, 73

        components, 74

        electrical components, 72

        implicit/explicit connections, 75

        reference designators, 72

        schematic representation, 72

definition, 1

Diecimila, 18

Duemilanove, 18

expansion connectors, 17

expansion headers, 85

female headers, 85

I/O board, 2

mechanical form factor, 86

officially licensed products, 19

power-supply section, 16, 75

    barrel connector, 76

    circuit evolution, 79

    input power conditioning, 76

    voltage regulator, 78

printed circuit boards, 21

processor

    decoupling capacitors, 85

    I/O drive capability, 84

    power consumption, 83

programmable LED, 85

RESET signal, 84

time base, 84

reset switch, 17

serial designation, 16

serial interface, 81

RS-232 interface, 81

USART peripheral, 81

USB interface, 17, 87

Arduino Mega 2560, 14

vs. Arduino Mega1280, 15

vs. Arduino Uno, 14

Arduino programming language

#define LED 13, 31

delay() function, 31

digitalWrite() function, 31

fdevopen function, 29

Hello, World program, 30

loop() function, 29, 31

main() function, 29

modern Hello, World program, 30

pinMode() function, 31

setup() function, 29

Arduino software, 25, 89

Arduino herritage, 91

Arduino-1.0beta4 prerelease package, 89

avrdude command syntax, 36

avrdude utility, 36

C programming language, 26

blinking the LED, 35

function definition, 27

header file, 27

Hello, world program, 26

libraries, 27

program statements, 27

punctuation, 27

self-documenting code, 27

semi-human-readable document, 28

standard output device, 27

Teletype/CRT-based terminal, 26

whitespace, 27

compiler, 31

avrdude, 32

avr-gcc compiler, 32

tasks, 32

device programming, 33

Arduino Bootloader, 33

test and debug, 33

hosts and targets, 25

installation, 91

logo, 89

multiplatform support, 90–91

open source software, 90

plain-text editor, 34

process, 91–93

programming language (*see* Arduino
   programming language)

repeat process, 34

splash screen, 90

user interface, 93

   edit menu, 94

   file menu, 94

   help menu, 97

   sketch menu, 95

   tools menu, 95–97

   web sites, 94

Word-processing software, 28

Arduino Uno, 2

   vs. Arduino Mega capabilities, 15

   drawbacks, 3

   expansion connectors, 6

   female headers, 85

mechanical form factor, 86

power supply circuit, 5

processor, 3

serial port, 5

shields, 9

Arduino Uno SMD, 3

Arduino USB, 88

Arduino-1.0beta4 prerelease package, 89

Atmel AVR, 39

   address spaces

      configuration fuses, 57

      data memory, 55

      EEPROM, 56

      general-purpose registers, 56

      input/output registers, 56

      program memory, 55

   ATmega328

      arithmetic logic unit, 50

      interrupt vectors, 52

      reset vector, 51

      SEI and CLI, 53

      SREG bits, 54

      vector table, 52

   clock systems, 54

device packaging, 40

  pins, 42

  surface-mount devices, 41

  through-hole DIPs, 40

internal peripherals

  analog inputs, 68

  external interrupts, 66

  general purpose I/O, 65

  Timer/Counters, 66, 67

  TWI, 68

  USART, 67

machine language instructions

  arithmetic and logic, 58

  bit manipulation, 64

  conditional branch instructions, 62

  data transfer instructions, 63

  limited instruction space, 61

  No Operation code, 64

  SLEEP instruction, 64

  unconditional branch instructions, 62

  Watchdog Reset instruction, 64

origins, 39

power pins, 43

alternate pin functions, ATmega328, 47

analog-reference pins, 45

digital and analog power supplies, 44

general-purpose I/O ports, 46

RESET pin, 45

XTAL1 and XTAL2 pins, 46

product datasheets, 40

tinyAVR family, 40

Audio sensors, 315

Autonomous robot, 305

■ B

Berne Convention, 230

Bipolar stepper motor, 310

Blinking LED, 165

  10W LED Driver, 179–82

  1W LED Driver, 178–79

  analogRead() function, 167

  analogWrite() function, 167

  current-limiting resistor, 166

  digital clock (*see* Digital Clock)

  Direct-Drive configuration

    20-LED bar-graph shield, 185

with LED driver circuits, 187–88

USART serial pin, 186

improvements, 167

IR remote control, 182–83

LED driver circuit, 174–76

LED Math, 174, 176

current-limiting resistor, 177

electrical power and voltage, 174

forward voltage, 176

map() function, 167

mostly optimized six-channel dimmer, 170

ADC peripherals, 171

Digital Input Disable Register, 172

Fast PWM and Phase Correct PWM modes, 172

for experimental purposes, 173

slew-rate limiting, 172

timer/counter peripherals, 171

multiplexing techniques, 188

Charlieplexing, 203–5

row-column multiplexing, 189–95

segment-digit multiplexing, 196–201

time-domain multiplexing, 202–3

slow enough, PWM frequency, 168

Fast PWM mode, 168

overflow interrupt, 169

Phase Correct PWM mode, 168

prescalar setting, 168

six-channel dimmer, 169

timer-overflow interrupt, 169

solderless breadboard, 166

TV-B-Gone, 183–84

Brushless DC motors, 309

Bus network, 290

■ C

CadSoft EAGLE, 251

Autorouter module, 252

direct-to-PDF printing options, 252

Layout Editor module, 251

parts, 252

Schematic module, 251

scripting language, 252

Charlie-plexing, 10

Clear Global Interrupt (CLI) Flag, 53

Clock prescale register (CLKPR), 127

Closed-loop systems, 317–19

Copyright, 228

C programming language, Arduino, 26

    blinking the LED, 35

    function definition, 27

    header file, 27

    Hello, world program, 26

    libraries, 27

    program statements, 27

    punctuation, 27

    self-documenting code, 27

    semi-human-readable document, 28

    standard output device, 27

    Teletype/CRT-based terminal, 26

    whitespace, 27

Cross compilers, 25

Cross toolchains, 25

Cross-platform development, 25

D

Data Register Empty interrupt, 134

DC motors

    commutation, 308

    H-bridge circuit, 308

    toy motors, 307

Device and process patents, 227

Digital Clock, 205

    accuracy, 210–11

    alarm function, 212

    flashing colon, 212

    Input Capture Event interrupt, 210

    prototype digitak clock, 207

    schematic representation, 206

    setup() function, 210

    solderless breadboard, 207

    user interface, 211

Digital signal probe, 129

E

Easily Applicable Graphical Layout Editor (EAGLE), 251

EasyTransfer library, 296

F

Firmata test software, 282

Flying robots, 307

Fully connected network, 290

G

GitHub, 226

Google Code, 224

H

Hardware design, 231

    Arduinos and shields, 247

        Arduino Duemilanove PCB, 251

        breadboard Arduino circuit, 250

        hardware compatibility, 248

        pocessor selection, 249–50

        power supply options, 249

        software compatibility, 248–49

    CadSoft EAGLE, 251–53

    infrared (IR) proximity sensor, 234

        compact version, 246

        connectors, 246–47

        improvements, 238–41

        IR emitter and detector, 235

        IR phototransistors, 235

        photodiodes, 235, 236

        printed circuit boards, 241–45

        prototype, 236–38

    learning requirements, 231

    adequate lighting, 233

    continuity tester, 234

    documentation, 233

    electrical connections, 233

    electronic components, 231

    oscilloscope, 234

    perfboard, 233

    prototype circuits, 233

    soldering, 233

    volt-ohm-amp meter, 234

Hardware peripherals, 133

    analog inputs, 152

        thermometer, 153

        voltmeter, 154–56

    digital input and output (I/O) pins, 139

        pin change interrupts, 140–42

        single pin change interrupts, 143

    external interrupts, 156

        ATmega2560 interrupts, 157

        ATmega328 interrupts, 157

        attachInterrupt() and detachInterrupt() functions, 157

        FALLING and LOW procedure, 158

        RISING procedure, 158

        signal-filtering capability, 157

tattle() function, 158

interrupt vectors

    for ATmega2560, 160

    for ATmega328, 159

PWM (*see* Pulse-Width-Modulation
    (PWM))

serial port, 133

    bare-naked interrupts, 139

    empty interrupts, 138

    ISR() options, 137–38

    nested interrupts, 138

    serial library, 134

    undefined interrupts, 139

    USART (*see* Universal
    Synchronous/Asynchronous
    Receiver/Transmitter (USART))

timers/counter peripherals

    ATmega2560, 144

    ATmega328, 143–44

    timer interrupts, 145–47

Hobby servo motors, 310

Infrared (IR) proximity sensor

    implementations, 234

    improvements, 238–41

    IR emitter and detector, 235

    IR phototransistors, 235

    photodiodes, 235, 236

    printed circuit boards, 241–45

        artwork, 242

        assembly drawing, 244

        components, 244

        double-sided PCB, 242

        drawbacks, 245

        drill files and drill tapes, 242

        layout techniques, 243–44

        silkscreen, 242

        single-sided PCB, 241

        solder mask, 242

    prototype, 236–38

Internet, 301–4

    Arduino web server, 303

    EtherShield library, 302

    microchip ENC28J60, 301

L

Launchpad, 225

Light sensors, 312–13

LilyPad Arduino, 20

M

Mesh network, 290

Microsoft's CodePlex, 225

Minicom, 96

Mobile robot, 307

Multiplexing techniques, LED

    Charlieplexing, 203–5

    row-column multiplexing, 189–95

    segment-digit multiplexing, 196–201

    time-domain multiplexing, 202–3

Musical Instrument Digital Interface (MIDI), 296

    Arduino MIDI keyboard, 299

    cable, 297

    hardware interface, 296

    serial.begin(31250) function, 300

N

Networking, 281

    doorbell circuit, 283–85

    EasyTransfer library, 296

    four-node-network, breadboarded Arduinos, 289

    Internet, 301–4

    MIDI, 296–300

    RS-232 standard, 291–95

    RS-485 standard, 295

    serial port, 281–82

    topologies, 290–91

    two-node dimmer network, 285–89

Noncontact sensors, 314–15

O

Open source, 229–30

Open-loop systems, 317

Optimizations, 99

    electronic measurements, 121

        Arduino performance, 121

        bit-toggle operation, 123

        CLKPR register, 127

        digital signal probe, 129

digital storage oscilloscopes, 125

digitalWrite() function, 122

power reduction methods, 128

toggling an I/O pin, 124, 126

low power/high speed, 120

serial communication

Arduino's Serial library, 107, 108

character strings, 111

configuration registers, 108, 109

data transmission, 109

printing integers, 112

shrink blink, 100

analysis, 103

binary notation, 103

code analysis, 101

code reduction, 105

DDRB, 102

measuring space-saving
optimizations, 100

pin toggling, 104

pinMode() function, 101

time, 105

using lower-level code, 106

space-saving optimizations, 99

SRAM, 112

Bare Minimum, 114

character strings, 118

data types, 117

measuring requirements, 113

memory sections, 116

variables, 117

P

Photo-sensitive resistors, 313

Pin-change interrupts, 140

for ATmega2560, 141

for ATmega328, 140

Posterous, 222

Project documentation, 213

audience, 217–18

automated documentation process, 217

hardware, 220

hardware documentation, 218–20

licensing

copyrights, 228

open source, 229–30

patents and trademarks, 227–28

public domain, 230

software, 220

source-code comments, 214–15

teamwork and collaborative development

    blogs, 221

    forums, 222

    project-hosting web sites (*see* Project-hosting web sites)

    revision control systems, 223

    wikis, 222

whitespaces, 215–16

Project-hosting web sites

    GitHub, 226

    Google Code, 224

    Launchpad, 225

    Microsoft's Code Plex, 225

    SourceForge, 226

Pulse-Width-Modulation (PWM), 133

    analogWrite() function, 147

    bitRead() macro, 149

    loop() function, 151

    pin change interrupts, 148

    reassigning outputs to any outputs, using interrupts, 150

    Timer Clock Select bits, Timer/Counter, 151

    Timer/Counter pins, Arduino Uno, 150

Q

QTouch library, 313

R

Radio control, 310

Return from Interrupt (RETI), 53

Revision control systems, 223

Ring network, 290

RJMP (Relative Jump) instruction, 62

Robot

    Arduino, solderless breadboard

        bumper switches and +5V power, 322

        control circuit, 320

        drive configurations, 322

        forward, reverse and stop speeds, 326

        measurement, 338–40

        motor math, 322–25

        open-loop servo null compensation, 331–33

        PWM hardware, 333–36

        schematic representation, 319–20

        servo smart functions, 326

        servo velocity function, 330

servo-driven wheel velocity, 327

straight-line motion, 337–38

turning, 338, 340–41

wheel motion, 336–37

wheel motors, 321

wheel velocity parameters-servo motor behavior relation, 330

audio sensors, 315

autonomous, 305

control systems

closed-loop systems, 317–19

open-loop systems, 317

electric motors and actuators

brushless DC motors, 309

DC motors, 307–8

servo motors, 310–12

solenoids, 312

stepper motors, 309–10

feedback filter, 354–57

flying, 307

indicators, controls, forms of communication, 315–16

light sensors, 312–13

mobile, 307

motion control, 307

noncontact sensors, 314–15

power supply, 306

small fan speed

control, 344–46

loop closed, 346–48

measurement, 341–44

quadrature encoders, 348–50

wheel velocity measurement, 350–53

touch sensors, 313–14

RS-232 standard, 291–95

RS-485 standard, 295

S

Sensorium, 305

Sensors

audio, 315

light, 312–13

noncontact, 314–15

touch, 313–14

Serial port

SoftSerial library, 281

Firmata test software, 282

Servo motors, 310–12

continuous rotation gear-motor, 311

error, 310

gear-reduction mechanism, 310

hobby, steps, 311

Set Global Interrupt (SEI) Flag, 53

SMDs. *See* Surface-Mount Devices (SMDs)

SoftSerial/NewSoftSerial library, 281

Software design, 255

    Arduino Core

        Arduino.h file, 265

        function prototypes, 265

        main.cpp file, 264

    Arduino libraries, 255

        header file LED.h, 256–58

        implementation file LED.cpp, 258–60

        keywords, 262

        LED library, 256, 260–61

        sample sketches, 261

    Atmel's AVR Studio, 276–77

    ATtiny13A, 262

        bootloaders, 267–69

        configuration fuses, 269

        fuse settings, 270–72

    Eclipse project, 278–79

    makefile, 273–75

tinyCylon

    boards.txt, 263–64

    delay() function, 266

    Larson Scanner, 266

    loop() function, 267

    setup() function, 266

Solenoids, 312

SourceForge, 226

SparkFun Arduino Pro, 20

Static random-access memory (SRAM), 112

    Bare Minimum, 114

    character strings, 118

    data types, 118

    measuring requirements, 113

    memory sections, 116

    variables, 117

Star network, 290

Status Register (SREG) Bits, 54

Stepper motors, 309–10

Surface-Mount Devices (SMDs), 41

▦ T

Tera Term Pro, 96

Toner-transfer method, 21

Touch sensors, 313–14

Toy motors, 307

Two-node dimmer network

LED brightness, pushbuttons, 285

loop function, 287

overloaded function, 287

Serial.available() function, 288

USART, 285

Two-Wire Serial Interface (TWI), 68

■ U

Unipolar stepper motor, 309

Universal Serial Bus (USB), 87

Universal Synchronous/Asynchronous Receiver/Transmitter (USART), 67

buffering, 134

Data Register Empty interrupt, 134

loop() function, 136

parallel interface, 134

Receive Complete interrupt, 135

Receive Complete interrupt handler, 136, 137

setup() function, 136

Transmit Complete interrupt, 135

usart_init() function, 135

■ V

Version control systems (*see* Revision control systems)

■ W, X, Y, Z

Wheel motors, 321

Wikis, 222

WordPress, 222